A WORLD OF WOMEN

Anthropological Studies of Women in the Societies of the World

A WORLD OF WOMEN

Anthropological Studies of Women in the Societies of the World

ERIKA BOURGUIGNON

and Contributors

PRAEGER SPECIAL STUDIES • PRAEGER SCIENTIFIC
A J.F. BERGIN PUBLISHERS BOOK

Library of Congress Cataloging in Publication Data
Main entry under title:

A World of women.

    A J.F. Bergin Publishers book.
    Bibliography: p.
    Includes index.
    1. Women—Addresses, essays, lectures. 2. Social
change—Addresses, essays, lectures. I. Bourguignon, Erika,
1924-
GN479.7.W67   301.41'2   79-11844
ISBN 0–03–051221–2
ISBN 0–03–051226–3 pbk.

Published in 1980 by Praeger Publishers
A division of Holt, Rinehart and Winston/CBS, Inc.
383 Madison Avenue, New York, New York 10017 U.S.A.

0 056 987654321
Printed in the United States of America

Composition by Publication Services

If anthropology has taught us anything,
it is to be wary of taking anything for
granted, especially the axiomatic values
of our own particular cultural heritage.

Victor Turner

CONTENTS

ALASKA

TABLES

FIGURES

PREFACE

In this volume, we have undertaken to present the lives of women in a dozen sociocultural settings dispersed over a large portion of the globe. The descriptions are based on original fieldwork by a dozen anthropologists, several of whom have maintained long-term associations with their people. In Brunei, in St. Kitts, in Yucatán, to cite only the most extended field series, changes and transformations in the communities and in the lives of individual women have been observed for as much as a decade. As this book goes to press, several of the contributors are renewing their ties with their friends of long standing.

It has been argued that women's lives center around their families and households, about the domestic and private domain. Where this is true, fieldwork involves admission to this sheltered area and participant observation of the activities of the women. This might mean attending women's belly-dancing parties in Saudi Arabia, learning to be a traditional midwife in Brunei, a medium in the Umbanda cult of Porto Alegre, Brazil, gathering wild plant food or cleaning game birds with Eskimo women, or following a group of scavenging children in St. Kitts.

This book grew out of a course on the Anthropology of Women that I have been teaching for a number of years at The Ohio State University. Several chapters were first presented to that class as reports by researchers recently returned from the field. The enthusiastic response of the students encouraged us to think that others might wish to share in what these fieldworkers had discovered. At the same time, I have sought to present these materials within a theoretical setting of issues in the current state of the anthropology of women's roles and status, and to draw together our findings to examine what we have learned by sampling this particular set of cultures. This volume, then, might be helpful to others teaching courses dealing with women in different societies. It may also serve in area courses on Afro-America, Latin America or the Mediterranean tradition, or in courses on culture change.

The book may, however, not only be of interest to anthropologists and their students, but also to the general reader, prompted by curiosity about other lifeways. Indeed, the materials we offer in these pages tell not only about women in far away places; more often than not, they may have direct implications for our own lives and those of our readers. Some of this relevance is related to the renewed interest in this country in ethnic identities and increased awareness of differences in traditional cultures. On the other hand, there are also the facts of culture change and of its impact on all aspects of our lives. Anthropological accounts of distant peoples permit us to see ourselves in others. They also help us to understand how what appear to be private and personal situations partake of the larger stream of cultural patterning and the forces that are at work in the transformation of societies. As is seen in a number of our contributions, the relation between tradition and transformation is often full of paradoxes. Radical steps in the reorganization of society sometimes take place in the defense of traditional values.

As I write these lines, the news media are reporting that a California jury has awarded a large sum in damages to a woman who sued her husband for defamation. The case is likely to make legal history in the furtherance of women's rights, for in the past it has generally been held that a wife cannot sue her husband except for divorce. Yet this advance in the cause of women was won in a case concerning a most ancient and traditional issue: the honor of a woman and her family centering about the virginity of a bride. The woman is a member of a Sicilian community, who had entered an arranged marriage. The husband, according to the plaintiff, had defamed her and her family by claiming that she had not been a virgin at the time of the marriage. The suit was brought to vindicate the honor of the woman and her family. The values were traditional, the means of redress were those of a society with different norms, and the outcome is innovative both for the Sicilian community and the larger society.

The concern with the values of honor and shame appear in several of the societies in our series. A discussion of the impact of culture change and the means people devise for coping with the transformations in their lives are dealt with by all. Three of our studies describe groups living within the borders of the United States, each facing a particular situation and coming to it from a special cultural background.

Many people have contributed to the making of this book: the individual women and their families, who allowed the contributors to study them, and the various agencies that gave support to the individual projects. These are acknowledged by the various authors. We also wish to thank the students at Ohio State and at several other institutions who have stimulated the presentations offered here. I am personally grateful to my collaborators for their willingness to participate in this common enterprise. I wish to thank my publisher, James F. Bergin for his interest and support of this project and my editor,

Judith Garvey, for her assistance in the production of the book. For bibliographic research, I am indebted to Susan McCabe. Jeanne Peebles prepared the Index and I wish to express my thanks to her for her painstaking work. To my husband Paul H. Bourguignon goes my gratitude for his encouragement and his wisdom and his own cross-cultural perspective on the lives of men and women.

Erika Bourguignon
Columbus, Ohio

A WORLD OF WOMEN

Anthropological Studies of Women in the Societies of the World

1 Introduction and Theoretical Considerations

ERIKA BOURGUIGNON

In this volume we bring together a dozen studies of women's status and women's lives in as many sociocultural settings. The chapters are arranged in a geographical order that takes into consideration some possible cultural and historical relationships among these groups. We begin with Sherri Deaver's study of modern Saudi Arabia, which places its emphasis on the eastern portion of that country and the urban upper-class women there. We next move to another Islamic society, but one outside the Arab world, namely the Malay people of Brunei, in northern Borneo, as presented by Linda Kimball. Here Islam meets the rice-based economies of South East Asia. From there we proceed to other Islamic societies, this time in West Africa. Margaret Saunders reports on the Muslim Hausa of Niger, and Risa Ellovich on the urban Dioula of the Ivory Coast. In both of these cases, Islam has encountered French colonial influences as well as traditional pre-Islamic tribal patterns.

From West Africa, we move to Afro-America, first to Brazil and then to the Southern Caribbean. Both Esther Pressel's study of the social relations between the sexes in São Paulo and Patricia Lerch's report on women in Rio Grande do Sul have as their contexts the rapidly growing Afro-Brazilian religion of Umbanda. In both of these cities, this religious movement attracts predominantly women as mediums, but its appeal is not limited to people of African ancestry. Religion is also the context of Jeannette Henney's study of women on the island of St. Vincent. The African cultural influences are less visible here. Where the cities of Brazil offer us glimpses into the complex social structure of South America's largest country, St. Vincent and nearby St. Kitts, discussed by Judith Gussler, show us veritable sociocultural microcosms.

We next move to the North American mainland. Our first stop is in Yucatán, where Felicitas Goodman presents the alternate life-styles of three Maya women, in rural and urban settings. In the United States, we meet women in three settings that illustrate the great range of social and cultural groups to be found in this country. We begin in the nation's capital. Here Margaret Boone shows us how Cuban women have found ways of adapting

1

to life in this country and have contributed to the successful adjustment of their families. The situation of Sarah Penfield, a rural grandmother in the Appalachian region of Southern Ohio is, in many ways, radically different. Focusing on a single woman and her own history of her life, Rosemary Joyce deals with an American way of life far removed from that of Washington, D.C. One might conjecture that Sara Penfield might find Washington less congenial than the urban middle-class Cuban women did!

Alaskan Eskimo women are discussed by Lynn Ager. Here, too, we are in the United States, yet again in a setting most Americans would find unfamiliar. Ager stresses the economic role of Eskimo women in the traditional pattern as it is still apparent in spite of the rapid encroachments of industrial society.

Our studies, then, deal with women's lives in sociocultural settings that range from the traditionally hunting and gathering Alaskan Eskimo to women in large cities, such as Brazilian women in São Paulo and Rio Grande do Sul and Cuban women in Washington, D.C. Although these sociocultural groups vary widely, all but two are part of large, complex, nation states. These are the two small, self-governing Caribbean islands of St. Vincent and St. Kitts. With the exception of the United States, all the societies represented here are part of the developing world. Yet in some respects even Appalachia and Alaska may be thought of as belonging to that category. Here the one possible exception appears to be the case of the Cuban women in Washington.

The sociocultural settings discussed in this volume do not represent a sample carefully drawn to permit the statistical test of any of the numerous propositions concerning women's status that have emerged in the literature. We can, however, discuss the applicability of certain concepts, the implications of certain formulations. We are able to explore some aspects of women's lives in different circumstances, to raise questions and to draw some comparisons.

The materials presented here are part of larger researches that were conducted under different circumstances and with a variety of primary goals in mind. In order to give the volume coherence and to allow us to make theoretical as well as ethnographic contributions, we agreed to address three central concerns. These were chosen, at least in part, because of their prominence in the literature. The three themes are the role of women in the *subsistence economy*, the utility and applicability of the concepts of the *public* and *domestic domains*, and the impact of *culture change* on the lives of women and their status. Beyond these core concerns, each paper pursues matters directly related to the characteristic features of the particular society and the special interests of the individual ethnographer.

THREE CORE PROBLEMS

By way of introduction, we may briefly review some of the salient issues concerning our three core problems. A number of authors have dealt with the economic roles of women in traditional societies and various hypotheses have been advanced. As Hammond and Jablow have pointed out,

> however sparse the ethnographic treatment of women, the one aspect of their lives that has regularly received attention is their work. In most primitive and peasant societies, the work that women are engaged in is so highly visible that it comes to the notice of almost every observer (Hammond and Jablow 1976:61).

Sexual division of labor and the relative percentage contribution of men and women to subsistence vary widely among societies, so that attempts at a direct linkage between reproductive biology and work roles are, at best, simplistic and tend to be culturally biased. Indeed, Ernestine Friedl has suggested that it may be more useful to

> consider first how the energies of adult women are used for the acquisition of subsistence and for other economic tasks, and, then, once these requirements have been established, to see how child-spacing and child-tending are accomodated to the requirements of the women's tasks (Friedl 1975:8).

The assumption of the primacy of reproduction derives to a considerable extent from the idea that birth control and child-spacing are modern practices, unknown to "primitives," and from the image of the Victorian woman bearing a child a year. Yet there is evidence to show that child-spacing is widespread in traditional societies. For example, according to Nancy Howell (1976) the birth interval among the nomadic hunter-gatherer !Kung is about four years. This case illustrates Friedl's point, for !Kung women nurse their children for a long time, and then continue to carry them on their backs. Pregnancy and the care of an infant cannot be combined with this practice at the same time as working actively at gathering plant food, which constitutes the major part of the people's subsistence.

Child-spacing is often achieved by means of a prolonged taboo on sexual intercourse after the birth of a child. This may be combined with an extended period of nursing and also with polygyny. Of the 304 societies coded for this variable in the *Ethnographic Atlas*, 38 percent have a postpartum sex taboo of a year or more (Bourguignon and Greenbaum 1973: Table 34). In some parts of the world, however, the percentage of societies making use of this child-spacing technique is much greater: 67 percent in Sub-Saharan Africa, 43 percent in the Insular Pacific.

At a level of greater cultural complexity and a different type of economy, compared to the !Kung, the Nupe women traders—as described by Nadel (1952)—also show an example where work takes precedence over childbearing and child-care. Another dramatic case of a similar sort is found in rural Haiti. Murray and Alvarez discuss some of the implications of the fact that the internal marketing system in Haiti is in the hands of women. They note that, since women have great economic opportunities as traders, childbearing is an economic liability, for "under current late-weaning practices a woman's economic activities are brought to a halt for more than a year and a half when she bears a child" (Murray and Alvarez 1975:122). In the community they studied, there was "quite a remarkable female absenteeism." The women's trading activity leads to a situation where the men raise crops and live in the village with the children, while the women spend much time on the market circuits. There is a "home-based world of men and a market-based world of women" (Murray and Alvarez 1975:121).

It should be noted here that the definition of what is masculine and what is feminine varies among societies as does the actual work that is performed by men and women. For rural Haiti, Murray and Alvarez note:

> The internal market system affects the norms governing sex roles in such a fashion that successful entrepreneurial behavior becomes expected of the female as a normal component of her general role as wife and mother. A woman is judged socially (and hence comes to judge herself) by the criterion of success in trade. Thus, in effect, the rural Haitian definition of "femininity" includes as a central component a notion of economic skill and productivity (Murray and Alvarez 1975:121).

Women's economic activities as itinerant traders affect their childbearing, for as Murray and Alvarez (1975:122) put it, there is a "formidable opportunity cost" in the presence of an infant. By contrast, we see that for the lower-class women of St. Kitts, as described by Gussler (this volume), children represent a potential lifelong economic asset. This is one important reason why even with the presence of modern means of birth control and an active campaign for their dissemination, the birth rate is high, infants are closely spaced and girls begin to bear children very early. Children, in this situation, represent one element in a complex strategy for economic survival of individuals in a setting of frequently matrifocal, consanguineal households.

There are striking contrasts between the vigorous trading activities of Haitian women, the struggle for economic survival of Kittian women, and the situation of upper-class Saudi women, as described by Deaver (this volume). They have no role at all in economic production, and live in total seclusion from the outside world. Indeed, they carry this seclusion and isolation with them when they move beyond the walls of their homes by means of the device of veiling and clothing that covers them fully. Here, several factors are at work: the presence of Islamic orthodoxy, the existence of a class structure and the high status of these women and their families within it, and the existence of urban centers.

There are three other Islamic societies among those described in this volume. These are the Brunei Malay of northern Borneo (Kimball), the Hausa of Niger (Saunders) and the Dioula of the Ivory Coast (Ellovich). There is considerable variation among them in the roles played by women, and all diverge greatly from the Saudi pattern. Among the Hausa, for example, Saunders tells us that some wealthy men are able to follow the orthodox pattern of secluding their wives. Yet even these women, who are restricted to their homes, may be producers of craft items, such as pottery, for a marketplace that they themselves will never visit. It is interesting, moreover, that among the Hausa, Saunders tells us, wife seclusion has increased in recent years, for it reflects both greater wealth and a validation of the prestigious position occupied by wealthy families.

Sanday (1973;1974) has sought to relate women's status to their role as economic producers. She defined status as "the *degree* to which women have decision-making power that affects activities at the economic and/or political levels" (Sanday 1974:192). High female status involves the cumulative effect of the following four factors: female control over things, demand for things women control (and, often, produce), female political participation, and finally, capping the list, female solidarity groups devoted to female political or economic interests.

Sanday correlated her criteria for female status with the percentage contribution to subsistence by women. In a pilot study of 12 societies, she found women's status to be low where their percentage contribution was either low (30 percent or less) or very high. A middle range, involving a balance in the share women and men contributed to the total subsistence appears to be most predictably associated with high status of women, as that is defined by Sanday. From this perspective, it is interesting to read the descriptions offered by our authors of the economic roles of women in the dozen situations presented here. What kinds of work do women do? How do they contribute to subsistence, directly or indirectly? What kind of control do they have over their produce and over what they own? Do women participate in the political sphere? Are there female solidarity groups? Furthermore, we may ask, how do women perceive themselves and their own situation? Is there a predictable link between subjective assessments and the objective criteria offered by Sanday?

Ernestine Friedl has suggested an additional aspect of the relationship between economics and status. She has argued that "it is the right to distribute and exchange valued goods and services to those not in a person's own domestic unit (extradomestic distribution) which confers power and prestige in all societies" (Friedl 1975:8). Contributing substantially to production will increase the likelihood of having the right to such distribution. Production then, is seen as leading potentially to extradomestic distribution, which in turn leads to, or increases, power and prestige.

Friedl's suggestion, like Sanday's research, hinges on a distinction between two "domains" or "spheres": the *domestic* (or *private*) and the *public.* These terms appear to be so familiar, to embody such commonsense distinctions, that they have been widely used in the literature dealing with women's status. They have, however, received only minimal definition, or analytic treatment. Sanday (1974:190) says: "The domestic domain includes all activities performed within the realm of the localized family unit." The concern here, then, is with "activities". The "realm of the localized family unit" appears to refer to a specific place and personnel. By contrast, "the public domain includes political and economic activities that take place or have impact beyond the localized family unit and that relate to control of persons or control of things." Gonzalez (1973) has urged the consideration of an intermediary domain, which she terms "supradomestic" and that lies somewhere between the two. The domestic domain tends to be identified by most writers with the women's sphere and the public domain with that of men, although this second identification is not quite as automatic. Rosaldo writes: "'Domestic'. . . refers to those minimal institutions and modes of activity that are organized around one or more mothers and their children; 'public' refers to institutions, activities, and forms of association that link, rank, organize, or subsume particular mother-child groups" (Rosaldo 1974:23). In her discussion of men and women in a village of Southern France, Reiter observed that "women spend their time . . . within a realm defined as their own . . . the realm of their households." This is a physical place and the women carry on a variety of activities within it. Yet, in pursuing her analysis, Reiter shifts to what she terms the "private" domain and concerns herself with "the importance of kinship in the women's lives" (Reiter 1975:253). Kinship, however, explicitly goes beyond the "realm of the localized family unit." Indeed, it is one institution that links, organizes, or subsumes, indeed often ranks, particular mother-child groups. This phrase, it will be noted, in fact constitutes Rosaldo's definition of the *public* domain! Could it be that in a complex, modern state society, such as that of France, kinship may be part of the private domain while in some kinship-dominated, "primitive" societies it may in fact be the public domain? Returning to Reiter, it should be stressed that she points out that subjectively, the women of the village, and she herself, perceived the private sphere of the women as being separate and distinct from the more public, highly differentiated spheres where men predominate in activities within the economy, politics, or the church (Reiter 1975:253). Reiter comments parenthetically that "the lives of men and women are, of course, integrated, in a holistic view of the way society actually operates" (Reiter 1975:253).

The question raised by Reiter concerning the subjective perceptions of the local women and of the American anthropologist is worth considering. We have seen in this discussion that a variety of concepts seem to have entered our discourse: activities, institutions, social units, physical structures (households or houses), and localitites. The definitions are shifting and somewhat slippery. Yet the contrast between the domestic/private, on the one hand, and the public, seem to be self-evident, and therefore merit our attention. This very fact, however, should make us suspicious and alert to the possibility that we may be dealing here with one of those unanalyzed cultural axioms, to which we need to pay special heed if we are to avoid a Western cultural bias in our work. Specifically, it is important to distinguish between the self-perceptions of people, their own theory of their society, which may be highly revealing to the anthropologist and an analytic tool that will have equal utility everywhere.

Elizabeth Janeway (1971) has neatly analyzed the underlying Western social mythology in her book *Man's World, Woman's Place*; indeed, she has done so in the very title. It is, after all, we who have grown up in modern industrialized Western society who have been taught early two old saws: "Woman's place is in the home," and "It's a man's world!" Many societies probably do actually set up such oppositions. But are they always made up of pairs of terms that mean the same things and cover the same ground? What is a "home?" Basing themselves on the work of the French historian Philippe Ariès, both Janeway and Reiter point to the recency of the small, nuclear family household in France. Janeway contrasts it with the social microcosm of the manor. This was, in fact, a community that included both kin and non-kin. Its large-scale economy represented a practically self-sufficient unit. It had little in common with the modern nuclear family residing in its private home. What of the kibbutz or the Russian collective farm? The papers in this volume present other variations on this theme. For example, Gussler notes that in St. Kitts a household may have a variety of compositions, and some may include unrelated individuals.

If we have difficulty in defining the "domestic domain" we have corresponding problems in delimiting a "public domain." Sanday (1973) speaks of it involving the economic and/or political. Reiter (1975) includes the church. Friedl makes it more inclusive, by contrasting "domestic" with the "extradomestic." Gonzalez (1973) suggests a third domain, at least for the United States, namely the "supradomestic."

Since these definitions present so many difficulties, it would seem wise at this stage of our investigation to seek to discover what domains are, in fact, recognized in particular societies. In other words, we need to proceed first with an emic analysis, making sure not to superimpose our own subjective evaluations and interpretations on those of the people we study. We may then be ready, on the basis of such data, to move with greater assurance toward a judgment of whether or not the concepts of "domestic"/"private" and "public" domains are useful analytic tools and, furthermore, whether they cover the entire spectrum of institutions and activities in given societies or whether other such domains might need to be considered. It is only then that we may be able to discern what links may exist between specific domains and the role definitions of men and women, and, perhaps also, of individuals at different points in the life cycle.

Much of the anthropological literature appears to tell us that men are everywhere superior and dominant, and women everywhere play subordinate roles; we must ask what the evidence is and what it means. One example may serve to illustrate the point. Rayna Reiter, on the basis of fieldwork in a village in southern France, tells us that "male dominance is an unconscious but cultural fact that village men internalize in the larger arena as well as in the home" (Reiter 1975:273). In contrast, women in this community are said to "perceive the public arena as sites of great play-acting. The men are seen as overgrown children strutting around and holding on to places and roles that are really quite silly; these have less value than their own homes and roles as family cores" (Reiter 1975:258). The views of women and of men in the community are, clearly, at some variance. Reiter, however, stresses the observation that the village is part of a large society, in which the state has ultimate power, so that from the perspective of the wider framework, the domestic arena of the women and their power in it is, at best, marginal. Describing a community in northwestern France, Susan Rogers, (1975) presents rather comparable data, but interprets them in quite a different way.[1] Rogers tells us that in her village women wield considerable power in the domestic sphere and significantly influence the decisions their husbands make. She argues that in this complex class society the domestic sphere is, in fact, the only one where the villagers have power, but this sphere is controlled by the women. The women, however, allow the men to believe, or to pretend to believe, that it is they who are dominant. Rogers concludes that what is seen here at work is not male dominance, but the "myth" of male dominance.

Comparing these two studies we might say that the stress of one author, Rogers, is on the village community, and that of the other, Reiter, is on the larger society. Their analyses, consequently, are framed within a different set of orientations and lead to the presentation of different pictures. It seems that, focusing at the local level, Rogers takes the women's views seriously, whereas, focusing on the relationship of the village to the state, Reiter sees the villagers, both male and female, as ultimately powerless. The women's image of their world is therefore an illusion.

Rogers argues that the "myth of male dominance" may exist in many traditional societies. What happens when the women behave in a way that may be seen by the men as a challenge to their claim of dominance? The case of the Nupe of Northern Nigeria, as described by Nadel (1952), comes to mind. In this patrilineal, Islamic West African society, many married women are itinerant traders, and their economic position may often be superior to that of their husbands, who are agriculturalists. As a result, the men are often in debt to their wives and the women take on major economic responsibilities, which according to traditional rules, are male obligations. Furthermore, to be itinerant traders women leave young children behind or attempt to limit their childbearing. This, too, is resented by the men, who consider such behavior immoral. Yet neither on the economic nor on the reproductive level can the men do anything about the situation. The men claim that the women's trading activities are recent innovations and that their views represent the true values of the traditional society. Nadel, however, was unable to find evidence for an earlier period in which such trading did not exist.

Among the Nupe there are widespread beliefs in witchcraft, and interestingly, it is women who are said to be the witches, who are thought to be organized into a society that parallels the society of the women traders. In the majority of the specific cases Nadel collected, the witch was an older domineering woman and the victim a younger man. The men also have a secret society, which, they say, has the power of "cleansing" villages of witchcraft. Nadel considers these beliefs an expression of hostility of the men against the women, whose activities they openly resent. We might say the "myth of male dominance" has been destroyed by the overt actions of the women. Another myth has been created as an alibi, to supplement the weakness of the traditional ideology: the myth of the female witches and the male heroes who defend the traditional mythology of male dominance.

An interesting footnote to Nadel's analysis is offered by the following: Some years ago, when I discussed Nadel's account with a class, a Nigerian student commented that Nupe women did indeed have great renown as witches. As a rationalist (he was a mathematics major), he said, he did not believe in witchcraft, but thought the women had themselves spread that rumor because it gave them protection on their distant travels. The myth of witchcraft, then, might serve both the men, who explain by it their loss of dominance, and the women, who may use it as a protective device.

Culture change represents our third central concern. All the sociocultural groups dealt with in this volume are involved in changes of different kinds, although the rapidity and intensity of the changes vary. The modifications of the conditions of life affect women in numerous and significant ways, and we see some of the problems but also some of the ways of coping with them. In some instances, such as that of the rural and urban women among the Brunei

Malays (Kimball), the Dioula women in town (Ellovich), and the rural and urban Yucatec women (Goodman), we find that more than one life-style exists and that there appears to be a certain amount of choice available. We may, therefore, be able to think of such alternate life-styles as constituting so many adaptive strategies employed by individuals to deal with their particular situations.

Various specific questions may be asked with regard to sociocultural and economic change: How is the position of women altered? Is it improved, or, to the contrary, is it worsened? Is change stressful and disorientating, or, primarily, liberating? Is it more stressful for women than for men, or vice versa? How are the relations between men and women affected? Is the distribution of authority, power, and prestige changed? Is the quality of interpersonal and familial relations altered? Culture change is likely to involve modifications in a whole series of aspects of life, of which economic changes are likely to represent only one segment, albeit often the most visible. We observe contact with other groups, or at least, their products, awareness of other worlds and of alternatives, some degree of Western education and a change in levels of aspiration. Often, but not always, men are more rapidly and intensively exposed to changes, than women. When this happens discrepancies may develop between their perceptions, their expectations, and their values. Their total behavioral environments may be so modified, that, in effect, men and women cease to live in a shared world, and a degree of alienation may result. In this country, we have heard a great deal about a "generation gap." One might well speak, in some instances, of a "gap" between the sexes, with regard to their cultural worlds.

There exists a sizable literature, anthropological as well as popular, that claims that women's status improves with "modernization," "westernization," greater societal complexity, and so on. This seems to be a variant of the theme that women in traditional societies are downtrodden, a version that may well have been influenced by one or more forms of "male bias" or simple ethnocentrism on the part of Western observers. Divale (1976) sought to test the theory that female status will increase with societal complexity. He confirmed it in a holocultural analysis of 31 cases, once he was able to correct for observer bias. He concludes that high female status appears at all levels of societal complexity, while low status occurs primarily in less complex societies. It should be noted that the key element in this study is ethnographers' judgment of women's status, rather than some standard criteria established by the comparativist. Moreover, it does not follow that women's status will necessarily improve when societies become more complex. However, it does appear probable, on the basis of available observations, that "westernization" leads to a modification of women's status in the direction of greater similarity to that which exists in the West. This is, however, not necessarily synonymous with "improvement."

Perhaps the most searching look at this issue has been taken by Sidney Mintz. With regard to internal trade in West Africa and the non-Hispanic Caribbean, he asks:

> If female role-playing is associated with [internal] trade, and if the relative importance of such trade is declining as the whole economy grows, what implications does this growth carry for the future sex-role differentiation of women? (Mintz 1971:251).

Mintz notes the extensive trading activities of women in such countries as Haiti and Jamaica, and in West Africa, and discusses their great economic skill and complete independence. In the contemporary situation, women traders tend to use their profits for the primary education of their children. In the case of daughters, such education leads to jobs as teachers, nurses, welfare workers, and so on. Mintz comments that such low-level salaried jobs

> represent a sharp shift away from individual enterprise, risk-taking, and independent endeavor of certain sorts...this direction [of change] is particularly telling for women since in societies of the West African and non-Hispanic Carribbean sorts, the idea that a woman conducts at least a major portion of her economic life independently is deeply embedded and generally accepted by all ...*independent* economic activity means just that—and a salary paying job does not confer independence upon the female in quite the same way that trade does (Mintz 1971:265-66).

Mintz concludes by asking rhetorically:

> Who is more modern, more western, more developed: a barefoot and illiterate Yoruba market woman who daily risks her security and her capital in vigorous competition with others like herself; or a Smith College graduate who spends her days ferrying her husband to the Westport railroad station and her children to ballet classes? If the answer is that at least the Smith girl is literate and wears shoes, one may wonder whether one brand of anthropology has not been hoisted by its own petard (Mintz 1971: 267-68).

The contrast between the American upper-middle-class suburbanite and the West African market woman may demand too much of an imaginative leap from the reader. In West Africa, however, such contrasts do appear side by side. Ellovich's chapter on the urban Dioula provides illustrations of the changes discussed by Mintz.

The discussion by Mintz may be related to that of Sanday, although their perspectives differ somewhat: a shift to clerical jobs is a move away from independent economic productivity and a lessening of control over economic resources. At the same time, as Ellovich shows for the Dioula, a loss of economic independence for women may be linked to status and prestige in the westernized sector of a West African society. Here status is not acquired by being an independent woman, but by being the wife of a high-status man. In this situation, two systems of values have come into contact, and different criteria are being applied. Goodman tells us that in Mexico the daughter of a Maya peasant woman who moves to the city may think of dependence on her husband's income as the proper way for an urban woman to live, and of work initiatives as demeaning. On the other hand, the "modernizing" village woman may find in the economic changes that her community and region are undergoing the opportunity for the development of entrepreneurship. In effect, her husband becomes her agent, because his work would be impossible without her literacy and her business acumen. Yet in contrast to the Afro-Caribbean woman, she does not acquire economic independence as a result of her activity.

The changes experienced by the people and to which they react or adapt occur not only within the framework of the local community. For many, short or long-term moves are involved. This applies to the Maya woman in the city just referred to. On a larger scale, it applies to the Cuban women in Washington. Their successful adjustment, which was vital for the adjustment of their families, was made possible, Boone argues, by their creative utilization and modification of their preexisting roles as middle-class Cuban women. It is particularly interesting that Boone finds evidence of conscious decisions as part of this process of transformation.

It has been argued that the continuity of roles between the old and the new society has often given women greater adaptability than men in situations of contact and change. In this respect several of our authors confirm what other observers have reported previously. For example, Louise Spindler (1962) has shown that Menomini women, at all levels of acculturation, demonstrate greater continuity in roles and values than men. She relates this to the preexisting flexible pattern of female roles, in contrast to the rigid public roles for men, as well as to the greater requirement for men to confront white society and to come to terms with it. For the Menomini, however, to a greater extent than for the Cubans, these differences in the continuity of sex roles led to some disharmonies in the relations between men and women.

Physical mobility appears in some of our other studies as well. In the Caribbean, in St. Vincent (Henney), and St. Kitts (Gussler), for example, many people leave for work in other countries, and for those who remain behind remittances play a significant role in their ability to survive. For Brunei Malays (Kimball) not only do Western-educated children of rural parents move to the city, but some daughters receive higher education in far distant countries. As a result, there are great differences in the life experiences of parents and their children. In two of our cases we deal with elderly women who look back over the span of long and productive lives. This is the case of Goodman's Eusebia and Joyce's Mrs. Penfield. Here change is measured in a lifetime, and not limited to the observational data available to the ethnographer. Mrs. Penfield not only describes changes, but Joyce's analysis shows us her frequently ambivalent feelings about them.

What institutions are available to people to deal with the changes they face, to cope with stresses, and to make the most of the transformations of their societies? The Western reader is likely to think of schools, and indeed that schooling is a subject that appears in these pages: the literacy, or even the advanced education, that people strive for, or seek for their children. Our studies also show the importance of the family in supporting individuals as they confront the world: the networks of the Kittian women, who "adopt" as it were, individuals as needed and their reliance on relatives who may physically be far away, or the central concern with the family of Cuban and Brazilian women. There is, however, another institution that appears to play a key role in several of our studies, and that is religion. The Apostolics in Yucatán, the Shakers in St. Vincent, and the Umbanda cult groups in São Paulo and Rio Grande do Sul all play a key role in the lives of the women, in ways that a perspective based on American denominational churches may not lead one to expect.

In the following chapters, then, we explore the lives of women in a dozen different sociocultural contexts. Culture change, the public and the private domains, and the economic role of women are discussed, and various facets of the societies are illuminated. At the end of the volume, we shall seek to assess what we have learned from these descriptions, and how our understanding has been enlarged.

NOTES

1. Various aspects of this picture of sex roles, and of the relations between women and men in French family life are confirmed by autobiographical and fictional accounts. See, for example, the 1978-79 French bestseller, *La Billebaude*. In this book the author, Henri Vincenot, describes his childhood and youth in a village in Burgundy during the years 1915-1930. Quite a different setting for family relations is provided by the opera *Louise* by G. Charpentier, which deals with a Parisian working-class family at the turn of the century. Here, too, the mother plays the decisive role in the domestic domain, while giving the father the impression that it is he who makes the vital decisions concerning their daughter's marriage.

REFERENCES

Bourguignon, E., and L.S. Greenbaum
  1973 *Diversity and Homogeneity in World Societies.* New Haven:
        HRAF Press.

Divale, W.T.
  1976 "Female Status and Cultural Evolution: A Study in Ethnogra-
        pher Bias," *Behavior Science Research* 11:149-68.

Friedl, Ernestine
  1975 *Women and Men: An Anthropologist's View.* New York: Holt,
        Rinehart and Winston.

Gonzalez, N.L.
  1973 "Women in the Jural Domain." In D.G. McGuigan, ed.: *A Sam-
        pler of Women's Studies.* Ann Arbor: University of Michigan
        Center for Continuing Education of Women.

Hammond, Dorothy, and Alta Jablow
  1976 *Women in Cultures of the World.* Menlo Park, Cal.: Cummings.

Howell, Nancy
  1976 "The Population of the Dobe Area !Kung." In R.B. Lee and I.
        DeVore, eds.: *Kalahari Hunter-Gatherers.* Cambridge: Harvard
        University Press.

Janeway, Elizabeth
  1971 *Man's World, Woman's Place: A Study in Social Mythology.* New
        York: Delta Books.

Mintz, S.W.
  1971 "Men, Women and Trade." *Comparative Studies in Society and
        History* 13:247-68.

Murray, G.F., and Alvarez, M.D.
  1975 "Haitian Bean Circuits: Cropping and Trading Maneuvers among a
        Cash-Oriented Peasantry." In S.W. Mintz, ed.: *Working Papers in
        Haitian Culture and Society.* New Haven: Yale University Antilles
        Research Program.

Nadel, S.F.
  1952 "Witchcraft in Four African Societies: An Essay in Comparison."
        American Anthropologist 54:18-29.

Reiter, Rayna
  1975 "Men and Women in the South of France: Public and Private Do-
        mains." In R. Reiter, ed.: *Toward an Anthropology of Women.*
        New York: Monthly Review Press.

Rogers, Susan
  1975 "Female Forms of Power and the Myth of Male Dominance: A
        Model of Female/Male Interaction in Peasant Societies." *Ameri-
        can Ethnologist* 2:727-56.

Rosaldo, M.Z.
   1974 "Women, Culture and Society: A Theoretical Overview." In M.Z.
         Rosaldo and L. Lamphere, eds.: *Woman, Culture and Society.*
         Stanford: Stanford University Press.

Sanday, P.R.
   1973 "Toward a Theory of the Status of Women." *American Anthro-
         pologist* 75:1682-1700.

   1974 "Female Status in the Public Domain." In M. Rosaldo and Louise
         Lamphere, eds.: *Woman, Culture and Society.* Stanford: Stan-
         ford University Press.

Spindler, L.S.
   1962 *Menomini Women and Culture Change. Memoir 91.* American
         Anthropological Association.

Vincenot, Henri
   1978 *La Billebaude.* Paris: Denoël.

PART I

ISLAMIC SOCIETIES

2 The Contemporary Saudi Woman

SHERRI DEAVER

Saudi Arabia is a country about which most Americans know little, and concerning which they hold a variety of misconceptions. In this chapter for the first time a woman anthropologist tells us about the Saudi woman and her world. The author delineates her position in the context of the contemporary society. A number of significant aspects of that society are presented, allowing us to understand the overall picture. Deaver gives special emphasis to the oil industry, the dichotomy between rural and urban populations, the pervasive force of Islam in everyday life, and the importance of kinsmen and family honor. The great influx of money, resulting from the oil industry, has brought about selective modernization as well as an increase in the seclusion of women. On the basis of her interactions with Saudi women, the author is able to show quite clearly that, from their point of view, sexual segregation is not equivalent to inferiority, low prestige, or powerlessness.

The purpose of this chapter is to explore the position of women in contemporary Saudi Arabian society. Our discussion will include both the behavorial and conceptual position of the woman in addition to her relationship to the rest of society. As we consider the modern Saudi woman it is important to realize that she lives in one of the most conservative of all present-day Islamic states. As a result of this she can be viewed as exhibiting, most strongly, the ideals that define the woman in Islamic thought. She is held responsible for maintaining the honor of the group by maintaining her own purity. This conceptual obligation results in behavioral traits that range from veiling in public to belly dancing for an all female audience. It is important to note in this context that while an upper-class Saudi woman might go unveiled in public and perhaps even to a nightclub in Beirut or Cairo, never would or could she do so in Arabia.

Modern Saudi women are of intrinsic interest to Westerners, if for no other reason, because they do veil and belly dance. These two behaviors have generated two widely contrasting stereotypes of the Saudi woman. She is portrayed either as a sensual, mysterious, wildly cavorting creature—the belly dancer—or as a secluded, downtrodden prisoner of an intensely male-dominated religious system. Both stereotypes, like all stereotypes, have some minor basis in reality, but both are also incredibly misleading. Veiling per se does not make one powerless any more than the ability to swivel the hips in a patterned fashion makes one a "free spirit" uncontrolled by societal norms.

When considering the modern Saudi woman two things must be kept in mind. First, sexual segregation can not necessarily be equated with a superior-inferior relationship. Second, a positive self-image does not require overt power in the public domain.

Sexual segregation permeates modern Saudi society. It is ideologically grounded in the Islamic belief system and in basic conceptual categories of the Saudi worldview. This sexual segregation is replicated in the social, economic, and architectural systems of the society. It results in the definition of male and female domains, which, on at least one level, are coterminous with public and private domains. This dichotomy is present in both the rural and urban settings. It is notable, however, that it seems to be more pervasive among the sedentary populations. The more pervasive nature of sexual segregation co-occurs in the urban context with an emphasis on formulaic orthodoxy, the absence of women from the economic role of producer, and with the constant physical proximity of nonkinsmen.

Limitations of This Study.

It is necessary at the outset of our discussion to place several restrictions on the following description. First, comments will be confined to Saudi women with only brief references to Western (mostly American and British) and East Asian women residing within the kingdom. Second, it should be noted that only the information concerning the sedentary populations is the product of ethnographic research by the author. Further, the vast majority of this information was collected between 1970 and 1972 in the Eastern Province (see Figure 2.1).

The fact that this information comes from the Eastern Province creates two further limitations on the data. First, the Eastern Province of Saudi Arabia is the site of the oil industry and its concomitant Western influences. Second, the Eastern Province is regarded by many Saudis as deviant when compared to the rest of the kingdom. This deviance, in the Saudi view, derives from the presence of the resident alien population created by the oil industry, and the relatively high percentage of Shia Muslims in the area. Shia refers to one of the major divisions of the Islamic community, which regards descent from the prophet as a defining attribute for political leadership. The vast majority of Saudis belong to the other major division of the

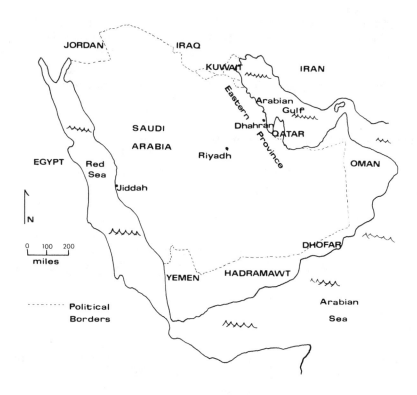

Figure 2.1: The Arabian Peninsula

Islamic community, Sunni, which regards descent from the prophet as a source of prestige but not a necessary prerequisite for political power. The Shia in the Eastern Province are regarded by the majority Sunni as inferior in terms of orthodoxy and unreliable in terms of political alliance.

Another limitation to our discussion of Saudi women is a little more difficult to pin down. As stated previously, the data on the rural segment of the population come from secondary sources. All of these that deal directly with Saudi nomads are the reports of males. This does not necessarily make them inferior or not useful. It simply is necessary from the outset for the reader to realize that this too will create a bias in the data. It is axiomatic that there are two social worlds in Middle Eastern societies, one male and one female. Therefore, ethnographers in the Middle East are confronted with a twofold problem from the outset. First, the scope of information they are allowed access to will be limited by their own sex. Second, the informants' access to information will be dependent on their sex. Thus, it is very easy to get a situation where a male ethnographer talks to male informants and produces a description that says almost nothing about females (see Cole 1975, for an example). The reverse is also true as I found in my field experience. Since this chapter deals specifically with women, the latter is not a problem. The former is. The reader is thus cautioned that the data on rural women contained herein are limited in detail and come from the male point of view.

Method of Presentation

With these limitations in mind our aim is to understand the Saudi woman both conceptually and in terms of behavior. Our further aim is to understand her relationship to the rest of Saudi society. To do this we will first consider the context in which she lives, modern Saudi society, in terms of both traditional and modern characteristics. Second, an ideal of the Islamic notion of female will be constructed by posing a series of overdrawn conceptual dichotomies. Using this ideal as a template we may explain the conceptual constraints on the Saudi woman that will be behaviorally defined by her society. The dichotomies that will be of primary concern to us since they underlie Saudi society are male/female, public/private, honor/shame, and their many transformations.

MODERN SAUDI SOCIETY

In order to understand the position of the modern Saudi woman we must turn to a necessary overview of modern Saudi society. To understand "the woman's place" we must, of course, understand the wider context—Saudi Arabia today. Several traditional aspects of Saudi society will be our first concern. These traditional factors include: (1) the separate but symbiotically related rural and urban segments of the population; (2) the pervasive force of Islam in Saudi society; and (3) the importance of kinsmen and the concept of family honor.

Traditional Rural-Urban Continuum

In Arabian history and postglacial prehistory there has always been a dichotomy between the nomad and the oasis dweller. One segment of the population has engaged in animal husbandry as a major subsistence strategy, while their sedentary counterparts have been dependent on agriculture. In the past the relationship between these two segments of the population has been based on the classic trading and raiding pattern. The nomadic segment of the population has been tied to the sedentary segment by the bonds of trade, religion and kinship. The oasis dwellers have been dependent on the nomads as consumers of agricultural products, clientele for religious specialists, and as defenders of their property and territory (Doughty 1936, Musil 1927, Dickson 1951, Cole 1975). The nomadic populations are limited by the size of their herds, which in turn are limited by access to water. The sedentary segment of the population is limited by access to arable land.

Islam in Traditional Saudi Society

"Saudi Arabia is the one country where Islamic heritage is most obvious and most jealously guarded, where the tenets of Islam are most adhered to and where Muslim law is most strictly observed" (Ghul 1966:10). The particular form of Islam dominant in Saudi Arabia is the Muwahhidun sect of the Sunni branch.

Literally Muwahhidun means unitarian. Critics of the movement/sect refer to it as Wahhabiya or Wahabbi and consider its members to be fanatics and puritans. Whatever name is used, it refers to the teachings of the prophet/reformer/teacher 'Abd al-Wahhab who lived from 1703-1787 A.D. or in the Arabian calendar from 1115-1201 A.H. The doctrine of this group emphasizes the oneness of Allah, a rejection of all intermediaries between God and man, and the equality of all men (and women) before Allah. Further, Allah is considered all knowing and all powerful and has ordained all that has and/or will occur in the realm of man.

The Muwahhidun started as a reform movement to purify Islam. As it grew it became an integral component of the expansion of the Saud family and hence eventually one of the foundations of the modern kingdom (Rentz 1972). The present-day state of Saudi Arabia is a theocracy, although it is not formally regarded as such. The Koran is the basis of the legal system. The King of Arabia is the Imam (religious leader/teacher) of the Muwahhidun, and the 'ulema (council of religious scholars) is consulted on matters of political policy.

Currently there is great tension between the traditionalist and those who would secularize the government. This is a very complex issue and one beyond the scope of this study. However, the significance of the Muwahhidun is impossible to overemphasize. Perhaps an example will illustrate the extreme conservatism of this sect and its far-reaching influence in Arabia today.

> The assasination of King Faisal was not an attempt to overthrow the monarchy. It arose out of a conflict between two branches of the ruling family and represents an atavistic throwback to the most fundamental aspects of Islam. A number of years ago, King Faisal issued an order to suppress all active opposition against the introduction of television. When a group of conservatives under the leadership of a member of the royal family threatened to attack and destroy a station, the police fired into the crowd and killed its leader. Because King Faisal refused to deliver the officer who had fired the fatal shot to the relatives of the slain man for execution (as is provided in the Koran), he himself became a target for revenge (Knauerhase 1977:34).

Two things are important in our example. The dispute centered around the introduction of television into the kingdom. The most conservative

Muwahhidun consider it to be sacrilege since television reproduces images thus impinging on Allah's domain. King Faisal, considered a liberal on this question, allowed television into the country. However, he heavily restricted programming. Television broadcasting is discontinued for 20 minutes during prayer call. Cut from all programs are all sexual scenes and mentions of alcohol. Sexual scenes in this context mean bodily contact between members of the opposite sex who are not kinsmen. Nudity is banned from the screen. Most programming consists of the cut versions of 1950s American serials, Egyptian soap operas, and the local news. Only male Saudis appear on television. So, even though King Faisal's directive concerning television is at one level liberal, the Muwahhidun "puritanical" influence is clear both in terms of programming content and in terms of when broadcasts are allowed at all. One further example to illustrate this is that in 1970 when the first graduation ceremony at the College of Petroleum and Minerals was broadcast for two nights in a row in a display of national pride of government-sponsored "progress," all women in attendance (wives of foreign faculty) were kept behind a screen and completely off camera.

Second, we notice in our example that King Faisal died in the context of a feud. "It should be not forgotten that Islam is a faith and a divine law, and that the enforcement of this law is a fundamental tenet in a truly Muslim society" (Ghul 1966:12). The Koran is the basis of law in Saudi Arabia. Self-help is legitimated by the Koran. It is the responsibility of the family wronged to correct the situation, by force if necessary. Once again the conservative nature of the Muwahhidun state is emphasized. Secular law as such does not exist in Arabia.

Today according to the most orthodox followers of 'Abd al-Wahab, it involves unbelief and heresy to accept the presence of cameras, tape-recorders, television, and so on. It is *shirk* (polythesism) to use the name of the prophet in an oath. It is not enough to state the Islamic creed to become a convert. Public prayer is obligatory. Tobacco, drugs, liquor, and pork are taboo, and within the kingdom there is relatively strict enforcement of these taboos. Allegiance to the government is in large part based on personal faith in a religious leader. This is particularly true among the nomads [Bedu] (Cole 1975).

One further attribute of the Muwahhidun state must be considered—the religious police or Mutawwah. The Mutawwah are common figures in the urban setting. They are self-appointed missionaries of truth and regard it as their duty to monitor propriety and everyday behavior of all people in the public domain.

> Public social behavior is still monitored by the committee for Encouraging Virtue and Preventing vice (hay'at al-amr b'il Ma'rūf w'al nahi 'an al-munkar), commonly known as the mutawiyin (volunteers). These morality police have been a part of urban life

in the country since the first Saudi state was established in the eighteenth century, when they were used by Wahhabi religious authorities to enforce observance of the puritanical social behavior as well as the devout religious practices promoted by the Wahhabis. Even in the middle of the twentieth century in Riyadh, although they no longer entered private homes to stop smoking or playing music, or to get them to go to the mosque, the mutawiyin did enforce these and other habits in public places (Rugh 1973:19).

In Dhahran in the early 1970s these volunteers made sure stores shut during prayer call and showed particular concern with people's general appearance and attire while ignoring music and smoking for the most part. Men with sideburns were forced into barbershops, and women were tapped on the legs with walking sticks when they appeared in public with their legs uncovered. Many students at the college felt it their responsibility to report to the Mutawwah on the behavior of their faculty. This led to the elimination of joint student-faculty viewing of movies shown by the college. The students' reporting to the Mutawwah also resulted in the deportation (24 hours notice) of one of the faculty who had admitted to these students that he was an agnostic. These and similar activities of the Mutawwah provide the major basis for the outsider's criticisms of the Saudi state as being both puritanical and fanatical.

In terms of women the Muwahhidun community calls for strict seclusion, complete covering when appearing in the public domain, premarital chastity, and postmarital fidelity. Violation of any of these tenets will bring retribution from the male kinsmen. In extreme cases this retribution may include death. It is both the right and the obligation of the male kinsmen to insure the proper behavior of their female kinsmen.

> Beirut, Lebanon, March 3, 1973–A man who choked his 15 year old daughter to death because she "flirted with boys" has just been released from prison on a presidential pardon after serving nine months of a seven year sentence (New York Times, p. 8).

The man involved was a Saudi. Had he done the same thing at home, there would have been no penalty.

Islam has been and is a pervasive force in Saudi society. It underlies the political system of the kingdom. It structures its legal system. It is a source of conflict centering around how to apply Islamic principles to a changing world. It serves to regulate everyday behavior, including dictating details such as what constitutes proper diet and dress.

Kinsmen and the Concept of Honor in Traditional Saudi Society

In the foregoing discussion of religion in Saudi society we made many references to kinsmen, that is, male kinsmen have the obligation of monitoring the behavior of female kinsmen, King Faisal was killed in the context of a

feud—a family affair, and so on. The importance of having relatives, kinsmen, is, and was in the past as pervasive a factor as is religion. One must have
kinsmen to survive. They take you in when you have troubles. They defend
you when you are threatened. But perhaps most importantly they are responsible for your behavior. A Saudi is not an individual who may act freely on
his own impulses; rather his behavior is structured by the fact that his actions
will reflect on his kinsmen. It is in this context that the notion of family
honor becomes important. The honor/prestige/status of the group is threatened or increased by the actions of its component individuals. This is of
particular significance when considering the position of women in this society
since it is the responsibility of the female to remain pure in order to maintain
the honor of the group. If the female does not remain pure, that is, does
something shameful, the family loses honor until the males correct her behavior. For example in 1977 one of King Khalid's brothers "drowned one of his
daughters in a swimming pool when he learned that she had been to bed
with a man before her marriage" (*New Republic* Feb. 1978:8). Premarital
sexual activity is shameful by Saudi standards.

Modern Changes in Saudi Society

Flying into the Eastern Province today is a little like being caught up in the
middle of one of the early science fiction films of the 1950s. The first sight
that greets the incoming visitor is a series of huge flares that burn perpetually
in the desert night. These are the natural gas wells that burn continuously.
These flames symbolize dramatically the place of oil in contemporary Arabia.
They are burning because fuel is in such abundance that waste is not a relevant dimension for decision making. They are burning because the gas is
"dirty," poisonous, and the secondary elaboration of the oil industry is unavailable locally "to clean" the gas—and so it burns. There is so much oil that
crude is used to stabilize the sand so that it will not drift on the roads.

Two of the major effects of the oil industry have been a tremendous
influx of wealth into the kingdom and many technological changes and material gains in large part funded by this influx of wealth. The oil revenues are
controlled by the government. In 1938 goverment oil revenues were .2 million
dollars; in 1948, 31.5 million; in 1960, 333.7 million; and in 1975, 25,675.2
million dollars (Knauerhase 1977:7). The influx of wealth into the country
from the exploitation of oil is currently creating a situation in which,
" . . . Saudi Arabia will emerge in the next few years as one of the financial
centers, perhaps the 'banker of the world'" (Schmidt 1974:93). This oil
money is funding the development of medical, educational, and transportation facilities. It has allowed for the massive importation of Western technology and material goods—everything from Lipton flow-thru tea bags to Chev-
rolet Impalas to F-15 jet fighters.

The oil industry has created a series of jobs that call for highly trained
professionals. This has resulted in an influx of foreign technicians that form a

resident alien population. "In the early 1970s about 300,000 foreigners worked in Saudi Arabia...by 1980 approximately one out of three workers will be a foreigner" (Knauerhase 1977:9).

The Eastern Province has borne the brunt of this foreign "invasion" or "development." Aramco, the Arabian-American oil company has set up three major camps, planned self-sufficient communities for the foreign technicians. One of these camps is located in Dhahran. Dhahran is not a town in the Western commonsense definition of that term. Rather, it is a locality that contains a series of separate living units. The Aramco camp is only one of these units; University of Petroleum and Minerals is another, but inhabitants of all units say they live in Dhahran and often refer to just their living unit as Dhahran. For clarity we shall retain the label Dhahran only for the locality even though this would seem arbitrary to the inhabitants.

Senior Camp looks very much like a 1950s version of a Southern California middle-class suburb. The gardeners, however, wear skull caps, and a majority of vehicles in the driveways have four-wheel drive. This community is inner directed. Within its walls (seven feet high, totally encircling the compound) are schools, restaurants, grocery stores, bowling alleys, and so on. There are third-generation Aramcons living in Senior Camp who speak no Arabic. Contact between the members of this foreign technician community and Saudi society at large is almost totally through males and basically limited to the economic sphere. An employee-employer relationship exists between the manual workers (Saudis) and the engineers, drillers, and geologists (non-Saudi) with the latter holding the dominant supervisory positions. At the office administrative level as opposed to the field administrative level there is official codominance and a generally friendly atmosphere that both sides work hard to maintain.

Outside this direct economic context Aramco in general and the foreign technicians in particular have had less effect on everyday life than might be supposed. This is a result of the Saudi's often ambivalent, if not hostile, attitude toward the foreign community. Senior Camp, for example, is regarded as a sort of pollutant to the true Muwahhidun state. It is the source of liquor, drugs, prostitutes, homosexuals, polytheism, black-market bacon, and so forth. The ambivalence of the situation is created by the fact that it is also the source of many positively evaluated material items in addition to sophisticated Western medical aid and jobs. So while Senior Camp is polluting to the proper way of life, it also offers advantages in terms of technology and material goods. Many Saudis, like their third world counterparts in many other areas, would like to take the technology and its jobs while rejecting the rest of the Western influences.

One of the major underlying rationales for the creation of the University of Petroleum and Minerals (another part of the complex called Dhahran) was to train a cadre of Saudi engineers to take over the slots now filled by foreigners. This would ultimately end Saudi dependence on foreign technology and thereby remove a polluting influence by terminating the foreign presence. Also the establishment of the university would create a suitable Muwahhidun environment in which to study and thereby stop the "brain drain" by saving the student population from the West.

In reality there seems to be little mutual respect on either side. Aramcons often regard the Saudis as barbarians and constantly tell "Saudi jokes," which usually center around a Saudi coming to some catastrophic fate because he refused to think for himself and relied blindly on religious faith. One of the current examples of this centers around a Prince who had crashed a jet fighter because he didn't put his landing gear down. When asked why he didn't pull out when the tower warned him of his problem, he replied, *"Inshallah,* if God wills I shall live, I will; if not, I shall not." Thus, the Saudi was/is constantly portrayed by the Aramcons as inferior, since he does not at least attempt to be independent and take care of himself. The Saudis are well aware of the Aramcon attitude.

The everyday influence of the Aramco community is further limited by the fact that when members do venture out they are often regarded negatively. Many cannot or will not bargain. This results in their being considered boorish at the least and stupid at the worst. Females tend to maintain their Western clothing styles, which leads to them being perceived as shameless, meaning, of course, from the Saudi point of view, that their men have no honor. Add to this that they do not follow the true faith and the fact that the Saudi's ethnocentrism is matched if not exceeded by that of the Aramcon and a situation is created where there is relatively little positive personal contact between the two groups.

Changes in the Rural-Urban Continuum
The distribution of wealth derived from the oil industry has radically changed the symbiotic relationship between the sedentary and nomadic sectors of the population.

> The traditional relationship between the Bedouin and the wider society can be characterized as one of mutual interdependence. Just as the Bedouin depended on the city for many essential services, the traditional city (and the village) depended on the Bedouin for protection. In recent decades, these services have been taken from the Bedouin...and transferred to the centralized state (Cole 1975:106).

It is the oil industry in Saudi Arabia that supports the hegemony of the house of Saud. Now there is a middleman, the centralized government, between the sedentary and rural segments of the society. Further, the oil revenues support the National Guard, a major source of jobs and income for the nomads today. Here again the government takes on the role of middleman.

As stated previously the nomadic population has been limited by the size of its herds, which were limited in turn by access to water. The introduction of the drilling technology associated with the exploration for oil has led to much geological survey activity and the drilling of new water wells. This has changed traditional migration routes and may lead to an increase in the nomadic sector of the population (Aramco 1968, Cole 1975). The sedentary segment of the population was limited by access to arable land. The oil industry has changed this by providing a new basis for sedentary adaptation— industrialization. As a result, towns are growing. With the influx of oil money has come an increase in the kind and availability of consumer goods, which has served to further demarcate the boundaries between the two adaptations. The urban population, while becoming more dependent on the outside world, is accumulating more new material items faster than the Bedu (Cole 1975: ch. 7). The Bedu, of course, have been tremendously affected by the introduction of trucks, four-wheel drive vehicles, and by the new water wells drilled by the new technicians. The unevenness of the modernization process is recognized by each group but evaluated very differently by each. The urban population tends to regard the nomads as uncivilized, country bumpkins. On the other hand, the nomads regard their relative independence from the oil industry as the only reasonable adaptation. "The oil wells...can be blown up in thirty minutes and with no money, all those people in Dhahran and Riyadh would die from lack of food. Why, they would not even have enough gasoline to leave and go back to their homelands" (an Al Jaber man in Cole 1975: 155). Further, the Bedu perceive themselves to embody the Arab virtues of generosity, hospitality, self-help, and honoring kinsmen (Cole 1975). "They reject the city as physically and socially polluted and prefer the desert where they can live what they habitually describe as a pure and clean life" (Cole 1975:16). The town Saudis on the other hand pride themselves on their sophistication and categorize the Bedu as wild. For example, the Bedu life is romanticized as being truly Arab, but, while it is proper to talk of a great grandfather who was a Bedu, such relatives of closer geneological depth are selectively ignored. Further, each group regards itself as being more properly Muslim than the other. The nomads regard the urban people as too concerned with form and not enough with spirit. On the other hand, the town Saudis often regard the emotionalism of Bedu religious activity as a sign of fanaticism.

In addition to these differences, the impact of the oil industry has created a further contrast between the sedentary and the nomadic peoples— the relative freedom of women. As economic adjustment continues the economic roles of women are, of course, adjusted. Ironically, in this case, "Westernization/modernization" is increasing the pervasiveness of seclusion in the more Westernized sector by removing urban women from the role of economic producer. On the other hand, the Bedu women have more markets to attend thereby decreasing seclusion in the least Westernized sector of the society. Traditionally, when the urban, sedentary adaptation was based on agriculture women took on the role of economic producer by modifying the raw material grown by the men into the products necessary to fulfill the needs for food, shelter, and the socially critical hospitality. This involved work both inside and outside of the home. In the industrialized-based communities, however, females have lost this role to a larger extent. Processed foods are increasingly available. Often prefabricated Western-style home furnishings are desired as insignias of status. More and more of the products once controlled by women are now simply bought in the marketplace.

All of the jobs in these communities from rigger to clerk to nurse are forbidden to women since they involve contact with male nonkin. Thus the woman in the new urban situation becomes more secluded, since she has less legitimate opportunities to venture into the public domain.

In addition to modifying the relationship between the rural and urban sectors of the population, the oil industry is having one further effect on the societal structure of modern Saudi Arabia. Internally, the influx of wealth from the oil exploitation is creating a growing, if small, middle class. It is difficult to assess the significance of the new middle class, since the changes associated with growth of the middle class in developing nations are in some cases actually made by the upper class in Saudi Arabia to improve its national image abroad.

> The introduction of television, the gradual change to a GMT time system, the adoption of an economic plan and its use of the Gregorian calendar, the spread of secular education and of public schooling for girls—all of these innovations were opposed by conservative religious leaders but took place anyway during the past decade. The rising New Middle Class did not demand these changes but was pleased that they occurred, and the growing importance of this group is undoubtedly a factor in these developments...The New Middle Class is still numerically small and, as long as economic development and some social change have occurred, it has eschewed demands for political change (Rugh 1973:7-20).

This is an *emerging* middle class. While its influence is felt disproportionately to its numbers in the economic and political spheres of Saudi life, the same can not be applied to the social sphere and in particular the status of women:

> Although Saudi girls are aspiring to a secular education, their social life is still strictly regulated. They must still wear veils in public places, and generally cannot be seen by adult males outside the immediate family. Foreign wives are usually exempted from this rule, and even a few Saudi wives of foreign-edu-

cated Saudis are to be seen at private parties of close friends. But this is a tradition that will not disappear overnight; even a Western education does not make a man tell his Saudi wife to be the first to uncover her face on the streets of Riyadh (Rugh 1973:18).

One of the keys to understanding modern Saudi society is to understand the effects of the oil industry. It has brought tremendous amounts of wealth into the kingdom. This wealth underpins the current political structure, which involves the centralized government taking on the role of middleman between the sedentary and nomadic populace. It has created an emerging middle class. The oil money underlies the development plans of the kingdom and is thus the basis for the projected growth of schools, hospitals, and so on. Further economic effects include the creation of industry-related jobs and essentially a new base for the sedentary adaptation. With the importation of the technology for this oilfield-based adaptation has come the immigration of a class of technicians who bring with them Western material goods, ideas, attitudes, and values. The often negative assessment of the foreign technicians by the Saudis and vice versa has limited the influence of this group outside of direct economic concerns.

MODERN SAUDI WOMEN

With this overview of both the traditional and modern aspects in mind, let us turn to a consideration of some of the key aspects of Islamic society as they specifically relate to women.

What is an *Islamic* woman? First, she is female. Both male and female are qualitatively distinct entities in Islamic thought. They share a sensual nature, which creates a unity between them. Also unity is created between them since both were created by Allah. The sensual nature of male and female is not assumed to be controllable through a simple force of will. Thus, outside agencies are needed to control this aspect of maleness and femaleness. Males, according to the Koran, have the qualities of strength, ability for judgment, and abstract reasoning. Females, on the other hand, can easily be lead into temptation. Therefore, to control sensuality it is necessary for males, through their strength and judgment to control the vulnerable females. Thus, the Koran states, "men are in charge of women." The mechanism most commonly employed by men in Islamic societies to establish control has been and is seclusion and veiling. The male/female dichotomy in Islamic society is at once complementary and hierarchical in structure. The categories of male and female are complementary since it takes both to define the unity created by Allah. They are hierarchical with the male as dominant (but not superior) since men have the qualities that enable them to control the qualities of women (see Table 2.1).

Table 2.1

Male and Female Qualities

Male	Female
sensual nature	sensual nature
created by Allah	created by Allah
strong	weak
ability for judgment	easily tempted
abstract reasoning	emotional

One transformation (alternate expression) of the male/female dichotomy is outside/inside, which results from men secluding women in an effort to control their sensual nature. Females are thus associated with the concept of inside, males with outside. Inside is, at one level, coterminous with the house or home, while outside is coterminous with the public, political, and social areas, the market and mosque. Thus, a further transformation of this dichotomy is home-house/market-mosque.

This transormation brings us to the second major dichotomy characteristic of Islamic society—public/private. Public space is male space. It is the area of business and political activity. Mosques are also in the public domain. Thus, economic, political, and religious activity are associated with the male. Private space is associated with females, kinsmen, gardens, and intimate relationships. The private domain may be seen as a kind of retreat, a sanctuary. Those people who are most trustworthy and who can be counted on to support you—kinsmen—are associated with the private domain. Women are the only source of new kinsmen and consequently belong to the private domain. To protect this sanctuary of the private space is the duty of all males. This is accomplished architecturally through externally opaque surfaces, tightly controlled access areas, and internal courtyards to provide private outside space. These three themes are characteristic of traditional Islamic vernacular architecture. When females do move into the public domain, they carry these barriers with them in the guise of extremely modest clothing, especially the veil. Transformations of public/private thus include male/female, outside/inside, market/home, nonkin/kin, danger/security, and distant social relationships/intimate relationships.

One further dichotomy is critical to the understanding of Islamic society—honor/shame. Honor is a male attribute, shame a female one. Any behavior resulting in the blurring of one of these sets of categories results in shame. Allowing a male nonkinsman in the garden when female members of the family are present, females unveiling in the public domain, intimate social relationships for either sex in the public domain, and so on, all involve a blurring of this cognitive structure. All challenge the Islamic ideal of the way things should be, and thus create the shame. One is honor bound to correct this imbalance in the ordained structure of the world.

> Honor is a crucial ingredient of every society. In Islamic cultures (and in many pre-Islamic Mediterranean cultures) male honor is closely linked to female purity: this requires virginity for the unmarried, fidelity for the married, and continence for the divorced or widowed. This conception of honor means that the behavior of an individual woman affects not only her own reputation but also that of her husband, her father, her brother, indeed that of all her male kin (Stiehm 1976:277).

In short, the unity of social life in Islamic society may be thought of as being organized in terms of a series of contrasting and complementary categories (see Table 2.2). All of these dichotomies are interrelated in the Saudi concept of the world. Hence, any dichotomy can be a transformation of any other. When balanced these categories define the world as it should be and honor is maintained. When imbalance occurs, shame results. The dichotomies or sets of categories are complementary, since it takes both of each set to define social life. They are hierarchical since Allah has ordained the male is in charge of the female and shame must be redressed to maintain honor. From this most general consideration of characteristics of Islamic society we must consider the Saudi woman and her position in her society (see Table 2.2).

Table 2.2

Complementary Categories of Social Life	
male	female
public	private
nonkin	kin
outside	inside
danger	security
market	garden
distant social relationships	intimate social relationships

In modern Arabia sexual segregation permeates the society. It stems ultimately from the Islamic definition of the world and is manifest in all spheres of the society.

This sexual segregation is found in the economic sphere. Woman's place is in the domestic domain. Women are responsible for all economic activities concerned with domestic maintenance. Traditionally women in the urban setting may have engaged in more extradomestic economic activities, but today with wage-labor in the oil industry replacing agriculture in many cases,

women are engaging in fewer of these activities. On the other hand, Bedu
women retain their extradomestic economic roles.

> There is a clear division of labor, but both sexes perform activities
> mainly associated with the other sex under certain conditions.
> Women are concerned with taking down, setting up, and transport-
> ing all household items...Men are mainly concerned with herding,
> milking, and watering camels, but women perform any of these
> tasks...Both men and women attend markets and buy and sell
> products (Cole 1975:79).

Nomadic pastorialism in contrast to industrialization necessitates the active
cooperation of all members of the group, male and female. The household is
an economic adjunct to the herds while it need not be to the oil rig.

A sedentary Saudi woman, then, tends to be more secluded than her
nomadic sister. She prepares or directs the preparation of all food and drink.
Through this economic role, she, like her nomadic sister, can dramatically
limit a man's ability to be a proper host. In this way she has power in the
male sphere without being a part of it. In towns, she may go to market if she
is without young kinsmen or servants to do this for her, but where possible it
is always more desirable to have the men of the household make outside
purchases. Having to do your marketing is a sign of low status and associated
with being poor. Nomadic women, on the other hand, go freely to markets
and participate avidly in trading. With the inflow of money from National
Guard salaries, the Bedu have increased their purchasing power at the same
time new material items have come into the markets. These two factors taken
together seem to have created a situation where the Bedu are coming more
often to market.

Socially, sexual segregation is signaled by the fact that in public there is
no social interaction between the sexes. Women are not seen in coffee houses.
Even if the males and females are close kinsmen they are not supposed to
overtly acknowledge each other in public (see Fernea 1965 for a parallel
situation). For example, a man might drive his wife to a medical clinic and
even in some unusual cases let her be treated by a male doctor, but he will
not accompany her from the car to the door of the clinic or demonstrate his
concern in any other public way. This segregation has created problems for
the adoption of Western medical technology. Female doctors are extremely
rare and, of course, all foreign (as are all of the nurses). This has led to a
situation where it was reported by a reputable physician that Arabian women
were superior to Western women since there was no cervical cancer reported
for the population. Another way of explaining the absence of cervical cancer
is simply that for women who have their passport pictures taken with the veil
on, a pap-test is beyond unthinkable.

Social life involving nonkinsmen centers in the home for the women. On
those occasions when males and females are in the visiting party, the women

entertain in one segment of the house, men in another. If only women make up the visiting party then the whole house is theirs. Male servants are treated as socially neuter by the upper class. They may see women unveiled but must retire as soon as their duties have been performed.

It was pointed out at the beginning of this discussion that one of the Western stereotypes of the Saudi woman is that of the wildly cavorting, sensual creature-the belly dancer. It is certainly true that they regard themselves as sensual beings. Wildly cavorting, on the other hand, has nothing to do with everyday Saudi female reality. Saudi women belly dance in their homes (private, female space) for audiences made up of either their nuclear family or more commonly for female guests (kin and nonkin). Only a prostitute would dance before male nonkin or in the public domain. Thus, the modern Saudi belly dancer is not some free-spirit breaking all the rules, but rather another expression of the rules resulting in this case in explicitly sexual exhibitionist behavior being restricted to a unisexual (all female) or a nuclear family setting. This is simply a logical result of protecting the honor of the group by secluding that which might bring shame.

In the belly dance the female's sensuality is explicitly displayed as is her beauty, her ability to dance, and her gold. The dance involves the dancer's careful control of arm movements which, while never restricting her pelvic movements, encircle her upper torso to best display her best jewelry. The hips rotate a full 360 degrees at various speeds while the torso is shimmied in a linear fashion. The eyes are downcast and the hair is often used as a drape or foil. The dance is flirtatious, entertaining, and fun. It further serves as a legitimate mechanism whereby the woman may display her best clothes and jewelry to her peer group without overtly challenging the egalitarian ideal of behavior. As the dancer moves she positions herself so each part of the audience may inspect her attire, especially her gold. According to Saudi women, the only jewelry worth having is gold. Gold is given to women on all occasions. If the situation calls for a gift from a male to a female, there is never any questions what it will be. It may be a bangle, ring, watch, and so on, but if the male can possibly afford it, it will be gold. Gold means security to the modern Saudi female. It is a sign of the continuing affection, concern, respect, and protection of her male kinsmen. It is also always legally hers. No one, not even her kinsmen, may take it without her permission. In times of stress it is easily converted into cash. So in the belly dance the woman is displaying an important marker of her status, her gold.

Children prepuberty seem to be socially neutral. They may move between the male and female entertainment sections within the house. However, outside the home the situation is modified. While male children may be seen in coffee houses on infrequent occasions, female children are not. This is the case even before the female is veiled which is usually about ten years of age, though the age varies widely. Also it should be emphasized that the process of seclusion is gradual. It is not uncommon to see a young girl trying to wear the abaya with limited degree of success. It may billow about her disregarded as she plays only to be pulled tight at the approach of a stranger. (Cole 1975: ch. 3).

The segregation of the sexes is also repeated and replicated by the vernacular architecture of Saudi Arabia (Rapoport 1969).

> The inward-looking Arab house, open to the calm of the sky, made beautiful by the feminine element of water, self-contained and peaceful, the deliberate antithesis of the harsh public world of work, warfare, and commerce, is the domain of woman. The name in Arabic "sakan," to denote the house, is related to the word "sakina," peaceful and holy, while the word "harim," which means woman, is related to "harem," sacred, which denotes the family living quarters in the Arab house (Fathy 1969:77-78).

House form is of particular interest here. Both the nomadic and the sedentary housing forms show the same concern with the allotment of space in terms of a sexual division. Saudi house form replicates the segregation of the sexes. Among the sedentary population the first noticeable division is that between the street (public domain) and the house (private domain), and is marked by a wall. These walls average about seven feet and are opaque. They contain no windows and generally only one door or gateway. Moving through the door gives entrance to the gardens in which females may move around minus abaya and veil if only females or kinsmen are present. Access to the interior of the house is through the front door for visitors.

The interior floor plan varies widely, but that area immediately accessible via the front door is male/public/nonkin entertaining space and will be used by females entertaining only if the group is entirely female or if it contains only close kinsmen. The more elaborate homes also include internal courtyards which serve to create more private, female space.

If the house does not have the separate surrounding wall as in the case of the new apartment buildings and prefabricated Western houses, this same basic concern with creating private, female space is maintained. Roof gardens or walled-in balconies serve the apartment dweller. On hot evenings it is the usual sight to see sheets hung in the roof areas to divide the space so visitors of both sexes may enjoy the night air. In these apartment dwellings without the separating wall, there are few if any windows on street level. Those that exist are opaqued. In the case of the prefabricated Western-style houses, drapes are always drawn tight. Male visitor access is through the front door only, while females may also use back and side doors as well. In these "prefabs," entertaining nonkin of both sexes creates logistic problems for the hostess. One common way of solving this today is to drape a sheet or curtain in the living room to create two spaces. That space with direct access to the front door is male space. In all cases the area immediately accessible via the front door constitutes male/nonkin/public space so that structurally at least female space can be characterized as being behind male space.

These architectural constraints then create a double threshold to insure the honor of that which is within, the women—the only source of new family members. The first major threshold is between the public and private domains, the second between nonkin and kin. Permission is necessary to cross the first; kin ties determine the ability to cross the second.

The internal space, whether created by the wall, lack of windows, or drawn drapes may be characterized as female, private, kin space. When only family members are home, the females may move freely in and out of the different sections of the house. A female may go outside uncovered if she has a garden, roof, or internal courtyard. Her access to these spaces is limited only by the entrance of nonkin who are male. When she moves out of these precincts, she will don the abaya and veil, which create a small, private, secure space that will not be violated by kinsmen once she is in the public domain. Thus, she remains socially invisible in the male sphere.

According to the traditional sources, Dickson, Doughty, Musil, and Thesiger and the most recent ethnographic report on the Bedu, *Nomad of the Nomads*, the same architectural constraints hold true for the nomadic populations in Saudi society. Although there is no wall to mark the first threshold between the public and private domains, there is a generally recognized distance at which nonkinsmen must signal their arrival so that camp members may arrange themselves in their proper quarters (Dickson 1951; Cole 1975). It is necessary to announce in some fashion that the outside world is about to intrude.

Structurally, the tent is divided into male and female compartments with the male compartment being the conceptual front (see Figure 2.2). Male visitors approach from the west, which brings them to the male compart-

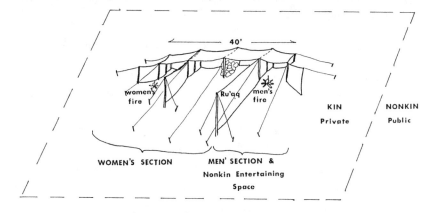

Figure 2.2: Nomadic Architectural Arrangement

ment, and confine their visiting to the male area of the tent if they are non-kinsmen. There is a hierarchy of rules concerning the control of the kinsmen who may cross the second threshold, the divider (Ru'ag), between the two compartments.

> When male guests arrive at the bayt, the women curtail some of their movements outside their part of the tent, depending on their degree of relationship with the visitors, the duration of the visit, and their actual need to leave the tent...If the visitors are not from the Al Murrah, they simply shake hands with the men and do not greet the women at all. If, however, the women know the visitors, they may greet the men verbally from their side of the tent. Any women who arrive with male visitors go directly, and from the back side of the tent, to the women's section. If they are Al Murrah women, the men of the bayt go to them at some time during the visit to greet them (Cole 1975:76-77).

When the female is outside the female compartment, as she apparently commonly is among the Al Murrah, she wears an abaya and veil thereby creating again her own mobile female, private space. According to Cole, (1975:76), women move about freely in their herding and household chores and attend urban markets regularly. While Cole attributes "more freedom" to the nomadic women, if we treat the camp as private space since it is definitely kin, female, and secure space, this apparent contrast is reduced. This, of course, does not explain the Bedu woman's greater access to one sector of the public domain—the market. Perhaps the nomadic woman's active participation in the economic pursuits associated with pastoralism explain this difference between the urban and nomadic women.

In general, sexual segregation permeates modern Saudi society. Women do not drive cars, eat in public, or pray in the same mosque as men. In many public buildings, while there are bathroom facilities for men, there are none for women. The architectural system then defines public space as male space. A woman outside her home is covered from head to foot by a black veil and abaya or loose fitting cloak. Style of covering varies from community to community but it is everywhere obligatory. Non-Saudi women who appear in public without these coverings are defined as shameless and their husbands as fools and honorless. This sexual segregation is ideologically based as is shown by these Koranic passages:

> And tell the believing women to lower their gaze and be modest, and to display as their adornment only that which is apparent, and to draw their veils over their bosoms, and not to revel their adornment save to their own husbands or fathers or husbands' fathers, or their sons or their husbands' sons...(XXIV:31).

> ...And when ye ask of them (the wives of the Prophet) anything, ask it of them from behind a curtain. That is purer for your hearts and for their hearts...(XXXIII:53).

...Tell their wives and their daughters and the women of the believers to draw their cloaks close around them (when they go abroad). That will be better, that so they may be recognized and not annoyed...(XXXIII:59).

In terms of basic categories of worldview, sexual urges are perceived by Saudis as uncontrollable. Therefore, it is necessary to seclude one of the sexes to protect the society from chaos. Being defined as female includes the duty of avoiding shame (sexual impurity) thereby maintaining the honor of the family. Being male involves the duty of protecting the honor of the group by respecting female kinsmen and protecting them from outsiders.

Male/Female: Ranking or Complementary Distribution

There can be no doubt, then, that sexual segregation permeates modern Saudi society. It is based in Islamic tradition and the basic cultural definitions of gender, space, kin, and honor. In everyday terms it regulates access to space and social and economic activities. To establish the existence of separable domains (whether native, analytical, or both) does not show anything about the relationship between the domains. In many recent discussions of women's roles, it has been commonly assumed that a public/private distinction must necessarily imply a superior-inferior relationship (Rosaldo and Lamphere 1965). This assumption of ranking seems to stem from a politically motivated egalitarian idealism and the assumption of ranking as *the* organizing principle of social organization and social thought. In many cases, undoubtedly, this assumption of the priority of ranking as an organizing principle is valid. However, in the Arabian case this assumption of ranking is not only misleading but in fact in conflict with the data.

The public/private dichotomy in Arabia is homologous with the male/female, nonkin/kin, danger/security, honor/shame dichotomies. These are sets of complementary pairs that define a world created and controlled by an all-knowing, all-powerful supernatural that has and will continue to ordain everything that has or ever can happen. Members of each of these pairs, male/female, public/private, and so on, are conceptualized as being qualitatively distinct. They are not on a continuum. They do not grade into each other. From the Saudi point of view these are discrete categories with their own attributes. One controls the other, that is, "men have charge of women," but this does not change their qualitatively distinct nature since male and female are equal before Allah according to Muwahhidun doctrine. Since male and female are equal, qualitatively distinct categories, ranking them is nonsensical. They are not comparable and, therefore, cannot be scaled relative to each other. To impose Western categories of inferiority/superiority then makes no sense. It is in this context that we can understand that the Western woman who goes out uncovered is regarded as a whore. A whore is a kind of woman. She is notably not categorized nor treated as a man when she invades the public domain but rather as that kind of woman who either has no kinsmen or very deficient kinsmen. A whore has no shame, therefore, she either has no kinsmen to protect her or her kinsmen have no honor.

Self-esteem and the Public Domain

Finally in this chapter we should note that high self-esteem, a positive self-image, does not require overt access to power in the public domain. First, Saudi men do not regard women as inferior. Rather, they are regarded as the repository of family honor. Women are kin and are therefore due respect, honor, and consideration. Second, Saudi women do not regard themselves as inferior to men. Part of their status is a function of that of their male kinsmen. This is neither inferiority nor subordination since the male's status is dependent on the purity of the females. Seclusion is regarded by females as an avenue to purity, thereby maintaining the honor of the family which creates security. While several Westernized Saudi women have indicated to me they would like to modify the woman's place in their society, when I examined their positions, they did not propose breaking down the public/private dichotomy. Rather, they proposed setting up schools for women who were poor and/or without kinsmen.

Part of the high self-esteem of Saudi women comes from their recognition that they are the only source of children, one of life's delights from their point of view. Barren women are an object of pity. Most urban Saudi women I knew assumed the women's movement meant not wanting to have children. The seeming demand of some Western women to be freed of their joy/duty is regarded as a symptom of mental illness. To limit the number of children is considered reasonable, but to choose never to have any is quite literally unthinkable. It is not a recognized option for a reasonable human being.

Reactions to Women's Lib

In Dhahran many Saudi women of the middle and upper classes have come in contact with the notion of women's liberation through the broadcasts of the Aramco radio station, news reports on television, and personal contact with foreign women, both from Aramco and the college community. Women's liberation for the most part is regarded by these Saudi women as non-sensical. Who would want to act like a man? Why take on more responsibilities than you already have? A few women rejected women's liberation on the basis that it would mean a loss of control, of power. In this context these urban women were very aware of their power to control the hospitality of the household. Since all business is at least partially a matter of social graces intertwined with kin ties and the reputation of the family, this power is no less significant for not being overtly displayed in the public domain. The same phenomenon has been noted among rural Islamic populations:

> Among the Bedouin of Cyrenaica men may boast of their dominance over women...but they are constrained in their actions by

the control women possess over the preparation of food, the provision of hospitality, the comforts of shelter, and the reputation for honor (Nelson 1973:555).

According to Nadia H. Youssef, feminism in the Muslim world is doomed to a very slow start. She deduces this because "The very women who could provide the leadership for such a movement, those with education and high social standing generally have little inclination to do so because they suffer the fewest disabilities under the present system" (1976:214). In the Arabian case, these are also the women with the most to lose. If they unveil they lose status, adversly affect their families' honor, and hence destroy the base for their own security. So it is not surprising that the women who talk of change seek contexts where they can express their individuality without endangering their protected positions. In Lebanon this creates a high percentage of female artists and in Arabia it creates women who want to start a sexually segregated school for the poor who are without the benefit of kinsmen and hence of a lower position.

REFERENCES

Anon.
    1978   "Saudi Duty Time." *New Republic* 178 (Feb):8.
ARAMCO
    1968   *ARAMCO Handbook: Oil and the Middle East.* Dhahran, Saudi Arabia: ARAMCO.
Bourdieu, Pierre
    1966   "The Sentiment of Honour in Kabyle Society." In J.G. Peristany, ed., *Honor and Shame.* Chicago: University of Chicago Press.
Cole, Donald Powell
    1975   *Nomads of the Nomads.* New York: Aldine.
Dickson, H.R.P.
    1951   *The Arab of the Desert.* London: Allen and Unwin.
Doughty, Charles
    1936   *Travels in Arabia Deserta.* London: Johnathan Cape.
Fathy, Hasan
    1969   *Gourna: A Tale of Two Villages.* Cairo: Ministry of Culture Publications.
Fernea, Elizabeth W.
    1965   *Guests of the Shiek.* New York: Doubleday.
Ghul, Mahmud A.
    1966   "Islam is a Faith and a Divine Law." *Emergent Nations* 2:10-12.

Knauerhase, Ramon
    1977   "The Economic Development of Saudi Arabia: An Overview."
            Current History 72:423:6-10.

Musil, Alois
    1927   *Arabia Deserta.* New York: American Geographical Society.

Nelson, Cynthia
    1973   "Public and Private Politics: Women in the Middle Eastern
            World." *American Ethnologist* 6:551-63.

Rapoport, Amos
    1969   *House Form and Culture.* Englewood Cliffs, N.J.: Prentice-Hall.

Rentz, George
    1972   "Wahhabism and Saudi Arabia." In D. Hopwood, ed.: *The Ara-
            bian Peninsula: Society and Politics.* London: Allen and Unwin.

Rosaldo, M.Z., and L. Lamphere, eds.
    1974   *Woman, Culture and Society.* Stanford: Stanford University
            Press.

Rugh, William
    1973   "Emergence of a New Middle Class in Saudi Arabia." *Middle East
            Journal* 27:7-20.

Schmidt, Dana A.
    1974   *Armageddon in the Middle East.* New York: John Day.

Stiehm, Judith
    1976   "Algerian Women: Honor, Survival and Islamic Socialism." In
            L.B. Iglitzin and Ruth Ross, eds.: *Women in the World.* Oxford:
            CLIO Books, pp. 229-41.

Thesiger, Wilfred
    1959   *Arabian Sands.* London: Longmans.

Youssef, Nadia H.
    1976   "Women in the Muslim World." In L.B. Iglitzin and Ruth Ross
            eds.: *Women in the World.* Oxford: CLIO Books. pp. 203-17.

3 Women of Brunei [1]

LINDA A. KIMBALL

The Malays of Brunei, on the northern coast of Borneo, are a Muslim people who represent the extremes of Islamic expansion in the islands of Southeast Asia. Kimball's intimate portrait allows us a glimpse into the life of women in this society. A strong drive toward modernization has been undertaken, yet for all of universal free education, most Brunei Malay women today follow a life pattern that, in its essentials, remains unchanged. The overwhelming fact of a woman's life is the day-to-day chores of cooking and child care and the interminable demands these chores make. Although some women hold technical jobs in the modern sector, most remain fundamentally oriented to their traditional domestic roles. They leave it to the men to deal with the outside world, which is perceived as rather hostile. The larger kinship network remains important and Islam the firm faith. However, in their own families, women make important economic and social contributions. They are not demeaned by sexual segregation. They are aware of their own power and prestige as competent individuals.

Brunei women live in a land of tradition and modernity, of splendid royal pageantry and satellite ground station. Some old women, it is said, have never set foot on dry land; some young women study at Oxford University. All call home a land of charm and beauty set on the west coast of Borneo between the interior highlands and the vast expanse of the sea.

The sea gave Brunei its former greatness as the center and ruler of a vast trading empire reaching from Java and the Malay Peninsula to the southern Philippines, around most of coastal Borneo and beyond. Like other trading empires in the Indonesian archipelago region Brunei held control of sea-lanes, favorable harbors, and strategic river confluences. The hold over inland regions was limited to a monopoly over their trade with the outside world, and did not include any significant political control. So different was this type of "empire" from those history knows well on the vast expanses of the continents that it warrants further study. For it should be noted that some old Brunei traders went the sailor's traditional "girl in every port" one better; they had a wife and family in every port, perfectly permissible under Islam so long as the wives did not exceed four in number. Of course, gossip says that wives often exceeded four and concubines were rather more. The coming of European traders demolished the old indigenous trading routes with the result that the Brunei trading base disintegrated over a century ago and with it some of the traditional life. Yet memories of the past are important to people even today; women still talk about how life was for their great great grandmothers, and many people still live in the houses built on piles driven into mudflats that cluster together to constitute *kampong ayer,* the Water Village of Bandar Seri Begawan, a water village that today differs little from the way it was during the height of the Brunei Malay empire.

During that centuries-long time of Brunei Malay empire ascendancy, ocean going vessels plied to and from the capital bearing goods from China, India, and beyond. As late as 1849 the crib-work of berths capable of holding 600-ton Chinese junks was visible in Bruneitown (the old name for Bandar Seri Begawan, which did not take on its new name until 1971), and the overgrown remnants of Chinese pepper plantations could still be found in the hinterlands.

In the perspective of Borneo, "hinterlands" means "upstream." Traditionally, the Brunei Malays lived only in Bruneitown, following the occupations of trading, fine craftsmanship, and fishing. Each occupational group clustered in its own section of kampong ayer; and each such section had certain distinctive features of dress, customs, and language. Their orientation was toward the sea and its trade routes. They considered the upstream "hinterlands" a rather fearful place best avoided, an attitude still found among many of the senior generations and sometimes expressed rather openly by old women. The Brunei Malays traded with the Kadayans to obtain rice and other agricultural products. A Moslem group linguistically and culturally very closely related to the Brunei Malays, the Kadayans lived on the land areas in the near vicinity of Bruneitown and grew rice, which they traded to obtain goods the Brunei Malays made, such as brassware, knives, and cloth, or imported from overseas. Beyond the capital region lived more remote groups, linguistically and culturally quite distinct from the Kadayans and Brunei Malays. Among these were the Muruts of the upstream area of the Temburong district, eastward and inland of the capital. Much feared headhunters, they would mount canoe-borne raids on the city. Old people still recall the tales of how the ominous thump, thump, thump of several hundred canoe paddles hitting the dugout freeboard in unison on the backstroke signaled the advent of a raid and the need to scurry to shelter. But all that is long past. Before World War One an epidemic of smallpox and cholera so drastically decimated the population of Murut longhouses in Temurong and elsewhere that it effectively destroyed local Murut culture. At about the same time Europeans started dividing off Temburong district for rubber plantations.

As the estates developed, the job openings attracted many people. Kadayans moved in to grow rice on the now vacated Murut lands. Brunei Malays moved in to tap, trade, and in some cases take up rice farming. They learned the farming techniques from the Muruts and the associated ritual practices from the Kadayans. Because these transplanted Brunei Malays were now rice growers, an occupation traditionally associated with the Kadayans, their relatives back in the capital sometimes mocked them as being "riverside Kadayans." There does, in fact, seem to have been some Brunei Malay Kadayan intermarriage in the remoter past and there was more when both groups had settled in Temburong; however, an individual's ethnic identity is determined quite simply by that of the father. Thus, if a Brunei Malay woman marries a Kadayan man, the children of the union will be Kadayan. Until quite recently most Brunei Malays in Temburong lived in the traditional Brunei Malay multifamily house as opposed to the Kadayan single-family house. After World War II the large rubber estates no longer existed, having been broken up into small holdings. As the rubber price has steadily declined, reaching such lows in recent years that tapping is not worth the effort, many Brunei Malays have left Temburong and returned to Bandar Seri Begawan while many Kadayans have remained. This process of Brunei Malays returning to the capital may be seen in the case of one girl of Fire Rock Village, Temburong.

Miriam binte Hassan (not her real name), which means daughter of Hassan, grew up in a typical multifamily Brunei Malay house in Fire Rock Village. Like other Malay houses in the village hers was built on the land but near the river, and stood on pilings that elevated the floor some eight feet off the ground. A ladder gave access to the roofed verandah in front. A door in the middle of the verandah led into the reception room that reached the full width of the house. A door in the back wall of the reception room opened on to the corridor in the middle of the house that led to the kitchen at the rear of the house. Three rooms opened off each side of the corridor. When Miriam was young a family lived in each of those six rooms, but as she grew up one after another of the families left till at the time of Miriam's marriage only her own family lived in the house. While Miriam was still in school many multifamily houses in Fire Rock Village were abandoned altogether as their inhabitants died off or returned to kampong ayer. No trace now remains of these houses because the Malays believe that evil spirits, *hantu*, take up residence in abandoned houses and to prevent this tear down all deserted houses, often reusing the good wood for new construction and burning the rest in cook fires. Miriam's family, like all others in the village and most in Bandar Seri Begawan, used and still use wood for cooking. Miriam and her siblings paddled a dugout canoe to the village school each day during their primary education, then stayed at the government boarding school in the capital for the higher grades. When not schooling in the village, Miriam spent all her vacations at home, being brought home and taken back by the department of education taxi-boat. Like many girls Miriam was engaged before completing the higher grades. Schooling is free in Brunei but follows the British and European pattern of competitive admittance to middle and upper school; many pupils do not complete high school and even fewer go on to college or university. Some go to normal school for teacher training, and quite a few men go to vocational and technical school. But not uncommonly, girls of sixteen-eighteen become engaged and drop out of schooling to marry, a pattern Miriam followed.

Original plans called for the wedding to be in Fire Rock Village, but eventually the plan was changed because the relatives of the husband-to-be all lived in kampong ayer and did not want to make what seemed to them the long and venturesome trip upstream. Also, the prospective groom had a job in the city, and the still followed custom of the groom coming to the house of the bride and staying there to live would have been impossible for him to observe. So rather at the last minute, for Miriam's father had already rebuilt the rickety dock in front of his house, the wedding site was changed to kampong ayer. Miriam stayed at the house of her mother's sister, which was conveniently next door to the house of the prospective groom. The wedding week itself had the full panoply of Malay ceremonies and festivities, parallel ceremonies taking place at the house of the bride and groom. One day during the wedding week the groom and the father of the bride signed the marriage contract, *akad nikah,* which in and of itself constituted the legal and Islamic formalizing of the marriage. But as at most weddings, signing of the formal instrument was but one small part of the main celebration whose culmination was the great day of feasting when the groom was brought in procession to the house of the bride there to sit in state with her on a dais in the *bersanding,* which is the highlight and central moment of the wedding; after that the couple are considered well and truly married although actual consummation will not take place till three nights hence. Miriam and her husband lived in the wedding house for some time, then later moved next door to the house where her husband had been. Less than a year after marriage Miriam had her first child, born at home with a government midwife and several traditional midwives in attendance. After the birth Miriam spent the customary 40 days with a warm stove, made of an old five-gallon kerosene tin, by her side to keep her from getting "cold." This classificatory "cold," the same as the "cold" associated with upstream areas beyond the reach of the tides where Malays rarely go, is considered apt to make Malays sick or even kill them and thus was something to be avoided. On the other hand, the non-Malay peoples who live in those upstream-beyond-the-reach-of-the-tides areas are considered "able to stand the cold." At the end of the 40 days postpartum period, Miriam's mother held the traditional feast in honor of a daughter's first child at which the new mother and her husband were dressed in finery and briefly sat in state much as they had at their wedding. A year or so later Miriam bore her second child. Miriam, her husband, and two children now live in kampong ayer, while Miriam's parents and younger siblings still live in Fire Rock Village.

Some young brides are unhappy at being tied down with children and housework; others seem happy with their lot. But a bright youthful bride tends to look worn and no longer young after six or seven childbirths even though the calendar may say her age is in the twenties. Women have mixed feelings about bearing child after child. On the one hand, they may at times enjoy the children and have the satisfaction of fulfilling their culturally approved role. On the other hand, it is work. Childbearing wears them out, and many say that now that children go off to school, having children is just a chore because the satisfaction of a house full of young people who also did most of the work is no longer there. The parents, instead of being able to enjoy their progeny, now must do all the work and also scramble to get the money needed to meet the childrens' expenses. Childless women will go to great lengths seeking fecundity; women with many children may seek abortions. Certain indigenous medical practitioners, *dukun*, induce abortions by going through a ritual and then piercing the bag of waters; but women are known to have died from bleeding because the *dukun* was not skillful enough in the ritual chants needed. Drinking large amounts of a certain tonic or taking certain potions are other methods. Government maternity clinics provide modern birth control procedures for those who desire it. In the past, child mortality was high, but modern health measures have lowered the mortality, and a youth boom is underway. The schools can cope with the influx, but the problem of where they will all find employment is major and unsolved.

Old women say that in the period between the two World Wars great changes in female behavior took place. It used to be that women prayed behind a curtain so that no man could see them, but now that is not so, though women do pray apart from men. It used to be that a woman would never touch the hand of a man other than her father, grandfather, or brother without putting a cloth over her hands so that there was no direct contact. But now that is not so. Many of those same old women know how to read the *Koran* and Malay written in Arabic script, but are unable to write. Their parents would not have them taught to write because daughters would only use the knowledge to write love notes and did not need writing anyway. They note that girls were once kept secluded, but that since World War II girls go to school and so mix with boys in a manner previously unthinkable. Once women stayed at home and would not go out except to visit close neighbors or attend weddings and childbirths; now women go to the store and are seen in public. Old women say that females used to be meek, quiet, retiring, and not forward, very different from what they are today. Although women are less sequestered than they once were, some of the other supposed differences have a "things were better when I was young" air about them, as well as reflect ideal values.

For although more sequestered, women seem to have often managed to boss, nag, and otherwise influence their husbands. Some of the Englishmen in Brunei around the turn of the century reported that at times when they had gotten the men to agree to do something, such as take a trip upstream, the men would later back out saying that they were willing but their wives would not let them. One may question the veracity of those explanations since saying that you would like to do what you agreed to do or are being asked to do, but so-and-so will not let you or so-and-so will be angry is an accepted polite manner of refusing without offending anyone. In any given case the person to whom such a refusal is made usually has a pretty shrewd idea of whether or not the explanation given is a polite one or a statement of plain fact. But the Englishmen would have had no such knowledge, both because they were foreigners and because they were men.

Even today some very old men will greet white people with a right-handed salute and the phrase *tabi tuan,* Acknowledged Sire, a phrase one uses should one encounter a *hantu,* evil spirit, so that the *hantu* being pleased at the acknowledgement will not harm one. The greeting is perfectly logical. After all, white people do look almost like *hantu;* they have pale skin and fair hair, only white people have pale eyes whereas *hantu* eyes are flaming red. This also explains why white people do not fear *hantu* the way Malays do—because they look so much alike. On the other hand, a white person who does start fearing that kind of thing gets very scared very fast. Englishmen who looked so much like *hantu* would certainly not have been allowed near a man's family.

And they were men. There was very much a separation of the sexes, which continues in clear but less extreme form today. For men the main gossip and communication centers are the mosque or prayer-house verandah, the docks, and the front room and verandahs of houses. If a woman passes within earshot, the conversation stops or changes tenor. By the same token women also stop or change their conversation when men approach. The main centers of female gossip are the back rooms of houses and particularly the kitchen.

The kitchen is usually the largest single room in the house. Small kitchens of single-family upstream houses may be only seven feet on a side, while the large kitchens of big multifamily kampong ayer houses may be 20 feet by 30 feet. A few upstream village houses follow the Kadayan custom of building the kitchen as a separate outbuilding elevated only a few feet off the ground. But most Malay houses have the kitchen at the back of the house. The kitchen in such cases is a step or two lower than the rest of the house. Various cupboards and closets may line the walls of the kitchen as well as some tables. In a few houses a kerosene-fired refrigerator is a luxury convenience. Stoves are wood-burning with an occasional kerosene or bottled gas burner or oven as a rarely used convenience. The traditional stove is elevated on legs above the floor and has two stove rods on which the pans sit above the cooking fire. The wood supply may occasionally be stored below the cooking surface, but is most commonly found stacked above the cooking area, which although it may seem a fire hazard does serve to keep the wood dry because of the rising heat and smoke. Dry wood is an important consideration in a land where high rainfall and muggy humidity can make dry kindling a problem. Some houses have a cement stove-bed, others a wooden one covered with a layer of sand or dirt. Somewhere near one of the kitchen walls will be an open slatted area in the kitchen floor near which is stored the water in jars. Kampong ayer houses now obtain water from spigots in public standpipes, but in the past all drinking water was carried, usually in bamboo tubes or pottery jars from a spring located near the site, with washing water being drawn from the salty river at high tide. Fire Rock Village houses for the most part carry water up from the river, the wells formerly used for drinking water have fallen into disuse, and only a few houses have ingenious systems to run rainwater off the roof through gutters and conduits to the storage jars or drums in the kitchen. In times of low rainfall when the river water is brackish, Fire Rock Village folk obtain sweet water from a spring on the hill upstream of the village. The slatted hole in the floor is the drain; near it dishes are washed, vegetables cleaned, and other chores involving water done. However, laundry is usually done at the river dock in Fire Rock Village or on the open platform area back of the house in kampong ayer. The main work and socialization area of the kitchen is the large empty space in the middle of the floor. Even a large kampong ayer kitchen, in which each family has its own little stove and cupboard nook along the side of the kitchen, will still have a large empty space in the middle. For everyday cooking and working women will sit or squat on the always clean floor. But when guests come mats are laid down for them; for, although shoes are always left outside the house, unless someone has just washed for praying and is wearing special slippers in, and the house floors of smooth hardwood or occasionally linoleum are kept scrupulously clean, it is the custom to lay down mats for guests, the exception being if they sit on chairs in modernized reception rooms. But even if the guests are women who have been seated on the chairs, proceedings have a way of adjourning to the kitchen or the rear of the house with everyone comfortably ensconced on nice mats. Women sit with their feet tucked under them and slightly to one side, the cross-legged position being proper only for men, and legs straight out in front proper only for tending infants, who are laid on the outstretched legs with their heads toward the woman's feet and their feet toward the woman's body. Squatting is proper only when engaged in work or going to the toilet. For jobs such as scrubbing floors or laundry, preparing vegetables, cleaning fish, or tending gardens women squat rather than stoop, kneel, or use a table. If men not of their immediate family are present, young women inside a house will sit properly on the floor to do work. To one accustomed to sitting on the floor a chair is uncomfortable, and women sitting in chairs are apt to tuck their feet up under them in the position they would use in sitting on the floor. Hospitality demands that a guest be offered something to eat and drink. As soon as a guest comes the hostess or her daughter or other close female relative puts the kettle on and makes a snack ready.

Sitting in the warm kitchen with a nice hot cup of tea or coffee and some snacks on a miserable, rainy, chilly day can be the most cozy and enjoyable experience imaginable. Over refreshments, as well as cigarettes and betel chew for those who take them, passes conversation and gossip that touches on many topics. In Fire Rock Village the crops, the weather, and children, as well as the doings of various people form the main content of conversation. In visits to kampong ayer some discussion of local events may take place, but usually women catch up on family news. If an anthropologist full of questions happens to be present, the conversation may range a bit more widely, but that does not seem to be a normal circumstance. At most tea times with several women present, conversation generally remains within the safe range of family and local happenings, often including detailed discussion of an upcoming or recently past wedding. Deeper and more searching discussions take place only in the comparatively rare circumstance when two women who are close in friendship, regardless of what their kinship tie may or may not be, have a private conversation with no one else but small children present. Then they may discuss ideas, feelings, and opinions in a rather detailed and searching manner and also enjoy one another's companionship as only close friends can. Let a third party approach, and pleasant chat of a moment ago becomes the everyday polite social conversation.

An important part of a woman's life are the meals she cooks. Brides take great care to cook their husband's rice in the moderately hard and dry fashion that Brunei Malays like, not soft the way Malaysians are said to like it and not mushy the way Europeans eat it. Rice is food, and food is rice. To enquire, "what did you have for dinner" meaning, what accompaniment was there for the rice, one asks, "what fish?" A standard cooking ingredient is *blachan,* fermented shrimp paste, which seasons vegetables and, when combined with soy sauce, vinegar, pepper, onion, and garlic, makes a pleasantly piquant side dish to go with rice. The rather extensive use of blachan is a distinctive and delicious feature of Brunei Malay cuisine. The proper etiquette of eating rice and other foods with one's fingers in the traditional Malay manner is just as elaborate and demanding as the etiquette of those who eat with chopsticks or with knife and fork. The serving of feasts and banquets demands proper service as well as abundant and tasteful food. For example, in bringing the servings from the kitchen to the diners, the dishes should be piled on the carrying tray in a symmetrical and aesthetically pleasing manner. When removed after the meal is completed, the dishes should again be stacked pleasingly on the tray.

Female gossip after a wedding or other major feast will dwell at length and in detail upon the proprieties or lack thereof in the presentation and serving of the food as well as upon quality, quantity, flavor, and attractiveness of the food served. The family that had the wedding will discuss who helped them or did not, and how much, as well as describing the last minute difficulties they overcame to make everything go well. The behavior, dress, and attitude of the guests also come in for their full share of analysis. To be sure such gossip does pass the time of day. But it also has a certain regulatory function. Knowing that they will be picked upon in detail if they do not conform to the accepted norms for guest behavior, guests dress and act in the appropriate way. Also, since such discussion is a proper one for large female tea times, women hear the opinion of others and find out how their own opinions compare. Nearly adult girls are usually present and from the tenor of conversation absorb the cultural values it reflects. Interestingly, the actual cooking of wedding feasts is usually done by men rather than by women. However, it will have been the mother of the bride who had the task of assembling the food as well as the cooking and serving utensils and had the time-consuming task of preparing the rice and spices for use in cooking. Near the time of the feast other women will come to help in the preparation, much of the work being done by older girls who have already acquired the necessary skills. On the day of the grand feast and on the wedding day itself men take over the cooking. Everyday cooking, however, is the domain of women.

One aspect of cooking is its potential as a woman's weapon. The husband or male head of the household must always be served the first portion of food from each pot, a propriety carefully observed since failure to observe it is believed to bring misfortune upon the household. Quietly amongst themselves women say that one reason men do not beat up their wives too much is the fear of being poisoned. The fear of poisoning and accusations of same are rather widespread. Old women say that in the past in the very crowded multifamily houses, fears and accusations of poisoning were much more rampant than they are now. But even now any mysterious illness is apt to be attributed to poisoning or to a malevolence deliberately sent to harm someone. All in all food is a central object of much conversation and thought. Generally, the people of Fire Rock Village eat a larger quantity of food at each meal than do those of kampong ayer. This may be due in considerable measure to the fact that Fire Rock Village people live a much less sedentary life than do those of kampong ayer. Some old women of kampong ayer can sit virtually motionless for hours at a time in a manner that upstream women find intolerable. Because they have spent most of their lives squatting or sitting with their legs tucked under them, very old women may be unable to straighten up to a fully erect position and thus walk about in a hunched over, bent-kneed shuffle. Some people are thin, some plump, and many in between; but except for illness and a few exceptional cases, the extremes of emaciation and fatness do not occur. Although the diet differs considerably from what Western-oriented nutritionists might find ideal, it is nourishing and delicious. In this respect the people of Temburong have an edge, in that most have gardens from which they get fruits and vegetables, and there is considerable semiwild area right next to the villages in which can be found some delicious vegetables, such as the pakis fern or the bungar green, which go eminently well with rice. Also, many Tamburong people grow their own rice, which has a far better taste than the bland polished rice sold in the stores and which is the mainstay of most kampong ayer folk. The woman's role in obtaining the family rice is not everywhere the same.

The Fire Rock Village woman does half or more of the rice raising, almost all the work except for the clearing and burning of the fields. She gardens, may raise some fruit trees, tends the family chickens, and gathers edibles such as greens, mushrooms, and fruits from the woody areas neighboring the village. She thus plays a major economic role in the family, although the cash-earning jobs, if any, are done by the husband. Kampong ayer and city women do not directly raise or produce food. They may do some handicrafts for cash, but traditionally it was the man who usually obtained the food through trade or fishing. Some older women worked as itinerant boat peddlers of foods and miscellaneous goods, but that occupation is rapidly vanishing as kampong ayer women now go to the store and are no longer so tightly cooped up in their houses. Many of the younger kampong ayer women, particularly those with postprimary education, work at salaried jobs in the city. The Malay phrase for those who work at such employ is that they *makan gaji,* eat a salary. Their income, and particularly the goods and foods they buy with it, may form a significant portion of the family income. In the past it would have been inconceivable for any women with children to occupy themselves at any task but child care. However, now many young women continue working even though they have borne children. The particular arrangements vary, but in general the woman's mother or mother-in-law is the one who tends the infant or young child while its mother is out working. On return home the woman greets her offspring and then sets about the waiting chores of washing, cooking, and cleaning, although her mother may have done some of these. Whether or not a woman works at a salaried job outside the home and whether or not she also has children to care for, all the housework, cleaning, and cooking is done by the women. Washing is done by hand since very few homes have washing machines. Families wealthy enough to have washing machines usually hire servants to do the wash instead.

One of the most wearisome chores for any mother is the nighttime care of infants and children who do not sleep. Custom demands that crying infants be tended to immediately; should a mother not instantly spring to it, some older woman will waken her and make sure that the infant is tended to as it ought to be. Tending squalling infants and conducting older children to the toilet, as well as the occasional all-night sessions spent up with sick children deprives many a mother of her sleep. The concept of letting a child cry itself to sleep is unheard of; such children must be rocked in their baby-sling and sung or crooned to until they fall asleep. An experienced mother sleeping by the baby-sling may, without waking up, put out her arm and start rocking the sling when the baby cries; only if the baby persists in crying will the mother come awake. An incident in the Fire Rock Village Chinese store one day pointed out clearly the Malay insistence of immediate attention to a crying infant. The storekeeper's wife was attending to some customers when her infant asleep in a crib in the store suddenly awoke and started crying. The shopkeeper's wife continued her business, intending to let the infant cry until she had time for it. But the Malay women she was waiting on told her she should tend to the infant right away and ceased transacting any business until the shopkeeper's wife had tended to it and quieted it. Until they are a year old, infants are carried in a sling at the mother's side. After that they are carried on the hip, developing an automatic reflex of hanging on with their legs. Young children may actually fall asleep and have their heads bobbing about in slumber but still be grasping with their legs. Children are loved, cared for, and shown fondness; but adults talk about children or in front of children; only occasionlly do they talk to children. Children are children, to be taught and raised; it is adults who count in the society. As infants and toddlers girls and boys are treated alike. But girls are expected to start helping with household chores, and kept to it, at an earlier age than are boys. Girls of five or six will be responsible for tending younger siblings while boys of that age have no tasks to do. Older boys may be asked or expected to do certain chores, but no issue is made of it if they do not. Girls of that age, on the other hand, will be chided if they do not do their share of the work. On the other hand, poor scholastic performance is not considered a major catastrophe for a girl, while boys may be under very strong direct and particularly indirect pressure to do well in school so that they can later get a good job. Every effort is made to continue a boy's schooling to the highest level he can attain, while a girl may be pulled out of school even if she is doing very well in order to help with the chores around the house.

Mothers say that a son is always theirs, but that a girl at marriage comes under her husband's orders and so is lost to her mother. Once she is married, a girl must ask her husband's permission to go anywhere, even to visit her mother, and must obtain her husband's permission before undertaking any major activity or any activity outside the home. This is scrupulously observed, particularly until the couple has been married several years. At that time the wife has come to know what her husband will and will not approve of, and may, for example, call on neighbors without obtaining the prior permission of her husband. If after four-five years of marriage a couple has no children, they will usually adopt a child. Belief has it that adopting a child often causes a couple to have children of their own. Childless couples may try Indian, Chinese, Western, and Brunei Malay medicine as well as pray at the sacred graves of renowned holy men in an effort to have progeny. Some couples remain childless; others have children none of whom live to maturity. One kampong ayer woman famous for her cooking and particularly her baking, had had six children none of whom lived past childhood. A child may suddenly lose one of its parents. One woman, famous for her prize-winning chicken kurma, chicken with a delicious coconut milk sauce, dropped dead without warning one morning. One woman who had borne 17 children died after a short illness. Within a month of her death villagers were suggesting to the widower that he ought to remarry. Children who have lost their father may have a particularly hard time of it since their mother's new husband is not their natural father and thus has only the most minimal obligation to them. Gossip tells of stepparents who neglect their stepchildren and of how hard it is to lose a parent. The lot of orphans is described as being even harder; they may be given scarcely enough to eat, but that is all; unless their elder sibling, grandparent, or paternal or maternal aunt or uncle looks after them, their lot is bitter. Tales are particularly rampant of how in the "bad old days" it used to be a particularly rough lot to be an orphan. In the cases observed stepchildren seemed to be rather well treated, but those were children who had lost their mother and still had their natural father to look after their interests.

Whether the child is male or female the biggest and most important ceremony in its life will be its wedding. Men may sign the formal marriage contract, but it is women who boss the wedding. Sometimes the father of the bride or groom seems almost to be a bemused spectator in the midst of all the hustle and bustle of the festivities. He does house repairing and other heavy work, but it is apt to be the wife who has decided what repairing needs doing as well as all the other details of the wedding. During the wedding men tacitly, but never openly, acknowledge the directorship of women.

A woman who dies in childbirth goes to heaven, just as does a man who dies in a holy war against infidels. Women often fear birth, particularly their first one. A first pregnancy is surrounded with many rules of do and don't in an effort to ensure an easy birth. But althrough the cultural ideal demands that a woman be a mother, in the past many women did not marry because their family was unable to find a husband who met all their exacting requirements. Such women lived with one of their married siblings and helped with the child tending. They depended for their food and clothing as well as other needs upon the generosity of the man of the household they lived in. Only some of those women would work as itinerant vegetable sellers or produce handicrafts that supplemented their subsistence.

Some women worked as midwives. The traditional midwife training was one of bearing children oneself, observing births, and learning the special skills from another midwife. Today some women go to the government training program for midwives, which teaches all of the latest scientific knowledge and the technique of midwife management of accouchement. Most women still give birth on a specially constructed low wooden platform in the house with one or more midwives present, which may or may not include a governmental scientifically trained midwife.

In the past most trance healers were women, generally women of ages sixteen to the twenties. In a special session they were possessed by *manbang* spirits or *hantu*, and while in trance they spoke out cures and treatments the spirit was giving. Such women often had many material goods because people gave large gifts for their mediumistic services. Some trance curers were also men, but women predominated. A female trance curer used lots of fragrances and flowers so that she would always smell sweet and so be pleasing to the familiar spirits. But because a woman in trance knew no shame and might run about naked, some parents did not want their daughters to become a trance curer and would hold a special ceremony in which an established trance curer came and took the spirit that was trying to possess the girl. There seems to have been some tendency for trance curing to run in families.

Certainly *dukunship,* the nontrance, nonpossession, intellectually oriented medicinemanship did tend to run in families. Both men and women were *dukun. Dukun* were the primary source of medical care, being present at and tending the various ailments and crises of life from birth to death. If midwives were having trouble managing the birth, the *dukun* was called in. In a sense *dukun* were often the intelligensia of village life. Their treatments involved diagnosis and application of a body of anatomical, physiological, cosmological, and pharmaceutical knowledge, which although differing in many respects from that of the modern Western medical doctor held an analogous position as the body of knowledge upon which treatment was predicated. *Dukun* learned much of their art, particularly that of diagnosis, through firsthand observation of an established *dukun* at work; in a sense this and the detailed discussions that followed in private constituted a form of clinical training. Only an older woman would receive such indigenous medical training. The transmission of the one particular piece of information, which constituted the transmission of the healing power of dukunship, took place in a private session; and no public event or announcement marked the occasion. A woman might be a fully trained and qualified *dukun* for several years before anyone apart from her and her teacher knew of the fact.

In the past *dukun* training was the only "advanced" training other than *Koran* reading available to women. Today education has markedly broadened their potential opportunites. But the "single career girl" is not one of the choices available. A woman may work while single, but the presumption is always that she will marry, although she may continue in her job after marriage. But for most women the sole career of a lifetime still remains home and children. The woman may have a good education and enjoy reading, but her place will be in the home. City women may have some time to listen to the radio or TV while working, but the village girl will spend much of her time in raising rice and gardening. Some women earn money by taking in sewing, and for one reason or another some never marry. But single or married, a woman's world is basically in the home, while much of a man's world lies outside the home.

Today many alert mothers will insist that their girls get a good education so that if something should happen to their husbands they will have an education to fall back upon. For young and old alike the women of Brunei realize that the world they live in is changing and that they will have to live with whatever the future brings. Brunei is a beautiful land of great promise, but the surrounding world has numerous problems. Brunei Malay women know that their traditional literature has something to say about times of troubles; and some of them read into the unhappy world news, the disastrous decline in rubber prices, and other events the signs which indicate that *hari kiamat*, judgment day, is coming. These women say that, yes, life was difficult during World War Two—when the Japanese held the area, but in time that passed; things are different now, the world seems on a downhill slide, and one should be assiduous in one's religious duties. Others disagree and say that the signs are not so grave as that; it is just that with so many newspapers, radios, and televisions, we are more aware of troubles all over the world. The discussion goes on as life goes on along the rivers and in kampong ayer by the great golden-domed mosque that stands as a message of peace over the land of Brunei.

NOTES

1. My fieldwork in Brunei lasted from October, 1969, to September, 1971. Over half the costs were self-funded, the remainder were supplied by a travel grant from the graduate school of Ohio State University and an ACDA grant through the National Academy of Science. From 1972-1974 I was a senior Fulbright Exchange lecturer at Universiti Kegangsaan, Kuala Lumpur, Malaysia; during this time my three visits to Brunei totaled six months' length. During the summer of 1979 I spent two months in Brunei.

Many thanks go to those in Brunei whose help and cooperation made this study possible: Pengiran Sharifuddin, Lim Jock Seng, the Government of Brunei, officers and staff of the Brunei Museum, the State Secretary, Fire Rock villagers, and my host family.

4 Women's Role in a Muslim Hausa Town (Mirria, Republic of Niger)

MARGARET O. SAUNDERS

This study of a Muslim group in a West African country shows us something of the interaction between the Islamic ideals and practices and the ancient West African traditions, which give women a significant measure of economic independence.

The Western stereotype typically has seen Muslim women as having no choice but to submit to male domination. The position of Muslim Hausa women in the town of Mirria partially contradicts this image. The author here shows us that women exercise limited but important power within the marriage relationship as well as in the economic sphere. Men need wives not only to provide domestic services but also to maintain their own status as social adults. Yet the dissatisfied wife can break up her marriage. The combination of polygyny and a high divorce rate means that getting and keeping wives is a constant concern for Hausa men. We see that, although women in this society are excluded from political and religious affairs, they are by no means powerless.

This chapter examines the status of women in Muslim Hausa life as observed in Mirria, Niger Republic, between 1973 and 1975.[1] Mirria data support a general thesis that women exercise power, although often not recognized authority, when women control desired goods and services. Both the working rules of Hausa marriage and the economic roles of Mirria women give women some control over such assets. They thereby provide a basis for limited types of female power that contradict the inferior formal status accorded to Muslim Hausa women.

Roles open to Mirria women are discussed in terms of the public domain-private domain distinction which has been suggested in recent literature in women's studies. Contrasts with the position of women in other Hausa sub-cultures are noted, since Mirria differs both from pagan Hausa communities and from the Muslim Hausa communities of Nigeria. For example, despite Islamic orthodoxy, less than one Mirria wife in ten was secluded in 1974.

THE SETTING

Approximately 25 million native speakers of the Hausa language are scattered across the savanna of northern Nigeria and adjoining areas of the Niger Republic, as well as in special Hausa wards of other African cities.[2] The central Hausa homeland today covers an area about 400 miles from east to west between Lake Chad and the Niger River. Hausaland extends from about 40 to 100 east longitude and from about $11°$ to $14°$ north latitude with annual rainfall ranging from about 40 inches in the south to about 20 inches in the north.

Within this area, peoples of diverse ethnic origins have become acculturated to a very generalized "Hausa civilization" which incorporates a wide range of variation.[3] Subcultural variations may be visualized as a continuum. Patrilineal pagan Hausa-speakers living in dispersed households fall at one end, and bilateral urban Muslim Hausa at the other. Political and religious organization, the kinship system, and settlement patterns all vary across this range. Despite diversity, a number of basic cultural elements occur in all or most Hausa-speaking settings. One of these is the ideal of male dominance and proper wifely submission—an ideal which is not always reached in practice.

In sum, "Hausa" is best taken as a linguistic group. Hausa speakers share cultural features that stem from their common adaptation to the savanna environment, to a city-state political framework, and to the religious and social influence of Islam.

Mirria lies in gently rolling open sandy country of the Sahel zone, near the northeastern edge of Hausa-speaking country. Beriberi territory begins to the east of Mirria, while Bugaje and Tuareg ethnic groups predominate to the north. Ethnic boundaries are not clear-cut. Bugaje and Fulani from small nearby communities may be recognized by their distinctive dress at Mirria's large Sunday market, which draws buyers and sellers from a 15 or 20 mile radius. Most permanent residents of Mirria speak Hausa as their first language. A few, mostly school children or adult men, are also fluent in French, the national language. As a county seat Mirria also houses government officials drawn from all of Niger's ethnic groups. Occasional teachers recruited from other African countries and a few European or American volunteers complete the ethnic array.

Mirria County *(arrondissement)* is one of five making up Zinder State *(département)*, one of seven states of the Niger Republic. Mirria County covers approximately the territory once ruled by the present royal dynasty as a small independent kingdom. Today the county is divided into 16 *cantons* or districts. Mirria District is headed by the traditional *Sarki* or king; it contains 35 recognized villages plus Mirria town and its outlying hamlets. The 1974 census of Mirria town listed 7,139 residents in 888 official households.

Neither county employees nor temporary residents are in the census; total population may be estimated at 8,000 in June 1974.

Mirria was founded in about 1774, when the present ruling dynasty settled beside a hamlet called Bilmari whose people were Hausa-speaking hunters. A band of marshland occupied by orchards and truck gardens still separates Bilmari from Mirria proper, although they are administered as one town. Mirria lies at the bottom of a shallow valley several miles wide, surrounded by its millet fields and by a tracery of paths leading to other villages. The major east-west national highway links Mirria with other cities, especially the state capital at Zinder just 17 miles away.

The narrow streets that wind between the high mud walls of Mirria households give the town a deceptive air of untouched tradition. Deceptive indeed, for Mirria has never been isolated from the world. It formed a part of the Bornu Empire in the nineteenth century and of the French colonial empire in the twentieth. A French military camp brought soldiers from all parts of French West Africa and their French officers to Mirria from 1939 till independence. Many Mirria residents make the pilgrimage to Mecca. Some still go overland, but others go by charter flights from Niamey or from Kano, Nigeria.

Urban-style, mud-brick houses and a large population of horses, a traditional status symbol, show that Mirria is a prosperous town. Millet and peanut crops succeed in most years, while garden and orchard crops from the Mirria marshland bring extra cash income. Convenient motor access to Zinder allows Mirria agricultural products to be marketed easily. A new wave of prosperity began when county offices were moved from Zinder to Mirria's vacant army buildings in 1966. Mirria entrepreneurs promptly built new houses to rent to county employees.

The Mirria economy, like that of most Hausa communities, follows a typical peasant pattern based on grain farming and other agriculture, a well-developed market system, and occupational specialization. As Hill (1972) notes, there is no Hausa "subsistence" sector as such, since virtually any commodity may be bought or sold as household fortunes vary. Nearly every Mirria male farms. Members of the traditional elite such as the king and important Koranic scholars oversee farming done by their dependents. Most members of the modern elite such as teachers and county administrators are strangers in Mirria and consequently do not own fields there. Both sexes practice craft occupations as additional sources of cash income.

Most Mirria households own one or more millet fields, where they plant staple grains (millet and sorghum), often intercropped with cowpeas which are planted between the rows of grain. Peanuts, the major cash crop in Mirria, compete with the staple grains for space in the household fields. Most fields are cultivated every year, with some use of manure as fertilizer. Tillable uncleared bush land within walking distance of Mirria is rare.

Some Mirria men also own gardens in two marshy areas *(fadama)* near Mirria, but many households have no members who own garden land. Local usage distinguishes gardening *(kaptu)* from farming *(noma,* literally "hoeing"); gardening is considered to be a craft occupation. Extensive irrigation ditches, which predate the colonial era, distribute water from springs and wells. Some of the garden crops are used in traditional Hausa cooking, while others were introduced by the French. With irrigation, some garden plots *(garka)* can be planted year-round; others flood during the rains.

Usually, however, gardens are deserted for millet fields *(gona)* during the short rainy season, which begins in May or June and ends in September. The rest of the year is so dry that Mirria's flat rooftops can be used for storing hay. Crop yields vary from year to year, depending both on total rainfall and on its distribution throughout the growth cycle for each crop. During the latest West African drought, Mirria rainfall dropped from 568 mm (22.4 inches) in 1968 to 208 mm (8.2 inches) the following year. Millet yields fell from 419 kilograms of threshed millet for each hectare of land in 1971 to 160 kilograms in 1972.[4]

The basic Hausa social unit is the household whose members share a single walled compound. Both the group and the compound are termed *gida.* Ideally, several small houses built around a central courtyard shelter a number of related men with their wives and children. The household holds farmland, *gandu,* which is farmed collectively under the direction of the household head, the *mai gida.* This is usually the senior male of the domestic group. He bears public responsibility for the entire group, for example in seeing that the taxes of all household members are paid.

This ideal extended-family household of overlapping residential, economic and legal entities is only partially realized in practice, since many pressures work for the separation of the kinsmen making up such a group. Brothers or sons who live together may divide the farms and cultivate separately; or men who have built separate compounds may still farm in *gandu* with their father or brothers. Neighboring compounds often do house kinsmen, but lack of vacant land in older wards of Mirria forces men to build new compounds away from kin. Some households were relocated during the widening of a few main streets in the 1970s. Both residential and agricultural choices represent individual strategies rather than absolute cultural limits.

ON "PUBLIC" AND "DOMESTIC" DOMAINS

One may readily distinguish public and domestic domains in the Hausa setting, but it is not clear whether we increase our understanding of the Mirria community by using these categories. Although women hold substantially more power in domestic affairs than in public affairs, legitimate authority in both cases is attributed to men. Men fill high-status positions in domestic organization as well as in public affairs. Female power in the domestic sphere derives from the ability of any woman to disrupt the small-scale organization of the household group. Despite reservations, I shall adopt the definitions proposed by Sanday and examine female status in Mirria in terms of the two domains.

The group which most clearly possesses an exclusive domestic domain in the Hausa setting is the *gida,* compound or household. Although individual members, or subgroups such as one wife and her children, have some activities such as craft occupations which are private to themselves, the basic Hausa social unit is the *gida* as a whole. The household resembles a corporate group; its subunits do not. Ideally the *gida* holds farmland and pays taxes as a single unit, whose members inhabit a single compound. The household head represents the entire domestic group in community affairs, especially politics and religion. Seclusion of wives within the compound walls (the exception rather than the rule in Mirria) gives symbolic expression to the domestic-public boundary.

In Mirria a neighborhood is to some degree an extension of the domestic sphere of its residents. A wife who never goes to market may pay day-time visits to the compound next door, or sit at her own doorway to chat. Many activities, such as marriage, involve several households but less than the entire community. Marriage decisions privately made within two households must be followed by public ceremonies which involve only a portion of the Mirria community, primarily neighbors and kinsmen of the newlyweds.

The household is the largest kin-based group which has exclusive common affairs in Mirria. Beyond this level, informal kinship links reinforce many other social relationships, but these ties are not structured through organized kinship groups. Only the royal Sosaibaki dynasty displays a corporate lineage organization in Mirria today.[5] As among most Muslim Hausa, Mirria residents trace kin bilaterally, through both parents. Some preference is given to paternal kin *(dangi wajen uba)* over maternal kin *(dangi wajen uwa).* For example, most Mirria households are formed around a patrilineal core of a man and his sons or brothers, while children belong to the father if a marriage ends in divorce.

The Public Domain: Politics, Religion, and Economics
Community-wide public affairs focus around three institutions in Mirria: politics, religion, and economics. Both politics and religion involve Mirria residents in extradomestic groups, and these groups are invariably male. Sacred and secular authority reinforce each other. Both sexes, however, play important roles in market-oriented economics in Mirria.

Administrative organization in the Niger Republic groups households into successively larger units of village or ward, town, district, county, state, and nation. Mirria District and its subdivisions follow traditional Hausa political organization based on a hierarchy of named offices (*sarauta*) which are inherited patrilineally. At their head is *Sarkin Mirria*, the traditional ruler. He also holds the title of *Chef du Canton*, a low administrative position in the modern government. County, state, and the nation itself are based on colonial administrative units and operate in French, the national language.

A traditional status distinction between rulers (*masu sarauta*, those with offices) and commoners (*talakawa*) still holds true in Hausaland. The categories are defined pragmatically: persons in power are "rulers" regardless of their origins. In Mirria members of the modern elite may receive traditional signs of deference such as the respectful greeting used for kings.

Despite tales of a few female rulers, Hausa women hold limited roles in traditional administration.[6] A woman serves as household head only when there is no adult male to fill the role. Women never serve as ward or village heads. Nor do they fill titled offices other than a few titles reserved for a close female relative of the king or for the head of local courtesans. In Mirria the only such title was *Magajiya*, held by a sister or cousin of the *Sarki*; her office had few duties or powers. A woman was indirectly responsible for the creation of the male title *Marafa*, which was first granted to the nonroyal husband of a Mirria princess (*maira*).

Employment in the modern sector also favors men and places women at a clear disadvantage. Some government services in Mirria hire women as nurses, teachers, development workers, and secretaries. All of these positions are also held by male nurses, teachers, and so on, while men also fill a range of other positions in which no women are found. A woman served as director of one primary school during a part of the research period, but most such positions are held by men.

The national constitution of 8 November 1960 promised universal suffrage for both men and women. One account of local elections in another Hausa area of Niger implies, however, that at least in rural areas, women took no part in elections.[7] No further elections have been held since a military government took power in 1974, but the new government encouraged a number of activities in honor of the International Women's Year in 1975. These occurred primarily in the capital city, Niamey.

More of the county services available in Mirria are used by men than by women. Most services used by women serve both sexes, while women rarely use other services such as those which deal with agriculture. Only one office, the women's section of the rural development service, was devoted exclusively to women. In addition to its out-patient clinic for adults of both sexes, the local medical center offered maternity and child health services for women.

Women as well as men also make active use of the judicial system. Women appear as plaintiffs, defendants, and supporters in disputes heard at any level, from the *Sarki's* customary law hearings to the Justice of the Peace court in Zinder. Although women take a spirited role in the arguments in cases concerning themselves, they rarely appear as formal witnesses (Fr. *témoin,* H. *shaida*) in the records of the Zinder court. This reflects the Muslim Hausa view of women as legal minors. For women, the most important function of the judicial system is in regard to divorce. Although a husband may divorce his wife by simple repudiation, only the courts can grant a woman a divorce which her husband refuses to pronounce.

At the elementary entrance level, school enrollment is approximately balanced by sex.[8] Early courtship followed by marriage at 13 or 14 years adds extra hazards to the educational process for girls. A few years of primary classes devoted to learning French, and basic literacy in French, are soon over. Young women claim that these foreign skills are soon forgotten once they leave school, since a young wife has little occasion to use them. Only employed women and wives of men in the modern elite are likely to move in French-speaking, literate circles.

Fewer girls than boys complete the six years of elementary study. The imbalance is greatest at secondary and upper levels, however. Competition for secondary school entrance is stiff for both sexes. In June 1974, some 365 county youngsters took the entrance exam for admission to the *College d'Enseignement General* (CEG); only 88 were admitted. This school opened in Mirria in September 1973 with an enrollment of about 200 boys and 21 girls. Two girls were from local families, two were daughters of government employees assigned to Mirria, a few were from bush villages in Mirria County, and some were from Zinder. The following year all first-year female students were assigned to a new CEG in Zinder, so the Mirria CEG enrolled only 11 girls and 235 boys in 1974-75. Students entering CEG range from about 13 to 15 years in age, and the program requires four years. Many parents, and many girls, do not wish a girl to be in school at this age.

Even if a young woman completes secondary school, she needs further training to win a professional position as a nurse, teacher, and so on. Few salaried positions exist for either men or women who have completed only elementary studies or part of secondary studies. Several young Mirria women who had not completed CEG studies worked as unpaid volunteers at the county office building to learn typing and other clerical skills. They hoped to be hired if paid positions became available. Young men compete for the same low-level clerical jobs.

Sexual maturity creates problems for never-married women whether they are students or employees. As one employed wife explained, a girl who keeps her reputation while also qualifying for a job has excellent marital prospects, since men are well aware of the advantages of a double income. But sexual activity may seriously harm one's marriage prospects. Traditional Mirria wives gossiped about unmarried employed women with the explicit assumption that they would already be married had they not acquired reputations for being sexually active.

As in most of the Islamic world, Mirria religious activity is segregated by sex. Female religious activity takes place within the household, while the public exercise of religion is a male-dominated activity. Men pray and study in groups, in public settings; other than a few postmenopausal women, women do not. Daily prayer, Friday congregational prayers, the celebration of religious festivals, and Koranic study all show this difference. Elsewhere in Hausaland non-Islamic religious activities such as the *Bori* spirit–possession cult bring women together in groups, but such activities were not found in Mirria.[9]

A close relationship between sacred and secular authority in Mirria is shown in several ways. First, the palace and the central or "Friday" mosque stand next to each other facing a single central public square. Both the top county administrator (*Sous-prefet*) and the traditional king (*Sarki* or *Chef du Canton*) symbolically lead the congregation in all community-wide religious observances such as Friday prayers and the annual Islamic festivals. Religious leaders also hold titles which are a part of the Mirria *sarauta* hierarchy of offices.

Men from some wards may arrive at Friday prayers in groups which represent wards or neighborhood mosques, as do some men from Bilmari, an area of Mirria. Further, the community wide Friday prayers are essentially the concern of political adults, that is, of household heads. Young boys often accompany their fathers to the mosque and carry their prayer mats for them, but youths and young men are not proportionately represented in the crowd that gathers for Friday prayers.

Most Mirria men perform at least one of the five daily prayers as part of an all-male group at one of the many neighborhood mosques.[10] Mosques vary from mud-brick buildings to simple mat-covered areas marked off by a row of stones in the open air. Forty or more men blocked one main street for prayers at dusk each evening. In contrast women pray alone, within the compound and often inside their bedrooms. Since no one sees their prayers, possibly women vary more than men in observing this religious duty.

Koranic schools which meet out-of-doors around huge millet-stalk fires are a prominent feature of Mirria night life during the nonfarming months from November through mid-April. Several large schools have separate classes for children and for advanced adult students. Adult students meet with the head *malam* (Koranic scholar, teacher, cleric) to read and study a text of Islamic law or poetry in Arabic, often from hand-copied manuscripts. Children learn the Arabic alphabet and memorize Koranic verses in Arabic from wooden slates. Girls were observed among the students of only one Mirria school. Adult women never study in such a setting. A few Mirria wives are tutored at home by a *malam* approved by their husbands, often a relative.

Both neighborhood mosque congregations and adult study groups are forms of voluntary association open only to men. Mirria women are expected to observe the five daily prayers except during their menstrual periods and immediately following childbirth. Women must also keep the fast at Ramadan, give alms as they are able, and join in family celebrations of the *Id el Kabir* and *Id el Fitr* festivals. Women who can afford to do so also make the pilgrimage to Mecca, as do prosperous men.

Women are excluded from important public roles in either political or religious organization. The case of economics is more complicated, since the division of labor allots market-oriented as well as household-oriented productive activities to Mirria women.

In Mirria, as in Hausaland generally, some economic activities are carried out by the household as a group. These are most often limited to growing staple grains for household use and cash crop for paying household taxes. In good years a Mirria household may actually be self-sufficient in grain, but its members still pay taxes, purchase clothing, and interact in social situations that require cash exchanges. Even the household grain crop may be sold to meet such obligations.

Virtually everyone but the very old and very young also practices a personal income-producing occupation directed at nondomestic markets. For men, personal farming or gardening is one possibility, on fields which they own personally or on plots allotted to them from household lands. Craft activities and wage labor are other sources of personal income for both sexes. Although women control personal incomes through their craft occupations and business enterprises, women are concentrated in low-income, small-scale economic endeavors. Only a few women have succeeded in accumulating the capital necessary for large-scale trading or building of rental housing. Most men are wealthier than are most women, and men control most land and houses.

Hausa women participate in agriculture to a degree which varies with the extent of urban Muslim influence. According to Barkow (1973:67), Maguzawa pagan Hausa of the Zaria, Nigeria, area say "Our women feed us," since the harvest from the private plots farmed by the women of the compound ideally feeds a household through the entire dry season. In much of the Niger Republic, but not in Hausa areas of Nigeria, even Muslim women farm.

Mirria women have withdrawn from active farming within the past generation. Today their agricultural role resembles Chinas' (1973:31) description of a Mexican Zapotec village where "men are the producers and women are the processors and vendors of the men's production." Mirria girls and women help with limited tasks at planting and at harvest, but they do not hoe, the central task in local farmwork. If Mirria women own fields, they ordinarily lend them to their husbands or to male relatives. One woman hired laborers to cultivate a field, which she planted in millet for household use. Few women (or men) have the cash income to follow suit. In Mirria large-scale sales of grain, cowpeas, peanuts, and truck crops are usually handled by men. Women retail these crops in small quantities for one meal or a few days at a time, together with spices and sauce ingredients.

Women process virtually every food crop at some stage. They thresh, pound, and winnow grain to remove grains from the head, loosen husks, and separate chaff from the grain. Women pound again to loosen the seed coat. In bush villages women produce flour by hand using grinding stones (*dutsen nika*), but most Mirria households have flour ground at one of the power mills in town. Women produce peanut oil, the major food oil used in Mirria cook-ing, by hand as a specialist craft. Female potters produce the water pots and cooking pots used in food processing. Although women milk cows, butcher-ing and herding are male occupations. Cooking for the domestic group or for the market trade in prepared foods is the final stage in food processing. Cooking is so strongly a female specialty that a wifeless man must buy his meals at market or depend upon generous friends and relatives.

Few members of either sex achieve great wealth, but in a town like Mirria the colonial era brought opportunities that increased the economic differen-tiation among members of the community. Peanuts and truck crops became sources of cash income. The army base and the location of a county seat at Mirria increased this trend.

Mintz (1971) has suggested that new opportunities introduced by eco-nomic development and the growth of modern economic sectors often benefit men rather than women and may even serve to put women at a relatively greater economic disadvantage. This has been true in Mirria. We have already noted that women are at a disadvantage in pursuing the educa-tion necessary for salaried positions in the modern sector. Men rather than women benefit from employment which does not require education, such as wage labor for the county. Gardening and farming activities, from which most Mirria men derive a substantial portion of their cash income, have become closed to most women over the past generation at the same time that cash income from these activities has increased.

M. G. Smith (1965:127) distinguished three levels of exchange in Hausa life: the complex of ceremonial or "gift" exchanges (which in fact are virtual-ly obligatory), commercial exchanges within the community, and commercial exchanges beyond the local community. In Mirria the three levels are far from distinct. Cash received in gift exchanges often flows into an individual's craft occupation aimed at local sales, or into market purchases of imported cloth or other goods. Gifts in the ceremonial exchange system (*biki*) are often of cash, so that every wedding or naming ceremony among one's kin or neighbors calls for ready cash. The *biki* system is thus one of the driving forces of the Mirria commercial economy.

Hausa commercial activities are not limited to fixed market places. Innumerable female petty traders retail kola nuts, spices, clabbered milk, sauce ingredients, and prepared foods from head trays or from mats at their doorways. Others sell a similar stock at the small daily food market, where male butchers also sell their wares. Male petty traders stock table-tops in likely locations with candy, cigarettes, matches, and similar items. Several small permanent shops, owned by men, stock soaps, perfumes, and miscellaneous imperishable items. Bulk sales of Mirria garden produce are often arranged by male wholesalers from within private households. More "hidden" trade occurs in small-scale retailing conducted by busy wives from within their compounds.[11] In sum, the large Sunday market is only one of many settings for exchange in Mirria.

Mirria data support Sanday's (1974) contention that economic power alone does not guarantee high status in the public domain for females. She has suggested that four factors are necessary for women to hold high public status. Only two of the four are present in Mirria. Mirria women clearly exercise "material control" over items beyond the domestic unit. There is also a "demand for female produce" in Mirria. But we have seen that female political participation is lacking. Nor are there female solidarity groups devoted to female political or economic interests. Most Muslim Hausa men hold more economic power than their wives just as they dominate public political and religious activities.

The Domestic Domain

Activities which go on behind the compound wall and affect primarily the domestic group may be viewed as a separate domestic sphere in Mirria. They contrast with public activities, which either subsume households in larger groups or are based on groups other than the household. The household is the focus of domestic activities.

Mirria households can be defined in several ways using legal, economic, or residential criteria for household membership. Those who farm *gandu* fields together and eat from the household granary may not all live within a single compound. Formal jural authority represented by census households may remain intact after fields and compounds have been divided. Not surprisingly, census households are larger than are either economic or residential units. Some 44 per cent of a sample of households from the 1968 Mirria census included dependent married men, but only 12 per cent of a smaller sample of residential groups housed two or more married men.

By any of these criteria for household membership, patrilineally related men form the stable backbone of Mirria households.[12] Mirria women form a transitory population circulating from household to household as daughters, then wives, then dependent sisters or mothers as they move through the marriage system. A woman typically changes both her residence and her census household with every change in marital status.

Hausa concepts of the "good" woman focus upon domestic female roles. Modesty, obedience to father or husband, and skill in domestic tasks such as cooking are desirable traits for a Mirria woman. Islamic piety serves to reinforce the image of the obedient, submissive wife. It is typical of this ideal that a wife is expected to kneel to serve her husband's meals, which he eats alone or with male friends.

The domestic roles open to a Mirria woman are determined by her stage in the life cycle and her marital status. In Mirria both sexes pass through five named life-cycle stages. As in many other cultures, Hausa roles for the immature and for the elderly show less distinction by sex than do roles for mature, vigorous adults. Terms at each end of the age spectrum reflect this fact, since terms for infants, children, and old persons are formed for both sexes from a single root.

For women the categories are:

jaririya: birth through toddler, a nursing, back-carried baby (weaning occurs at 18-24 months);

yarinya: girl child through about age 10;

budurwa: marriageable girl prior to first marriage, eligible for courtship, about 10-14 years old; ends with first marriage;

mace: woman, applicable only after marriage (according to some informants, only after childbirth);

tsohuwa: old woman, visibly past the age of reproduction (this stage is reached later than the actual menopause).

There are similar categories for men, but the adult male stages are reached at later ages than the adult female stages:

jariri: birth through toddler, a nursing, back-carried baby;

yaro: boy child through about 14 years;

samrayi: youth from adolescence through marriage and the birth of one or two children; ends gradually with increasing maturity;

mutum: person, especially used for adult married men;

tsoho: old man whose head hair is gray (at this age a man may leave part of his beard unshaved).

A man of thirty might still be regarded as a "youth." His twin sister at that age might be considered a "woman" and be celebrating the marriage of her daughter.

Although first marriage is an essential rite of passage for both sexes in reaching adulthood, additional terms are necessary to specify the possible marital statuses open to adults once they have been married. For women these include:

amarya: bride, especially from first marriage to birth of first child; a woman is termed a "bride" each time she remarries;

mace: wife, especially after birth of first child; eventually used for mature women who achieve social motherhood through foster children;

zawara: marriageable widow or divorcee who lives with relatives until she remarries;

karuwa: courtesan or *femme libre,* a widow or divorcee who lives alone or in a courtesan's compound providing entertainment and sexual services for male suitors; she may eventually remarry and return to the *mace* status.

The marital status terms for men are:

ango: groom or newly married man, used each time a man marries;

miji: husband, a term related to *namiji,* male of any species;

goboro: wifeless formerly married man, applicable only to a divorced or widowed man who has no other wives at present, thus no one to provide the wifely services such as cooking which are necessary for an independent household (rarely used in Mirria except in a joking, semiscornful way).

The terms for both lifecycle stages and marital statuses reflect the importance of marriage in a woman's life. First, marriage is the basic rite of passage, which simultaneously transforms a girl into both wife and woman, although full *mace* status may wait until motherhood is achieved. So basic is the married status for adult females that the term *mace* is used for both "woman" and "wife." Marriage is the normal state for women; nonmarried adult females require separate terms. A physically mature female who has never been married is an anomaly in Hausa society; we have seen that this discourages the education of most girls beyond the age of puberty.

Few restrictions limit the choice of spouses open to Mirria residents; a man is only forbidden to marry the sister of any of his present wives and certain close relatives. Courtship is easiest within the area served by the Mirria weekly market. Some 60 per cent of all wives in the 58 compounds of a residential survey came from Mirria town, and another 23 per cent were from nearby villages. Mirria women also marry out in all directions, but suitors from bush villages are at a disadvantage. Mirria women prefer not to hoe farms or grind flour by hand as village wives must do, and they know that larger towns offer more commercial opportunities for crafts or petty trade.

First marriages are usually arranged by the families of marriageable girls and youths, while the spouses themselves exercise greater choice in later unions. For this reason, first marriages are more likely than later ones to be with cousins or other kin. Marital histories of 30 Mirria women included some 22 unions described by the woman herself as *armen gida* (kinship marriage) of 69 total marriages. However, 15 of these kinship marriages were first marriages for the bride—half of all first marriages.

A Mirria girl enters her first marriage at about 14. She is expected to be a virgin and may be rejected should she prove not to be, in contrast to greater premarital sexual freedom among pagan Hausa in Niger. Marriage may occur before the girl's first menstruation, which fosters the belief among some Mirria residents that menstruation is a result of intercourse. One informant explained that she was married, had one menstrual period, and then became pregnant with her first child without realizing what was happening. She recalled that her girlish figure suddenly changed as her breasts enlarged, a typical symptom of early pregnancy.

The groom at a girl's first marriage may be a young man of 20 or 25 who is also marrying for the first time, or he may be a much older man taking an additional wife. For a man's first marriage, however, there is a strong preference for a previously unmarried bride. Only then can he complete the elaborate rite of passage leading toward social adulthood. In later marriages his bride may be a widow or divorcee, or a young unmarried girl.

Households follow a well-known developmental cycle as young men marry, have children, and establish independent compounds to which sons or younger brothers may in turn bring their wives. Marriage is the essential first step on a man's road to independence. Married men headed 88 per cent of the 160 households in a 20 per cent sample of the 1968 Mirria census, and 76 per cent of the households in a separate residential survey of 58 compounds. Only 19 per cent of census units reported their heads as younger than 35 years, 58 per cent as between 35 and 54 years, and 23 per cent as 55 years or older.

Being a wife is a labor-intensive role. Food preparation alone is a lengthy and tiring daily task. Cooking is the primary duty of a Mirria wife toward her husband, who is expected to provide her with millet and with the money to purchase ingredients for the sauce served over the staple grain dishes. A wife must carry water from the spring and gather fuel, unless her husband purchases both. She is also responsible for household cleanliness, dishwashing, laundry for herself and her children, and general child care if children are present. She may help with some farm tasks at planting and harvest. Finally she is always at the beck and call of her husband for such services as spreading mats for his guests.

Not surprisingly, some Mirria women choose to enter polygynous, and occasionally secluded, marriages. Despite their air of male dominance, both polygyny and seclusion clearly reduce a wife's workload. In a polygynous household, cooking duties follow a strict rotation of two days at a turn for each wife. Sexual privileges coincide with cooking duty. Since one wife cooks for the husband and all the wives and children, her co-wives have less work during those two days. Co-wives have more time for their own craft occupations, social activities, personal grooming, and other activities of their own choosing. Each wife has a private bedroom, but all share the courtyard and cooking area.[13]

A man who can afford to support several wives is also likely to be prosperous enough to be more generous than other men. Women informants unanimously named generosity with cash and other gifts as the most important attribute of "the good husband." Men stressed obedience first among the wifely virtues, and a polygynous husband can be more demanding of his wives in this regard than can other men. He can divorce one wife without becoming a "wifeless man" dependent on others for his meals, and he is in a better position than a poorer man to court and win a new wife.

The Hausa term for co-wife is *kishiya,* derived from *kishi,* jealousy. Obviously there is much potential for jealousy in plural marriages, especially since the wives usually live in the same household. But it is equally possible for women to work out harmonious, amicable relationships from which all the wives benefit. Since divorce offers a way out, women who cannot get along are not forced to remain together indefinitely. Co-wives often help each other with pounding grain much as sisters may visit over work in an American kitchen. Women who have been co-wives for some time may name each other as close friends and continue to visit each other if the husband divorces one.

The husband's ability to distribute gifts and sexual satisfaction evenly helps in keeping a household peaceful. Co-wives are mutually jealous of their husband's outside affairs. The wives of one neighbor threatened to beat any "other" woman until she returned whatever gifts the husband had given her to them, the rightful owners of the husband's sexual attentions.[14] But even a monogamous wife is not assured of exclusive sexual access to her husband, since he may visit local courtesans or pay court to a widow or divorcee.

Table 4.1 shows the distribution of monogamy and polygyny in the entire Mirria Census for 1974.[15] Only one husband in five had two or more wives, while only 3 per cent had three or more wives. But polygynous men account for one-third of all married women.

Of the 1,910 married women in the 1974 census, only 154 Mirria wives were said to be secluded. Four-fifths of these women (82 per cent) were in polygynous marriages. Seclusion has been increasing since the beginning of this century, when only the king and one Koranic scholar are reported to have secluded their wives. In deciding whether a man secluded his wives, the minimum measure used by male informants was whether the wives went to market. The withdrawal of women from farming at Mirria fits into the pattern of increasing seclusion, even though most women still go out freely.

Informants of both sexes invariably insisted that secluded marriage (*armen kuble* or *armen tsare*) was "better" than nonsecluded marriage. Even women who would have refused a suitor who practiced seclusion gave this an-

Table 4.1 Plural Marriage in the 1974 Census of Mirria*

A. Spouses in Monogamous and Polygynous Unions in the 1974 Census

| | Married Men | | Married Women | |
	#	%	#	%
Monogamous Unions	1,267	81.2%	1,267	66.3%
Polygynous Unions:				
2 wives	248	15.9%	496	26.0%
3 wives	37	2.4%	111	5.8%
4 wives	9	0.6%	36	1.9%
Total Polygynous:	294	18.8%	643	33.7%
Total Unions	1,561	100.0%	1,910	100.0%

B. Measures of Polygyny in the 1974 Census	
Measure	1974 Census
Incidence (p): polygynists per 100 married men	18.8
Intensity (w): wives per 100 polygynists	218.7
General Index (m): married women per 100 married men	122.4

*The 1974 census included 7,139 persons in 888 households.

Source: Unpublished Census Registers,
town of Mirriah, Niger, May–June 1974.

swer. The superiority is explained in religious terms: Allah says that other men should not see one's wives.[16] But seclusion also reduces the workload of a wife, since it relieves her of chores outside the household. Since only a prosperous husband able to be generous is likely to attempt seclusion in Mirria, seclusion clearly offers economic benefits to the wife, who continues to practice a trade or craft from within the household.

Ronald Cohen (1971:182) has suggested that seclusion "separates the wife from the community and links her closely to her husband (and his authority)." This may be true in communities where most adult women are secluded, but in Mirria seclusion does little to separate a woman from a wide network of social ties with other women. Her unsecluded women friends may visit her freely, while her husband cannot entirely forbid her to go out.[17] With her husband's approval, she may pay social calls any night after dark and occasionally participate in daytime activities such as marriage festivities for relatives.

Men hold the positions of greatest authority within the household in Mirria just as they do in public affairs. In their domestic roles of husband, father, and household head, men expect obedience and respect from their subordinates of either sex, including wives. A man achieves full social and political adulthood only as an independent household head, a status available only after marriage.

A woman exercises some formal authority within the household over her dependent children, her junior co-wives if she has any, and her daughters-in-law. As senior wife of the household head, or *uwar gida,* a woman may administer the cooking and food division, and general household management, for a large household, commanding respect for her competence in this role. But a woman becomes a household head only by default, for lack of an adult male to fill the role. Of the eight sample households which were headed by a woman in the 1968 census, none contained any married, hence socially adult, men.

Although only one Mirria man in five is polygynous, these men account for one-third of all wives. Thus one wife in three has co-wives. Since some compounds house two or more married men, several wives are present in many households. A mother or sister of the household head may also live in the same compound. Women and children eat together, apart from adult men. Women work with other women and relax with other women.

The Mirria domestic sphere is marked by formal male dominance, segregation of the sexes, and residential arrangements which often provide women with female companions, coworkers, and rivals. A wife is officially under the authority of her husband and the head of his household. Yet her economic and marital roles actually give a Mirria wife substantial power, especially at the domestic level.

SEX, STATUS, AND POWER IN MIRRIA

Social status may be defined in terms of authority an individual holds, the actual power he or she exercises, the degree of respect one receives from one's fellows, or some combination of all three.[18] Here the Hausa view of women as social inferiors of lower status than men contrasts with the actual position of Mirria women in economic and domestic life.

The standard description of the system of social status for Hausa men comes from M. G. Smith (1959; 1965). He described northern Nigeria, but similar factors could be observed in social ranking in Mirria. Inequality is a basic fact of Hausa social life. Even within the household, men relate to each other as superiors and inferiors, not as equals. Differences in wealth exist even in small villages where all residents are commoners. In a complex community like Mirria, men move in a system that allows for wide differences in status based on birth as a "ruler" or a "commoner" combined with occupation, wealth, and piety.

Just how women fit into the Hausa status system has been debated (Yeld 1960; Smith 1961). A Hausa woman is under the legal authority of her father, her husband, or even her adult son. Her achievements of wealth or piety take second place to her ascribed biological status as a woman, although such factors affect her ranking among other women. Smith (1961:57-58) concluded that the status of a woman was determined by her generation, age, marriage order among her husband's wives, her marital career, ethnicity, descent, fertility, the position and prospects of her offspring, and differences in wealth. Of these only her economic success and her total marital career are subject to much control by the woman herself.

Hausa women rarely hold positions of authority in either public or domestic affairs. Women of the Mirria royal family serve as pawns in alliances sealed through marriage, not as titleholders and administrators. Women have even fewer roles in the public domain than do dependent men, such as a married son still living in his father's compound. As Rosaldo (1974: 29) has pointed out, "we find, in most societies, relatively few institutionalized roles for women ..." One result is that there are fewer sources for differences in status among women than among men.

Mirria women in general related to each other more nearly as equals than did men. There are, however, significant differences in wealth among Mirria women. Most women control only a small personal income derived from petty trading or craft activities, while a few unusual women undertake economic ventures on the scale of successful male entrepreneurs. A woman may earn criticism and gossip for such success, rather than respect, although her economic power will be acknowledged.

Hausa marriage dramatizes the formal subordination of women in many ways. First, a woman is a legal minor who cannot arrange a marriage on her own. Regardless of her age, a woman must be represented by a male marriage guardian, although mature widows or divorcees often make their own marital decisions and then obtain the guardian's consent. Further, the binding ceremony or "marriage tying" (*darmen arme*) represents a contract between two groups of men, that of the bride and that of the groom. Neither spouse is present at this event. Instead men representing each spouse exchange a sum of bridewealth (*sadaki*) from the groom's kin to those of the bride in front of witnesses. The groom's representative must reply to formal questions affirming the groom's ability to feed, clothe, and house his bride, and a religious official leads the men present in a prayer. The marriage tying establishes a legal marriage and takes the same form for first and later marriages. The celebration surrounding this event is much more elaborate for first marriages, however.

Additional sexual asymmetry occurs in other aspects of Hausa marriage. One man may have up to four legal wives; in the past some Mirria men also had slave concubines. A husband may seclude his wives, restricting their freedom to leave the compound. This reinforces his status as a devout Muslim as well as a properly respected husband, although in Mirria seclusion is considered appropriate only for members of the nobility, respected Koranic scholars, and a few other prosperous men.

A husband has the right to pronounce a divorce if he wishes, regardless of the wishes of the wife. If a wife desires a divorce, however, she must either provoke her husband into divorcing her or pursue a divorce through the courts; she cannot pronounce a divorce. A man may remarry as soon after being widowed or divorced as he can gather the necessary financial resources for a new marriage. A woman in contrast must observe delays fixed by Islamic law and local custom before she may remarry. The delay serves to determine the legal father of the child should the woman be pregnant when the marriage ends. She must wait until her third menstrual cycle after a divorce (about three months), but four months and ten days after the death of a husband. A widow is expected to spend this time in mourning; she wears old clothing, leaves her hair unbraided, bathes infrequently, avoids public places, and in general must avoid being attractive to new suitors. No similar demands are made of a widower, who may resume normal activities after a week of formal mourning.

Despite the formal advantages of men in the Mirria marriage system, a wife holds a significant degree of power through her ability to threaten to break up the marriage. A Mirria woman remains married by choice; in Thomson's phrase, "willing consent" is the basic working rule of marriage in this part of Hausaland (1976: 144).

Divorce is no idle threat. Of the total of 69 marriages reported in the marital histories of 30 Mirria women, 34 unions (49 per cent) had ended in divorce. If only the 45 marriages which had already ended are considered, 76 per cent had ended in divorce and only 24 per cent by the death of the husband. While 25 of 30 women had never been widowed, only eight had never been divorced. Although divorce predominates as the means of ending marriages, many women make at least one enduring match. Eleven of the 24 currently married women had been married to their present husbands for 15 or more years, and four more had been married for at least seven years.

A divorce may be initiated by either spouse, but procedures differ by sex. Formally men have the advantage: a husband may divorce a wife by simply declaring their marriage at an end, whenever he chooses to do so. Yet in fact, husbands often resist divorce even when a wife is being purposely disobedient. For the 80 per cent of Mirria men who are monogamous at a given point in time, a disagreeable wife may be preferable to the dependent state of having no wife at all.

Convincing a new wife to enter marriage is an expensive project for a man. Courtship requires a constant flow of small presents, from kola nuts and perfume to cash. At a time when a day's agricultural labor earned a man a-bout 62 cents or 125 CVA, the sum spent in courting an unmarried girl in the Maradi area of Niger might exceed 150 dollars or 30,000 CVA (Nicolas 1971). Only a small fraction of this goes for the formal bridewealth exchanged at the marriage tying which is the only sum the husband may reclaim if the wife seeks a divorce. If she has borne him a child, even this sum is not refunded; he has the right to keep the children. Should he divorce her, he has no claim to any reimbursement.

An unhappy wife may first attempt to provoke a divorce by repeated disobedience. If her husband ignores the misbehavior, she may try other tactics such as running home to her parents or flagrant adultery. Some disputes end in reconciliation rather than divorce.

However, the wife may refuse to return to her husband and instead seek a divorce through the courts. Both traditional and modern officials first try to reconcile the couple, or, failing that, to convince the husband to pronounce a divorce. Regardless of the husband's wishes, a wife who persists in demanding her freedom will ultimately receive a divorce from a court such as the Tribunal de Première Instance in Zinder. Her stated reason may be no more than "I don't want any more of him"; or it may include such legitimate complaints as beatings or failure to provide millet, the staple grain. A new suitor, or the woman's own kin, help repay the former husband's bridewealth.

Paradoxically, polygyny is one of the factors underlying a wife's power to break up a marriage. Polygyny substantially increases a woman's ability to find new suitors, since nearly every adult male in Mirria is potentially seeking additional wives at any point in time. Since a divorcee is as suitable as an unmarried girl for later marriages, any woman who has yet to pass the menopause can confidently expect to find other suitors if her present husband fails to meet her expectations. The younger and more attractive the woman, the more likely she is to appeal to other men who may prove more generous or less demanding than her present spouse.

If plural marriages were forbidden by changes in Niger's family code, one effect might be to discourage women from seeking divorce since it would drastically reduce the availability of potential new husbands. A woman with little chance of remarrying would be likely to prefer a partially satisfactory spouse to none at all. On the other hand, men would be forced to divorce more frequently if they wished to continue to take new wives from time to time. Forbidding polygyny might actually reduce the alternatives open to Mirria women, at least in the short run, if such a law were to be enforced.

Divorce is not the only way for women to interfere in marriage plans made by men. Even a very young bride has a potential veto power over a marriage arranged against her wishes. If she persistently resists the advances of her husband to avoid consummating the marriage, or runs away to a sympathetic relative and refuses to return, eventually a divorce will be pronounced. In one Mirria case, the girl's mother finally obtained a curse against the marriage from a local *malam* (Muslim cleric), at which both the father and the prospective husband gave up the marriage plans.

For most women, divorce or widowhood is followed by a new marriage soon after the required waiting period is completed. Most women spend the months as a *zawara* living with a mother, brother, father, or other relative. However the role of *karuwa* or courtesan offers another alternative for young, attractive widows or divorcees. It offers more independence and more sexual freedom than the roles of wife or daughter also open to young adult (that is, previously married) women. Renting a room of her own among strangers, or moving into a courtesan's compound (*gidan karuwai*) identify a woman as a *karuwa.* A widow or divorcee may be sexually active, as shown by occasional illegitimate births, but so long as she lives with relatives a woman is not considered a *karuwa.* Ordinarily a *karuwa* has previously been married at least once.

A *karuwa* rejects the authority of both husband and kin. Typically a woman finds it easier to flaunt family authority from a safe distance and moves to another community to live as a courtesan. Her kin are embarrassed nonetheless. Although a courtesan may marry and return to the role of wife, most Mirria women gossiped critically about the women they named as former courtesans.

Another basis for female power in Mirria results from the economic activities of Hausa women. A woman has a recognized right to her own economic activities independent of those of her spouse and free of his control, which again contradicts the formal lines of male dominance. The husband is obliged by Islam to support his wife, but has no claim on the income from his wife's private endeavors. Should he borrow from her, the loan must be repaid. If he wants doughnuts which she has prepared for sale at market, from grain or flour she provided for herself, he must purchase them unless she chooses to offer them as a gift. A wife controls the goods she brought with her at marriage (primarily furniture and household goods) and takes them with her if the marriage ends.

We have already seen, however, that women in general hold less economic power than do men in Mirria. Typical occupations open to Mirria women are described in Table 4.2. Few of these occupations offer large profits that allow one to accumulate enough capital to move into large-scale enterprises. A woman is likely to receive a larger lump sum through the cash and kind *biki* gifts offered at ceremonial occasions such as the naming ceremonies for one's children, than through most female craft specialities. The few women who conduct large scale trade or build rental housing for government officials received their initial capital through generous spouses, inheritance, the ceremonial exchange system, and possibly past courtesanship, rather than the typical female occupations.

Table 4.2 Occupations of Mirria Women: Some Typical Examples*

A. Traditional Sector

Labor
    daka: pounding grain for pay
    sussuka: threshing grain for pay

Sale of Foodstuffs or Prepared Foods
    toya: frying and selling various sorts of doughnuts such as *waina* (millet cakes) and *pankasou* (wheat cakes)
    hura: preparing and selling *hura* (cooked millet flour mixed with sour milk and water), a common mid-day meal
    tuwo: preparing and selling *tuwo*, the standard evening meal, of various types of cooked grain flours served as a stiff porridge with a sauce of vegetables, spices, and meat if available
    maka: making macaroni for sale from flour and water using a small hand-operated press, dried in the sun
    mai gujiya: producing peanut oil by hand as a home industry and selling the oil (*mai gujiya*) and its by-product *kulikuli* (fried peanut meal balls)
    saye-saye: petty retailing from one's doorway of the typical female stock of spices, sauce ingredients (tomatoes, onions, dried leaves, red pepper, and so on), seasonal fruits (mangos), and kola nuts

Other Traditional Occupations of Women
    commerçant: large-scale retail sales of a stock also suitable for men, sold at weekly markets
    gine tukwane: making and selling at market various types of pottery: *tukwane*, cooking pots; *gargoletti*, a type of water pot; and so on.
    karuwanci: courtesanship (practiced by formerly married women)
    kitso: braiding women's hair into the various elaborate braided hair styles typical of Mirria Hausa fashion (*kitso,* hairdo)
    mai gida: landlord of rental housing, restricted to a very few well-to-do women; also practiced by men
    talle: hawking, the most common occupation of young girls, also practiced by older women; typically involves hawking of kola, cigarettes, and so on, from a head tray in public places

*Table 4.2 is continued on the next page

B. Modern Sector

instituteur: teacher (primary school level). Also practiced by men.
infirmière: nurse. Also practiced by men.
secretaire: secretary. Also practiced by men.
telephoniste: switchboard operator. Also practiced by men.

Such occupations are only open to educated women with a minimum of six, and for many positions ten or twelve, years of education. Most women practicing these occupations in Mirria are not native to Mirria.

There are at least three reasons for the difficulty women in Mirria experience in achieving more than modest economic success. First, women in general do not control either farmland or houses, although women occasionally own these items. Without farms or gardens, women are excluded from the agricultural endeavors from which most Mirria men receive much of their cash income. Further, a woman has a relative shortage of labor inputs for her own personal enterprises. For most of her adult life, much of her available energy is devoted to the labor-intensive role of dutiful wife. Most of her available labor (her own plus that of children or foster children), is devoted to her wifely domestic chores.

In addition to these constraints, a cultural factor seems to be at work. Hausa cultural values held by both sexes serve, as in the United States, to limit the aspirations of Mirria women. In Mirria as in the United States, it takes a woman of unusual initiative to carve out a larger than usual role for herself even in the relatively open field of economic endeavors. Even women who are clearly very able businesswomen are restrained by their own image of the proper Hausa woman. They hesitate to make moves which result in criticism and gossip by other women as well as men. Hard work, shrewd intelligence, some luck in obtaining capital, and a deaf ear to such criticism are ingredients in the success of the few women who have achieved a larger than usual degree of economic power.

Since their husbands are more successful than other men, wives of elite men hold less relative power than do other Mirria women. Among the traditional elite, wives lead lives similar to those of nonelite women. Even if the husband is prosperous, these women perform domestic chores, such as sweeping the women's quarters of the palace. Outside help is limited to such tasks as threshing and pounding grain, which are performed by hired female labor. These wives are more likely than their neighbors to have two or three co-wives, and to be secluded. Preadolescent daughters or foster-daughters serve as sales agents for the typical female occupations which they carry on from within the household. Some daughters as well as sons are enrolled in school.

Top male county officials such as the Sub-prefect, his administrative assistant, and secondary school professors may choose from a range of marital options that allow for much variation in the style of family life. Some marry educated women who also hold professional positions, and agree to an *alliance* or "wedding ring" marriage which restricts traditional rights to polygyny and to divorce by repudiation.[19] Polygyny and seclusion are less frequent among the modern elite, although some officials practice both.

The ideal of Mirria's young professional men is a monogamous union with an educated, employed woman. Of the employed women who were married, most were partners in unions of this type. With their joint income, such couples are affluent by both local and U.S. standards. They enjoy elegant clothing in Hausa and French styles, battery-operated record players and tape recorders, homes furnished to Westernized tastes, and even automobiles or motorcycles.

One case to the contrary came to my attention. The first marriage of one Mirria girl who became a schoolteacher in the 1960s was arranged by her family with a moderately prosperous older relative. She taught at schools in Zinder and in Mirria during this marriage, which ended in divorce after several years. When she was posted in Zinder, the husband rented a room there for her and joined her there when he attended the large weekly market in Zinder every Thursday. She later became subject to periodic spells of insanity said to be caused by *iskoki*, (s. *iska*) due to medicine (*magani*) used by jealous co-wives in a later marriage away from Mirria. It is tempting to view this as an expression of the conflict between the role of Hausa wife and that of professional woman.

In the ideal case, the wife hires a houseboy to take over domestic chores, which are still considered to be her responsibility.[20] The couple may entertain jointly and take some meals together, in contrast to traditional sexual segregation in these activities. These couples are more likely than others to use modern methods of birth control to limit or space children.[21] Maternity leaves and government family allowances benefit the couple when children arrive. Since government services move their personnel frequently, finding jobs in the same locality is a common problem for these couples.

Even if she is not employed, the wife of a civil servant may expect her husband to provide a houseboy as a status symbol to take over much of the work of cooking, marketing, and so on. A teenaged wife then languishes in boredom until children arrive or until she finds a craft compatible with her husband's status. Such wives retail prestige goods, such as Djerma weavings from western Niger, or practice needlecrafts of European origin such as knitting baby garments, crocheting caps, or embroidering bed covers for sale. Child care, suitable occupations, and household management occupy older wives of modern elite men.

Since educated men far outnumber educated women, most civil servants must take wives who are not employed away from home. Some wives have completed several years of school, others have no formal education and do not speak French. Even among the modern elite, wives may be excluded from official or semiofficial social functions such as an evening play performed by secondary school students. The Sub-prefect may entertain official guests at a dinner served in the dining room by his cook-steward, while his wife and children eat in the family quarters. Female civil servants attend official functions along with their male colleagues. Regardless of the wife's education, families of civil servants make more use of medical services than do others. They usually encourage both sons and daughters to remain in school until they qualify for professional jobs.

CONCLUSIONS: FEMALE POWER IN MIRRIA

The inferior formal status of Mirria women is illustrated by the ideology of male dominance, the exclusion of women from public political and religious affairs, and the greater authority of men within the household. Yet women hold some power, despite their lack of authority, in the economic sphere and within the marriage relationship.

Indeed because the dissatisfied wife has alternative options, acquiring and keeping wives is a constant concern of Mirria men. Sums spent in courtship, marriage, and gifts to wives affect the local cash economy over and above the direct productive activities of women. This is a relative power, however. A woman can change from one husband to another, but she can do little to change the working rules of Hausa marriage and relations between the sexes. She may reject male authority in the role of courtesan, or live within the culturally approved female roles of daughter, wife, and mother.

Despite such limits, a Mirria woman does not see herself as powerless. In consequence, women have strong self-esteem which belies their supposed inferiority. Within the limits of their culturally shaped aspirations, Hausa women are self-confident actors. Their willingness to stay married visibly affects the male world in which wives are a prerequisite of adult status.

Sanday (1974:192) has suggested that the economic role of women in a given society is critical to their overall status in the public domain, including political organization. Their economic roles may even be critical to the recognition of women as social adults (Sacks 1974:219-22). Both authors conclude that the low degree to which women achieve power in the public domain in most societies is linked to a tendency for female production to be oriented to domestic group needs rather than toward the larger public. Hausa data support Sanday's observation that public economic roles for women are not sufficient to cause high public status.

NOTES

1. Research was supported by grants from the Fulbright-Hays Doctoral Dissertations Abroad program and from NIMH and authorized by the Niger Republic through the Institut de Recherche en Sciences Humaines, Niamey. Most research was conducted in Hausa.

The classic study of a Hausa woman's life is *Baba of Karo* (Smith 1954) which spans a period from about 1890-1950. Other data on Hausa women may be found in works by Barkow, A. Cohen, Faulkingham, Greenberg, Hill, Monfouga-Nicolas, G. Nicolas, Piault, Raynaut, M. G. Smith, Thomson, Trevitt, Trevor, Yeld, and others. An excellent short ethnography of Muslim Hausa is found in M. G. Smith 1965.

2. Recent estimates vary from 15 million (Hill 1972) to 30 million (Faulkingham 1970). The language includes a number of mutually understood dialects.

3. Barkow 1973 argues that the degree of cultural or subcultural variation makes "Hausa civilization" more accurate than "Hausa culture."

4. Figures courtesy of Mirria County Service de l'Agriculture, annual reports for these years.

5. Smith 1965 and Faulkingham 1970 note the tendency in other Hausa communities for groups holding political power to maintain corporate descent groups.

6. Queens are said to have ruled at Daura and at Zaria (Smith 1964); at least the Zaria queen is probably an actual historical figure.

7. The constitution appears in Peaslee (1965:577-588.) Faulkingham (1970: 65-66) describes a local election near Madaoua. All members of the pre-1974 local party committee in Mirria were male.

8. Figures on the proportion of Mirria children ever enrolled in school were not available. Many local parents are skeptical of the value of Western education and only enroll a child if ordered to do so; other parents encourage both sons and daughters to attend. In earlier years, far more boys than girls were enrolled even at the elementary level.

9. The *bori* cult bears a resemblance to the African-influenced Brazilian possession cults described in other chapters. The social function of *bori* seems to differ between pagan and Muslim Hausa (contrast Faulkingham 1975 with Monfouga-Nicolas 1972). Mirria informants claimed that no one in Mirria had inherited *bori* spiritis, but it is possible that the cult is practiced clandestinely. Since it is openly practiced elsewhere in Niger, this seems unlikely. A few post menopausal women participate in public Islamic prayers.

10. "Mosque" refers both to the congregation and to its place of worship.

11. Hill 1969 uses this phrase; Cohen 1969 gives details of large-scale housetrade in the Hausa community of Ibadan in Nigeria.

12. Many different relatives are included in the Hausa usage of terms such as "son" and "brother" and their French glosses used in the censuses. Households may include maternal kin of nonkin clients as well as paternal kin, but most are formed around a core of a man and his sons or brothers. As noted above, there is a strong patrilineal bias in descent despite recognition of bilateral kin ties.

13. Occasionally a man marries a second or third wife without having a separate bedroom for her in his compound. He must then rent a room for her elsewhere in Mirria, where he joins her during her two-night turn of sexual privileges. A few women were married to husbands who had another home and wife or wives in other towns.

14. For case examples of co-wife relations in Mirria, see Saunders 1978, Chapter Five.

15. Spot checking and a residential survey of one neighborhood indicate that most married adults are accurately reported in the census, which is essentially a tax list. Most known cases of under reporting in either the 1968 or the 1974 census concern children under age 15, the age of tax liability.

16. This also explains why secluded wives go out after dark, when the lustful eyes of other men see less well.

17. The *Sarki's* wives leave the palace only for childbirth, in deference to the many powerful spirits which inhabit the palace and threaten death or abnormality to the newborn (servant women also avoid childbirth there). But other wives are under an obligation to attend ceremonies, especially mourning, in their natal families. A husband may not refuse permission to attend such events.

18. Authority here means legitimate power, while power is the ability to enforce compliance with one's wishes, whether one has the right to compliance or not.

19. Female informants (a teacher posted to Mirria and a woman married in Zinder) gave this description of civil marriage, locally termed *alliance* marriage. In addition to Islamic ceremonies, the marriage is registered at the Zinder city hall (*mairie*).

Educated women of Niger's modern elite typically share the common Western view of polygyny as a symbol of male oppression.

20. Since the houseboy would be taking over her duties, the wife should pay his salary, according to one young single male official.

21. Oral contraceptives and the rhythm method were used by some civil servants in Mirria. Young male officials felt that uneducated wives would ob-

ject to the use of birth control, since children in general are highly desired and viewed as a blessing from Allah. Traditional child spacing depended upon late weaning (18 to 24 months) and a prohibition of intercourse with a nursing mother. Today Mirria women say that intercourse may be resumed as soon as the required 40-day period of special bathing has been completed after childbirth.

REFERENCES

Barkow, Jerome H.
1971 "The Institution of Courtesanship in the Northern States of Nigeria." *Genève-Afrique* 10:58-73.

1972 "Hausa Women and Islam." *Canadian Journal of African Studies* 6:317-28.

1973 "Muslims and Maguzawa in North Central State, Nigeria: An Ethnographic Comparison." *Canadian Journal of African Studies* 7: 59-76.

Chinas, Beverly L.
1973 *The Isthmus Zapotecs: Women's Roles in Cultural Context.* New York: Holt, Rinehart and Winston.

Cohen, Abner
1969 *Custom and Politics in Urban Africa, a Study of Hausa Migrants in Yoruba Towns.* Berkeley: University of California Press.

Cohen, Ronald
1971 "Dominance and Defiance: A Study of Marital Instability in an Islamic African Society." *Anthropological Studies 6.* Paul J. Bohannan, ed. Washington, D.C.: American Anthropological Association.

Faulkingham, Ralph H.
1970 Political Support in a Hausa Village. Ph.D. dissertation. Ann Arbor: Michigan State University, University Microfilms (#71-18,201).

1975 "The Spirits and Their Cousins." Amherst, Mass.: University of Massachusetts, Department of Anthropology, Research Report #15 (October 1975).

Goody, Jack
1972 *Domestic Groups.* Addison-Wesley Modular Publications, Module 28. Reading, Mass.: Addison-Wesley Publishing Co

Greenberg, Joseph
1946 *The Influence of Islam on a Sudanese Religion.* Monograph. American Ethnological Society. New York: J.J. Augustin.

Hill, Polly
    1969   "Hidden Trade in Hausaland." *Man:JRAI* (New Series) 4:392-409.
    1972   *Rural Hausa, a Village and a Setting.* Cambridge: Cambridge University Press.

Mintz, Sidney
    1971   "Men, Women, and Trade." *Comparative Studies in History and Society* 13:247-69.

Monfouga-Nicolas, Jacqueline
    1972   *Ambivalence et culte de possession: contribution à l'étude du Bori hausa.* Paris: Editions Anthropos.

Nicolas, Guy
    1965   *Circulation des richesses et participation sociale dans une société hausa du Niger.* Bordeaux: Centre universitaire de polycopiage.
    1971   "Un aspect de l'économie ostentatoire en Afrique Noire." *Cahier de Sociologie Economique* 1 (second série, juin 1971).

Peaslee, Amos J., ed.
    1965   "Constitution of Niger." *Constitutions of Nations,* 3rd. rev. ed. Vol. I. Africa. The Hague: M. Nijhoff, pp. 578-88.

Piault, Colette
    1965   "Contribution a l'etude de la vie quotidienne de la femme Mawri." *Etudes Nigeriennes* 10.

Raynaut, Claude
    1972   *Structures normatives et relations électives: étude d'une communaute villageoise haoussa.* The Hague: Mouton.

Rosaldo, Michelle Zimbalist
    1974   "Woman, Culture, and Society: A Theoretical Overview." In *Woman, Culture, and Society.* M.Z. Rosaldo and L. Lamphere, eds. Stanford: Stanford University Press, pp. 17-42.

Sacks, Karen
    1974   "Engels Revisited: Women, the Organization of Production, and private Property." In *Woman, Culture, and Society.* M.Z. Rosaldo and L. Lamphere, eds. Stanford: Stanford University Press, pp. 207-22.

Sanday, Peggy R.
    1974   "Female Status in the Public Domain." In *Woman, Culture, and Society.* M.Z. Rosaldo and L. Lamphere, eds. Stanford: Stanford University Press, pp. 189-206.

Saunders, Margaret O.
    1978   Marriage and Divorce in a Muslim Hausa Town (Mirria, Niger Republic). Ph.D. dissertation, Indiana University. Ann Arbor, Mich.: University Microfilms.

Smith, M.G.
1959   "The Hausa System of Social Status." *Africa* 29: 239-251.
1961   "Kebbi and Hausa Stratification." *British Journal of Sociology* 12:52-64.
1964   "The Beginnings of Hausa Society, AD 1000-1500." In *The Historian in Tropical Africa.* Vansina, Mauny, and Thomas, eds. London: Oxford University Press for the International African Institute, pp. 339-57.
1965   "The Hausa of Northern Nigeria." In *Peoples of Africa.* James L. Gibbs, ed. New York: Holt, Rinehart, and Winston, pp. 119-55.
1968   "Political Anthropology: Political Organization." *International Encyclopedia of the Social Sciences,* Vol. 12, pp. 193-202.

Smith, Mary F.
1965   *Baba of Karo: A Woman of the Muslim Hausa.* New York: Praeger.

Thomson, James T.
1976   Law, Legal Process and Development at the Local Level in Hausa-speaking Niger. Ph.D. dissertation, Indiana University. Ann Arbor, Mich.: University Microfilms

Trevitt, Lorna
1973   "Attitudes and Customs in Childbirth amongst Hausa Women in Zaria City." *Savanna* (Zaria, Nigeria) 2:223-26.

Trevor, Jean
1974   "Family Change in Sokoto, a Traditional Moslem Fulani/Hausa City." In *Population Growth and Socioeconomic Change in West Africa.* Caldwell et al., eds. New York: Columbia University Press.
1975   "Western Education and Muslim Fulani/Hausa Women in Sokoto, Northern Nigeria." In *Conflict and Harmony in Tropical Africa.* G. Brown and M. Hiskett, eds. School of Oriental and African Studies, Studies on Modern Asia and Africa #10. London: George Allen and Unwin, Ltd., pp. 247-70.

Yeld, E.R.
1960   "Islam and Social Stratification in Northern Nigeria." *British Journal of Sociology* 11:112-28.

5   Dioula Women in Town: A View of Intra-Ethnic Variation (Ivory Coast)

RISA S. ELLOVICH

Like the preceding chapter by Saunders, the present contribution offers us a view of women in a West African Islamic group, and it, too, suggests that a revision of some old notions of women in this society as oppressed and controlled may be in order. Ellovich focuses on the alternative life-styles of Dioula women in the Ivory Coast city of Gagnoa. Here she finds that another set of ideas also requires reconsideration. Some of the early literature on African urbanization had predicted that towns would offer women greater economic and social opportunities than they had known in rural areas. Also, they were expected to develop a new set of attitudes and behaviors similar to those of urbanized Westerners. The author, however, discovered, and is able to show us, that Dioula women who live in the city of Gagnoa are not following Western models of behavior. Quite to the contrary, they seem to be careful to maintain their Dioula tradition within the urban context. In significant respects, however, the move to the city and often into the modern sector as well, has reduced rather than increased the status of Dioula women.

The new urban centers of Africa are places of great variety. Populations in town represent a diversity of ethnic groups and languages, their environments a plethora of options. For urban dwellers or those migrating to the city from rural areas, the town is at once a source of traditional and changing ways, African and non-African phenomena, familiar and unfamiliar events. How people choose to behave in town thus reflects a series of choices they make from among the alternatives they perceive to be available.[1]

The city is a locus for maintenance of tradition and for potential change in African society. The coexistence of old and new in town, of diverse groups and arenas of action, allows residents to choose between traditional ways and nontraditional, both in specific situations and as a general life-style. For members of a single ethnic group, what consequences has this array of potential options and constraints for their continued identity as ethnic group members?

This chapter focuses on variation within an urban ethnic group, the Dioula of Gagnoa, Ivory Coast, and the relationship of this variation to both sociocultural and biographical factors. Specifically, Dioula women and their lives in town are discussed. What has been the effect of the city on Dioula women? Has their status changed? Of what significance is the variation in their behavior? Do the behavioral variations reflect a change in Dioula norms or, rather, a flexible continuity of traditional Dioula expectations?

The Dioula identify themselves as culturally and behaviorally distinct from non-Dioula. They do this by evaluating their own behavior and that of fellow members in terms of its congruence with established Dioula norms. This Dioula cultural code is not monolithic; rather, it encompasses a range of variants. Dioula urban dwellers may behave in different ways all of which are acceptable to and supported by other members of their group. Individual courses of action reflect both the influence of this code and the influence of environmental factors. These factors, in turn, constitute a vehicle for both cultural continuity and change.

This general framework for approaching the question of Dioula urban behavior becomes more complex when the parameter of gender is added since the spheres of action and of solidarity in traditional Dioula society are in many respects gender-linked. To assess the significance of behavioral strategies used by urban Dioula women, we must take into account the traditional code characteristic of their rural predecessors and contemporaries.

The Dioula are an Islamic African population most noted for their success as traders throughout former French West Africa.[2] Originally from the Mande region of present day Mali, the Dioula were among some of that area's population to convert to Islam after initial contact with Moslems in the eleventh century (Trimingham 1968:10). Dioula migrated to the Ivory Coast during the fifteenth and sixteenth centuries, settled in the northern savannah regions, and resumed their occupations of farming and trading (Tauxier 1921:70,207, 211; Marty 1922:79; Delafosse 1931:52-53; Joseph 1944:64; Holas 1965:32-33; Lewis 1970:57). It was their trading activities that took them further south on business in search of markets for their salt, cattle, and grain in exchange for local produce, especially kola nuts (Marty 1922:67, 400). However, the Dioula maintained their permanent homes in the north. In successive migrations they reached the forest regions of the Ivory Coast around the time of French pacification. The urban centers the French established were ideal for Dioula commercial activities and the Dioula began settling in towns like Gagnoa at the turn of the century.

Traditionally the Dioula were rurally based farmers. Some men were also long-distance traders for part of the year. While long-distance trading was basically the province of men, certain women owned slaves whom they delegated to trade on their behalf (Launay 1977:418). Women also engaged in small-scale local trading of products such as homespun cotton yarn and surplus garden produce such as gumbo, red pepper, and peanuts. Nevertheless the primary economic base of most families remained farming with some herding, and households based on extended family membership constituted the units of economic endeavor. Indeed these households were the most important units of Dioula society. They supplied their respective members with both economic and social security (Tauxier 1921; Delafosse 1931; Marty 1922; Labouret 1934; Joseph 1944; Holas 1965).

The household group was headed by the father or the oldest male in the patrilineal line. This man had authority and responsibility which extended to all spheres of the individual household member's life. He made all essential decisions about punishment for wrongdoers, expulsion for consistent serious offenders, and death for unfit children (Labouret 1934:55-60). His responsibilities included assuring adequate food and clothing for family members, payment of family debts, negotiation of brideprice payment, arrangement of marriages, and generally, "…guarding and administering the common property of the family"[3] (Labouret 1934:56).

The division of labor was by sex, age, and ability. Men were responsible for tilling the soil, for herding, hunting and fishing. Boys helped their fathers with their garden work and with raising chickens and goats. Young men formed group cooperatives which helped their members fulfill their agricultural obligations to their fathers-in-law or their future fathers-in-law. These obligations included clearing new fields. Women did the agricultural work of planting and harvesting the crops and did some selling of produce. As well, they were responsible for domestic chores and for educating young children. Girls helped their mothers in the fields and with the selling.

Property was owned communally and privately depending upon its nature. The land and herds were the communal property of the patrilineage. Products of the land were also communal property. Private property included personal effects such as clothing and jewelry; religious items such as prayer mats and water ablution pots; and household wares such as baskets, pots, and cooking implements.

Communal property was controlled by male members of the patrilineage. Private property could be owned by both men and women. Men owned their clothing and religious objects. Women owned property including livestock and jewelry purchased with their market earnings, clothing, and household wares which were given to them at marriage.

When a man died his belongings, communal and private, and his debts passed to his oldest living brother, then to his oldest brother's sons, and finally to the man's own sons. Failing these lines of succession, property was inherited by daughters and, in extremity, by wives. Only if a man had *no other* descendants did his wife inherit his property (Tauxier 1921: 226). Children inherited from their mothers: boys getting a full share; girls getting half a share of her property (Tauxier 1921: 243).

Marriages were arranged between the fathers and male relatives of the prospective son's-in-law family background; his ability to offer a substantial bride-price; and his ability to support his future wife. Although cross-cousin marriage was preferred, other men of the Dioula group were considered appropriate spouses, if they were Moslem. Sometimes a girl was promised at birth to a future groom. Generally the consent of the girl was acquired by her father prior to his finalizing the arrangements with the groom's father or emissary.

After marriage a woman resided in her husband's compound, sharing domestic tasks with her husband's other wives if he was polygynously married.[4] These tasks were done in rotation by each of the wives. The senior wife had some special responsibilities in the compound. It was she who established the rotation pattern among the wives and directed their domestic work. However, a husband was expected to treat each of his wives equally.

A wife owed her husband strict obedience. Even to leave the compound she was expected to ask her husband's permission. As a sign of respect she never used her husband's name in addressing him. Rather she would refer to him as "master of my home" or, using teknonymy, as "father of X."

The husband and his family were ever present in the married life of a woman. If a husband died, his brother had the right to marry his widows. Indeed, because bridewealth had been paid, it was expected that widows would not return to their father's household but would be maintained by and remain married to someone in the deceased husband's family.[5] Children belonged to the father and the father's family. Even children born to a woman during a long absence of her husband belonged to that man and not to the genitor proper. In the case of divorce, a woman would care for her children until they could manage without her, around the age of three, at which point they would be returned to the former husband's house to be raised by his family.

If marriage and filiation seem to have been dominated by the man and his family, it is interesting to note that in divorce Dioula women did have some clear-cut rights. Divorce by mutual consent was unheard of; yet, there were various grounds upon which a husband or wife could terminate a marriage. Husbands could divorce wives for the following reasons: infertility, adultery, lack of virginity on the wedding night, pregnancy at the time of marriage, constant fighting, and insulting the husband's mother. On the other hand, wives could divorce husbands for the following reasons: impotence, nonsupport, excessive violence, desertion, and insulting the wife's parents (Tauxier 1921: 244-45).

In seeking a divorce, a woman had recourse to her patrilineal kin: her father and her brothers. Thus, Dioula women had some power; however, this power rested in the woman's ability to influence her male relatives, to influence the men who controlled her world. Likewise, because a woman's activities were accomplished mainly in the household, her strategies to effect change or redress an imbalance there were limited to influencing the men in that domain: her husband, his brothers, her sons. If a woman were seriously dissatisfied with her husband, she could refuse to cook for him. By so doing, she also would be refusing to sleep with him. By disrupting the order of the household work in refusing to act in the fashion expected of a married woman, she could make her point effectively.

A postmenopausal woman who did not necessarily cook for or sleep with her husband could use a similar tactic, refusing to talk to her husband if she were angry with him. If her co-wives were sympathetic to her cause, they too could stop talking to the husband.

More commonly, however, Dioula women stood alone in their acts of persuasion and dissidence. Co-wives did not necessarily have much in common except a husband whom they shared among them. While interviewing Dioula about polygyny, I heard a recurrent remark, "Co-wives are jealous of one another and cause fights among themselves." These fights were often over apparently trivial matters; yet they upset the balance of the household for a day or two. Occasionally when asking details about an occurrence with a co-wife, the children of another wife would answer, "That is not our business. She is my father's wife but not my mother." Lamphere's remarks (1974: 109) seem applicable to the Dioula when she suggests that in societies where lineages prevail and where domestic and political spheres are separate, women rarely cooperate with one another because their interests do not coincide. Dioula women act on their own behalf and usually do this alone when dealing with their husbands.

If one were to assess status according to Sanday's (1974: 191) definition, "(1) the degree to which females have authority and/or power in the domestic and/or public domains; and (2) the degree to which females are accorded deferential treatment and are respected and revered in the domestic and/or public domains," the traditional Dioula woman had some status in the domestic domain and virtually no status in the public sphere. Dioula women had no domestic authority. Their farming activities allowed them limited power but their fathers, husbands, or husbands' families had direct control over their labor and the products therefrom. Their domestic power lay primarily in their ability to influence the males who had authority over them. In the public world of politics and religion, the only nondomestic activity available to women lay in selling the surplus of their gardens. In terms of authority, then, Dioula men were in control both domestically and publically. In this sense, an

"...asymmetry in cultural evaluation of sexes" (Rosaldo 1974: 17) existed in Dioula society. Dioula women lacked "...generally recognized and culturally valued authority" (Rosaldo 1974: 17).

However, there is no mistaking that Dioula women had value and were respected in their society. A woman's father could command substantial bride-wealth for his daughter; a woman's consent was obtained before marriage arrangements were finalized; a woman's importance in the process of homemaking and childrearing was recognized; and a woman's rights in divorce were acknowledged. The Dioula woman was accorded respect in all these areas falling within the domestic domain. As Rosaldo has indicated on a more general level, women in patrilineal societies are often in the anomalous position of being

> ...seen as unnecessary or superfluous, yet at the same time vitally important to men: they are needed as wives, as sisters to be exchanged for wives, and as procreators who reproduce workers and heirs for the group. Because they are important, they are powerful, yet theirs is a power opposed to formal norms (Rosaldo 1974: 32).

The limited power and ensuing respect shown women in the domestic domain indicates some, if not a pronounced degree of, status for Dioula women.

In the contemporary urban setting of Gagnoa, Dioula women have retained much the same overall position. They have increased neither their independent economic activities nor their participation in political and religious activities outside the home. Yet changes have occurred over the last 50 years that have affected the status of urban Dioula women and the strategies available to them.

During this time the Dioula population of the Ivory Coast has shifted for the most part from being rurally based agriculturalists and part-time traders to being urban-based, full-time traders and businessmen. The paved road from the capital, Abidjan, to Gagnoa and the new cash crops in the area have put the Dioula in an excellent economic position. They have become the major trade link connecting the furthest northern areas of the Ivory Coast with the southern regions and connecting Bété farmlands to the French established urban centers.

The urban setting placed Dioula in contact with many other African ethnic groups, with Europeans, with the new money economy, and with urban services such as schools and hospitals. Initially the Dioula became involved with the city and its activities by being the area's major entrepreneurs. Their successful trading ventures led to the organization of a strong transporters' union in town (Lewis 1970) which has allowed the Dioula to control much of the overland trade and transport in the region. Some of their children attend public schools, receiving an essentially French education, which enables them to be employed not only in Gagnoa but throughout the Ivory Coast and in France in occupations never before followed by Dioula.

Their preeminence in the business world and their newly acquired skills and jobs have facilitated Dioula mobility: socioeconomic, occupational, and residential. The migration of rural Dioula to the city and of urbanized Dioula to other cities has affected the traditional Dioula family. At minimum, this mobility has altered the composition of Dioula residential units. Where all extended family members used to live in one household in one town, one now finds residential splintering of that family. Members may live in different cities; in different quarters of the same city, or in different houses in the same quarter. Another reason for residential separation of family members is the high cost and shortage of urban dwellings. Traditionally an entire extended family would live in a compound; indeed, established Dioula urbanites, those having been in towns like Gagnoa for several generations, often own a compound. However, there are a limited number of these housing units in such towns, and there is little space available for building compounds of adequate size. Generally, European-styled homes and apartments do not have enough rooms to accommodate a large extended family. So, recently migrated urban Dioula, faced with the difficulty of finding appropriate housing for their families often are forced to separate family members, sometimes into nuclear family units, which then reside in another family's compound or in a European-styled house.

With the extended family living in disparate households scattered throughout one or several neighborhoods in a city, it is difficult for the household head to exert as much authority on family members as his traditional role entailed. While his daily routine in town might allow him frequent contact with family members, the control he wielded previously over the behavior of each individual has been weakened by residential separation.

Not only has residential unity been compromised, but the members of the family no longer form a single production unit either. Individuals do not always work for or with their parents, their family, or their lineage. Some family-run business persists. However, many Dioula are self-employed, work for European companies, or for the government. Usually urban Dioula do not engage in farming. If part of a Dioula family's lineage continues to reside in its natal village, a rural lineage member may grow crops for the urban part of the family. This would be done in exchange for monetary support of the village or for providing transportation for produce to the southern markets. Thus, the communally organized, strong family group which characterized the Dioula at the turn of the century is not necessarily the case for Dioula in town today. Many urban Dioulas own property individually and treat their earnings as their own, not their family's.

In light of such changes in social organization, residential pattern, and economic activities, some scholars predicted an impending disruption of traditional family structure in town (Tauxier 1921; Labouret 1934; Baker and

Bird 1959; Little 1959; Marris 1962; Aldous 1965). Some suggested that certain Africans would try to emulate the European model for marriage and family life with individual mate selection and monogamy (Little 1959; Marris 1962; Little and Price 1967). In fact the changes in Dioula family life which have occurred have little to do with such emulation; neither do they reflect breakdown to Western-style nuclear family units.

Although a modification of traditional family behavior may be occurring, this modification is not necessarily the radical change some of the literature has suggested it to be. Further, this modification in behavior seems to be supported by traditionally held values. The customary values are being maintained and appear flexible enough not to have become insignificant. They functioned in the past to support Dioula farming families and communities; they function as well in the present to support the coexistence of urban residence, new occupations, social mobility, and maintenance of extended family ties. This flexibility in Dioula norms and the blend of traditional and nontraditional behaviors that it allows for within the rubric of "being Dioula" is a key to the range of behavioral alternatives one observes among town-dwelling Dioula women.

Certain areas can be examined in the urban context to focus on the contrasts and similarities between traditional and present-day behavior patterns. These areas include spouse selection, authority structure, economic organization of the household, and women's involvement in the public sphere of activities.

Although some individuals in town marry spouses of their choosing, more than likely they request parental assent prior to the marriage. Obviously, it is still important to have family support for an intended marriage. Also, the independently chosen spouse often fulfills traditional Dioula dictates. Spouses ideally should be Dioula, Moslem, preferably from the same natal village, and from respected families. As for the monogamous marriages, some of which are performed by civil ceremony in the town hall,[6] they may well be a consequence of economic exigency rather than of acceptance of European patterns. Maintaining a polygynous household in town can be expensive. Monogamy may suit the urban individual's budget better.

In monogamous households where independent mate selection has occurred, the husband still appears to be the unquestioned head of the house. He continues to command respect and obedience from his wife. This apparent vestige of the traditional Dioula family system is consistent with the differential subsistence and social roles played by men and women in the urban setting. Men, who were traditionally charged to feed, shelter, and clothe their families with the resources at hand from the family's communal efforts, are still maintaining their families but solely by their own resources, and not by reliance on the contribution of all family members. The responsibility for the economic support of urban families falls on men. In this sense, the male role has increased in importance from the traditional pattern. Women, who traditionally were the essential labor force for agricultural work now are petty traders, salaried workers, or are unemployed. It is not the responsibility of urban women to provide the agricultural labor force necessary for the economic survival of the family group. In this sense their role, and subsequently their status, has changed rather drastically.

Both Friedl and Sanday have suggested that women's status largely is predicated on the part women have in the subsistence technology of the group (Friedl 1975; Sanday 1974). Women can be expected to have relatively high status when they are not only involved in but when they control production. Since urban Dioula women play a less important role in subsistence, their status has decreased. Whereas traditionally men and women were partners in maintenance of the group, having complementary roles in subsistence activities, men now have taken on the larger share of group maintenance (Boserup 1970: 191) and women help or not, dependent on their abilities and inclinations.

Most of the new economic opportunities theoretically available to women are actually very difficult to attain. To become a salaried employee for the public or private sector, for example, a midwife, nurse, teacher, or shop girl, a woman must have had some formal education. This means that her father approved of her matriculation, not so common an occurrence among Dioula men, and that someone was willing to pay for her school fees. It also means that the woman had the perseverance and ability to attend school regularly; to keep up with the work; and to make acceptable grades enabling her to advance through the school system. Since Dioula women's education is seen as less essential than men's, many women never attend school at all. Those who do are not encouraged in their endeavor, and they are saddled as well with many household chores which do not allow them adequate study time. Consequently, a Dioula girl who begins school often never completes the elementary grades. A woman with two or three years of education does not find a salaried job with ease. She is considered to be insufficiently trained for this type of work.

Ironically, men with comparable limited education are more likely to be employed. In a situation of competition for a desired job, a Dioula man would have greater success than a woman for several reasons. Because Dioula men traditionally are expected to support their families, they would ostensibly be in greater need of employment than women. Dioula men not only try to reserve good jobs for themselves, but they try to keep women away from salaried employ because these jobs so often entail a woman's "...working under the authority of a foreign man" (Boserup 1970: 190). Further, there "...may be a preference on the part of the representatives of European firms to deal

with men" (Mintz 1971: 265). Thus, low level civil service and clerk jobs calling for some education are almost always filled by men, not women. "In Africa...the modern sector is virtually a male preserve" (Boserup 1970: 190).

Beyond the fact that women may not be able to avail themselves of new
possibilities presented by the urban milieu, one can question the relative value
of these jobs for women anyway. Mintz has suggested that these new occupations may well make women less, rather than more, independent than they
were formerly (Mintz 1971). Women who are self-employed in the market
have more independence than do salaried women. Traditionally, market
women's earnings were their own. Since their exact earnings were not known
to others, few personal demands could be placed on their money. Salaried
women, on the other hand, "...are committed to more expenditure and less
capital accumulation accordingly" (Mintz 1971: 266). "...A husband cannot
safely tamper with his wife's conduct of her trading business, while he may,
indeed, lay serious claim upon her earnings at a job without endangering her
performance" (Mintz 1971: 266). Thus, women in traditional economic pursuits and in traditional life styles appear more independent and perhaps better off than women who have entered the modern sector as wage earners.

However, even women following traditional economic pursuits may be in
a deteriorating economic situation in town. With reference to small scale trading Boserup states "...this sector seems to be so overcrowded that the earnings
of most women must be extremely small" (Boserup 1970: 191). Robertson
points to a reduction in financial cooperation and support among Ga market
women in Accra which "...has probably worsened their financial position"
(Robertson 1976: 132). And Lewis reports on a similar worsening of the e-
conomic position for the majority of Abidjan market women (Lewis 1976).

So, while Dioula men are more and more involved in the public sphere of
life, making a living and being politically involved, women are not. While
men's roles expand in the public sphere, women's roles actually seem to be lessening in this area. Ostensibly, a woman's roles within the home have not
changed. However, her importance in educating her children has decreased because her children, especially her male children, attend school and are educated
there to enter a system about which she knows little.

The economic and social roles Dioula men play now are essential to the
family's existence. Dioula men's status has remained the same or has increased
accordingly. Dioula women's roles have diminished in the economic sphere
and have been modified in the home to a point where Dioula women may be
seen to have less status now than they did in the past. Being stymied because
of inadequate opportunities, inadequate preparation, and inadequate economic
support from their families, Dioula women can ill afford to break ties with
their families, their ethnic groups, the African community. In response to
their loss of status, they seem likely to uphold tradition and to conform to

traditional ethnic expectations for the security, economic and social, that they offer her. Dioula women's behavior is variable; yet underlying it is a retention of tradition and ethnicity.

Three particular cases can be used to illustrate some of the above mentioned points. On one level these cases indicate the variety of behavior manifested by Dioula women in town. On another level the similarity among these women indicates a strong retention of ethnic identity through traditional behavioral patterns.

These women, whom I shall call Awa, Mariam, and Fanta, were Dioula, in their twenties, born in Gagnoa. Their respective families were from the same natal village in the north of the Ivory Coast. They had spent their childhoods in town and were married at the age of eighteen. At the time I knew them they each had at least one child.

Awa had no formal education and could speak no French. She was a petty trader by profession, although she did not pursue this career with any apparent enthusiasm. When she had the money or could borrow it from her husband, she invested in popcorn which she would cook, package, and then sell in front of one of the movie theatres in the evenings. Her father had arranged her marriage to a Dioula man from a relatively prominent family. At the time, her marriage was monogamous, but she looked forward to a day when she would be the senior wife in a household. She lived in the compound of her husband's family and visited her mother daily.

Mariam had six years of education and spoke French well. She was employed by the government at the local women's center[7] and had worked there for five years. She had met her husband while attending school and they had decided to marry. Her parents had objected, not liking the fellow very much, but they had acquiesced and her father arranged the marriage after much insistence by Mariam. She lived with her husband, a school teacher, and their two children in a European-styled home in an African quarter of town. Mariam did not want to be married polygynously, stating, "Polygyny is illegal, and, furthermore, it destroys the home." Her husband, however, was a well-known woman chaser, and spent little of his free time at home with his family. Mariam retained strong and very warm relations with both her parents and saw them as often as she could.

The third woman, Fanta, had had three years of formal schooling, and she could speak French with some ease. Her father vehemently had opposed her attending school so she had done this clandestinely, while living for a time with her older brother in Abidjan. She was a seamstress by profession, having been an apprentice for some time in a seamstress shop. She had not practiced her profession, however, since her marriage because of frequent residential changes, which did not allow her to establish herself in any community, and because of lack of encouragement on the part of her husband. Her father too had arranged her marriage to a Dioula man from a prominent family. She had given her consent initially to this marriage but had changed her mind, choosing instead to elope with another man. Her father refused to recognize the legitimacy of their relationship and severed all ties with his daughter. She lived with her husband in his home and visited her mother secretly and only at times when her father was not in town. Her marriage was monogamous, and both she and her husband seemed determined to keep it that way. When asked about polygyny she said, "It is not right for me. I am not interested in that form of marriage and I do not want my husband to take another wife."

Awa in many ways represents an traditional Dioula woman who has been brought up in town. Her Dioula background prepared her for an arranged marriage, a polygynous household, an occupation as a petty trader. The urban milieu has had minimal effect on her upbringing or on her behavior. The main difference between Awa and a rural Dioula woman is that Awa does not contribute to the subsistence maintenance of the family through farm labor. Her husband has full responsibility for the family's sustenance. Any profits she realizes from her economic activities are hers alone, as is the case with rural Dioula women. What the urban setting has done is to effect a change in her status from being a family member who contributes significantly to family maintenance to being a family member who depends heavily on her husband and his family's resources for her survival. Her male children who may attend government schools will be less guided by her dominance in the domestic sphere because of her ignorance of the system they are being trained by and for. Her daughters, who will probably be denied formal education by her husband, will be more likely to come under her direct influence and may well be traditional Dioula women themselves.

Mariam appears to be the least traditional woman of the three cases. Her years of schooling have prepared her adequately for salaried work in the public sector. She even has a savings account at the bank separate from that of her husband. She is aware of new laws governing women's status and marriage, especially the Civil Code established in 1964 which made polygyny illegal. Yet, the work and the financial contributions she makes to the maintenance of the household also cast her in the traditional role of woman as laborer.

In an equally traditional vein, she feels that working in the public sector changes nothing about women's care of their homes and children. "Salaried work changes nothing in the manner and style of life of a Dioula woman." So, in the domestic sphere she maintains a traditional relationship with her children and her husband. When asked about children's education, Mariam responded that boys ought to be encouraged further in school than girls because "men are superior to women."

Obviously, Mariam has elements of the nontraditional and traditional in her urban life. She chose her husband independent of her family's wishes, and then her father arranged for the brideprice payment and the marriage. She has a monogamous marriage, which she favors, but her husband has a lover in town with whom he spends much of his leisure time. Mariam is aware of this situation and has conflicting responses to it. On the one hand, she says she would accept another wife if her husband chose to marry again. On the other hand, she holds that polygynous marriage destroys home life. Her acceptance of the idea of a second wife, presumably her husband's present lover, gives vent to her hope for a more stable marriage. With the added responsibility of another wife, her husband might be deterred from additional extramarital liaisons and might spend more time with his family. Yet, ideally, she would prefer a nontraditional, monogamous marriage with a faithful husband.

Her apparent nontraditional status as a salaried worker belies a much more complex behavior pattern. In light of her difficult marital situation, it is small wonder she maintains very close ties with her parents. The only available recourse for security appears to be in the traditional system with those persons whom she trusts the most, her mother and father.

Fanta has many of the trappings of a nontraditional Dioula woman. Her schooling, her occupational training, her defiance of paternal authority, and her independent mate selection all mark a break with traditional Dioula expectations for a woman. In these ways she has been influenced by the urban milieu. Ironically, she is not unlike Awa in that she too does not contribute to family maintenance. She too has rights to any profit she might make as a seamstress. However, there is a difference between them in that Fanta does not practice her occupation. By being unemployed, she is totally dependent upon her husband and his family.

Her husband has a prestigious job in the government and has high status in Dioula and in Ivorien society. She participates in this high status because she is his wife; however, she does this at the expense of total financial dependence on him. She has gained status socially but has lost it economically. Her own economic status is lower even than that of Awa. Mariam and Awa make money which is theirs alone. They have some independence. Fanta has none of this. The city which allows for socially upward mobility of which she, by association, is a part has actually stripped her of economic and social independence.

So, Fanta, although apparently a woman changed in part by the urban milieu and by the opportunities the city presents, is less independent than most traditional Dioula women and has less status than they. In fact, in spite of the nontraditional ways she manifests, Fanta has followed some basic Dioula tenets which make her akin to traditional Dioula women. Her willingness to defy her father's authority in arranging her marriage and to risk banishment from the family appear to be rash acts, contrary to Dioula values. However, in analyzing the decisions and actions involved, one can note that Fanta indeed was behaving in Dioula ways.

She adhered to ethnic dictates in her choice of a mate. Her father had chosen a Dioula man from the same natal village as they; a devout Moslem; a man with an excellent job and good future before him. Whom did Fanta choose as an alternate? The man with whom she eloped is also a Dioula from the same natal village as her family; he is a devout Moslem and a man with a prestigious government position which almost guarantees him an excellent future. So, in her choice of mate, she deviated not at all from the traditional norms. Her only nontraditional act was that *she* chose her mate.

What allowed her to behave in this nontraditional way? Fanta had not acted on whim in terms of her marriage. She had consulted all members of her family, excluding her father, and found they all supported her. Indeed these family members tried to exert pressure on the father to change his mind and accept his daughter and her choice of husband. With the support of her entire extended family, Fanta felt more secure in her behavior. Here, the extended family (without her father) seems to have acquired the authority and respect traditionally relegated only to the male head of household. What this woman did was to adjust the older system of marriage arrangement and respect for father's authority to work to her advantage. She transferred the authority normally placed in her father onto her entire extended family. Had they not supported her, I doubt she would have behaved as she did. However, Fanta had the weight of tradition behind her in her decision and in her actions.

Although on one level both Fanta and Mariam appear to be nontraditional, urbanized Dioula women, on another level they are as Dioula as their counterpart, Awa. Although acting in different ways, all these women identify strongly with their ethnic group. Moreover, they are all acknowledged as proper Dioula by their fellow Dioula.

These urban women, members of the same ethnic group, manifest divergent behaviors which are identified and accepted as Dioula. This speaks to the flexibility of ethnic norms which can be employed appropriately in a variety of ways. The disregarding of older expectations and the developing of new behavior has not occurred to any large extent in the African urban environment. This may be true in part because the city, which theoretically offers more economic and social opportunities, may actually offer fewer of these opportunities. Instead of becoming more independent in town, many women may become more dependent. In light of this growing dependency a Dioula woman would do all she could to follow traditional ethnic dictates. She would not be in a position to risk exclusion by her family, lineage, or ethnic group as she derives her only security from these very groups. And, as of the present, there are no alternative sources of security. The retention of ethnicity in the urban milieu is a strategy for women in a new environment where they may be losing status and a measure of economic independence.

NOTES

1. I would like gratefully to acknowledge the encouragement and helpful comments of Judith Friedman Hansen, Bob Launay, Joan Scott, Kent Maynard, Margaret Saunders, and Erika Bourguignon. The fieldwork upon which this study is based was carried out between December 1972 and June 1974 in the Ivory Coast and was supported by a Fulbright-Hays Predoctoral Dissertation grant.

2. It is critical to note the perspective of authors writing about traditional Dioula culture. Most were colonial officers or persons writing from a colonialist perspective. Their contact with Dioula women was minimal and their remarks reflect this. A vision of women as an oppressed and controlled group dominates this literature. We do not know whether this stereotype was upheld in actuality. Indeed, this essay's comments about present-day Dioula women's strategies and status may well be applicable to this earlier period.

3. "...sa charge principale consiste à garder et à administrer le bien commun."

4. It should be noted the Dioula have not followed the practice of purdah or seclusion of wives as have some other Islamized African groups like the Hausa about whom M. Saunders has written elsewhere in this volume. Trimingham (1959: 176, 189) has suggested that, among people whose women engaged in farming, wife seclusion did not exist, whereas among cultures where slave labor was present and where women did not farm, they were secluded.

5. This is a breach of Islamic law which, although allowing for the levirate, does not demand its practice. "Islam rules that widows are free to marry whom they please..." and this may or may not include the deceased husband's brother (Trimingham 1959: 169). The continued operation of the levirate among the Dioula is an example of the persistence of customs which predate Islamization and the successful coexistence of traditional African customs and Islam among some peoples (Trimingham 1959: 40, 126, 169-70).

6. Salaried workers who marry according to the Civil Code of 1964 receive financial benefits, called "allocations familiales" (family allocations), for their households and their children. This helps explain why these people would choose to marry in a civil ceremony.

7. The nearest American equivalent to this center is the YWCA. Women and girls attend classes to learn skills such as sewing, cooking, and reading.

REFERENCES

Aldous, Joan
    1965   "Urbanization, the Extended Family and Kinship Ties in West Africa." In *Africa: Social Problems of Change and Conflict.* Pierre van den Berghe, ed. San Francisco: Chandler Publishing Company, pp. 107-16.

Baker, Tanya, and Mary Bird
    1959   "Urbanization and the Position of Women." *The Sociological Review* 7:99-122.

Boserup, Ester
    1970   *Woman's Role in Economic Development.* London: George Allen Unwin Ltd.

Cohen, Michael A.
    1974   *Urban Policy and Political Conflict in Africa.* Chicago: The University of Chicago Press.

Delafosse, Maurice
    1968   (orig. 1931) *The Negroes of Africa.* F. Fligelman, trans., New York: Kennikat Press, Inc.

Friedl, Ernestine
    1975   *Women and Men.* New York: Holt, Rinehart and Winston.
Holas, B.
    1965   *La Côte d'Ivoire Passé-Présent-Perspectives.* Paris: Librairie Orientaliste Paul Geuthner.

Joseph, Gaston
    1944   *Côte d'Ivoire.* Paris: Librairie Arthème Fayard.

Labouret, Henri
    1934   *Les Manding et leur Langue.* Paris: Librairie Larose.

Lamphere, Louise
    1974   "Strategies, Cooperation, and Conflict Among Women in Domestic Groups." In *Woman, Culture and Society.* Michelle Zimbalist Rosaldo and Louise Lamphere, eds. Stanford: Stanford University Press, pp. 97-112.

Launay, Robert
    1977   "Joking Slavery." *Africa* 47:413-422.

Lewis, Barbara
    1970   "The Transporters' Association of the Ivory Coast. Ethnicity, Occupational Specialization, and National Integration." Ph.D. dissertation, Northwestern University. Ann Arbor, Mich: University Microfilms.
    1976   "The Limitations of Group Action among Entrepreneurs: The Market Women of Abidjan, Ivory Coast." In *Women in Africa.* Nancy J. Hafkin and Edna G. Bay, eds. Stanford: Stanford University Press, pp. 135-56.

Little, Kenneth
1959 "Some Urban Patterns of Marriage and Domesticity in West Africa." *The Sociological Review* 7:65-82.

Little, Kenneth, and Anne Price
1967 "Some Trends in Modern Marriage Among West Africans." *Africa* 37:407-24.

Marris, Peter
1962 *Family and Social Change in an African City*. Evanston: Northwestern University Press.

Marty, Paul
1922 *Etudes sur l'Islam en Côte d'Ivoire*. Paris: Editions Ernest Leroux.

Ministère du Plan
1967 *Region de Daloa, Gagnoa. Etude Socio-Economique*. Tome I. Abidjan: Ministère du Plan.

Ministère du Plan: Datar
1975 *Document Provisoire. Livre Blanc du Centre-Ouest*. Abidjan: Ministère du Plan.

Mintz, Sidney W.
1971 "Men, Women, and Trade." *Comparative Studies in History and Society* 13:247-69.

Robertson, Claire
1976 "Ga Women and Socioeconomic Change in Accra, Ghana." In *Women in Africa*. Nancy J. Hafkin and Edna G. Bay, eds. Stanford: Stanford Univesrity Press, pp. 111-34.

Rosaldo, Michelle Zimbalist
1974 "Woman, Culture, and Society: A Theoretical Overview." In *Woman, Culture, and Society*. Michelle Zimbalist Rosaldo and Louise Lamphere, eds. Sanford: Stanford University Press, pp. 17-42.

Sanday, Peggy R.
1974 "Female Status in the Public Domain." In *Woman, Culture, and Society*. Michelle Zimbalist Rosaldo and Louise Lamphere, eds. Stanford: Stanford University Press, pp. 189-206.

Tauxier, L.
1921 *Le Noir de Bondoukou*. Paris: Editions Ernest Leroux.

Trimingham, J. Spencer
1959 *A History of Islam in West Africa*. London: Oxford University Press.
1968 *The Influence of Islam Upon Africa*. London: Longmans, Green and Company, Ltd.,

PART II

AFRO-AMERICAN SOCIETIES

6 Spirit Magic in the Social Relations between Men and Women (São Paulo, Brazil)

ESTHER PRESSEL

In this chapter, the author introduces us to the complex subject of Brazilian sex roles, as she discovered it in the modern city of São Paulo. The stereotyped sex roles center about the themes of virility and virginity, which reflect aspects of the ancient Mediterranean honor/shame complex. Pressel describes eight case studies of individual men and women caught up in the confining net of these stereotyped roles, which inhibit the satisfactory expression of personal feelings. For the problems that result for the individuals, such as male impotence and female hysteria, relief is sought, and found, in the Umbanda and Quimbanda spirit possession religions. The author argues that these religious settings cannot be categorized as belonging exclusively into the feminine domestic domain or into the masculine politicoeconomic domain. Instead, the spirit possession religions offer a *neutral* locale and cultural belief system, which satisfy individual needs of both men and women; at the same time, they support the larger traditional Brazilian view of sex roles.

Brazilians, in discussing the topic of religion, frequently observe that their countrymen "have two religions." They use this phrase to indicate that they are officially Catholic, but at the same time are also interested in one or several of a multitude of Brazilian spiritist religions.[1] These religions focus their ritual activity on mediums who are said to be possessed by spirits of the dead. At public and private sessions, the spiritual entities diagnose and cure illnesses and help solve personal problems of clients who have come for aid. During an eleven-month field study[2] of the Umbanda spirit possession religion in 1967, I was struck by the openness with which the Brazilian news media discussed spiritism; by the great quantity of books published by spiritists; and by the ease with which individuals discussed their personal experiences with spirit possession religions with me. Since nearly all Brazilians list their religion as Catholic for the census, it is impossible to know with any certainty the exact number of persons who have the dual religious commitment. I have the impression, however, that at least 50 per cent of the Brazilian population has had contact in one way or another with spirit possession religions.

UMBANDA AND QUIMBANDA

The two Brazilian spirit possession religions that I examine here in terms of certain social relations between men and women are Umbanda and Quimbanda. Nearly all of my field work was focused on Umbanda in the metropolis of Sao Paulo (Pressel 1973, 1974, 1977). The symbolic content of Umbanda is varied and complex. It includes cultural elements from African and indigenous Indian religions, from the French spiritism of Allen Kardec, and from Catholicism. Umbanda is one of the more recent additions to a long tradition of syncretic Brazilian religions, for example, Batuque, Xango, and Macumba. These earlier religions were and are followed primarily by lower-class Afro-Brazilians. Umbanda differs from its predecessors in that its members in Sao Paulo tend to be upwardly mobile and are generally in the upper-lower and middle classes. Descendants of Europeans account for perhaps as much as 50 percent of Umbanda membership in Sao Paulo. Although Umbanda originated in the earlier part of this century, it seems to have more rapidly expanded into nearly all parts of Brazil beginning in the 1950s.

At the public sessions of Umbanda held twice each week, both men and women enter trance states of varying depths, and are possessed by spirits of dead Afro-Brazilians (*prêtos velhos*) and Brazilian Indians (*caboclos*). At less frequent intervals, spirits of dead children (*crianças*) possess Umbanda mediums. Since these three Umbanda spirits had led good lives while still incarnate, upon death they obtained heavenly "light." They exclusively perform white magic (*magia branca*) for their clients, such as helping an individual with his personal problems or curing an illness. The spiritual *consulta* (consultation) may deal with the usual aches and pains, nervous tension, fatigue, as well as "heart" and "liver" ailments. There is always the working person's problem of getting or keeping a job. Some businessmen also feel the need for some spiritual assistance when confronted by new decisions. Family quarrels, difficulties in love affairs, and even poor scholastic grades are brought to Umbanda centers.

In addition to the three spirits with "light," a fourth type of spirit known as Exu,[3] possesses a medium approximately once each month. This spirit has its origins in West African Yoruba religion, and was brought to Brazil by slaves from that area. According to Bascom (1969:79), Exu is the youngest and cleverest of the Yoruba deities. Acting as a messenger, he delivers sacrifices prescribed by a diviner to the high god Olorun. Exu, being a trickster deity, can start fights or cause "accidents" to occur. In Brazil, Exus and their feminine counterparts known as *pombagiras* are somewhat devilish characters who like to drink hard liquor, curse, sing lewd songs, and tell off-color stories. Exus differ from the other Umbanda spirits in that they are spirits of persons who had led especially wicked lives prior to their death. As a result, these spirits did not go to heaven, and are said to be without spiritual "light."

Exu spirits come in two varieties, and it is at this point that the second spirit religion, Quimbanda, enters into our discussion. Quimbandists work almost entirely with Exu spirits—and the worst kind of Exu, at that. For a specified fee or an expensive present, such as liquor or French perfume, Quimbanda Exus are said to perform antisocial acts such as wrecking a marriage, crushing a business competitor, or causing a man to become sexually impotent. Quimbandists work with *magia negra,* or black magic. In contrast, Umbandists claim that their Exus do not indulge in such dastardly behavior. Umbanda Exus are viewed more as reformed characters. They are said to be working their way through a sort of heavenly parole system by performing only good magic to counteract the evil Quimbanda magic. By doing enough good works, the Umbanda Exus hope to find themselves closer to heavenly "light," or so the theory goes. It is not always easy to say what is "good," and what is "evil," magic. Obviously, a spirit work designed to increase one's business may be detrimental to another businessman. Furthermore, there is something of a continuum between Umbanda and Quimbanda. A particular Umbanda center, therefore, may lean somewhat in the direction of Quimbanda when it comes to matters of Exu spiritual works.

EXUS IN SOCIAL RELATIONS BETWEEN MEN AND WOMEN

During the year of field work in Brazil, I became aware that certain problems brought to Umbanda Exus could be delineated in terms of social relationships between men and women.[4] A pattern emerged in which men consistently utilized Umbanda Exus to counteract the evil magic said to be sent against them by Quimbanda Exus employed by women. This sequence of events, or parts thereof, is illustrated in the seven cases which follow.

Case 1 (Roberto) Early in the year, four of my major informants invited me to attend a private session that they were planning to hold for a male acquaintance of theirs. He was about 35 years old and of Italian descent. During the short bus ride to the apartment of Roberto,[5] the purpose of the session was explained to me. Roberto and his father operated a small industry of things made from plaited straw, principally hats and ladies' purses. During the past year Roberto had become somewhat independent of his family, buying his own apartment. Sometime earlier, he had started to make his own hats, purchasing the plaited straw from his father, and selling the finished products independently. Recently, however, he had been unable to find a sufficient number of retail sellers. In the Brazilian idiom, he had *caminhos fechados*, that is, his paths had mysteriously been blocked. I soon learned that this generally meant that someone had paid an evil Exu spirit of Quimbanda to obstruct his enemy's progress. The purpose of this private Umbanda session was to discover what had happened and to reopen Roberto's paths.

We arrived at Roberto's apartment about 9:00 p.m. The four mediums included João, a 30-year old man, who was cook and waiter in an exclusive beauty salon; Juvenir, a 25-year-old male, who was an accounting clerk in the offices of a major Brazilian airline; Maria, a 37-year-old female, who operated a small beauty salon; and Cecilia, a 52-year-old woman, who was the wife of a taxi driver. They explained to me that the spirits like company. Therefore, they had invited me and three others to this private session.

Cecilia, the oldest and most experienced medium of the group, assumed the leadership role, telling the men to arrange a temporary altar from a work bench covered with a white sheet. Each of us lighted a candle for our guardian angel. We placed the candles on a plate which was carried to another room. Someone turned out the lights and the four mediums began to dance in a counter-clockwise direction around a glass of rum and a lighted candle placed in the center of the floor. They clapped hands to the rhythm of the song which they were quietly singing for their Exu spirits. Then the two male mediums picked up the glass and candle, carrying them to the terrace. The objects were left just outside the back door to placate any maleficent Exus of Quimbanda who might have been lurking in the vicinity and who might have been jealous of the rituals of the Umbanda Exus of these mediums. A few minutes later, Maria was possessed by her male Exu spirit, "Sete Escade," and Cecilia was calling her Exu through song. She stood in place, putting most of her weight on one foot and balancing her body slowly forward and backward about five times. Her eyes were alternately closed or staring at an unmarked spot on the wall. Suddenly, head and chest jerked once or twice in opposite directions. As she slowly straightened up her body, we could see that her face had been transformed into the devilish countenance of "Marimbondo," her male Exu. He wore a crooked smile and as he slowly began to open his eyes, Marimbondo shouted in a low rasping voice, *"Boa noite!"* ("Good evening!"). When he heard the somewhat weak response from the audience, Marimbondo shut his eyes, furrowed his brow and with great aplomb loudly emitted intestingal gas to show his displeasure. Everyone laughed and as Marimbondo opened his eyes, he began to scold everyone, saying that he wanted to hear a strong *"Boa noite"* from each person. We complied. The two Exus began to make their round of individual greetings, extending alternately left and right forearms and hands stiffened into hooklike forms characteristic of Exus to each member of the audience, who stood up to respond in a like manner. By this time, Juvenir had lighted cigars, which he gave to Marimbondo and Sete Escade. Marimbondo looked around, asking if there were nothing in the house to drink. Roberto provided some rum.

The preliminary greetings finished, Marimbondo began to converse with Roberto, who explained his financial problems to Cecilia's spirit. Roberto also said that he felt depressed and tired. Nonchalantly flicking his ashes to the floor, Marimbondo picked up a handful of manioc meal from the altar. Telling Roberto to stand in an open space in the room, he sprinkled the meal over Roberto's head. The two moved away from the spot and Marimbondo began to inspect the pattern of the meal which had fallen to the floor. After a few minutes of scrutinizing the manioc from different angles, the Exu bent over and with several sweeps of his hand outlined the head, two breasts, and hips of a woman. Marimbondo straightened up and announced to Roberto that his problems were due to his ex-fiancee. She had payed an evil Exu of Quimbanda to block all of Roberto's roads to success soon after their engagement had been broken off five years ago. Roberto confirmed that he had broken off the engagement and that his difficulties had begun about that time. As the two continued to converse, Marimbondo accepted another glass of rum and another cigar. Sete Escada, who had been discussing the problems of the others in the room refused more rum, saying that he wanted only water now.

Marimbondo placed Roberto facing the closed front door. Juvenir was told to mix together a small amount of gunpowder and manioc meal. It was wrapped in a piece of paper which Marimbondo placed on the floor behind Roberto. The Exu flicked the live coals from his cigar onto the paper. The ensuing explosion broke up the evil spiritual "fluids"[6] which had plagued Roberto, sending them through the door. Marimbondo asked Roberto how he was feeling now. He responded with a smile that he was fine. The two continued to discuss the case, Marimbondo maneuvering the conversation until he had learned that Roberto had been sleeping with the woman in question. He asked Roberto whether his sex life had been the same since the engagement had been broken off. Roberto replied that it had not been very satisfying. With a sinister laugh the Exu announced that he was sending Roberto to the bathroom to urinate. Furthermore, since Roberto had so much evil fluid to get rid of he was ordering all of the men in the room to assist Roberto by urinating, too. A line formed outside of the bathroom door.

This ritual in the bathroom finished, Marimbondo once more placed Roberto facing the front door. The Exu stood behind Roberto. Pouring a small amount of gunpowder into his own hand, Marimbondo instructed Roberto to concentrate on all of the things that he wanted for the future, now that all obstacles had been removed. A few sparks from Marimbondo's cigar ignited the gunpowder held in his hand. The ensuing explosion terminated Marimbondo's business with Roberto and he began to converse with and amuse the others in the room at his leisure. During the months which followed, Roberto said that his business affairs gradually improved. He took some interest in women after this session.

Case 2 (Luis) Several months after I had begun my fieldwork a 40-year-old man, Luis, who was a solidly middle-class proprietor of a modern electrical store, and his wife were the supposed victims of Quimbanda Exu works. The wife underwent an operation on her internal organs. While she was in the hospital, a nurse incorrectly administered some medication and severely burned the abdomen and thighs of the patient, putting her on the critical list for a few days. Sometime later Luis was out driving his Volkswagen van when it skidded on the wet pavement. The door jarred open as the vehicle collided with another car. As Luis fell out his head struck the pavement, and he was knocked unconscious. He suffered a broken nose and a gash on his head that required a number of stitches. It was significant to Umbandists that the gash was on the left side of the man's head, because Exus are said to be "of the left side." Furthermore, seven stitches were required, which is the magical number associated with Exus! Members of the Umbanda center where Luis served as financial director held several special sessions for him and his wife, which I attended. The good Exus of Umbanda undid the black magic of the Quimbanda Exu. The Umbanda Exus claimed that it was the husband's disappointed mistress who had paid a Quimbanda Exu to victimize her former lover and his wife.

The ex-girlfriend did not attempt to harm Luis's business, as had occurred with Roberto in Case 1, but she supposedly was interested in doing away with his wife. The situation was regarded as especially odious by two married male friends of Luis, particularly since they shared with him the expenses of a special apartment *"para brincar"* ("for playing around"). The men normally brought their girlfriends here. Believing that Luis's rejected girlfriend had sent a Quimbanda Exu against Luis, they felt that their shared apartment was filled with bad spiritual fluids which might harm them as well. They therefore asked Cecília (see Case 1) to perform a purification ritual for them and their defiled apartment, which she did.

Case 3 (Mr. N.) Another example came to me from a Brazilian friend, who described her uncle's personal problems with Exu spirit works which he claimed were directed against him by women. The uncle, Mr. N., was an older man and a university graduate who worked in the civil service. Mr. N. had had a very warm and close relationship with his wife until two years ago, when she had suddenly died from cancer. The family believed that he had had frequent and satisfactory sexual relations with his wife and that he had never stepped out on her during his marriage.

It was truly a marriage of love and the stuff that romantic stories are made of. When Mr. N. was a boy, his family was of the upper middle class and white. As was the custom of well-to-do Brazilian sons, he began his first sexual experimentations with the family maid—a mulatto ten years older than he, and with a child by a husband who had left her. However, the relation between the two turned out to be one of serious love. But, because of the family's social position, it was impossible for Mr. N. to openly live with his true love—a married woman with a child, a mulatto, a servant.

When it became evident to the family what was happening, they sent their servant away from the house. Not wishing to sever their relationship, Mr. N. financially maintained his love and her child in a separate house, visiting her during the week, but continuing to retain his official residence in his family's house. Some years later when the mulatto's husband died, she and Mr. N. were married. His family never knew of the marriage, and Mr. N. continued to retain his official living quarters in his father's house.

About twelve years ago, when Mr. N's mother died, the family was looking for a female housekeeper to manage the servants, and they asked their former mulatto maid to return. She agreed and came to live at the house in the status of servant. For various reasons, Mr. N.'s niece, Amélia, was especially close to the new housekeeper, who once secretly told her of the marriage to Mr. N. Amélia was very pleased with the marriage and refused to keep still. She told both her "new" aunt and the rest of the family that it was wrong for the woman not to assume her rightful position as wife and as mistress of Mr. N.'s household. With a minimum of fuss this was accomplished, and the couple had lived happily together for some years until her death.

According to his niece, Mr. N. was profoundly shocked by his wife's death, and became withdrawn, refusing to go to movies or to engage in any other forms of social activity. She felt that he exhibited signs of paranoia. Recently, he had fired a very competent house servant for no apparent reason. When his niece questioned Mr. N. on this matter, he responded that he had found two crossed sticks in the back garden. He believed this represented a Quimbanda Exu work aimed at him. The servant, Mr. N. claimed, desired him as a lover. Also, in recent months, he thought that certain single women in his office wanted to marry him for his money. One day, he found a strange looking box in his office desk drawer. Since he believed that it contained the paraphernalia from an Exu work directed against him by one of the women, he picked it up with great fright and threw it out the window without examining the contents. To make the women in his office "jealous," he asked his niece to call him during office hours to make "pretend love talk" over the telephone.

Amélia became quite worried when her stepcousin—the stepdaughter of Mr. N.—informed her of additional difficulties. Mr. N.'s office supervisor had indicated that he was concerned about her stepfather's mental health, suggesting that he should see a psychiatrist, or be hospitalized. The stepdaugher and niece, although very worried about Mr. N.'s behavior, agreed that two avenues should be explored before suggesting psychiatric aid to him. They believed that his problems stemmed from the shock resulting from his wife's untimely death, as well as from the absence of sexual relations. Therefore, the two young ladies thought it would be good to arrange a better-class female "companion" for Mr. N.—one with "a good education and a more delicate sense of male-female psychology than one normally finds in the ordinary woman of the streets." At the same time, they felt it would be helpful to talk with an Umbanda medium about Mr. N.'s fears of Exu works. Hopefully, they could get him to attend a spirit session to help counteract what he believed to be Quimbanda black magic. I left Brazil during the planning stage, and unfortunately am not aware of the final outcome. However, the sequence of events further validates the pattern in which it is assumed that women direct Quimbanda black magic against men, followed by men going to Umbanda Exus for help.

Case 4 (Thales) Generally, my informants were reticent about providing examples out of their own lives of Exu sessions having to do with relations between men and women. On the other hand, they could be coaxed fairly easily into discussing the involvements with Exu works of their friends, who were also my informants. They may have attended such a spirit session or, in some instances, they simply leveled accusations of black magic against their friends. Whenever two or more persons independently provided information on the same individual, I included the case in my developing list of male-female Exu works. In one of these cases, my informants claimed that one of their male friends, Thales, was suffering from sexual impotence sent by an evil Quimbanda Exu.

Thales was an ambitious young man who had left his family of northern European extraction living in the southernmost state of Rio Grande do Sul to look for a job in São Paulo. At first, he had worked as an electrician. He preferred to learn what he could at one job and then move on to another where he could learn something new and different. He had served in the army for a year, and was recently discharged when I first met him. He was 21 years old at the time, and had obtained employment as a servant in a very wealthy home. Although his salary was nearly equal to that of some male office workers, his position was regarded by some of his friends as being somewhat lower in status. Thales, however, observed that as a live-in servant he had no expenses for room and board. He saw the financial advantage to his job, and was saving his money to open a small shop specializing in men's clothing.

Sometime before entering the army, Thales had participated as a spirit medium in an Umbanda center. He had liked a mulatto girl who at the time was also a spirit medium in his Umbanda group. The relation between the two evidently had been close, for when the girl had become ill, Thales had paid for various medical expenses. The relationship had not lasted, however. The cult leader at this particular Umbanda center had been a strict woman, and Thales's young ladyfriend eventually had had a serious disagreement with her. The younger woman then left the group. Next, the cult leader's *caboclo* spirit had told Thales in a public spirit session that he should not see the girl again. Thales had responded that he would look after his own affairs and had told the cult leader's spirit not to meddle. Soon after, Thales had entered the army. The cult leader held a special ritual to separate Thales and his spirit to prevent possession during his military service.

While in the army, Thales stopped seeing the young woman, and did not resume the old relationship after getting out of the service. At 21, he had a good job, but was not moving along in life as fast as he would like. He was searching for an acceptable (and accepting) wife. But, he reportedly told Cecilia that he was impotent. Since he had stopped seeing his earlier girlfriend, he believed that she had paid a Quimbanda Exu to bring him this particular misfortune. During the few months that I knew Thales, he did not ask for an Umbanda session of white magic to counteract the evil work of his ex-girlfriend. I suspect this might have been due to a certain ambivalence toward Umbanda that Thales evidently felt. He refused to participate as a spirit medium on a regular basis. Furthermore, when he did attend sessions, he nearly always was possessed by Exu spirits who disrupted the religious proceedings. This frustrated the cult leader to the point of suspending Thales temporarily from her group of mediums. In this setting, then, Thales seemed somewhat reluctant for Umbanda help in overcoming his sexual difficulties.

Case 5 (Maria) In the last three cases we turn our attention to Exu works which focus more on the women involved. In this case of Maria (see also Case 1), friendly—and sometimes unfriendly—accusations of Exu works against men were made by nearly all those who knew her. Maria was 37 years old and liked to think of herself as a "true" Brazilian, being of mixed Italian, *bahiano* (Afro-Brazilian) and Amerindian ancestry. As a child she had worked in the fields in the countryside of São Paulo. When she was 25 years old, she came to the big city to work as a servant in a private home. She says that she had taken some acting lessons, and claimed to have acted in several productions. She had lived with a man for several years and had given birth to his son. The child died before reaching the age of five.

In more recent years, however, Maria's love for the theatre was transferred to her oftentimes dramatic spirit possession experiences. She noted that her participation in Umbanda gave her a feeling of peace and tranquility which enabled her to forge ahead in her present profession of beautician.

She owned and operated her shop. Maria claimed that if ever she failed to work as an Umbanda medium with her spirits doing charitable works for others, business in her shop would slow down considerably. For this reason, Maria was rarely absent from the regular weekly spirit sessions at the local Umbanda center.

This vivacious woman evidently had done quite well for herself financially for she was in the process of getting money together to make the down payment on an apartment at the time I knew her. It is interesting that at this time Maria's spirit would directly ask specific individuals to repay loans which his medium (Maria) had lent to them. Since one does not usually directly question the actions of possessing spirits, nothing was said on the spot. But later, people complained, even to the point of questioning the authenticity of Maria's possession. They believed that a good Umbanda spirit would never go so far as to request money on behalf of his medium. In addition to the sort of manipulative behavior just described, Maria often and openly admitted that when business slowed down, she dispelled the evil "fluids" in her salon by exploding gunpowder, lighting a candle, and saying prayers.

There was no doubt in Maria's mind that her religion had helped her in her personal advance from fieldhand's daughter to modern business woman. She tended, however, to talk more about her spirits doing charitable works for others than actually occurred. I believe this fact, coupled with her (and her spirit's) somewhat manipulative ways, was what probably led her friends and acquaintances to accuse her of using Exus to snare a husband. If there were some hostility attached to the accusation, Quimbanda spirits were said to be involved in her black magical works. Her closer friends who understood Maria's frailties in her pursuit of wealth and a husband tended to emphasize her role in Umbanda and spoke merely of Exus in a general way.

Case 6 (Four Unmarried Girls) In the final two cases mentioned here, my major informant, Cecilia (see Case 1), was said to perform strong Exu works for women. Some years ago, four young ladies had asked Cecilia to help them get married. In the story that my other informants related, Cecilia's Exu, Marimbondo, took the girls and several musicians and assistants to a forested area outside of São Paulo. Since the event had occurred some time earlier, and because Cecilia did not especially care to elaborate on her participation in such Exu works, I have very few details on this incident. But, one part was regularly talked about, namely, that Marimbondo asked the ugliest male musician, a drummer, to urinate in a cup. The girls were then told to drink this "love potion." Furthermore, the three who complied eventually married, while the lone abstainer remained single. I might add as a footnote that magical rituals are very idiosyncratic among mediums, and that not all Brazilian women securing Exu assistance in landing a husband must observe Marimbondo's ritual peculiarities!

Case 7 (Virgínia) The women in the first six cases have all been unmarried. The present example differs in that the woman was married, but recently separated. Virgínia was 35 years old and of Italian and Portuguese ancestry. The family had done well in Brazil. Her brother had studied science in the university, and Virgínia had been graduated from normal school. The family had been in contact with Umbanda three or four times before Virgínia began attending Umbanda sessions after her husband left her. She found the middle-class cult leader at the center I was studying compatible and helpful. Virgínia was encouraged to learn the role of spirit medium. And, whenever her young sons misbehaved, Virgínia was to telephone the cult leader about their problems. Then, at the next public session, the cult leader's spirit helpfully reprimanded the boys. Furthermore, the cult leader and a few trusted assistants conducted a secret Exu session to help bring back her husband. Cecilia admitted to helping with this private session, but she and the cult leader discouraged me from inquiring into the details of the session.

THE PATTERN OF EXU MAGIC IN RELATIONS BETWEEN MEN AND WOMEN

A general pattern of events emerges from the data in the preceding section. First, it is interesting to note that in all seven cases, single women were involved. In the first six cases, they were unmarried, and in the seventh, Virgínia was separated and alone because her husband had left.

Second, the women in each of our seven case studies were said to have gone to a medium for Exu black magical assistance. In all cases the woman wanted to make her relation with a man more secure. Usually, she wanted him to marry her. Virgínia, the only married woman, wanted her husband to return to her. An often discussed magical means of accomplishing this is to cause the man to become impotent with women other than herself, as in the cases of Roberto and Thales. There was an added difficulty in the case of Luís, for he was already married. No matter to the rejected girlfriend, and everyone shuddered at the boldness with which the Exu struck at Luis's hospitalized wife. In two of the cases the women were said to have gone to extreme measures of revenge when it appeared that they would not get to marry their ex-lovers. Roberto's financial affairs were wrecked, and Luís was nearly killed in an auto collision. In some of the other cases, the attempts to secure a husband do not involve such dastardly activities. In fact, in Mr. N.'s case it appears that only an awful lot of wishful thinking was put forth on the part of this older gentleman for some sexual activity to fill his lonely life.

In most instances, my informants claimed that the women had gone to Quimbanda Exus, but the data are somewhat contradictory. For example,

Maria's less charitable acquaintances accused her of practicing Quimbanda black magic to secure a husband. Her closer friends admitted only that she used "strong" Exu magic. Cecília worked with Umbanda Exu magic to help the young ladies secure husbands and to aid Virginia in hopefully bringing back her husband. Late in this chapter, I discuss Cecília's attitude toward these sorts of spiritual activities.

To what extent women *actually* requested magical services from Exus is open to speculation. As anthropologists are more than aware, a witchcraft accusation and the reality of witchcraft practice are two different things. Also, it is possible that a woman may only threaten a man with Quimbanda works; for example, it was reported to me that one woman informed her lover in the heat of an argument that she had hidden a lock of his hair and a sweat-stained shirt. She said that she would not hesitate to give them to an Exu if he continued to visit his wife!

The third and final part of the larger sequence of events occurred when the man, suffering from various problems supposedly caused by an evil Quimbanda Exu, went to a good Umbanda Exu to obtain countermagical assistance. This step actually happened in the first two cases reported in this chapter. My informants conducted several special sessions for both Roberto, the hat-maker, and Luís, the appliance store owner. In the Case 3, the niece and step-daughter of Mr. N. were ready to suggest this next step to him.

BRAZILIAN SOCIAL ROLES FOR MEN AND WOMEN

In attempting to explain the particular sequence of events discussed above, it is useful to consider some observations made by Emilio Willems (1953: 340-42) on the cultural roles for Brazilian men and women. Willems refers to these cultural expectations for sex roles as the "virginity" and "virility" complexes in middle-class Brazilian families. A summary of parts of his article follows.

According to Willems, the virginity complex is a cluster of values around which the female role is centered. Interviews conducted by Willems over a period of 12 years indicated that even liberal-minded men would not marry a deflowered girl. If a man should unknowingly marry a woman who was not a virgin, he could use the Brazilian law (Codigo Civil Brazileiro, Articles 218, 219, IV) to have the marriage adjudged void. Traditionally, when a woman's chances for marriage were gone, she had two alternatives. She could become a spinster in some relative's home, or she could become a concubine or practice prostitution.

A married woman is also restricted sexually. She cannot engage in any activities which could be in any way interpreted as inviting the attentions of men other than her husband. A man has sexual monopoly over his wife. There are sanctions against an unfaithful wife which are comparable to those against premarital sexual relations discussed above. If a husband finds his wife and her lover *in flagrante delicto,* he is supposed to go into a raging fit. According to Willems it is legally acceptable for the husband, in such an emotional state, to severely beat or even kill the lovers. Even if the husband does not resort to such drastic measures, it is almost inevitable that he will insist on a legal separation. Until very recently (1977), divorce was not permitted in Brazil. Therefore, the woman could not remarry. The man, however, was, and still is, expected to take a concubine, and no damage would be done to his reputation.

The virility complex is a set of values around which the male role is centered. Early and frequent sexual activity for men is regarded as not only healthy, but also as an essential attribute of manhood. Chastity in a man is ridiculed and is a possible sign of impotence. Marriage, as long as wife and children are economically cared for, does not channelize or restrict sexual intercourse for a man. According to Willems:

> It is not surprising, therefore, that the Brazilian male learns to build up his self-esteem largely in terms of sexual prowess. Erotic adventures obviously perform the function of bolstering up his ego. Obviously, institutionalized prostitution becomes an indispensable corollary to a social order wherein males are encouraged to indulge in promiscuous sexual relationships and respectable females are expected to accept severe restrictions regarding their association with men (Willems 1953: 343).

In view of the foregoing data from Willems, it seems to me that the normal sequence of events of Exu sessions which involves relations between men and women is a function of the statuses of the sexes in Brazil and of the Brazilian cultural image of male and female behavior. The unattached single woman (unmarried, separated, or left alone by her husband) lacks a respectable social status. As such, she may become the scapegoat for a variety of personal problems and illnesses that might plague a man. Given Brazilian cultural expectations, it is naturally assumed that the woman, accused of initiating an Exu service, is not an innocent party. Unless she has a particular job skill and the personal character to withstand malicious gossip, the only other thing she could be expected to turn to is prostitution or concubinage.

Furthermore, Willem's comments on the virility complex help explain the absence of cases in which a man initiates a Quimbanda Exu session, followed by a countermagical Umbanda session held by a woman. A man who must resort to the assistance of Quimbanda spirits to control his relations with women is automatically negating his virility. A man is able to handle his relationships with mere mortal women, *but* he is powerless before the supernatural Quimbanda spirits sent by a woman to bring him harm. Under the latter circumstances a man is justified in seeking the aid of Umbanda spirits to counteract the Quimbanda Exus. When I asked my informants whether they had ever heard of a male lover using a Quimbanda Exu against a woman, and the woman then asking for countermagical assistance from an Umbanda Exu, only one case could be cited. Although the entire story of this single deviation from the norm was not remembered in detail, my informant added that the man involved was regarded as "crazy" for doing such a thing. It seemed to be the exception that proved the rule.

The extreme situation just described is changing somewhat. In the years since Willems reported his observations on the virginity and virility complexes (1953), as well as the intervening years since I did my fieldwork (1967), there has been an increase in the participation of women in education and in nondomestic employment. According to Vaz da Costa (1974):

> The 1972 National Household Sample Survey, for example, re-
> veals that of Brazil's population ten years and over almost a mil-
> lion more women than men are attending school (5.4 versus 4.5
> million). Other data show that women comprised 47 percent of
> the university enrollment in 1972, as compared with 37 percent
> in 1969, only three years previously. The 400,000 women attend-
> ing universities have entered into all fields of advanced study.[7]

Robock (1975: 12) tells us that women comprise 29 percent of the labor force, with heavy employment still in the service fields, and that their participation in industrial, governmental, commercial, and professional employment is growing as more educated women enter the job market. However, one should be cautious in assuming that such changes automatically bring about an improved status for women. As Mintz (1971: 267) has noted, "...it may be that some forms of modernization are regressive, in that they actually reduce individual prerogatives for members of one sex." This is especially true if women are educated to fill only the middle echelon of service jobs, and are not regularly placed in significant decision-making positions.

THE ROLE OF THE WIFE IN MALE-FEMALE EXU MAGIC

Most of the case studies described in this chapter have been focused on single women who were interested in securing their relationship with an unmarried man. In Case 2, however, a married man, Luís, was involved. Throughout all of the proceedings, his wife played the traditional role of quiet suffering as described by Willems. For as long as Luís generously provided for her and their children, she had no recourse. I never ceased to be amazed at the openness with which the entire matter was conducted. She regarded it as her husband's natural right to have a mistress, but both were very distressed by the extreme measures the ex-girlfriend took to bring Luís back to her. One should not be so surprised at the willingness of the wife to play this *marianismo*

(Maryism) role vis-a-vis the man's *machismo* role, for the prejudice in favor of the wife's saintliness guarantees her the support of the community (Stevens 1973: 98). Furthermore, there is some question as to whether the virginity-*marianismo* complex will ever be reduced in importance as more women enter the modern job market. As Stevens (1973: 99) points out:

> When women work outside of their home, *marianismo* makes it plain that no employer, whether he or she be a corporation president, a university dean, or a government official, has the right to ask a mother to neglect a sick child in order to keep a perfect attendance record at the office, classroom, or factory. The granting of sick leave to a mother of a sick child is not so much a matter of women's rights as a matter of the employer's duty to respect the sacredness of motherhood which the individual woman shares with the Virgin Mary and with the great mother goddesses of pre-Christian times.

To what extent Brazilian women will continue to stick with their traditional woman's role in the future will depend in part on their employer's willingness to sustain it in a growing impersonal industrial economy.

Even at the present time, though, we would be mistaken to assume that all Brazilian women enjoy their traditional role. In some marriages, the wife is unwilling, at least subconsciously, to accept the social norms of *marianismo.* Such was the nature of Marimbondo's medium, Cecilia (see Cases 1 and 6).

Some 20 years ago, Cecilia's husband had a mistress who supposedly paid an Quimbanda Exu to perform a service against him. Cecilia claimed that he went berserk, selling his possessions, and smashing in his car with his bare fists. Her neighbors told her that she should urge him to seek help at an Umbanda center. When he refused to go for a spiritual consultation, Cecilia decided to attend an Umbanda session herself. The cult leader informed her that she needed to develop her mediumistic abilities to help her husband. Cecilia said that she did not want to become a medium, but felt that it was the will of God.

Several events indicate that Cecilia had some difficulty playing her role as the faithful Brazilian wife at this time. In a dream she had before fully developing her mediumship, she and her husband were fleeing into a wooded area. Pursuing them was her male Amerindian spirit, carrying a spear. The Indian caught up to them, and attempted to seize her away from her husband for the purpose of sexual relations. Another revealing incident involved Cecilia's being possessed by the spirit of a dead boyfriend, who assured her that she had married the right man. This latter event occurred at approximately the same time Cecilia finally decided to regard her mediumship in Umbanda in a more positive light. And, in becoming more accepting of herself, she no doubt became increasingly certain that her decision some years earlier to marry her husband was indeed a sound one. These feelings were then psychologically projected onto the behavior of her possessing spirit (ex-boyfriend), who brought her feelings into consciousness by means of his public statement. Cecilia continued to work on developing her mediumship over a period of some 20 years, and presently is a very highly respected Umbanda medium.

Today Cecilia's husband faithfully spends most of his nights at home, having given up his mistress. The two of them appear to have a very loving relationship in which he, at least superficially, maintains an authoritarian status. Umbanda provides Cecilia with a means of meeting a wide variety of people outside her home. She told me that her mediumship has made her a "free woman," for as long as she tells her husband she is at Umbanda sessions, he allows her to stay out until 3:00. Nor does he become upset if the Umbanda people she is with are men. In fact, Cecilia's husband seems to enjoy listening to Cecilia's recounting of intimate details of the problems clients bring to her spirits!

Cecilia says that she has learned to recognize three stages in a man's life: (1) youthful love and courtship; (2) extramarital relations during early middle age; and (3) return to the wife in late middle age. Her spirits serve others in terms of this view of male behavior. Her Exu spirit, Marimbondo, enthusiastically states that he especially likes to get unmarried men and women together. Marimbondo is willing to perform a service for a single woman who needs some assistance in snaring an unmarried man, as in Case 6 of the four young women. Nor does Marimbondo object to helping a married woman such as Virginia get her husband back. Both Cecilia and Marimbondo view these sorts of Exu work as very strong Umbanda magic, although the men involved could possibly interpret them as Quimbanda black magic! Indeed, this is probably the reason Cecilia never cared to discuss in any detail the Exu works her spirits performed to help women secure husbands. On the other hand, Marimbondo refuses to help a single woman break up her lover's marriage, regarding this as a more typical Quimbanda ritual.

Interestingly, Cecilia's Marimbondo is also willing to assist men who have Exu difficulties in their extramarital affairs, but at the same time does not encourage such activities of men. In fact, in some instances Cecilia seemed to get satisfaction out of making a roving husband worry just a bit. For example, Alberto, one of the men sharing the apartment with Luis, was concerned that some of his more recent misfortunes were connected with the Exu magic of Luis's ex-girlfriend, and had asked Cecilia's possessing spirit about the matter. In telling the incident to her husband later that evening Cecilia laughed as she noted that her spirit had been unwilling to commit himself to an answer. In refusing to give Alberto a positive answer, Cecilia thought that her spirit left Alberto with some doubt and worry about just which women were using Quimbanda powers against him.

UMBANDA AS A NEUTRAL DOMAIN

In recent years much has been made of the concepts of "private" and "public" domains in explaining the general absence of legitimate power among women in economic and political spheres. There is no indication in Sanday's definitions of the place of religion, although some mention is made of a correlation between the percentage of deities who are female, and female contribution to subsistence ($r = .742$) in a cross-cultural survey (1974: 204). Also, there is a small correlation ($r = .300$) between the percentage of female deities with general powers over both males and females, and female status (1974: 205). But these sorts of data have more to do with the psychological projection of women's economic roles onto the religious belief system. Religion is not really considered in Sanday's article as a complex of social activities.

Rosaldo (1974: 23) has also used the concepts of domestic and public domains, viewing the public domain in a more general way than Sanday as "activities, institutions, and forms of association that link, rank, organize, or subsume particular mother-child groups." This could easily include religion. One problem, however, arises in applying Rosaldo's definition to Umbanda. Family units, or even for that matter mother-child groups, do not enter into Umbanda membership as they might in the Brazilian Catholic church. More often, it is individual members out of a family who join Umbanda. I think this is perhaps a minor objection, but one to keep in mind when we consider complex societies which tend to use voluntary association to a greater degree than smaller and more homogeneous traditional societies do.

Several things seem to set Umbanda off into a sort of "neutral" domain, which is neither wholly private nor public. Most important is the fact that Umbandists view themselves as members of a group that is something like a family. The mediums who belong to a particular Umbanda center refer to their leader as a *mãe* (mother) or a *pai* (father). In turn, the leader calls his or her mediums, who serve on a very personal basis, *filhos(as)* (sons and daughters). To some limited extent, the members view each other as brothers and sisters, but the emphasis is on the vertical relationship as found in the traditional Brazilian *patrão* (patron) system.

The fictional kin terms serve to neutralize what would normally be expected to occur between men and unprotected women outside of their homes. The element of sex to some extent is reduced by the use of kin terms. Therefore, Umbanda is thought of as a more or less acceptable and safe place for both married and single women to go to outside of their homes. This is not to overlook, of course, those husbands who prefer that their wives work at centers with a female cult leader. There appears to be some occasional jealousy and fear that a male Umbanda leader might gain the slightest possible control over one's wife.

Brazilian social life for women can often times be quite confining, and Umbanda seems to be an outlet for women like Ceci'lia who found it difficult to play a strictly passive and accepting role while her husband saw other women. When Virgi'nia's husband (see Case 7) left her, she found support for herself, and aid in disciplining her sons in Umbanda. The special costumes, and the dancing and singing which usually precede the spirit consultations are fun. They also help lift the novice mediums out of their mild states of depression. In learning to play the spirit roles (developing one's mediumship) the individual feels as if he or she is doing something to help alleviate the surrounding "bad fluids." Younger men are also susceptible to bad fluids and join Umbanda, but they often tend to drop out as mediums when they mature and find satisfaction in their work and marriages. However, they may decide to remain associated with a center, serving as a "director" who looks after the more mundane aspects such as collecting membership dues, keeping order in the center, and getting car rides for members when they visit another center as a group.

Both men and women gain a better sense of control over their personal lives in Umbanda. This happens in several ways. For one thing, the spirit's medium at first is allowed to say and do things on behalf of his medium, which seems to relieve psychological tension. Gradually, new spirit roles are learned, behavior is socially controlled, and at this point a medium's spirit may begin to give advice to clients during the consultation period. This can be a big boost to the medium's ego as the spirit may tell a client how to manage a difficult spouse or make suggestions on handling his or her children. Decisions related to employment, business, and money are also prominent in spirit consultations. We therefore note that matters from both the private-domestic and public domains are handled in Umbanda, thus supporting its position as a neutral domain in the Brazilian society.

Finally, we might inquire as to whether Brazilians view women in Umbanda as wielding legitimate power such as men seem to generally have in the economic and political parts of the public domain. Strictly speaking, I suppose that we would have to offer a negative response, for it is neither a male nor a female medium who gives advice or makes decisions for a client; instead, it is the medium's *spirit* who theoretically does all of the really important things. On the other hand, it is sometimes difficult for most people (both mediums and clients) to make a distinct separation of the spirit and medium. Many times I heard a person refer to a medium's name when discussing a particular bit of spiritual work. When I would ask if he didn't mean that the medium's spirit did thus and so, there was usually a quick "yes" and he would continue to speak on as if the two were one and the same. Separation of spirit and medium was usually more important when a medium felt it would be to his or her benefit not to be associated with a particular spirit decision or action. This was especially true whenever a spirit behaved in inappropriate ways! It seems to me that the ambiguity surrounding the question of whether medium or spirit, or both, have legitimate power serves to reinforce the notion that Umbanda is a neutral domain. It is a situation in which female mediums have legitimate power along with male mediums, or neither sex has any real power of their own as the spirits take over.

SUMMARY AND CONCLUSIONS

As a social institution Umbanda is recognized by the average Brazilian as a legitimate force. It works to reduce all of those features of humankind which are found in Quimbanda—corruptive, manipulative, evil, and illegitimate powers. Although our seven case studies (eight, if we include Cecília's husband) dealt with matters in which women paid Quimbanda Exus to disrupt men's lives, it should be noted that this is only one aspect of Quimbanda-Umbanda works. Men may also enlist the aid of Quimbanda Exus to manipulate other men. Similarly, women have been known to ask these evil Exus to harm other women. For example, the beautician, Maria (see Cases 1 and 5), claimed that some years earlier she had entered and won in a contest of coiffures. There were many well-known hairdressers who were envious, one or more of them sending Quimbanda black magic against Maria the following year. On the way to the next contest, the car carrying her seven models had a very bad accident, causing the most beautiful model to have her neck dislocated. One month later, Maria went to a Japanese palm reader, who told her everything that had happened in the car accident "as if he had been there himself." He also indicated that another beautician despised her and was afraid that Maria would defeat her in the contest. She therefore had paid an Exu to send a powerful work which would stop Maria's success.

We should also keep in mind that Exu works occurring between persons of the same sex or between men and women are not the most frequent types of spirit works in Umbanda. As indicated earlier there are three spirit types with heavenly light—*prêtos velhos, caboclos,* and *crianças*—which conduct most Umbanda consultations. But, there is less darkness and mystery associated with these spirits. Often they are not regarded as powerful as the Exus. I think this fact suggests that the social norms surrounding the sexual role behavior of men and women must be of quite tenacious and dark forces if one must resort to using Exu power instead of that of the more ordinary spirits.

Furthermore, although the virility and virginity complexes spell out the content of one's sex role in Brazil, not all individuals find it easy, or even possible to play out the prescribed male or female role. To help individuals manage such difficulties, cultural systems are equipped with "self-correcting mechanisms," to use the term of Paul (1967). Three such correcting devices found in Brazilian society are summaried here.

First, a single woman may become anxious when she is unable to secure a husband. She brings into operation a balancing device when she threatens her lover with the black magic of the Quimbanda Exus. If she should lose her man, the unattached woman can still carry out her threat, giving her at least the psychological satisfaction of revenge.

Second, a man may find that playing the prescribed virility role can become tiring, and even impossible, especially when he is beset with various kinds of economic, personal, or sexual difficulties. Although he is unable to deny his manliness, he can find a scapegoat in the unattached female lover, accusing her of Quimbanda witchcraft. An additional corrective mechanism lies in his utilization of the countermagic of the Umbanda Exus.

Third, the wife in the love triangle, as illustrated by Cecilia, may find it difficult to act out her role as the faithful spouse. A balancing mechanism in this situation is the psychological outlet she finds in the spirit roles she plays within the socially acceptable context of Umbanda sessions.

Thus, it is the Brazilian cultural definition of social roles for men and women which helps to support the spiritual dichotomy of Quimbanda and Umbanda Exus. In turn, the presence of these two spirit religions in Brazilian society reinforces a sort of "spiritual dichotomy" of men and women.

Finally, I briefly discussed the nature of Umbanda as being in neither the private nor the public domain but as existing as a neutral domain. It was suggested that three things support this view. First, the fictional kin terms used in Umbanda neutralize the normally expected overt sexual behavior between unchaperoned persons. Second, in the consultation process, Umbanda mediums-spirits deal with problems which come from both public and private domains. And third, there exists some ambiguity about whose legitimate power we are looking at in Umbanda. Is it both male and female mediums who are associated with behavior normally found only in the public domain of men? Or, does neither sex hold any legitimate power, having relinquished all of their own actions to their possessing spirits?

In closing, I hope that by focusing on individual case studies and psychological processes, I have shown that men and women as individuals require and use certain balancing mechanisms to correct for the social roles which their culture has provided for them. Furthermore, I think it is probably of some importance that these processes are carried out in a neutral domain which is neither the domestic world of women nor the public domain of men.

NOTES

1. See Bastide (1978) for an excellent review of Afro-Brazilian spirit religions. McGregor (1967) and St. Clair (1971) provide popular accounts of spiritist religions in Brazil.

2. The work reported in this chapter is part of a larger study that was supported by Public Health Service Research Grant MH 07463 from the National Institute of Mental Health. The project, entitled Cross-Cultural Studies of Dissociational States, was under the direction of Dr. Erika Bourguignon, of the Department of Anthropology, The Ohio State University.

3. I use the Portuguese orthography. The *x* is prounounced like the English *sh*, such that *Exu* is pronounced as "Eshu."

4. I wish to thank Dr. Erika Bourguignon for pointing this out while I was in the field. The final responsibility for the contents, including any possible errors, of this chapter, however, is my own.

5. This name and all other names of informants used in this chapter are fictitious.

6. Bad spiritual fluids, usually associated with Quimbanda Exus, are said to be responsible for illnesses and other personal misfortunes. A person who is healthy and free from anxiety and personal difficulties is thought to be surrounded by good fluids. See Pressel (1973) for further discussion of this theory of fluids.

7. As summarized by Robock (1975:11).

REFERENCES

Bascom, William
>   1969   *The Yoruba of Southwestern Nigeria.* New York: Holt, Rinehart and Winston.

Bastide, Roger
>   1978   *The African Religions of Brazil.* Baltimore: The Johns Hopkins Press (first published in France in 1960).

McGregor, Pedro
>   1967   *Jesus of the Spirits.* New York: Stein and Day.

Mintz, Sidney W.
>   1971   "Men, Women, and Trade." *Comparative Studies in Society and History* 13:247-69.

Paul, Benjamin D.
>   1967   "Mental Disorder and Self-Regulating Processes in Culture: A Guatemalan Illustration." In *Personalities and Cultures,* Robert Hunt, ed. Garden City, N.Y.: The Natural History Press.

Pressel, Esther
>   1973   "Umbanda in São Paulo: Religious Innovation in a Developing Society." In *Religion, Altered States of Consciousness, and Social Change,* Erika Bourguignon, ed. Columbus, Ohio: Ohio State University Press.

1974   *Trance, Healing, and Hallucination: Three Field Studies in Religious Experience.* Co-authored with Felicitas Goodman and Jennette Henney. New York: Wiley.
1977   "Negative Spirit Possession in Experienced Brazilian Umbanda Spirit Mediums." In *Case Studies in Spirit Possession,* Vincent Crapanzano and Vivian Garrison, eds. New York: Wiley.

Robock, Stefan H.
1975   *Brazil: A Study in Development Progress.* Lexington, Mass.: D. C. Heath.

Rosaldo, Michelle Zimbalist
1974   "Women, Culture, and Society: A Theoretical Overview." In *Women, Culture, and Society,* M.Z. Rosaldo and L. Lamphere, eds. Stanford: Stanford University Press.

Sanday, Peggy R.
1974   "Female Status in the Public Domain." In *Women, Culture, and Society,* M.Z. Rosaldo and L. Lamphere, eds. Stanford: Stanford University Press.

St. Clair, David
1971   *Drum and Candle.* New York: Tower Publications, Inc.

Stevens, Evelyn P.
1973   "Marianismo: The Other Face of Machismo in Latin America." In *Female and Male in Latin America,* Ann Pescatello, ed. Pittsburgh: University of Pittsburgh Press.

Vaz da Costa, Rubens
1974   A Participação da Mulher na Sociedade Brasileira. São Paulo (mimeo).

Willems, Emilio
1953   "The Structure of the Brazilian Family." *Social Forces* 31:339-45.

7   Spirit Mediums in Umbanda Evangelizada of Porto Alegre, Brazil: Dimensions of Power and Authority

PATRICIA BARKER LERCH

In this chapter, the author attempts to understand the great appeal of the Umbanda spirit possession religion for the Brazilian women she knew in the city of Porto Alegre. She argues that the role of spirit medium in Umbanda presents middle and lower class women the opportunity to transcend the confines of their ordinarily powerless social and economic status. The spirit medium role not only gives the woman an aura of supernatural authority, but also provides her with a network of clients and of information not otherwise available to her. As a result, she is placed in a position that allows her to control the extradomestic distribution of certain goods and services. Given the present ambiguous position into which Brazilian modernization has placed women, the Umbanda medium role is seen as alleviating certain of the less beneficial aspects of economic development.

Drawing upon materials collected in Porto Alegre, Brazil in 1974-75, this chapter analyzes the role of spirit medium in the religious cult Umbanda Evangelizada (evangelized or reformed). During fieldwork, the primary research methodology was "participant observation." Consequently, the research required active participation in and detailed observations of the lives and experiences of spirit mediums. Data obtained in this manner were enriched by formal and informal interviews with informants.

In every Umbanda center that was observed during fieldwork, approximately 80 to 85 percent of the mediums were women. It seems only natural to ask why this should be the case. If we look at the spirit medium role in terms of what benefits accrue to the role occupant we find that religious authority and economic power are among the two most important. Religious authority is conferred by a supernatural being known as a *guia* (guide) who is believed to possess his medium during the weekly *Trabalho de Caridade* (Work of Charity). The possession of the medium is usually accompanied by a trance or altered state of consciousness so that the spirit's identity is seen to replace the medium's. Economic power, that is the ownership or control of strategic resources, is a feature of the medium-client relationship. The spirit medium, via religious authority, has access to information concerning the resources of his clients and he can reallocate these resources if he so desires. Thus, the medium stands in a position of control over some important economic resources such as jobs and wealth.

Additional prestige is credited to the medium because this role is difficult to enter and continue in for any length of time. The training period, referred to as the development of *mediumidade* (medium abilities), requires fortitude and courage as well as the ability to withstand pain and suffering. The quality of *mediumidade* is ascribed and innate. While everyone is supposed to have some *mediumidade*, the role behavior of medium is learned.

The services rendered by Umbanda spirit mediums are important to the hundreds of clients who frequent the centers two or three times per week. By providing clients with an explanation for their problems, rendering valuable curing services, giving out information, and distributing valued resources, the medium performs a real service for society.

Thus, the status of women who are mediums is enhanced relative to nonmediums and clients. Since modernization, that is, economic development, has not yet benefited most Brazilian women and has even to some extent cut them off from traditional economic power, the popularity of the spirit medium role is understandable.

DOMAINS, POWER, AND STATUS

In discussions of the status of women in societies around the world, one major concern has been with identifying those roles and related activities which allow women access to power and/or authority.[1] Closely related to this concern is the distinction between two realms of activity in the private domain and in the public domain. According to Rosaldo (1974: 3), a universal asymmetry of the sexes has developed from the association of women with the maternal role and consequently with the private domain, and of men with those activities and roles taking place outside of this domain.

Private domain roles do not allow women access to power or authority so long as they focus inward upon the localized family unit and do not relate to the control of resources and of people outside this domain. Power can also come with the control over extradomestic distribution of a valued good or service. Thus, the presence of either economic power or economic authority will tend to enhance the status of women in the public domain.

Woman may be excluded from authority in the public domain by civil codes which prohibit them from entering into certain activities or roles that allocate authority to role occupants. This is the case described for Portuguese peasant women (Riegelhaupt 1967). Circumventing the formal role structure that is sanctioned by civil law is an informal system in which economic power in the public domain results from the occupancy of certain trading roles. The mechanisms granting women access to economic power include a sophisticated system of internal communication (that is, gossip) and a network of ties to male and female patrons living outside of the local community. The access to information through gossip and the ability to contact nonlocal patrons both enhance the status of Portuguese peasant women traders in their local community. Similarly, in Barbara C. Aswad's (1967) study of key and peripheral roles among noble women in a Middle Eastern plains village, internal communications are vital in conferring power to women. Peripheral roles fall outside of the authority structure of key roles, but they still have an important effect on decision making. Peripheral role occupants are able to use information that is obtained through gossip and unrestricted visiting patterns to secure favorable decisions.

It appears then that power and authority in the public domain are conferred by institutions or achieved by activities that provide access to valued goods and services. Such access becomes the basis for control over people and control over things. The sources of access may be through such indirect channels as an internal communications network like gossip and/or contact with nonlocal patrons.

Thus far we have only discussed economic power and its effect on status. We must now consider religion and how and where it fits into this domain distinction. It may be that religious behavior, roles, and activities form a separate domain. If so, some characteristics of the "religious domain" would be similar to those of the public domain. Religious activities might also take place and cut across both domains (the private and the public) making it necessary to consider the overlap of domains. According to A.F.C. Wallace (1966: 52), the underlying premise of every religion is the belief in souls, supernatural beings, and supernatural forces. When people's actions are guided by this premise, they are religious actions. Certain aspects of religious behavior such as prayer, music, taboo, or sacrifice take place in the private domain; others occur within the public domain. Religious behavior is in some instances social, that is, the adherents of a religion on some occasion come together as a group. As Wallace (1966: 65) points out, "no religion is purely an individual matter; there is always a congregation which meets on some occasions for the joint performance of religious acts." In this respect, religious activities fall within the public domain.

The role of Umbanda spirit medium takes place within the structure of roles making up the Umbanda cult institution. It is a cult institution in Wallaces' sense of the term:

> A cult institution may be defined as a set of rituals all having the same general goal, all explicitly rationalized by a set of similar or related beliefs, and all supported by the same social group (1966: 75).

According to Wallace (1966: 78) it is very difficult to discuss the 'religion' of a society since rarely does everyone operate under a unified system of beliefs. Rather in any one society there are a series of cult institutions, overlapping in membership and even in beliefs, which complicate the picture. This is true for modern Brazil where the Umbanda cult exists alongside the Catholic cult institution, the Kardec cult institution, and many Protestant cult institutions, to name just a few of the many that complicate the religious scene of Brazil.

The expectations that define the Umbanda spirit medium role involve actions affecting both domains; however, role behavior falls primarily within the public domain. An Umbanda spirit medium is expected to participate in such extradomestic activities as the weekly *Trabalhos de Caridade* ("works of charity") at the Umbanda center and the fund-raising luncheons and clothing drives. The public aspects of the role of spirit medium and the source of its economic power and religious authority derive from the complex interaction between the spirit *guia* ("guide") and the clients.

The clients and the mediums *con guias* ("with guides") form the core of Umbanda. Theirs is a reciprocal relationship which is beneficial to both partties. We can pose two questions. First, what is it that clients get from a medium *con guia*? Second, what do the mediums receive in return? The answers to these questions are explored in this chapter because in them we can begin to see the attraction that this role of spirit medium holds for some Brazilian women. Let us briefly preview what is to come. The answer to the first questions is somewhat more obvious than the second. The client receives special services and valued information and goods from the medium *con guia*. The services include: 1) an explanation for one's problems, 2) an access to curing services such as the *passe*, the *passagente*, the *banha descarga*, the *remedios*, and the astral operations. The valued information and goods include forewarnings about unfaithful husbands and help in finding employment.

What do spirit mediums receive in return from this relationship? A medium *con guia* is given recognition for possessing superior spiritual knowledge that is applicable to a wider range of situations. This is demonstrated by the fact that clients actively seek out the advice of mediums *con guias*. Thus, a spirit medium is a recognized authority on many matters important to life. A popular spirit *guia* (through his medium) builds up a steady clientele about whom he collects a large body of information that concerns the details of the lives and circumstances of his clients. This storehouse of information is used in some cases to find solutions to a few of his clients' problems. Finally, clients come from all walks of life. Therefore, a spirit *guia* knows both powerful and powerless people. Powerful people can be helpful to others, especially if they are grateful for help given to them by the spirit *guia.* To summarize, public recognition for superior religious knowledge combined with an internal communications network and access to potential patrons gives the spirit medium role considerable power and authority within the public domain.

RIO GRANDE DO SUL AND THE SOUTH

The three states of Rio Grande do Sul, Parana, and Santa Catarina comprise the smallest of Brazil's five major regions.[2] The social, cultural, and economic history of the South prompts many writers to refer to this area as "another Brazil" (Wagley 1971: 72). The economic development of the region has been one of steady growth since its colonization during the eighteenth century by Portuguese Azoreans and European farmers. According to the economist Stefan Robock (1975), the South never shared in the typical economic cycle of "boom and bust" that is so characteristic of the other major regions of Brazil.

Rio Grande do Sul is the largest state in the South region and is even larger than the two South American Republicas of Ecuador and Uruguay. Covering 3.3 percent of Brazil's territory, it measures some 478 miles from its easternmost to its westernmost point and almost the same distance from north to south. Bordering Uruguay and Argentina, it lies well below the tropics (falling between 27° S and 34° S). The state is primarily hilly and is crisscrossed by mountains and rivers. Joseph L. Love (1971) divides the state into three major cultural and economic regions: the Litoral, the Campanha, and the Cima da Serra (or simply the Serra). The Litoral, the smallest of the regions, consists of the coastal strip and the alluvial areas washed by the Lagoas dos Patos and Mirim; it extends from Torres in the north to Santa Vitoria do Palmar in the south, including the Jacuí River Valley as far west as Cachoeria. Both historically and presently, the Litoral is the most densely populated region. Despite its poor soils, it has become the locus of the state's exports, interstate commerce, and industry. The three largest cities of the state are located in this region. Porto Alegre, the capital, is furthest north at the junction of the Lagoa dos Patos and the Jacuí and Guaiba Rivers. Although it is the largest city with over one million people and the most important manufacturing center in the state, Porto Alegre cannot be reached by oceangoing vessels because of the shallowness of the lagoon's northern section. Items for export must travel by truck, train, or small ship to the only ocean port in the state, Rio Grande. Pelotas which lies south of Porto Alegre and just west of the lagoon is the second largest city. The strip of sandy beach running northward from Rio Grande (the city) to Torres presented an effective barrier against early attempts to settle the state. Since there are no rivers cutting across this sandy strip to the lagoon, the area remains isolated and sparsely settled. Except for resort cities such as Tranmandaí, small fishing villages are more typical of the coast. Along the western shores of the lagoon rice cultivation prospers.

The second region, the Campanha, is primarily composed of hilly grass-lands that are divided up into large *estancias* (cattle ranches). These ranches employ the *gaucho*[3] ("cowboy") whose image so permeates the state that *gaucho* is a synonym for *riograndense* (a person from Rio Grande do Sul). In the third region, the Cima da Serra, we find the richest soil in the state. Lying north of Porto Alegre, the Serra combines a high plateau, pine-forested region with rolling grasslands extending to the west. The Serra is the center of the European settlements referred to as the Colonial zone.

The people of Rio Grande do Sul come from many cultural and ethnic backgrounds, a fact which is today obscured by the dominant *gaucho* image. The Riograndense Indians, the state's first inhabitants, practiced a culture si-milar to other Tropical Forest peoples and spoke a language within the Tupi-Guarani family (Wagley 1972). Tupi-Guarani culture influenced the forma-tion of the western frontier life-style to a much greater degree than it did in the eastern Litoral, since the Indians of the Litoral were decimated early leav-ing no traces of their culture (Cesar 1962: 19).[4] During the sixteenth, seven-teenth, and eighteenth centuries, Rio Grande do Sul remain a sparsely popu-lated frontier area. In 1700 the first important migration south began with bands of adventurers from São Paulo known as *bandierantes*[5] who journeyed into the area capturing Mission Indians. Later in that century in order to se-cure the territory against Spanish domination, Portuguese settlers from the Azores were encouraged to immigrate into the state. According to the *politi-ca dos casais,* a policy of settling families and couples, Azoreans populated both the Campanha and the Litoral. Those settling along the Lagoa dos Patos (1740) founded the Porto dos Casais which later became Porto Alegre (1742).

The Negro first entered *Gaúcho* society as a slave imported to fight the Spanish. In 1725 a ship direct from the Guinea Coast of Africa carred a cargo of slaves destined to reinforce dwindling Brazilian troops already in the area (Cesar 1962: 30). Then in the year 1735, African slaves, who were brought south with a company of São Paulo *bandierantes,* participated in the con-struction of a highway which opened the way for trade between the South and the São Paulo merchants and landowners. However, through the first half of the eighteenth century, as long as the demand remained low, African slaves did not enter the state in large numbers. Finally, economic pressure on *estan-cia* owners made them look for a cheap labor supply for their ranches and their dried beef factories (*charqueadas*), and this stimulated the slave trade in the South. The 1775 census shows that one-quarter of the state's twen-ty thousand inhabitants were either black or mulatto slaves working chiefly as domestics and stockmen (Rout 1976: 82). This figure contin-ued to climb as the rapid growth of the dried beef industry made Rio Grande, Pelatos, and Porto Alegre the chief domestic producers of *charque* (dried beef). The census of 1814 puts the proportion of African slaves in the total population of the state as high as 30 percent or twenty-three thousand. Ninety percent of these slaves were committed to permanent service in the dried beef industry.

Charqueada slavery was unique in Brazil because the masses of unfree labor were urban and industrial. The slaves worked all year long without seasonal breaks for a minimum of 12 hours per day beginning at midnight and ending at noon. The emancipation of workers was fairly uncommon. A rapid influx of predominately male slaves prevented the creation of a large mulatto contingent such as existed in other areas of the nation (Rout 1976: 82-83).[6]

From 1777 to 1822 the *estancia-charqueada* socioeconomic complex dominated Riograndense society. Two major classes which were composed on the one hand of wealthy landowners, cattlemen, and *charqueada* owners and on the other by their workers—the African slaves and *Gaúcho* peons—were separated by an insignificant middle class of Azorean peasant farmers and shopkeepers. This small agricultural complex could not compete either economically or socially with the cattle complex (Love 1971). But just two years later in 1824 a significant transformation of *Gaúcho* society began when European peasant farmers immigrated into the state settling in the area known as the Colonial zone. The Brazilian emperor Dom Pedro I officially sanctioned this immigration. According to Jean Roche (1969)—95 percent of all the immigrants arriving between 1824 and 1870 were German. Some twenty thousand settlers founded towns north of the capital. Not until the era of World War II did German immigration again become significant. The Italian immigration reached its peak between 1874 and 1889 when sixty thousand people settled in the Colonial zone (Azevedo 1969). Since the land nearest to Porto Alegre was already taken by Germans, the Italians settled further north and west.

In summary we can see that the cultural origins of the people of Rio Grande do Sul are diverse. The Indian contributed heavily to the Western *Gaúcho* life-style, the Portuguese, the Germans, the Italians, and the Africans added to the culture of the Litoral and the Serra. Although it is true that the European immigrants and the *Gaúcho* life-style are generally thought of first when Rio Grande do Sul is mentioned, there has been substantial Afrobrazilian culture retained and practiced in the state. This is most clearly seen in the two African-derived religions of Batuque and Umbanda.

Batuque was first described by the American anthropologist M.J. Herskovits in 1943 when he visited Porto Alegre. Batuque is an Afrobrazilian religion similar to those practiced in the northern states and cities of Brazil, and it is heavily influenced by Yoruba and Dahomean religions of West Africa. Herskovits (1943) encountered 42 cult houses in Porto Alegre, and he estimated that approximately one-half of the cult houses were under the direction of female cult leaders. At the time of his survey, Herskovits (1943) found that Batuque drew its clientele primarily from the approximately fifty thousand Negroes in the city.

Umbanda[7] appears to have entered Porto Alegre and Rio Grande do Sul somewhat later than Batuque. According to the officials at the Union of Umbanda in Porto Alegre, Umbanda was introduced into the state between 1944 and 1949. Since that time, it has grown in popularity to the point where there are at least two thousand centers. Umbanda is also an African-derived religion, but it is a more syncretic or mixed form than Batuque. In addition to the African contribution, Umbanda incorporates beliefs and practices of Catholicism, Spiritism, as well as beliefs and practices from American Indian religions. Umbanda appeals to urban Brazilians of all ethnic and social-class backgrounds.

There are many forms of Umbanda being practiced in Porto Alegre. The type which is reported upon in this chapter is known as Umbanda Evangelizada. The devotees of Umbanda Evangelizada claim that it represents a purer form of Umbanda, being one that is devoid of the *fantasia* (fantasy) that in their opinion characterizes many other types of Umbanda.[8] Umbanda Evangelizada is characterized by a belief in spirit possession trance. Supernatural entities take over or "incorporate" the bodies of designated mediums. During this "take over", the identity of the human medium is replaced by that of the possessing spirit. We shall next look at the ritual and beliefs of this cult institution.

TRABALHO DE CARIDADE

The *Trabalho de Caridade* ("Work of Charity") is the major ritual of Umbanda Evangelizada. Following is a brief description that will reveal the major supernatural beings and the most important ritual elements. The *Trabalho de Caridade* is held at the Umbanda center twice weekly between the hours of 7:30 p.m. and 1:30 a.m. The mediums arrive early and they stop and chat with their friends before they retire to a small rear dressing room where they change into the plain white uniform typical of their center. One female medium attends the pharmacy, a small drug counter, at which herbs, perfume, candles, candy, and Avon products are sold during the evening. The male secretary hands out small numbered tickets to the visitors and the *sociais* (paying members) as they arrive. There are two separate numbering systems—one for *sociais* who are given numbers within the first series and another for the visitors who receive numbers in the second series. The secretary keeps track of how many clients wish to see the *Chefe, Pai Xangô,* and he limits this number to 20 per evening.

Each medium changes from street clothes into the uniform of the center. Men dress in plain white tunic tops and straight legged pants and women wear plain white dresses; both sexes wear white tennis shoes. Then as each medium enters the *sala de conga* (altar room), he or she stoops over to knock three times on the floor forming a small triangle. This simple salute to the altar and spirit entities is elaborated upon by some mediums who prostrate themselves full length on the floor in front of the altar. A short prayer may be recited in front of the altar. After the salute and the prayer, the medium walks over to a particular *ponto* (point or place) within the room where he or she will remain for perhaps the next four hours. The new developing mediums stand in parallel rows facing the altar until the *consultas* (consultations) begin, whereupon they assume the various roles of usher, *escrevedor* (writer of spiritual messages), and doorman.

Defumação occurs when a male medium assistant proceeds with the *defumação*–(censing)–of the center, the mediums, and the clients. This is done with special 'astral perfume' and incense. The incense consists of a blend of herbs burnt in a special censer. The 'astral perfume' is sprayed into the air in front of the altar, in the four corners of the altar room, and onto the hands of each medium. Finally it is brought out to the waiting clients and visitors. The censer of burning incense follows the same pattern. The purpose of the *defumação* is to help cleanse or discharge the mediums and the clients of any lingering evil fluids that they may have attracted to themselves during the normal course of their day. It is also a form of protection against the *espiritos sem luz* (spirits without light) which are believed to linger about the center during the *trabalhos* (works).

Calm music is piped through a loudspeaker system serving the altar room and the clients' waiting rooms. The male medium assistants place the *Chefe's* microphone in the middle of the altar room in anticipation of his *palestra* (lecture). Throughout this period of preparation, the mediums stand inside the altar room, concentrating in readiness for spirit possession trance. Depending upon what time they arrive, some mediums will stand for three to four hours.

Roupas para firmar (clothes for blessing) is called out by the *Chefe* as he walks from room to room greeting friends and clients. Some clients have with them the clothes of a friend or relative who is sick or troubled. These clothes will be blessed–censed–with incense and "astral perfume," and thus have the evil fluids discharged from them. It is believed that clothing picks up the vibrations of the person who wore them. So in the case of illness, an odor or aura is left in the clothes, which must be cleansed by a spirit medium if the person is going to recover. The clothes are brought to the altar where the *Chefe* or his assistant sprinkles "astral perfume" on them and places a few rose petals among them. They are then returned to their owner.

Radiações de luz (radiations of light) are collected from the clients by the male medium assistant or by the *Chefe*. These *radiações de luz* are small slips of paper which contain the name, the address, and the problem of a person who needs special help. They are submitted on the behalf of people who cannot easily attend the *trabalhos* themselves, if, for example, they are from another country. The name of the entity from whom help is being sought is also written on this paper. After the papers are collected, they are placed underneath a stone on the altar. The stone symbolizes *Xangô,* the spiritual protector of the center. It is believed that these messages will be transmitted during the *Trabalho de caridade* up to the astral plane where the various entities will attend to them.

"Greetings" occur after the preparations are finished, and the *Chefe* comes to the microphone to address the visitors. He begins by welcoming his "brothers and sisters" to the *Trahalho de Caridade.* In his opening announcement, he reminds the clients that the ritual *passe de caridade* is an important part of the Monday and Thursday meetings and that it is entirely for their benefit. The *passe de caridade* has the power to help them solve their problems. The only requirement, that they as petitioners must have, is a pure heart, one which is devoted solely to God and Jesus Christ and one which is free of evil thoughts and intentions. The *passe de caridade* and the *consultas* help a person counteract the negative influences of *espiritos sofredores* (suffering spirits) who are responsible for making one smoke, drink, and perform other misdeeds that can prejudice one's spiritual development.

During "opening prayer," the *Chefe* turns toward the altar to recite the opening prayer in which he beseeches God, the Virgin Mary, and Jesus to give all present the spiritual guidance they need, to allow the *entidades de luz* (entities of light), protectors, and *guias,* and all the spirits in the phalanges of the Warriors of Justice to descend into the center this evening. He repeats this prayer adding *Xangô São Jeronimo,* the protector of the fraternity, to the list of entities addressed.

The *Palestra* (Lecture) occurs on Mondays and Thursdays and lasts 30 to 45 minutes. The *palestra* generally covers a point of doctrine, but the *Chefe* can also use the opportunity to make announcements about upcoming events, to explain the meaning of Umbanda Evangelizada to those attending for the first time, or to point out that the *entidades de luz* do not smoke, drink, or dance. He may also discuss the origin of a particular *festa* for one of the entities.

Pontos Cantados are short hymns or prayers that invoke the power and the force of the entities. With each *ponto cantado* the mediums invite the entities to enter the center. The cult leader calls out each *ponto,* and the mediums sing each *ponto* according to the tradition of the center. In Umbanda Evangelizada *pontos cantados* are sung without drum or percussion accompaniment. Their cadence is deliberate and slow. It is important that each *ponto* be correct otherwise it will not have the desired effect upon the session; the words and melodies are practiced every Tuesday during the classes held for development. The song leader, a female spirit medium, must make sure that the mediums know the correct words and tempo for each *ponto.* The importance of this role cannot be underestimated since if the *pontos* are incorrect the entire session can be prejudiced.

The following entities are particularly important in the *pontos cantados* of Umbanda Evangelizada: *Ogum São Jorge, Nossa Sra, Iemanjá, Mãe Oxum* or *Virgem de Conceição, Oxôce São Sebastião, Xangô São Jeronimo.* In addition to these entities known as *orixás,* there are the *prêtos velhos* (old black spirits) in the *linha* (line) of *Pai Benidito, Pai Joaquim de Luanda,* and *Xangô.* Another *ponto* celebrates the power of "our *guias*" and another the *cabocla* (Indian spirit) *Jurema.* As each *ponto* is sung, one or more of the mediums have entered into an altered state of consciousness. When all of the mediums have received their entities, the consultations begin.

COSMOLOGY

The ritual elements comprising the *Trabalho de Caridade* are supported by a system of beliefs about man, the universe, and the supernatural. The universe is divided into two realms, that of the *plano astral* or astral level and that of the *plana terra* or the earthly level. The goal of each person is spiritual evolution from the earthly level to the astral level. This goal may be achieved through a finite number of incarnations whereupon after the twelfth and final incarnation, a person becomes a permanent spiritual being living on the astral level.

The pantheon of spirits worshipped in Umbanda Evangelizada represents a hierarchy of entities descending from the astral level down to the earthly level. Those closest to the astral level are filled with enlightenment, power, and goodness while those closest to the earthly level lack these traits, and they are responsible for human problems and suffering. God, Jesus Christ, the Virgin Mary, and the *orixás* and Catholic saints are on the astral plane. As we have seen, they are called upon to lend their support to the *Trabalho de Caridade.* The *orixás*[9] of Umbanda Evangelizada combine two separate religious traditions—the Catholic and the Yoruba. In Brazil's colonial past, Yoruba slaves and their descendants transformed their gods into the syncretic *orixás,* that today form a category of supernatural beings in which certain Yoruba gods and Catholic saints originally alike symbolically have now become fused in the *orixá*-saint equation. This common *orixá*-saint equation is further syncretized in Umbanda Evangelizada with the image of the soldier-warrior of Rio Grande do Sul's colorful military past. The *Gaúcho* is commonly depicted as a fighting cowboy who was recruited for the almost continuous external and internal wars of the last several centuries of the state's history. According to Francisco Oliviera Viana (1952), the *riograndense* is a warrior by education and inclination making every *Gaúcho* a soldier. Reflecting this tradition, the *orixás* are also *guerreiros* (warriors) who wage spiritual battles on behalf of their devotees. According to my informants in Umbanda Evangelizada the *orixás* were soldiers who fought against evil and for justice in several of their past incarnations. They have continued this fight as *orixá*-saints in Umbanda Evangelizada. The *orixás* head a complex of spiritual lines and phalanges in which the entities are ranked in descending order according to their possession of spiritual enlightenment. Since the *orixás* are so close to the astral plane and thus so powerful, they cannot "incorporate" spirit mediums without causing them great physical harm. Instead the various *orixás* send the lesser spirits which they command down to earth to do works of charity on their behalf. The major possessing spirits are the *caboclos* (Indians and indigenous peoples from around the world), the *prêtos velhos* (spirits of old black people), and the *crianças* (children, sometimes identified as Brazilian). The *caboclos* belong to many different lines among which are the *linha Jurema*, *de lua* (moon), *de sol* (sun), and *de fogo* (fire). One special line of *caboclos* known as the *Linha Demanda*[10] ("claim" or "fight") is believed to be effective against witches and sorcerers. The *Linha Demanda* was described as a spiritual police force whose responsibilities resemble those of the military police of Brazil. The *caboclos* have a reputation for strength and courage, and they often deal with those problems that require these traits.

The *prêtos velhos* also descend to work several times a week. Although they are important to Umbanda Evangelizada and are recognized for their special curing powers, there is no requirement that guarantees that every medium shall receive one. Considered to be more "suave" or calm than the *caboclos*, the *prêtos velhos* work on Saturdays with other calm spirits in the *Linha de Oriente*. *Prêtos velhos* are believed to possess the power to cure the effects of the *mau olhado* or evil eye.

The *criança* spirits descend into the centers of Umbanda Evangelizada on the last Tuesday of every month. Their arrival is celebrated with a party, complete with balloons, cookies, and candy. The *crianças* like to play on the floor and to fight with each other over the balloons and candy. Clients seek the advice of *criança* spirits because they represent purity and innocence.

Another category of spirits, the *exus*, must be mentioned. *Exu* spirits are believed to cause people problems. Although everyone is liable to *exu* possesion, it is not sought or desired because *exus* cause people to engage in antisocial acts. For example, a female *exu* spirit known as a *pomba-gira* may possess a woman and make her paint herself up and go out on the streets like a prostitute. However, if a husband and a wife are both possessed by *exus* then they will have a happy relationship. In the centers practicing Umbanda Evangelizada, the only recognition given to *exu* spirits is a special place near the entrance of the *sala de conga* that is known as the *ponto de encruzilhada* (place of the crossroads). Since a person entering from the street may have been under the harmful influence of *exu* spirits, that person must be relieved of such influences. The *ponto de encruzilhada* has the power to draw away such harmful influences. Marking the place is the flag of Brazil, which, as the symbol of the nation's strength, aids in the fight against the evil influences of the *exu* spirits.

The characteristic spirit possession trance behavior identified with each of these spirit categories reveals another distinction between Umbanda Evangelizada and other types of Umbanda. The spirit possession trance is very controlled and subdued. There is no possession trance dancing accompanied by drumming to induce the trance state and possession. The *caboclo* spirit's presence is recognizable only by the stern, flushed, face of his spirit medium. The *prêto velho* role is similar to that in other types of Umbanda and the medium walks with a curved back and works seated on a low bench. The *criança* spirit role is associated with playful behavior and childish antics. However, some mediums who receive these spirits never exhibit any of these more stereotyped forms of possession trance behavior.

ROLE STRUCTURE

The roles found within Umbanda Evangelizada include four basic types: the cult leader, the spirit *guia*, the spirit medium, and the client. The way in which the relationships between these roles is structured is related to the domain of action that we focus upon.

A cult leader can be either male or female, but women frequently outnumber men by a wide margin. Of the two thousand registered centers kept track of at the Union of Umbanda, 85 percent are headed by women. In order to enter this role, spirit mediums must receive a direct spiritual order from God or from their spirit *guia*. This spiritual order usually comes in a dream or a vision. The spirit *guia* of the cult leader assumes the role of spiritual chief and protector of the new center. The duties of a cult leader concern the organization of the Umbanda center and the spiritual development of the mediums.

The structure of Umbanda role relationships are determined by two domains of activity: the "material" and the "spiritual." The names of these domains derive from a distinction that Umbanda mediums themselves make between the *parte material* and the *parte espiritual*. The former refers to the physical or material body and the latter refers to the spiritual self and spirit *guia*. The "material" domain includes those activities performed by mediums when they are not "incorporated" by spirits. This mainly concerns the business affairs of the center such as paying rent and utility bills, buying supplies for the *trabalhos*, organizing the charity drives, collecting membership dues, cleaning and maintaining the building, decorating for *festas* (parties for the *orixás*), and preparing the *sala de conga* for the weekly sessions. The structure of role relationships within this domain resembles a centralized federation in which authority filters from the top down. The cult leader and the president of the *sociais* (clients who pay dues to belong to the fraternity) head up the chain of command. In order of descending authority there is the cult leader, the secretary, the male assistant to the cult leader, the mediums *con guias*, the medium *aspirante* (aspiring medium), the *cambonos* (new mediums), and the *sociais*.

The domain of the spiritual represents those activities performed while the medium is incorporated by a spirit *guia.* These include giving ritual passes and consultations. Most of these activities occur during the weekly *trabalhos* held in the cult house. In rare cases, they may also take place in a medium's home. The structure of role relationships within this domain form a loose confederation which is composed of the chief spirit of the entire center and the *guias* of the working mediums. The *guias* represent many different lines of spirits, each working with different powers and techniques of curing. The spiritual "boss" is technically the chief spirit of the cult leader. This spirit, usually a powerful *orixá* such as *Xangô*, is recognized as the protector and founder of the cult. The chief spirit has the authority to prescribe the order of the ritual, to determine the dress of the mediums, to define the limits of acceptable trance behavior, to limit the activities of the other spirit *guias* who work at the *centro,* and to loosely control the methods used in the *trabalhos* by the spirit *guias.* This authority is often tested and challenged by the other spirit *guias.*

It is accepted that the spirit *guia* has authority over the details of cures and strategies employed in problem solving, but even the spirit *guia* must accept the teachings of Umbanda Evangelizada. What we have here is an attempt by the cult leader to set up guidelines for the spirit role without actually denying the existence of the separate, strong personality of the *guia.* The cult leader tells the mediums that enlightened spirits never work evil or demand high payments for their services or direct their clients to place offerings to *exu* in the cemeteries or crossroads. These things are explained as self-serving directions of the *parte material* and not the *parte espiritual.* Those mediums who violate the rules are reprimanded, and if they continue, they are asked to leave.

Deviations from the expected possession trance behavior are not punished quite so severely because controlled trance is not within the reach of every medium. Even so, controlled trance behavior is still one of the major goals of development. Controlled trance behavior means the ability to retain an upright posture, open eyes, and a calm facial expression. Uncontrolled trance behavior is defined as anything which deviates from this behavior such as grunting, shouting, bending over suddenly, falling to the floor, shaking, trembling, dancing, and smoking pipes or cigars. Spirit possession trance is induced through intense concentration and repeated practice. Outside sensory stimulation is consciously blocked out as mediums stare with eyes open at a chosen spot on the floor. The only voice that they strain to hear is the cult leader's signaling the start and end of prayers, songs, and other ritual events.

The relationship between the spirit *guia* and the medium may take one of three forms: *incorporado,*[11] *encostado,* or *en transe.* A spirit may completely *incorporar* (to incorporate) the medium's body and assume control of all outward bodily manifestations. The medium is said to be *incorporado* (incorporated) by the spirit. The medium is referred to as the *aparelho* (apparatus) of the spirit. When the spirit leaves, the *aparelho* claims not to remember what has happened during the incorporation. This state of amnesia varies in intensity because some mediums claim that while *incorporado* they "see" themselves as an Indian or a warrior but their perception is distorted. One spirit medium said that she saw herself, as if from a distance, and she felt the power and strength of the *guia.* When there is a slight period of amnesia following incorporation, it seems to act as a role-segregating mechanism, which keeps separate the *parte material* from the *parte espiritual.* The following example illustrates how this role-segregating mechanism functions. Dona Bette's *guia* is in the *Linha de Oxoce,* and she handles many clients. One day at the supermarket two strangers approached Dona Bette and thanked her for some advice, which they claimed she gave them. Somewhat startled, Dona Bette told them that she was afraid they were mixing her up with someone else. In talking with them further she discovered that they were regular clients of her spirit *guia.* Dona Bette then explained to them that she could not discuss their problems or take credit for helping them since she, Dona Bette, was neither responsible for these events nor familiar with them.

A spirit may communicate with a person while it is alongside of, or *encostado,* the medium. When a spirit is *encostado,* it is not inside of the medium but next to the medium. The medium may receive directions and messages from the spirit and still be conscious and aware of her surroundings. Such spiritual messages are usually written down and read later at the *trabalhos.* Only rarely does a medium enter into a deep trance state that is referred to as being *en transe.* This state causes severe headaches and can make the medium sick. Being *en transe* is different from the other medium-spirit relationship in that the medium's spiritual self is believed to leave her body to journey to other parts of the city. One medium described a visit that was made by her "spirit" to a local hospital where her spirit performed an operation.

THE ROLE OF MEDIUM

A medium is a person through whom the spirits are believed to speak and communicate with people. The most basic attribute of this role is a quality called *mediumidade.* It is an ascribed characteristic that is inheritable and God-given. One cannot acquire it or get rid of it. A person can only develop it through study, concentration, spiritual guidance, and proper training. Both cult leaders and mediums claim that most people possess some *mediumidade,* but the amount depends upon *vidas antepassadas. Vidas antepassadas* or past incarnations determine both the level of *mediumidade* and its stage of development. The maximum number of *vidas antepassadas* is twelve. Cult leaders and highly evolved mediums are near the end of their required number. After they reach twelve, they are no longer reincarnated in material form but remain in spiritual form and dwell on the astral plane.

The development of *mediumidade* requires a special kind of person who is able to withstand a lot of pain and testing. A medium must be loving, kind, patient, motherly, moral, and pure. She should be able to endure pain and suffering. Suffering is believed to be a spiritual test that must be conquered and withstood without complaint. The examples of spiritual tests endured by informants include a long and painful throat condition, the obstruction of education because of unforeseen events, and marital problems. These tests themselves are often interpreted by the cult leaders as signs of *mediumidade,* too.

The *parte material* or physical body of a medium must be pure and healthy. The maintenance of this state involves a purification rite known as a *banha descarga,* which is taken before the medium comes to the center to work. The ingredients of the bath may be purchased at any one of the Umbanda stores in the city. The failure to observe this rite can result in a weakened and unprotected body that cannot withstand evil influences. In a woman's body the *banha descarga* keeps evil influences from attaching themselves to the female organs. The *banha descarga* functions to keep the material part of the medium healthy so that the medium can continue to work spiritually during the *Trabalho de Caridade.* A medium must also maintain a healthy body by refraining from smoking and drinking. High moral standards are to be observed in order to keep the medium pure, since purity is a necessary precondition for spiritual work.

A medium is expected to practice charity and to extend help to anyone needing it. Umbanda Evangelizada provides ways to do this through such organized activities as charity teas, clothing drives, and Christmas gift give-aways. The proceeds from these events are used to buy the material to make clothing for the poor.

New mediums are recruited into the role by the cult leader who identifies the signs first and then relays the information to the perspective medium. Although the signs vary, a number of them occurring in a person's life is taken as evidence of a spiritual call. Some of the signs are excessive crying or sobbing, prolonged illness, unexplained events, unsolvable problems, and unusual occurrences. A cult leader warns a perspective medium that resistance is dangerous. Resistance is often encountered in the husbands of future mediums because they do not believe in the *mediumidade* of their wives. Most female mediums and cult leaders agree that a married woman should have her husband's consent and cooperation, but if it is impossible to get it, the spiritual order ought to take precedence over this resistance. The development of *mediumidade* is often recommended by cult leaders and spirit mediums as a way to overcome problems. This is the case in the following example of a woman who was experiencing marital problems.

A young woman came to the center to receive help and advice concerning the drunkenness of her husband. He refused to attend with his wife so she brought along some of his clothes to be ritually cleansed of evil influences. When she entered the *corrente* (circle) of mediums, she was possessed by an *irmaozinho* (a little brother) spirit who threw her violently to the floor. The female cult leader sent the spirit away, enlightened, and she told the client that this spontaneous possession trance was a sign of undeveloped *mediumidade.* Mediums are known to attract backward spirits who seek enlightenment. These spirits linger in the medium's home disrupting the home life. In this case the drunkenness of the husband was attributed to this *irmaozinho* who had possessed the wife.*

In Umbanda Evangelizada the development of *mediumidade* takes three to four years, involving seven confirmations, attendance at classes for development, practice at weekly *trabalhos*, observation of other mediums, and guidance by the cult leader. The time commitment is enormous. A new medium usually attends all of the weekly *trabalos* and classes so that she can get adequate experience. This means that she is at the *centro* four evenings out of seven and all day Saturday. The Seven Confirmations are central to developing *mediumidade* because they mark the successful attainment of spiritual knowledge and assistance within specific lines. In Umbanda Evangelizada, the following confirmations are observed: the baptism, the Triangle of Fire, the Initiation, the *Trabalho do Mar* (Work of the Sea), the Confirmation of the *Cachoeira* (Waterfalls), the Confirmation of the *Pedra* (Stone), and the Confirmation of the *Pretos Velhos* and the *Linha de Oriente.*

THE CLIENT-MEDIUM RELATIONSHIP

The clients come to the trabalhos seeking spiritual cures and explanations for their problems. The average number of clients observed at the regular weekly sessions range between 200 and 250 and on special occasion it reaches almost one thousand. A major source of the clients' problems is believed to be the "disincarnated" spirits of dead people. They are called *espiritos atrasados* (backward spirits), *irmaozinhos* (little brothers), and *espiritos sem luz* (spirits without light). These spirits are neither good nor evil. They cause people problems because they cannot seem to help themselves find a way to evolve to a higher spiritual level. They wander about the earth searching for enlightenment. Sometimes, they are used by evil people to harm others but they themselves are not evil. It is believed that they are responsible for a wide

*All case reports in this Chapter are from unpublished Fieldnotes.

range of problems and usually a client does not discover that they are bothering him until he is told so by a spirit *guia.* A spirit *guia* is able to communicate with these spirits and find out just what needs to be done to get them out of the body of the client. An especially good medium can attract these spirits into her body, and when they leave, they are more enlightened and will not bother people anymore.

Espiritos mals (evil spirits) are another source of the clients' problems. These evil spirits originate with evil people, some of whom committed suicide. *Espiritos mals* intentionally do harm to people. Violent acts and outbursts are attributed to them. A spirit *guia* of a good medium can detect their presence in a client and can persuade them to leave the client alone. Sometimes this persuasion involves a spiritual and a physical fight. When an *espirito mal* leaves the client's body and enters into the medium's, it moves up through the stomach area and lodges in the medium's throat. It stays there for a few seconds and chokes the medium. Then it leaves the medium's body by going out through the top of her head. The medium jerks slightly and raises her arms.

A broad category of problems fall under the category of a *demanda* (claim). A problem classified as a *demanda* is traced to a specific *trabalho* aimed at the client by someone who is his enemy. This person may be jealous of the client or he may hate the client, so he sends evil spirits and misfortunes against him. The client becomes a victim of evil works and comes to the Umbanda center for help. The spirit *guia* that he consults with sets the forces of good against these forces of evil. The term *demanda* symbolizes this spiritual action.

Some problems are caused by evil fluids or influences which surround the client's body. Evil fluids can cause nervousness, stomach aches, indigestion and headaches. They can be picked up almost anywhere a person goes. The *mau olhado* (evil eye) can be another source of the client's problem. The *mau olhado* is a direct glance from the eyes which emits a force. When it is cast intentionally, it has the power to destroy its object. It can wreck wood tile floors, ruin careers, and distrupt engagements. The *pretos velhos* are good at detecting it. Statements of praise from people who may really be envious or jealous are a sign that it may have been cast. In the following case, a client's problem began with the *mau olhado* and was further complicated by an *espirito mal.*

A female client came to the *trabalho* of the *Linha de Oriente* on Saturday evening. During the session, she was violently possessed and thrown to the floor by an *espirito mal.* The cult leader stepped forward to question the spirit. He asked its name and its intentions. The spirit refused to answer at first, but then shouted out that it was going to destroy this woman and her family. The woman's husband was present and after the cult leader sent the spirit away, he gave the husband a ritual *passe* at the altar. The husband was told to take his wife home.

Later in the week Dona Bette explained the background of this case to me because she knew this woman well. They were *coma-dres*.[12] The woman's husband is a traveling salesman, and he was doing very well in his business until he aroused the jealousy of another person (unidentified). This jealous person put the *mau olhado* on him and ever since he has had problems. He began drinking, fighting with his wife, and fooling around with other women. His business dropped off. The client begged her husband to come to the *centro* for a *passe* but he refused, at least until that Saturday night.

So far then, we have seen that clients are given some explanations for their problems and misfortunes. But they also receive some special curing services from the medium *con guias*.

Despite the fact that each case is handled individually, there are some common services rendered in the cure. The three most commonly used are the ritual *passes*, the *passagentes*, and the *banha descarga*. *Passes* are given as a matter of course to every client who sees a *guia*. A *passe* consists of wiping away evil influences which cling to the immediate atmosphere around the body. The medium whips her hands around the client's body which draws the evil fluids away from it. A *passagente* involves three or seven mediums working together to cleanse the client of evil and to draw the possessing spirit into the body of one of the mediums. A *banha descarga* or ritual herb bath is prescribed as a follow-up procedure to the *passe* and *passagente*. It is believed to give added protection until the next visit.

Remedios (remedies) are also prescribed by spirit *guias*. These range from antacids which can be purchased at the pharmacy to herb teas made from lo-cal plants. Sometimes a client is told to collect a green plant known as *arruda* and to place it in a cup of water. The *arruda* and water are left by the bed of a sick person so it can collect anger which lingers in the atmosphere and which can case illness. *Arruda* is commonly associated with the *pretos velhos* who use it in their curing practicies. Rose petals placed in water and kept over night are believed to help upset stomachs. In the morning, the rose water is to be drunk by the patient.

Astral operations are a special service rendered by spirit mediums work-ing in the *Linha de Oriente*. I observed eight astral operations as they were performed by the spirit of a physician which possessed or incorporated the body of Dona Edi, a female cult leader in Umbanda Evangelizada. The clients came from her neighborhood and from Porto Alegre. The following problems were diagnosed by the spirit doctor of Dona Edi and were operated on spiritually over a three-month period: cancer of the stomach, a disorder of the prostate gland and stomach, a disorder of the female sex organs, and a kidney and bladder malfunction. These problems are believed to be spiritual disorders.

The astral operations were performed while Dona Edi was incorporated by her spirit *guia*, the doctor. The operating power rested in her right hand, which she held just above the afflicted area of the client's body. The operations lasted only a few minutes and left no scars or incision marks on the body. All of the cutting was done "spiritually" so nothing showed up materially. The astral operation took place within the center upon an operating table specially prepared for this purpose.

The preceding client cases demonstrate cures involving special services and explanations available to spirit mediums through their *guias*. These techniques of curing are probably more common than the kinds of solutions which are presented next. However, the solutions in the following cases seem to be equally valuable to certain clients who face personal and economic hardships. These cases were collected about the clients of one spirit *guia* in the *Linda de Oxoce* working through the medium Dona Bette. They demonstrate how the *guia* can use the storehouse of information which he has collected about the lives and circumstances of his clients to help solve problems for some other clients. They also show how some powerful clients can be potential patrons who can be persuaded by the spirit *guia* to use their influence to help people.

> Case Number 1: A young woman was deserted by her husband and left to raise her children without child support. She came to Dona Bette's *guia* for advice and help. He told her he knew why she was suffering so much in this life. In a past life, she had been a man who had also deserted his wife and family. This man's wife had to struggle to survive and to support her children. So, the punishment he received was to be reincarnated as a woman in the same situation. The spirit *guia* was not unsympathetic to the plight of the children who he believed were the innocent victims of this predicament.

This case demonstrates a comon problem for women, that is, the desertion by their husbands. It also provides an explanation for the problem in the sins of another life. The solution involves another client, and his problem is presented in the following case.

> Case Number 2: An elderly and wealthy man was a regular client of Dona Bette's spirit *guia*. For many years, he suffered from an 'illness' and by this time he was willing to do anything necessary to help cure himself. Dona Bette's *guia* told the man that if he

wanted to get better then he should contribute some of his wealth to help others. He was told to donate child support money to the children in case 1.

Here we have the solution of the client's problem in case number 1 being tied to the cure of an illness of a client in case 2. The spirit *guia* has in effect been able to reallocate specific resources and to rechannel them to the supposed advantage of both clients.

In case 3, which follows, we have an example of information in the form of gossip being used to forewarn a female client about the infidelity of her husband. Clients often say that they are told startling and surprising things by spirit *guias* who seem to know so much about them before they themselves know. Among the clients of one *guia* gossip is common, and it can be useful.

> Case Number 3: Donna Bette's *guia* told a female client that she was going to be in for a big surprise concerning her husband. The woman returned about one week later and recounted these events. She had difficulty with her husband for quite some time, and they were not getting along. One day during the week she was walking along the street when she spied her husband ahead conversing and walking with another woman. She quickly caught a bus to avoid meeting them face to face. The woman discovered that her husband was not going to work as he said he was but was instead going to this other woman's house during the day. The other woman was giving him money to come. The wife decided to confront her husband with this information, and then to ask him to move out!
>
> The husband went immediately to the other woman's house and related what had happened. As she listened to him, she decided that she did not want him anymore either. So now he had no one. In Dona Bette's words: "He chose the wrong road and he has to stay on it."

This case demonstrates another problem which women face in life, that is, the infidelity of their husbands. The solution to this problem was to forewarn the client about her husband. She was told about a surprise concerning him. In all likelihood she already knew that something was wrong concerning him as they had quarreled for some time. The spirit *guia* put her on the alert. She was able to save face by confronting him and telling him to leave, and in this manner punish him before he had a chance to desert her. In a small way perhaps this revenge would "cure" her of her problem by making it less painful to her.

The next case is somewhat different than the first three in that it involves the distribution of goods to a client from the common coffers of the Umbanda *centro*. A spirit *guia* does have access to certain common funds for helping out clients.

> Case Number 4:   Dona Bibiana lived alone with her young son. She was deserted by her husband and was employed as a cleaning lady. She was constantly ill and upset at work. She broke down in tears and sobbed so hard that her boss told her to go home until she felt better. Eventually, she was fired. She came to the *centro* to consult with the *guia* of Dona Bette. He listened to her problem and then directed her to the secretary who gave her some funds to tide her over.

This case again shows the problem of a lone woman trying to work and raise a child at the same time. The solution is a practical one, although temporary, involving the common funds of charity possessed by the center.

The final case which the *guia* of Dona Bette handled involves a young spirit medium, Dona Ira. She came to Porto Alegre from the interior and found employment as a domestic servant. At the time, she was relatively uneducated and barely literate.

> Case Number 5: Dona Ira always worked late at the Umbanda centro assisting the cult leader in the *trabalhos,* which in those early days sometimes lasted all night. Her employer, a wealthy Italian woman, grew annoyed with her late nights and she fired her. Dona Ira could not find another job. She turned to Dona Bette for help and Dona Bette provided her with a place to sleep and something to eat. Dona Bette encouraged her to begin the free adult night classes in the city and helped her to purchase some furnishings for an apartment. In return, Dona Ira worked as a domestic servant for Dona Bette.
>
> Dona Bette's *guia* was also concerned with the fate of Dona Ira. He knew of her desire to become a doctor and of her interest in medicine. He also knew of a former client of his who operated a chemical laboratory which processed blood specimens for the hospitals. When this client returned again to the *centro*, the spirit *guia* asked him to help find Dona Ira employment. He agreed to hire her in his lab. She was able to move out of Dona Bette's and rent an apartment with three other women.

This case demonstrates two levels of help which mediums and their *guias* can render to others. By helping Dona Ira find temporary employment within her home and by encouraging her to start school, Dona Bette began a permanent solution to Dona Ira's problems. The spirit *guia* used his influence and connections to get her a better job. The spirit *guia* has the ability to contact potential patrons and to influence them to help his clients. The case also shows how spirit mediums have the authority through their guias to reallocate goods (employment) in the public domain.

DISCUSSION

The role of medium is set within a role structure dominated by two domains of action—one material and the other spiritual. Within the material domain, the occupant of the medium role has the opportunity to move up through a hierarchy of roles to the respected position of cult leader. As she passes from the *cambono* position to that of medium *aspirante* to medium *con guia*, she gains a wide variety of experiences. She acquires organizational and administrative skills from the charity drives and luncheons. She learns how to interact socially with men and women from different social classes and ethnic backgrounds. The status of a medium within this domain depends upon recognized accomplishments such as the *vidas antepassadas* (reincarnations), the level of *mediumidade*, and the stage of development. Status is also influenced by the number of years of experience within Umbanda Evangelizda, social class, and sometimes ethnic background.

On the other hand, within the spiritual domain the medium's status is determined by her spirit *guia* and his talent for solving the problems of his clients and for attracting a large clientele. Spirits themselves are not ranked vis-a-vis each other. However, in certain matters, they do defer to the spiritual authority of the cult leader's spirit guia, but they are still autonomous entities. Status gained by a medium within the material domain is offset by the equality of the spirits within the spiritual domain.

In the eyes of their clients, the spirits and their mediums provide important services. They can answer the big question of "why is this happening to me?" The curing ritual follows a set pattern, which is common to each session and which is repeated each time a client visits. The repetition of this ritual seems to reduce the client's anxiety and assures him that this is a reputable establishment in which the *guias* know what they are about. It is similar to the standardized procedure that accompanies a visit to the doctor. There is a waiting period before the examination and consultation. *Passes, passagentes, banhas descargas, remedios* are always part of the standard treatment. In some special cases and for some qualified mediums, astral operations may be performed. These operations reassure the seriously ill person that something extra special is being done to help him or her recover.

The real and practical help with personal and economic problems that is offered to clients cannot be ignored. The significance of this kind of help for urban clients who are often alone in the city and who are left without patrons is considerable. (See Wagley 1971:106-7)

FEMALE STATUS AND MODERNIZATION

In our discussion of domains, power, and status, we saw that women who have access to economic power and/or authority in the public domain stand a good chance of experiencing a relative rise in social status. Sanday's (1974) evolutionary model of female status in the public domain suggests that the acquisition of economic power via control or ownership of strategic resources occurred as women were able to rechannel their energies away from private domain activities and into public domain activities. One would think that modernization would contribute in a positive way to the enhancement of female status. However, as we examine the role of the Brazilian woman in the modernization of Brazil, we find that while there have been some significant changes in the job opportunities and educational benefits open to women, modernization has not been entirely beneficial to all women.

Urbanization, plus rapid economic development and industrialization, produced an impressive rate of economic development for Brazil, which is being described by some as an "economic miracle." The miracle refers to an economic growth rate from 1968 to 1975 averaging 10 percent annually in real terms. According to Stefan H. Robock (1975: 1), a specialist on the Brazilian economy, "Brazil has increased its national output by an amount equal to its total cumulative economic growth over all the previous centuries of its history." Two separate studies of the participations of Brazilian women in this economic miracle show that although there has been a dramatic increase in the participation of women in education and employment categories previously reserved for men and that now women comprise 20 percent of the labor force, the employment of females is still heaviest in the service fields, including domestic service (Rubens Vaz da Costa 1974, cited in Robock 1975:11-12; Madeira and Singer 1975).

The Madeira and Singer (1975) economic report draws the following specific conclusions about female participation in the work force during the years 1920-1970. First, the number of jobs created for women through economic development is fewer than the number of women in urban areas who seek employment. Secondly, the growth of domestic-remunerated services employing women in typical female chores are still important sources of income for women with no skills or education. Third, there is hidden unemployment among women in urban areas because the majority of women are either unemployed or employed in socially unproductive work. Fourth, the transformation brought about by development had contradictory consequences for the economic and social status of women especially in the secondary sector and in the production services where the elimination of artisan and domestic jobs removed a large number of women from economic activities. Madeira and Singer (1975:496) estimate that in 1970 more than three-fourths of economically active women were found in subsistence agriculture and remunerated domestic work. They find this encouraging since in 1960 the proportion was more than four-fifths. According to the Sinopse Estatística do Brazil (1975) between 1940 and 1970 an average of 82 percent of Brazilian women were not counted among those active in economic affairs.

"Work" is defined as activity that is related to the production of goods and services (Madeira and Singer 1975:490). Activity identified as work becomes increasingly specialized during economic development and increasingly isolated from the home. Brazilian women are assigned house tasks which are not considered as "work" by Brazilian census takers and economists. Housework is not seen as contributing to social production, that is, economic development, and since so many women are engaged in housework the number counted as economically active is extremely low.

Implied in the Madeira and Singer (1975) report is a distinction between two spheres of activity: one of domestic tasks which is associated with women; and one of "work" or activities contributing to economic development which is associated primarily with men and only some women. Keeping their definitions in mind, let us look at "housework" in Porto Alegre.[13]

The activities performed by women within the domestic sphere include the *serviço de casa* (housework), domestic crafts, and domestic service. Housework is defined as the organization and running of a household. It represents the major domestic tasks ascribed to Brazilian women. The activities concern:

1. *Food:* tending fruit trees and gardens, shopping for daily supplies, preparation and serving of meals, cleaning up after meals, canning and storage of food;
2. *Clothing:* shopping for materials and/or finished clothes, designing, sewing, repairing, washing and ironing of clothes;
3. *House maintenance:* sweeping and washing floors, dusting and polishing furniture, yard maintenance, minor repairs;
4. *Early education and child-care.*

The serviço de casa is the responsibility of the *dona de casa* (housewife or owner of the house). The *dona de casa* has the power to allocate part of this work to other females such as her daughters or, if she has the resources, to an *empregada doméstica* (domestic servant or maid). Men and boys are not expected to help in the *serviço de casa*. This expectation is often reflected in the doubts single women have about being able to find a husband who will allow them time to pursue either their careers or their missions in Umbanda Evangelizada.

The role of full-time *empregada doméstica* is very attractive to lower-class rural women moving into the city. This attraction is based upon job security and the chance for upward social mobility. An *empregada doméstica* who is employed by an upper-class family is usually provided room and board plus a small salary. Although the monthly wages fall below the minimum wage of Rio Grande do Sul, the job gives women free time to pursue outside activities. Several spirit mediums were *empregadas domésticas,* and they were able to divide their time between their employment and the development of their *mediumidade* (medium abilities). Free time allowed some to better themselves by attending adult night school programs such as the MOBRAL[14] movement sponsors. The completion of night courses leads to higher paying skilled jobs.

Domestic crafts require skills traditionally associated with domestic production. These include knitting, crocheting, embroidery, designing and sewing clothes, and special food preparation. Domestic service (such as the role of *empregada doméstica*) is defined as employment within the domestic sphere in which traditional household work is performed by hired personnel. Domestic service includes some of the less skilled aspects of housework such as washing and ironing clothes, washing and sweeping floors, dusting and cleaning the house, and so on. It can also include the more skilled domestic crafts mentioned above. Domestic crafts and domestic service skills develop during the early training and education of girls who will eventually be expected to direct all housework. Domestic crafts were a very basic part of a young girl's training, especially among the women descended of European immigrant families of the Colonial zone. Take the case of Thelma for example:

> Descended from Italian immigrants to Rio Grande do Sul, Thelma grew up in a small town within the Colonial zone. Fifteen years ago she left her family in order to come to Proto Alegre where she lives now at the age of thirty-one. Thelma's upbringing was supervised by her father who believed that she should learn the traditional role of *dona de casa.* Encouraged by her father to leave school after the primary level, Thelma was apprenticed to an old immigrant woman who taught her to sew and design clothes, crochet and knit, embroider and cook. She resisted this role but her father would not allow her to pursue any other. Eventually, in the face of her father's opposition, she worked as an assistant to the primary school teacher. But in order to continue her formal education any further she had to leave home and move to another city and finally to Porto Alegre. In 1975, she was studying for the entrance examination of the medical school at the federal university.

Economic development eliminated some important cottage industries that enabled women to contribute to social production, gain some economic power, and to be counted as "working." In the following example, one Brazilian informant, Dona Bette, discusses the small domestic shirt factory that she ran from her home in the 1950s and 1960s. Utilizing her domestic craft skills of designing and sewing clothing, she employed several female assistants to sell the shirts for her on the streets.[15]

(Dona Bette is descendent of Italian immigrants to Brazil.) My husband and I moved to Porto Alegre about nineteen years ago. He is a carpenter, self-employed. Before we moved into this house (a well furnished three-story home), we lived in a smaller, more modest home. I used to make shirts there in my living room. I designed and cut out the patterns and hired several women to sew them up. A few more women sold the shirts for me out on the street. That is how I helped my husband send our two sons to the university and purchase this big house. I was always a very active woman.

Such cottage industries are being replaced in Porto Alegre by parallel industries manufacturing clothing and processing food. And as Madeira and Singer (1975) point out, some women have suffered from this aspect of economic development since the new industries cannot absorb all the female labor made available by the decreasing demand for the products of cottage industries.

CONCLUSIONS

The role of spirit medium in Umbanda Evangelizada of Porto Alegre is a public domain activity, since it includes activities taking place or having impact beyond the localized family unit. Religious authority is conferred on the role-occupant through a "spiritual connection." Economic power emanates from the complex interaction between mediums and clients. The source of this economic power lies in the access which the medium client relationship allows to an internal communications network and in access to nonlocal patrons. Spiritual authority validates the use of this power to reallocate resources among clients. The spirit medium role serves society by providing an explanation for problems, by answering the client's question of "why this should be happening to me" and by giving the public much needed ritual curing services. Women seem to be attracted to this role because of the above attributes and because, as of yet, they are excluded from economic roles offering similar benefits. Also, the Brazilian economic miracle is, at present, putting women in an ambiguous position. Certainly the relative status of a few women participating in social production and contributing to economic development has been enhanced, but the vast majority of women are still not a part of this. Economic development has meant the loss of certain profitable cottage industries in which traditional domestic crafts were employed, and thus, the loss of an important source of economic power for women.

The role of spirit medium contributes to modernization in the sense that it allows some women access to economic power in the public domain even if they are not employed in so called "social production." By offering women an avenue for social mobility, the Umbanda spirit medium role alleviates some of the less beneficial aspects of development.

NOTES

1. M.G. Smith (1960:18-19) defines power as "the ability to act effectively on persons or things, to make or secure favorable decisions which are not of right allocated to the individuals or their roles." Authority is "the right to make a particular decision and to command obedience."

2. According to the Sinopse Estatistica do Brazil, Sao Paulo is in the "Southeast" region along with the states of Guanabara, Rio de Janeiro, Espirito Santo, and Minas Gerais.

3. The typical dress of the *gaucho* included a broadbrimmed hat, a bandana (*lenco*), tall leather boots with accordian pleats at the ankles, huge jangling spurs (*chilenas*), heavy trousers (*bombachas*), and a *poncho.* He lived on meat cooked over an open fire (*churrasco)* and drank hot herb tea or *mate.* (Love 1971:11)

4. Tapes or Tupi-Guarani were placed on settlements or *reducoes* by Jesuit missionaries. These *reducoes*, known as the Sete Povos, were conquered in 1801 and their inhabitants became nomads, cowboys, and soldiers contributing manpower to the external and internal wars of the state. The cultural influence of the Guarani of the Missoes district, part of the Cima da Serra, was still so influential that as late as the 1830s Tupi-Guarani was still a major language in the area (Love 1971).

5. According to the Brazilian anthropologist, Arthur Ramos (1972:130) the bandierantes were composed of *mamelucos* or persons of mixed Indian and European descent.

6. The rapid influx of predominately male slaves prevented the creation of a mulatto contigent such as existed in other slave areas of Brazil. Caio Prado Junio, a Brazilian historian of the colonial period, is quoted by Rout here as pointing out that the "blacks were blacker, and the whites, whiter."

7. The African-derived religion known as macumba, once popular in Rio de Janeiro and Sao Paulo, is the immediate forerunner of umbanda. In fact umbanda in these areas is still known to outsiders as macumba. Macumba combined Yoruba beliefs with those from Angolese and Congolese religions (see Bastide 1978 and Pressel 1974 for a more complete discussion). Sometime in the past, macumba was influenced by a lower form of spiritism known as Kardecismo (Bastide 1978:315). Brazilian spiritism originated in Ceara and Bahia in 1865. It was primarily urban, and its dogma appealed to many different levels of society. The upper-class intellectuals and scientists were drawn by its metaphysical philosophy while the lower middle-class and lower-class people were probably attracted by its semi-upper-class stigma which gives it more prestige than either macumba or other forms of African-derived religions. This mixture of macumba and lower spiritism first occurred in Rio de Janeiro and later in other areas of Brazil--Minas, Rio Grande do Sul, Sao Paulo, Recife (Bastide 1978:315).

8. This seems to conform to Camargo's (1961) description of the varieties of umbanda that he surveyed in Sao Paulo. He arranged the beliefs and practices of umbanda along a continuum from the most traditionally African to those closest to Kardecism.

9. The syncretism of African gods and Catholic saints is a phenomenon typical of Afro-American religions in Cuba, Haiti, and Brazil (Herskovits 1937).

10. In Rio de Janeiro's umbanda and macumba centers, Yvonne Maggie Alves Velho (1975:48-49) found that a *demanda* is a war of the *orixas* waged for the benefit of people. It is very dangerous and it can even kill the person for which the losing *orixa* fought. *Orixa* is broadly used here to refer to any divinity or supernatural figure who enters into contact with a human through possession (1975:166).

11. The relationship referred to here as *incorporado* is similar to what Bourguignon (1976:8) calls possession trance: "a belief in possession that is used to account for alterations or discontinuity in consciousness, awareness personality, or other aspects of psychological functioning."

12. *Comadre* (co-mother) is a fictive kin tie in which two women are bound together by the fact that one is the godmother of the other's child.

13. The material on "housework" is drawn from formal interviews with 21 Porto Alegre women. The group interviewed included about an equal number of spirit mediums and noncult affiliates, that is, women who did not frequent umbanda at all.

14. MOBRAL stands for the Brazilian Literacy Movement and its goal is to reduce the illiteracy rate within a decade from 33 percent to less than 10 percent.

15. This role is similar to the processing-vending role of Isthmus Zapotec women. See Chinas 1967 for a comparison.

REFERENCES

Asward, Barbara C.
1967 "Key and Peripheral Roles of Noble Women in a Middle Eastern Plains Village." *Anthropological Quarterly* 40:139-52.

Azevedo, Thales de
1969 *A Colonização Italiana. Rio Grande du Sul: Terra e Povo.* Porto Alegre: Editôra Globo.

Bastide, Roger
1978 *The African Religions of Brazil.* Baltimore: The Johns Hopkins Press (first published in France in 1960).

Bourguignon, Erika
1976 *Possession.* San Francisco: Chandler and Sharp.

Carmago, Candido Procopio Ferrevia de
1961   *Kardecismo e Umbanda: Uma Interpretação Sociológica.* São Paulo: Livaria Pioneira Editôra.

Cesar, Gulhermino
1962   *Historia do Rio Grande do Sul. Periodo Colonial.* Porto Alegre: Editora Globo.

Chinas, Beverly L.
1973   *The Isthmus Zapotecs. Women's Roles in Cultural Context.* New York: Holt, Rinehart and Winston, Inc.

Herskovits, Melville J.
1937   "African Gods and Catholic Saints in New World Negro Belief." *American Anthropologist, New Series* 39:635-43.
1943   "The Southernmost Outposts of New World Africanisms." *American Anthropologist, New Series* 45:496-510.

Love, Joseph L.
1971   *Rio Grande do Sul and Brazilian Regionalism 1882-1930.* Stanford: Stanford University Press.

Madeira, F.R., and P. Singer
1975   "Structure of Female Employment and Work in Brazil." *Journal of Interamerican Studies and World Affairs* 17:490-96.

MOBRAL
1975   The Brazilian Adult Literacy Experiment. Educational Studies and Documents. No. 15 UNESCO.

Pressel, Esther
1974   "Umbanda Trance and Possession in Sao Paulo, Brazil." In *Trance, Healing, and Hallucination,* F.D. Goodman, J. Henney, and E. Pressel, eds. New York: Wiley.

Ramos, Arthur
1972   "The Negro in Brazil." In *Brazil, Portrait of Half a Continent.* T. Lynn Smith and A. Merchant, eds. Westport, Conn.: Greenwood Press.

Riegelhaupt, Joyce F.
1967   "Saloio Women: An Analysis of Informal and Formal Political and Economic Roles of Portuguese Women." *Anthropological Quarterly* 40:109-26.

Robock, Stefan H.
1975   *Brazil: A Study in Development Progress.* Toronto: D.C. Heath.

Roche, Jean
1969   *A Colonizacao Alema. Rio Grande do Sul. Terra e Povo.* Porto Alegre: Editora Globo.

Rosaldo, Michelle Zimbalist
1974   "Woman, Culture, and Society: A Theoretical Overview." In *Woman, Culture, and Society,* M.Z. Rosaldo and L. Lamphere, eds. Stanford: Stanford University Press.

Rout, Leslie B.
1976 "Race and Slavery in Brazil." *The Wilson Quarterly* 1:73-92.

Sanday, Peggy R.
1974 "Female Status in the Public Domain." In *Woman, Culture, and Society*. M.Z. Rosaldo and L. Lamphere, eds. Stanford: Stanford University Press.

Smith, Michael G.
1960 *Government in Zazau: 1800-1950*. London: Oxford University Press.

Vaz da Costa, Rubens
1974 *A Participacao da Sociedade Brasiliera*. Sao Paulo: (mimeographed).

Viana, Francisco Oliveira
1952 *Populacoes Meridionais do Brasil: Historia-Organizacao-Psicologra, II: O Campeador Riograndense*. Rio de Janeiro.

Velho, Yvonne Maggie Alves
1975 *Guerra De Orixa. Un Estudo de Ritual e Conflito*. Rio de Janeiro: Zahar Editores.

Wagley, Charles
1971 *An Introduction to Brazil,* rev. ed. New York: Columbia University Press.

Wagley, Charles
1972 "The Indian Heritage." In *Brazil. Portrait of Half a Continent*. T. Lynn Smith and A. Merchant, eds. Westport, Conn.: Greenwood Press.

Wallace, Anthony, F.C.
1966 *Religion: An Anthropological View*. New York: Random House.

8 Sex and Status: Women in St. Vincent

JEANNETTE H. HENNEY

In this chapter, the author focuses her study of Vincentian women on the Spiritual Baptist church and describes the ritual possession trance that is a central feature of the religious practice of this group. By comparing significant aspects of this behavior with the human sex act as described by Masters and Johnson, she adds a further dimension to our understanding of both altered states of consciousness and human sexual behavior. Henney analyzes the differential gratification available to lower-class Vincentian men and women both in the Spiritual Baptist cult and in the larger society. She notes that the women, with their augmented entrepreneurial opportunities, can enjoy greater public power, than the men who join the cult. This is in line with our observation of the economic independence of women in the Non-Hispanic Caribbean as well as in West Africa. The author suggests that, contrary to what has been argued in the literature, in this society, it is the men rather than the women who may find compensating gratifications in the cults.

As the public at large has discovered women, so too have the anthropologists. And, as is common in contemporary society, when a state of awareness is approached or achieved, a veritable spate of printed, spoken, and visual material dealing with one aspect or another of the subject can be anticipated—and has, indeed, appeared. But increased productivity tends to stimulate further thought and consideration, and tends to encourage innovative applications and approaches to one's own data. Hence, I have been encouraged to reexamine my field experience and my continuing interaction with several of my informants, and to attempt to describe and evaluate the status of women in the religious community that I studied. And since my principal concern was with states of altered consciousness as they occurred in that group, I further propose, in this chapter, to investigate possible relationships between the observed dissociational states and sex. I intend to outline briefly the activities of the congregation during a typical worship service and describe in some detail the behavior of those worshipers who become dissociated, considering not only the differential behavior of male and female worshipers in dissociational states, and the differential gratifications within the religious group that accrue to males and females through participation in dissociation, but also the similarities between their behavior while in an altered state and that of individuals engaged in sexual intercourse. I will also give some attention to the differential opportunities and statuses accorded to males and females in, and by, the larger society.

The religious group under investigation is found on the island of St. Vincent, one of the Windward Islands of the Caribbean, lying about 100 miles west of Barbados and 170 miles north of Trinidad. St. Vincent is a small island, only 11 miles wide and 18 miles long. It is exceptionally beautiful; vegetation is lush and well-watered; the mountainous terrain and periodically threatening volcano, Mt. Soufrière, the black sand beaches, and the changing sea add to the picturesqueness. Vincentians take considerable pride and pleasure in the natural beauty of the island. Some of the local folk theorists, in good geographical determinist tradition, even attribute the islanders' warmth and friendliness (for which they have a well-deserved reputation) to the fact that they live in such an attractive, bountiful, and congenial setting.

Although St. Vincent was subjected to alternating French and British control in the post-Columbian period when the various European powers were vigorously competing for riches, land, and supremacy in the West Indies, the island finally became part of the British colonial system in 1783. And today, St. Vincent has achieved the status of an associated state of the United Kingdom. Vincentians speak the English language, and the predominating Western influence on customs and institutions has been, and remains, English.

The composition of St. Vincent's population recalls the history of the island and calls attention to the importance of slavery during the early period of development. The census data for 1960 indicate an overwhelming majority of blacks:

Negroes	56,207
Mixed	17,444
East Indians	2,444
Carib Indians	1,265
Whites	1,840
Other	748

Of the total population in 1960—79,948—37,561 were males, 42,387 were females. Within seven years, however, the population of the island had jumped to 91,326.

St. Vincent fits the general family-household patterns that have been noted for other areas of the Caribbean. In 1960, 8,290 families of a total of 15,713 had male heads; 7,423 families were headed by females. Males over 15 years of age who had never married numbered 11,501 as opposed to 5,314 who were married, 360 widowed, 26 divorced, and 38 separated; 15,347 females over 15 years of age had never married, 6,152 were married, 1,267 were widowed, 30 divorced, and 33 separated. Legitimate births in 1964 numbered 897 while 2781 births were recorded as illegitimate.

The religious situation in St. Vincent is dominated by three major persuasions: Anglican, Methodist, and Roman Catholic. Combined, they account for approximately 90 percent of the church memberships on the island. A number of other religious options are available, however, although they report far fewer members. The one in which I was interested had an unrecorded number of adherents when the 1960 census data were gathered—it had been outlawed in 1912 and was only awarded legal status in 1965, a year before my first visit to the island. The members refer to themselves formally as Spiritual Baptists, although outsiders may apply the derogatory, but descriptive, label of "Shakers" to them. A number of Spiritual Baptist churches are operating on the island, and there is considerable visiting back and forth of the different congregations. Each church is autonomous, but the worship practices and beliefs of the various congregations are very similar. One ubiquitous feature is the incorporation of altered states of consciousness into their belief and behavior systems.

Spiritual Baptists are not restricted to St. Vincent. Simpson (1970) and Herskovits (1947) have reported on Spiritual Baptists in Trinidad. (The cult had apparently spread to Trinidad from St. Vincent, and my informants indicated that lines of communication were being maintained between at least some of the Trinidadian and Vincentian groups.) Smith (1963) mentions the presence of Spiritual Baptists in Grenada, also. And some of the Vincentian Spiritual Baptist congregations make periodic trips to various islands in the Grenadines (the tiny islands scattered between St. Vincent and Grenada) to conduct worship services, keeping in touch with believers and possible converts where it might be impossible to maintain a regular church because of the small population. The latest Vincentian Spiritual Baptist offshoot to come to my attention is in New York City. I have been informed that several qualified members of the Vincentian congregation that I studied are making lengthy visits to New York and are conducting services there.

The religious approach of the Spiritual Baptists is fundamentalistic and Protestant. They follow the Methodist order of morning worship closely, and use the Methodist hymnal (the prayer book and hymnal are published in Great Britain), but they also include elements in their worship services that would not be part of the usual Methodist service. The most conspicuous departure from contemporary Methodist procedure is the incorporation of altered states of consciousness. Dissociational states occur in a variety of contexts within the Spiritual Baptist religious system. They are evidenced by different behavioral characteristics and are interpreted differently depending upon the context. During a worship service, dissociation is a frequent occurrence. In this context the affected individual shakes and exhibits other visible and audible manifestations that are believed to be the result of possession by the Holy Spirit (this combination of belief and behavior was labled "possession trance" [PT] by the Cross-Cultural Study of Dissociational States.[1]) Dissociation (without an accompanying belief in possession, T, according to the Cross-Cultural Study of Dissociational States usage) may also occur during extended periods of isolation, in which case it takes the form of hallucinatory activity, and is interpreted as a journey taken by the spirit of the affected person. Visual and auditory hallucinations are also reported as the divine stimulus that motivates the unconverted individual to embrace the Spiritual Baptist religion. Dreams (see Bourguignon 1972, for a discussion of dream-producing sleep as a type of altered state of consciousness) containing certain culturally important elements may also serve the same function.

Spiritual Baptists' worship services can be divided into two principal parts. During the first part of the service, the Methodist order of morning worship is generally adhered to, with the addition of a few embellishments. The worshipers either read the conventional, prescribed forms from their prayer books or they recite the appropriate words from memory. (Many individuals bring both prayer book and Bible to the meetings.) They participate in the singing of hymns. All members of the congregation enter into the performance of certain rituals, such as parading through the prayer house shaking hands with everyone. For other rituals, such as the blessing of the corners and doorways of the prayer house, some worshipers perform while the rest watch and wait. Dissociational states have little opportunity to develop while the congregation is thus occupied with repeating responses, following Bible lessons, attending to their hymnals, and frequently changing positions—sitting, standing, kneeling, and moving about. On rare occasions a worshiper was observed showing the early signs of a developing trance, but in all cases the dissociational state was quickly aborted.

As the worship service progresses beyond this early period, however, the groundwork for the full range of dissociational states is laid. The second part of the service is much less structured. Hymnals, Bibles, and prayer books are laid aside. There are now no rigid forms that have to be observed or repeated. In addition to those individuals who have been officiating during the service, ordinary members of the congregation may also preach sermons, present testimonials, and offer prayers. If a person intends to present a sermon or testimonial, he or she will usually begin the performance by starting to sing a well-known hymn. The congregation then joins in. After the initial hynm, the speaker periodically interrupts the sermon or testimonial to introduce other hymns. When a hymn has been completed and while the speader is talking, though, the congregation continues singing or humming, maintaining a steady and monotonous musical background that may, however, change in intensity—sometimes becoming louder and more demanding, sometimes becoming softer and less insistent. If a person offers a prayer rather than a sermon or testimonial, he or she will chant or sing the prayer while the congregation chants a response at the end of each metered verse. States of dissociation can be expected to develop during activities of this nature.

The members of the congregation sit on narrow, rough, wooden benches. Very few prayer houses have benches with backrests. The worshipers keep their eyes closed or half-closed. Some individuals prop up their heads with their hands. Some yawn. They give the general impression of being half-asleep. They seem to pay very little attention to the speaker's words. This is not surprising, perhaps, since much of the content of sermons, testimonials, and prayers is repetitious—not only does the individual performing repeat himself or herself over and over again, but most performers repeat much of what others have already said. Occasionally, the congregation may even drown out the speaker with their singing and humming. But, although they may not attend to the person performing, neither do they seem to pay much attention to their own singing. They sing or hum in a mechanical way with little affect or interest invested in it. It seems to provide a device for blocking the intake of most outside stimulation (even as individuals who find sleeping under noisy conditions difficult can block out the noise with a special instrument that gives off a monotonous sound).

Dissociational states that occur during the worship service among the Spiritual Baptists may develop from a phase of lesser involvement to a phase of increased involvement, and from an individualistic level to a group level. When an individual exhibits the first symptoms of a developing state of dissociation, he or she may be the only one in the congregation doing so at the time. Or there may be several individuals, scattered through the prayer house, who are affected. The trancer may be one of the passive worshipers, or may be the person who has been preaching, testifying, or praying.

If the trancer is a member of the audience, he or she has been sleepily humming, singing, or chanting responses, and probably overtly emphasizing the rhythm established by the hymn or prayer—if seated, by rocking back and forth, twisting from side to side, tapping the feet, clapping the hands, or nodding the head, and if standing, by swaying from side to side, or by swinging about in a semicircle, pivoting first on one foot then on the other, while clapping the hands or slapping the Bible or prayer book. The first outward indication of a state of dissociation may be a convulsive jerk of one or both arms, shoulders, or head; a shiver, a shudder, shaking or trembling; a sudden shout, sob, hiss, or a series of unintelligible vocalizations. Or the person may suddenly stand up and dance in place. If several persons in the group are affected at the same time, in this initial phase, each individual will display a different set of symptoms. These spontaneous signs of inner lessening of external control have a random quality and lack the rhythmic patterning that develops in the next level of dissociation. In the beginning phase of the unfolding dissociational state, then, the characteristic signs, viewed either for the individual or for the group, are without regularity or order. It is interesting to note, however, that each trancer develops his or her own peculiar style, so that the movements and sounds of a particular individual can often be predicted and thus can identify the person, at this level. For example, one woman, who was observed repeatedly, would always drop her head on her chest as though dozing, then she would jerk head back while raising her arm with fist tightly clenched and shout "Hi! Yi!" When another woman was in this stage of dissociation, she would always shake her shoulders and jerk both arms forward and up, while sobbing.

If the person who has been preaching, praying, or testifying is the one who is affected, the first outward indication of developing trance may be a quaver in his or her voice. He or she may also jerk spasmodically, shake, or tremble, or interrupt the prayer, testimonial, or sermon with a yell. He or she may become restless and excited, and, if standing, may pace back and forth more rapidly. But at this stage trancers do maintain sufficient control to be able to continue speaking and to be understood.

The level of dissociation might not proceed beyond this first stage. The manifestations described might subside more or less quickly, perhaps to be repeated after another period of preparation. Or they might persist for some time with dissociation being maintained at this level. As more and more individuals become involved in first-level dissociational states, however, some trancers may begin to slip into the next phase. And although both levels of trance can—and may—continue simultaneously for a while, eventually all, or most, of the dissociated individuals will exhibit behavior characteristic of the second level.

At the second level, each trancer repeats his own unique action pattern quite rapidly, over and over again. For some individuals, only the head and arms are involved; for others, more of the body. Whether sitting or standing, most trancers bend forward from the waist, but if they are on their feet, they will also bend their knees slightly. They may shuffle their feet or hop, but they rarely wander very far from their places. Some trancers roll their eyes back so that only the whites show. Others keep their eyes closed. Some show signs of profuse sweating (which might not seem unusual considering the hot, humid climate and the physical exertion involved), but others engaged in the same activities, do not. Some trancers spray saliva, but none of them froths at the mouth. And there is no yelling or shouting at the second level as there was in the earlier phase. Furthermore, dissociated individuals at this level are much less susceptible to external stimulation than they are at the previous level—I observed repeatedly that the light from a flash bulb in no way disturbed second level trances, whereas the flash would disrupt first level trances.

Hyperventilation is characteristic of the second level of trance. One of the church leaders often achieved this level of dissociation when he was on his knees, offering a prayer. He would bend forward and put his knuckles on the ground, gorilla-fashion, almost touch his head to the ground, and then jerk back and up while gasping loudly. The sequence was rapidly repeated, over and over again. Another leader, when seated, would bend his head down almost to his knees, then jerk his head up and back. He would bubble his lips on the way down and audibly take in gulps of air on the way up.

Whatever idiosyncratic movements, sounds, or breathing peculiarities prevail, however, will be subordinated to the rhythmic beat that all trancers maintain at the second level. It is immaterial whether the dissociational states have developed during a prayer, sermon, testimonial, or hymn—in any event, there has been singing, humming, or chanting to provide the trancers with a beat. If dissociation develops during the singing of a hymn, the words, which were distinct and understandable at the beginning, slowly disintegrate into repeated syllables. These, it turn, become grunts and gasps, emitted in unison by the trancers and in time to the established beat, as the second level of trance is achieved.

In the first level of dissociation, the sounds made by the various trancers can be singled out on a tape of the proceedings and in many cases, as mentioned previously, the person responsible can be identified. A salient difference between first- and second-level trances is the solo as opposed to the group aspect. At the second level, the sounds are so well blended that it is impossible to identify anyone from the sounds alone; the trancers no longer sound like individual performers, but like a choir. Understandable speech, of course, is not produced in the second phase.

In situations where the worshipers are standing and are crowded together (as they might be if they had been singing a hymn at an outdoor meeting, for example), the corporate character of the performance is further enhanced. Not only are the breathing sounds in the second-level dissociational state kept to a precise tempo, but the motion patterns are also depersonalized and unified so that each trancer is reproducing the same movements as if in a chorus line. This was observed several times when the group was huddled together. Each trancer was bent over at the waist with knees flexed, breathing noisily and bobbing up and down in time with everyone else. This phenomenon seems to be very similar to the "trumping and laboring" described by Moore (1965:64) for several Jamaican revival cults: "a shuffling, twostep dance done to 2/2 rhythm, bending forward and up in rhythmic sequence, while sucking the breath into the body and releasing it with a grunting sound."

Eventually this smooth, aesthetically pleasing rhythmic performance gives way to a third level of dissociation in which movements and sounds are again random and spasmodic and without discernible pattern. If the trancers had been huddled together, some now wander away from the group, and then further undo the choral aspect of the phenomenon by interjecting idiosyncratic movements that ignore the tempo that had been established and maintained previously. Breathing ceases to be a disciplined group activity spaced at set intervals; irregularly timed yells and loud sighs obliterate the rhythm. But in contrast to the first level, the sounds produced now are not spotty occasional yells against a musical background. Trancers in the third level do not sing or hum. They produce gasps, groans, sighs, and shouts in profusion. They sound, and appear to be, bewildered and breathless. The scene is one of general confusion. However, no special treatment is required to bring the trancers back to normal, and states of dissociation at this phase can be terminated within a short time.

In comparing dissociational states as they occur among the Spiritual Baptists with sexual responses as reported by Masters and Johnson (1966), certain similarities are obvious.[2] Masters and Johnson have diagrammed the male and female sexual response cycles as progressing through four phases: excitement, plateau, orgasm, and finally resolution, which brings the individual back to an "unstimulated state." The developmental course of typical trances can be diagrammed as proceeding from a pre-trance, "normal" level, to the first level in which trance involvement begins to appear, through the second level in which the highest phase of the experience is reached, to the third level in which dissociation is lessening and dissipating, and then to a post-trance, "normal" level.[3] The sexual response diagram and the trance diagram are quite similar (see Fig. 1). Both phenomena build to a climax of maximum involvement, which then dissipates. In both, appropriate stimuli are requisite for development, and in both, relaxation and tension-reduction are outcomes.

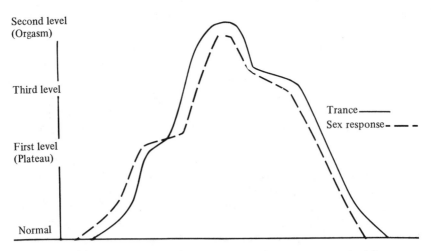

Figure 8.1. Development of a dissociational state compared with the male sexual response cycle, adapted from Masters and Johnson (1966:5).

Certain physiological reactions are also similar. Hyperventilation is common to both phenomena. And, unlike some Carribean religious groups, the Spiritual Baptists do not hyperventilate to induce dissociation. As in the sexual response cycle, hyperventilation occurs later in the course of the dissociational state and continues throughout the second level of trance even as it does through the entire orgasmic phase. Perspiring also occurs in both experiences, and, with trancers even as with persons participating in sexual intercourse, not all individuals are equally affected. Some trancers were observed who perspired copiously, others gave no outward indication of perspiring. However, perspiration does not appear late in the course of dissociation as it does in the sexual cycle, but may be observed at all trance levels. Spasmodic movements of arms, neck, face, and legs are also common features, but with the general body position being a factor in musculature involvement in both states of dissociation and sexual intercourse.

Diversions occurring at an early stage in the build-up leading to orgasm or second-level trance states can affect the progress of either phenomena. A developing dissociational state can be aborted or interrupted by inappropriate happenings. I have already mentioned the effect of light from a flash bulb, but occasionally just getting the camera ready was a sufficient disturbance to prompt an incipient trancer to become alert and turn, smiling for the picture. Masters and Johnson (1966:183) report that "a sudden loud noise, vocalization on an extraneous subject, or an obvious change in lighting, temperature, or attendant personnel may result in partial or even complete loss of penile erection" during the excitement phase of the sex act.

The Spiritual Baptist trancers resemble female participants in sexual intercourse in some ways. Females involved in sex are "capable of rapid return to orgasm immediately following an orgasmic experience if restimulated before tensions have dropped below plateau-phase response levels" and they are also capable of "maintaining an orgasmic experience for a relatively long period of time" (Masters and Johnson 1966: 131). Given the proper stimulation (as for example, a situation where most other trances have persisted at the second level, or where the rhythmic beat has either been maintained or, if not, has been quickly reestablished), trancers can slip from second to third level and then return to second-level trances repeatedly, provided they have not returned to a posttrance normal state in the meantime (see Fig. 2). And, like female sex participants, trancers may persist in a dissociated state for a relatively long period of time.

In contrast to the obvious differential behavior of males and females during a sexual experience, however, behavioral differences between dissociated males and females were indiscernible in the context of the Spiritual Baptist worship service. The various trancers had their own idiosyncratic motion and vocal habits, but these did not lend themselves to classification on the basis of sex. Nor did informants mention any sex dissimilarities in the observable phy-

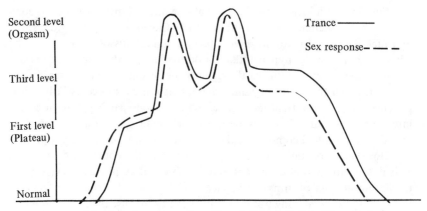

Figure 8.2. Development of a dissociational state with repeated returns to the second level of trance compared with a female sexual response cycle involving multiple orgasms, adapted from Masters and Johnson (1966:5).

siological aspects of the dissociational states that occurred outside the worship service, although they did report sex distinguishing characteristics of a different nature, which will be discussed later. However, it is quite possible that more refined observations and the collection of precise measurements for dissociational states, similar to the work that Masters and Johnson have done on sexual intercourse, might reveal not only sex differences in states of dissociation, but further interesting similarities between dissociation and sexual response as well.

According to the Spiritual Baptist belief system, both males and females are eligible to serve as hosts for the Holy Spirit, and the Holy Spirit may possess persons of either sex indiscriminately. (Numerically, more women than men appeared to be dissociated during worship services, but more women attend the meetings than men; the percentage of women involved in trance seemed to be about the same as the percentage of men.) The gratifications that individuals stand to derive from dissociational states, however, differ to some extent depending upon sex, regardless of whether the altered states are interpreted as possession by the Holy Spirit or not, and regardless of whether or not the trances occur within the context of the worship service. The Spiritual Baptist adherents are drawn principally from the lower class—the politically, economically, and socially less privileged portion of the society—those persons in the society whose prestige yearnings are satisfied least adequately and whose identity images are likely to suffer most. The Spiritual Baptist religion offers these individuals a number of advantages, among them the opportunity to achieve prestige within the cult and to bolster their identity images through the mechanisms of possession-trance and trance, and through the various offices that are available in the church hierarchy.

But let us examine in more detail the general social milieu of St. Vincent in which the Spiritual Baptists are submerged and also inspect more closely some of the beliefs and practices of the Spiritual Baptist church. We will then consider the apparent consequences of the Vincentian environment and the specific religious system insofar as they have relevance for this discussion. How are lower-class individuals, the most likely candidates for the Spiritual Baptist church, regarded by the rest of the society? What about differential treatment of males and females within and without the church? What kinds of opportunities and advantages are available to one sex or the other? How can the situation that prevails in the larger society be assuaged, or perhaps exacerbated, by the Spiritual Baptist church for its male and its female followers? How can the beneficial prestige that is available in the church be realized—how can an improved identity image be accomplished? And are these benefits equally available to both sexes, and equally sought by both?

Fraser (1975) has investigated the class structure of St. Vincent. He states that between 75 and 80 percent of the population, or perhaps more, fall into the lower-class category, "made up of rural and urban laborers, small-holders, share-croppers and tenant farmers, fishermen, and the unemployed" (p. 199). He goes on to say, however, that "individuals...have a fair degree of mobility throughout the system, and there have been cases of people rising from the very bottom to near the top of the social pyramid" (p. 198). And indeed, everyone either knows, or knows of, exceptional individuals who have made unusual leaps in socioeconomic status.

The instances of upward mobility that I was aware of included members of both sexes, but the mode of achievement was different for each sex. Several males were able to reach higher-status positions through the agencies of the educational system and the political system. One man qualified for scholarship assistance and became an attorney. At the primary level, education in St. Vincent is free. At the secondary level, various scholarships are available to cover or defray the costs of tuition, books, and board. Some are provided by the government, some by the Banana Association, the Town Board, the Old Girls, and so on. Those students who are eligible to apply for a scholarship are identified by their primary teachers. And the qualified secondary school graduate may obtain further education through a system of Island scholarships to the University of Jamaica. Another man improved his position by becoming active in politics and being elected to a high public office. The statuses of several women that I knew also improved substantially—not by their own efforts, however, but because they reflected their husbands' increased statuses. (Scholarships are open to females as well as males, but I did not happen to know a woman who had used this route to improved status.)

For the great bulk of the lower class, though, the amount of mobility—if, indeed, it occurs at all—will be much more modest, and many lower-class Vincentians view themselves vis-à-vis the middle and upper classes as being in a more or less fixed position. They might yearn to extricate themselves (or be extricated) from a depressed status, but for many of them the day-to-day existence is sufficiently demanding that little remains of their physical or monetary resources to invest in the kinds of activities that would be necessary and appropriate for upward mobility of any significant magnitude. They are not above presuming upon a former relationship to exploit those who have made some gains, however. The public official mentioned before was approached by several less fortunate individuals for temporary jobs when they needed money for a special purpose—"we has to beg him for a few days' work," which they were sure he would provide because "he teach me in school."

Members of the lower class who are also members of the Spiritual Baptist church may find in the church services additional reinforcement for their conviction that their socioeconomic position is relatively permanent and further support for their acceptance of that perceived reality. The message that is constantly being repeated in sermons, prayers, testimonials, and Bible lessons, is that they, the underprivileged, are actually God's chosen elite. Since they follow His word closely, they are destined for an eventual eternity in Heaven. On the other hand, those who strive for material possessions and high standing, and who are not doing the Lord's bidding—the upper classes—are doomed. Thus, the church devotees are provided with a rationalization for their position in the society, whatever their sex, although they are probably unaware of this latent function.

In spite of the fact that lower-class women may not be as likely as lower-class men to personally achieve a dramatic upward shift in status, nevertheless, they are, generally speaking, in a somewhat more comfortable economic position than men. Lower-class women on the island of St. Vincent, like women of other Caribbean islands and West Africa, have inherited an economic tradition of petty trading restricted to their sex (cf. Mintz 1960, 1964; Jahn 1968; Tanner 1974). Through this avenue of entry into the economic subfield of the public domain (see Sanday 1974), Vincentian women gain monetary rewards, but perhaps more importantly they also gain independence and self-esteem and a measure of contentment and satisfaction.

Very little capital or effort is required for a woman to set herself up in business. If she has access to a little land, she can plant a garden—even on a city lot, even on rented property. Growing conditions are quite favorable on the island; soil is fertile and rainfall adequate. Very soon, the surplus crop can be taken to market. St. Vincent does have some large farms[4] where male and female laborers work for wages and the crop—arrowroot, bananas, some Sea Island cotton and coconuts—is principally intended for export. But food crops grown for local consumption—breadfruit, root crops, and so on—are produced mainly on small plots of land, and sold in the local markets by women. A woman can realize additional profits if she raises a pig or two to sell. She can set up shop with a few candy bars and perhaps a charcoal brazier for roasting peanuts near a school where she can catch the pupils at recess. She can buy wholesale lots of various commodities as she is financially able, and then sell the items at retail prices. Nor are her endeavors restricted to the island of St. Vincent. If she feels so inclined, she may pack up her inventory, take a boat to the neighboring island of Bequia or one of the other islands of the Grenadines and sell her stock there. And she can stockpile part of her small profits over a period of time, and eventually she may be able to achieve a goal that is common among the women; she may be able to buy a little land and a house of her own.

The same channels of access to the economic domain that are utilized by women are not open to lower-class men. They are less able to operate independently as entrepreneurs and are more dependent on working for others. Women, too may be employed by others—as domestic helpers, as members of road-building crews (women carry gravel and sand in trays on their heads), as part-time workers when a banana boat is in the harbor ready to be loaded, and so on—but the other alternative is available to them, while it is not an option for men. A further possibility exists for some women—they may be supported adequately by their husbands and may not have to work if they do not want to, which is a source of considerable pride for a wife and is undoubtedly a great satisfaction for the male, since he is fulfilling the societal ideal. Because the economic conditions on the island are so dismal, most lower-class men yearn to leave, hoping for more lucrative opportunities elsewhere. Some of them are able to realize their desires. They may be hired by shipping lines, or they may find work in North America, England, or Trinidad. Emigration, however, is by no means restricted to males. Even though women generally seem to find more fulfillment and satisfaction with the local job opportunities available to them than men do, still some of them also find the prospect of leaving the island to work overseas very inviting.

Other cultural features also contribute to the independence, self-reliance, and generally more effective accommodation to the social system that is evident among the lower-class women. Childrearing practices provide differential experiences, challenges, and sanctions for boys and girls. Distinctive treatment begins with infants. Mothers will proudly remark that their boy babies are "so bad," and imply that the baby is too much even for an adult to control. Thus they indicate quite early the importance of the principle Wilson (1973: 227) found operating specifically among males in the area of social relationships on the island of Providencia, and which he labeled "reputation," defining it as "a standard of value, of moral measurement of a person's worth derived from his conduct with other people." Girl babies are not expected to be "bad"—they are supposed to be more docile and manageable than boys. From about the age of two, however, all children are expected to be obedient, respectful, and quiet. They are subjected to persistent nagging, frequently admonished to "hush!" and "be quiet!" (even if they are silent and still at the moment), and corporal punishment is a common sanction. Little boys, partly, perhaps, because of their earlier conditioning, seem to behave in ways that invite correction more often than little girls, but boys are given much more freedom and are able to escape from adult supervision sooner and more completely than girls. There is a strong tendency for boys to drop out of school early (thereby depriving themselves of a resource that might have been instrumental in bettering their future economic situation) and to spend much of their time wandering about with the peer group, which becomes increasingly important and influential for them.

Girls tend to continue their education longer. Perhaps the value of an education is more obvious to them given the kinds of economic opportunities that await them. Perhaps their early socialization experiences have rendered them more conforming. But, turning again to Wilson's (1973: 104) analysis of Providencia, which seems applicable to St. Vincent as well, perhaps because education is a component of that principle that he observed as being more important to women than reputation—"respectability," a constellation of values that serves as a rationale for stratification in the society. "Manners, good taste, and moral sensibility," accouterments of respectability, are conferred by education. Hence, women are more eager to acquire an education and its concomitant benefits. Wilson noted—though he cautions that it was only an impression—"that women far more than men were keen on their children going to school, and girls were given every opportunity for an education". My impression was the same. All my female informants stressed the number of years they had attended school and how much they had enjoyed it. Without exception they expressed regret that they had been unable to continue their education further, and many indicated concern and interest in the education of their children—to the extent that some of them were paying for a parochial school education in the lower grades even though free public school education was available at that level.

Girls are also kept busy at home, helping with younger children and with other tasks, and they are apt to be closely associated with their female kin group—mother, older sisters, aunts, and grandmothers—who can facilitate the girls' transition to adulthood in ways not available to boys. In addition to teaching them the ordinary domestic and social skills, they may eventually introduce girls to prospective employers or encourage them to become vendors. Not all girls, of course, are able to remain in school, supported by family. For some, work becomes an economic necessity at a fairly early age, which means, in addition, more freedom from home restraints. Many girls, working or not, become sexually active in their teens and pregnancy is common. But the kin group can usually absorb the new member, freeing the young mother so that she can continue to work.

Lower-class attitudes toward marriage and a family are emancipating mechanisms for both sexes. Legal marriage is regarded as highly desirable, especially by the women, being linked as it is to the female value cluster subsumed under "respectability" (Wilson 1973: 100). But neither sex considers legal marriage, in any way, essential. Marriage may not even be considered by a couple, or it may be regarded as an unattainable goal—at least for the moment. Couples may marry later on after several children have been born, or even after children have been raised. Many households include no adult males. Male consanguines may live elsewhere because of work or other attachments, and the adult females of the household may not have entered into any reasonably stable relationships with male partners. Some households that do include a male-female unit are nonlegal arrangements, although they may be quite stable. And some few households, of course, do include a married pair.

The birth of children is expected and welcomed by both sexes. There is no notion that a woman can have "too many babies", nor is any feeling expressed that children contribute to a woman's lot of "never-ending drudgery" as is reported for some societies (for examples, see Rogers 1975: 733). Both parents are proud of their offspring, legitimate or illegitimate. One pregnant informant introduced her 12 children to me with obvious pride and pleasure. Each had a different father, and some of the older girls were already reproducing according to the same pattern. A father, who lived most of the time in the city away from his rural home and family because of part-time job possibilities, showed the same pride when presenting his numerous offspring, although he expressed the common male concern that he was not providing for them adequately. Males find considerable satisfaction in being able to provide well for their children. Even in the case of illegitimate offspring, fathers will willingly contribute to their support insofar as they can.

Male-female relationships have a somewhat ambiguous character. Women are unquestionably self-assured and independent. Single women and women maintaining a relationship with a man, with or without a shared-household arrangement, are understandably apt to operate as distinct, detached entities in many situations. But even married women seem to conceptualize themselves as separate from the husband-wife unit. The first person singular is quite conspicuous in their speech: "*I* buy a house," "*I* sell *my* breadfruit," "*I* go to the meeting" (even though the husband is also going), "*I* send *my* children to the Catholic school," and so on.

Yet, when a group includes both sexes, the males are deferred to. In an informal, social gathering, the men will be seated while the women wait on them, serving them food and drink. The women will often vie for male attention, and try to amuse the men by being coy and silly. A woman may even attempt to provoke a man's anger and, quite deliberately, it would seem, try to force him into assuming a dominant position. One woman, on such an occasion, persisted in teasing the head of the church until he became so exasperated that he picked up a switch and gave her a half a dozen hefty strokes with it. Although she was still laughing, she was also crying and wiping her eyes—but she seemed satisfied that she had achieved her goal. In the formal church context, women in the congregation—those without offices in the church—will often vacillate between quiet attention and inattentive giggling and whispering. The disruptive behavior, again, appears to be a deliberate ploy to attract the attention of a man and to coerce him into assuming an authoritative, perhaps punitive, posture. The Pointer will usually oblige them by lashing at them with his strap or sanctioning their behavior in some other way. Thus, in ways such as these, women continue the process of shaping and perpetuating the ideal image of the male as virile, aggressive, active, and dominant that they had begun when the man was still an infant. And the men, although they obviously enjoy the status and role conferred upon them by the women, are often frustrated, then, by their inability to operate in the same capacity outside the church and class community and by the contrasting appraisal attached to them and their efforts by the larger society.

Thus, there seems to be no real struggle against male authority among lower-class women. Feelings of deprivation and discrimination that do exist seem to be more prevalent among men than women, and they seem to be generated more by the class structure than by differential access to power based on sex. Members of the upper classes may openly deride lower-class individuals, whether male or female, and tend to regard them with some contempt, characterizing them as lazy, slovenly, and lacking in intelligence. The resulting abused identity image can be somewhat more crucial for lower-class males than females since males may derive further corroboration of the stereotype from the economic domain, while females may find comfort in the contradictory evidence that their more successful economic ventures provide.

For those lower-class individuals who are also followers of the Spiritual Baptist church, there are teachings and practices that can ameliorate distress experienced in the larger society. The church community is an elite community. No one joins the church in the first place unless he or she has seen a vision, or had a dream or some other experience that can be interpreted as an invitation to join from the Holy Spirit. Those persons who become dissociated during the worship service demonstrate further, and quite convincingly, to themselves and to their fellow worshipers that they are worthy and righteous—since, according to Spiritual Baptist beliefs, the Holy Spirit only enters and shakes those individuals who are pure.

Additional corroboration of worth can be derived from the Spiritual Baptist ritual known as "mourning." Those members who participate in the ritual are eligible to fill certain offices in the church structure, but "going to mourn," like joining the church, is for special, selected persons—those who have received a sign from the Holy Spirit. "Mourning" involves remaining in isolation under conditions of sensory deprivation for an extended period of time, perhaps two weeks or more. During isolation, dissociational states occur in the form of hallucinations, which are interpreted as taking a "spirit journey." The hallucinatory content, reported by the mourner and confirmed by the Pointer, reveals the work in the church that the person is destined to perform, as well as the appropriate identifying uniform and equipment to which he or she is entitled. Division of labor on the basis of sex is largely maintained: women mourners discover that they are to fill a woman's position in the church, that they are to wear a dress of a particular color and style, and a head-tie of a certain color. Males, similarly, find that they are to fill male positions, and are to wear or carry the designating paraphernalia for their offices.[5]

The church also provides an opportunity for lower-class individuals to talk—any person, regardless of sex, can address the congregation and God in prayer, sermon, or testimonial—and to be the focus of attention. In the larger society, these people are denied opportunities for verbal expression with the expectation that others will listen. Yet they thoroughly enjoy talking and hold proficiency with language in high esteem—a trait they share with other Caribbean societies (see Wilson 1975). In the church, the desire or need to verbalize can be realized, and the talker can occupy center stage for a long period of time and be assured of an audience.

Generally speaking, women are subordinate to men in the church. Spiritual Baptists will recite Bible verses to support and explain discriminatory practices (for example, concerning the requirement that women cover their heads in church, or that a man should be head of a church). So, although women have opportunities to hold positions of leadership in the Spiritual Baptist church—which is in distinct contrast to the leadership opportunities for women in the large, organized churches on the island—their offices are still subordinate to the male office of Pointer. Furthermore, women greatly outnumber men in the church, yet all of the men have official positions, whereas the majority of women do not. And these women—never men—are the potential recipients of sanctions—at the hands of a male—for misbehaving during services.

Henry and Wilson (1975) surveyed the literature concerning the status of women in Caribbean societies and were convinced that women "by and large, play a subservient role to men particularly in economic and social areas...and that women frequently are forced to hide their potential talents and abilities" (p. 165). In lower-class fundamentalist religious groups, however, they discovered "one of the few areas in society where women find some measure of equality with significant others" (p. 190). In the Spiritual Baptist church context, it is true that some women do find some measure of equality (the Holy Ghost possesses and shakes males and females equally, both sexes are eligible for church membership and church office, and so forth), but for most of the individuals involved, a situation contrary to Henry's and Wilson's findings seems to obtain. We do not find the usual state of affairs with the men achieving dominance in the public domain and the women being in need of outlets such as religion to compensate for their concomitant insignificance in the public domain. In the lower-class Vincentian Spiritual Baptist community, women are relatively more important in the economic sphere and men tend to have more importance in the religious sphere. Religion, here, may indeed be functional as a balancing mechanism. But, with its emphasis on males and on the ideally appropriate subordinate position of women validated by the Holy Scriptures, it would seem to compensate lower-class men more than lower-class women for their lack of dominance in the public domain of economic and political affairs. The church may also serve as a compensatory device for some women, not, however, because their men outrank them in the public domain, but because they do not. The attitude of indulgent playfulness with which women assume the subordinate role has a conspicuously calculated quality about it. They may find, in the church service and in the church community, satisfaction for an acquired need to feel dependent and childlike, but, at the same time, they are catering to the male ego and continuing to press the male into the ideal mold.

It is interesting to note that the general sex-differentiated socialization practices carry over into the church context. Little girls, more often than little boys, accompany their mothers to the meetings, and the girls conduct themselves in a proper, acceptable way. They are quiet and unobtrusive to the point of being overlooked, which must be something of a feat since the meetings are very lengthy—some last all afternoon and evening. At one meeting where some little boys were present, two of them played quietly and unnoticed for several hours. But, as time went on, and they became more engrossed in their games and less attentive to their surroundings, they also became more active and noisy until they distracted the Pointer. He angrily directed someone to remove them, and shortly after sounds of slapping and crying could be heard. When the boys returned, they remained silent and subdued the rest of the evening. Such behavior as to attract sanctions was never observed with little girls.

The male who holds the highest position as Pointer of the church acquires additional power and prestige as well as increased duties and responsibilities. (As has been mentioned, at the time of the initial field research it was learned that only a man should be the head of a church—the few Spiritual Baptist churches with women in the top position were ridiculed). Dissociational states are of a different order for the Pointer. The Divine gives special abilities and insights to him as His agent for carrying out His will. The Pointer is believed to have a superior ability to speak in tongues (his "telephone line" to God), and is believed to be the only person in the church who can understand what all the other worshipers who have this gift are saying. The Holy Spirit may reveal information about the misdeeds of church members to the Pointer that he would not otherwise be in a position to know or discover. Then, while in an altered state and possessed by the Spirit, the Pointer may serve as an extension of the Spirit in meting out punishment to the wrongdoer. Thus, the Pointer's relationship with the supernatural is of a higher order than that of the ordinary worshiper. He is in closer communication with the Spirit. His privileges and powers are enhanced. But as the human mechanism through which the Spirit works he must also assume more responsibility. He not only judges and sanctions. He must be a decision maker—he evaluates the mourner's spirit journey and decides when the isolation period should be terminated, he determines when the baptismal candidates are ready for the rite, and so on. And he is also in a position to experience greater gratification for his prestige cravings that he cannot satisfy in the larger society than the untitled worshiper or the holder of a lesser office in the church.

SUMMARY AND CONCLUSIONS

The Spiritual Baptist church is one of a number of religious options open to lower-class individuals on the Caribbean island of St. Vincent. States of altered consciousness are featured prominently in the church services, during the "mourning" period, and are reported as a supernatural inducement to accept baptism and membership in the church or to submit to the "mourning" ritual. The states of dissociation that were observed in the church services developed in phases bearing considerable similarity to the developmental phases of sexual intercourse, with some aspects of the progression of the trance state being more like the female contribution to the sex act than the male component. Sex differences in overt trance behavior were not detected, but an analysis of the consequences of membership in the Spiritual Baptist church and participation in the positively valued trancing revealed differential benefits that might be acquired by males and females.

In Vincentian society, lower-class individuals generally lack influence and prestige. Their position of powerlessness may be sharply underscored by a tendency of the upper classes to openly ridicule and downgrade them. Lower class women, however, have been the fortunate beneficiaries of the West African pattern of female trading, and although their marketing ventures are on a relatively small scale, still the women do gain entry thereby into the economic arena. Thus, they have an opportunity that is not available to men to achieve a measure of financial stability, and, since the women tend to be oriented toward respectability, they are in a position, then, to fulfill some of the requirements for respectability at a material level. Hence, I have argued, lower-class women are apt to be more self-confident, more secure, and more satisfied with their perceived identity image than lower-class men.[6]

Men tend to be motivated by an emphasis on reputation rather than respectability—and women aid and abet this male orientation. That women may contribute substantially to the molding and shaping of the male personality has been noted by other investigators (for example, Mernissi 1975), and Vincentian women are no exception. They encourage and promote the qualities appropriate for the masculine reputation—virility, aggressiveness, achievement, and dominance—beginning with the infant and continuing into adulthood. But, by urging such role behavior on men, women contribute to male frustration since the female-encouraged identity image finds little validation in the larger society or at home. Most men are denied opportunities for independent or entrepreneurial statuses in the public domain, and their personal power is undermined by the economically more successful women.

The Spiritual Baptist church functions as a compensating and balancing mechanism for its members. Lower-class individuals can find in its teachings and practices a sense of self-worth, an opportunity for self-expression, and a more palatable perspective on their relationship to the other, better-endowed social classes. Men are compensated for their inferior public statuses by being especially favored in the church. Their unsuccessful attempts to attain the ideal male image, and particularly their inability to surpass and dominate women in everday life are balanced by the emphasis on male superiority and dominance in the church. Women can indulge themselves, meanwhile, in regressive behavior, and can temporarily assume a subordinate position with respect to the men.

We might question why more lower-class men do not join the Spiritual Baptist church if, indeed, it confers the benefits mentioned. Again, the importance of reputation for males and the economic limitations suggest some possible contributing factors. The Spiritual Baptist church is not highly respected by most Vincentians. And men, being employed by others, might feel that belonging to a stigmatized group would be disadvantageous in their economic, and reputational, struggles. Women would not be as likely to share that concern. And men might also be less attracted to a church (if they were attracted to a church at all) whose leader was only able to obtain part-time work than they might be to a religious group with a leader who was obviously successful.

But for the men who do join the church, the benefits seem clear. They may have to settle for reputation within the more restricted church community, but they also receive balm there for their injured egos. As for the women, although they appear to have relinquished a superior position to become subordinate for the time being, one has the impression that they are fully aware of what they are doing in catering to the men, and are enjoying what might be regarded in some ways as play.

NOTES

1. For a more complete discussion of this usage and the use of the labels, "T" and "P," see Bourguignon (Foreword in Goodman, Henney, Pressel 1974) and Henney (1968).

2. Much of the material in this section was originally presented in a paper (Henney 1972) given at the Symposium on Sex and Trance during the 1972 meetings of the American Anthropological Association in Toronto.

3. For a somewhat different conceptualization, see Henney (1974).

4. In 1961, according to the Economic Planning Unit's *Facts for Investors on Saint Vincent* (p. 28), the island had 32 farms of 100 acres or more, 390 farms of 10-100 acres, and 10,928 farms smaller than ten acres.

5. For a detailed description of the baptism and mourning rituals, see Henney (1974).

6. For a detailed discussion of the components of a person's identity image see Wallace and Fogelson (1965); for my application of their model to the Spiritual Baptist situation, see Henney (1973).

REFERENCES

Bourguignon, Erika
  1972 "Dreams and Altered States of Consciousness in Anthropological Research." In *Psychological Anthropology*. Francis L. K. Hsu, ed. Cambridge, Mass.: Schenkman Publishing Company.
  1974 Foreword. In *Trance, Healing, and Hallucination*. Felicitas D. Goodman, Jeannette H. Henney, Esther Pressel. New York: Wiley.

Fraser, Thomas M., Jr.
  1975 "Class and the Changing Bases of Elite Support in St. Vincent, West Indies. *Ethnology* 14: 197-209.

Goodman, Felicitas, Jeannette H. Henney, Esther Pressel
  1974 *Trance, Healing, and Hallucination: Three Field Studies in Religious Experience*. New York: Wiley.

Henney, Jeannette H.
  1968 Spirit Possession Belief and Trance Behavior in a Religious Group in St. Vincent, British West Indies. Ph.D. diss. The Ohio State University, Columbus, Ohio. Ann Arbor, Mich.: University Microfilms.
  1972 The relationship of trance and sex in a West Indies religious group. Paper presented to the Symposium on Trance and Sex at the 71st Annual Meeting of the American Anthropological Association, Toronto.

1973   "The Shakers of St. Vincent: A Stable Religion." In *Religion, Altered States of Consciousness, and Social Change.* Erika Bourguignon, ed. Columbus: The Ohio State University Press.

1974   "Spirit Possession Belief and Trance Behavior in Two Fundamentalist Groups in St. Vincent." In *Trance, Healing, and Hallucination.* Felicitas D. Goodman, Jeannette H. Henney, Esther Pressel.

Henry, Frances, and Pamela Wilson
1975   "The Status of Women in Caribbean Societies: An Overview of Their Social, Economic, and Sexual Roles." *Social and Economic Studies* 24:165-98.

Herskovits, M.J., and Frances S. Herskovits
1947   *Trinidad Village.* New York: Knopf.

Jahn, Janheinz
1968   "A Yoruba Market-Woman's Life." In *Every Man His Way.* Alan Dundes, ed. Englewood Cliffs, N.J.: Prentice-Hall.

Masters, William H., and Virginia E. Johnson
1966   *Human Sexual Response.* Boston: Little, Brown and Company.

Mernissi, Fatima
1975   *Beyond the Veil: Male-Female Dynamics in a Modern Muslim Society.* New York: Wiley.

Mintz, Sidney
1960   "Peasant Markets." *Scientific American* 203:112-18, 120, 122.

1964   "The Employment of Capital by Market Women in Haiti." In *Capital, Saving and Credit in Peasant Societies.* Raymond Firth and B. S. Yancey, eds. Chicago: Aldine.

Moore, Joseph G.
1965   "Religious Syncretism in Jamaica." *Practical Anthropology* 12: 63-70.

Rogers, Susan Carol
1975   "Female Forms of Power and the Myth of Male Dominance: A Model of Male/Female Interaction in Peasant Society." *American Ethnologist* 2: 727-56.

Sanday, Peggy R.
1974   "Female Status in the Public Domain." In *Women, Culture, and Society.* Michelle Zimbalist Rosaldo and Louise Lamphere, eds. Stanford: Stanford University Press.

Simpson, George E.
1970   *Religious Cults of the Caribbean: Trinidad, Jamaica, and Haiti.* Caribbean Monograph Series, No. 7.

Smith, M.G.
1963   *Dark Puritan.* Kingston, Jamaica: Department of Extramural Studies, University of the West Indies.

Tanner, Nancy
    1974   "Matrifocality in Indonesia and Africa and among Black Americans." In *Woman, Culture, and Society*. Michelle Zimbalist Rosaldo and Louise Lamphere, eds. Stanford: Stanford University Press.

Wallace, Anthony F. C., and Raymond D. Fogelson
    1965   "The Identity Struggle." In *Intensive Family Therapy*. Ivan Boszormenyi-Nagy and James L. Framo, eds. New York: Harper and Row.

Wilson, Peter J.
    1973   *Crab Antics: The Social Anthropology of English-Speaking Negro Societies of the Caribbean*. New Haven: Yale University Press.
    1975   *Oscar: An Inquiry into the Nature of Sanity*. New York: Vintage Books.

9 Adaptive Strategies and Social Networks of Women in St. Kitts

JUDITH D. GUSSLER

This chapter looks at the role of women in a generally poor plantation society in the non-Hispanic Caribbean, on the island of St. Kitts. Factors of poverty, migration, low incidence of marriage, and a high birth rate combine to make the lives of lower-class women difficult. Within this sociocultural system, children represent for men an affirmation of their masculinity and for women, potential support at later stages in life. Survival for a woman and her young children requires much ingenuity and diversification of effort. Women's strategies to "get by" include the development and utilization of a network of human resources. The author discusses the implications of these networks for lower-class women's social and geographic mobility, and she contrasts their form with those of middle-class women in the society of St. Kitts. The careful exploration and optimization of avenues of support, including the management of social networks, shows Kittitian lower-class women to be resourceful and often successful social actors.

A young friend wrote recently from St. Kitts:

> Righ [sic] now I am very broke I aint even have a cent to buy decoration for the house. Cant even get a job. If you do get a job they dont want to pay you sufficient money and some times they delay you. Its a lady living side me she cant walk so good it is she who do give me little change sometime to buy milk for them [the babies] and when she dont give me they would drink the plain boiling water...

I met this young woman in 1972 when I began field research on food distribution and social networks on the small West Indian island of St. Kitts.[1] When we met she was a child of 14; in 1977 she was a 19-year old unmarried mother of four children, living in poverty and ill health. While her plight is more serious than that of most other young women, they all share some of the problems of trying to raise families in a society where employment opportunities are scarce and incomes are low. The common difficulties faced by the women of St. Kitts produced in me both personal concern and anthropological curiosity. I sought to find why, in this generally poor nation, these young women are often relatively more deprived than some other categories of people and what actions they (the women) take to ameliorate their situation.

In this chapter, I will describe the major sociocultural and historical parameters of resource distribution, and discuss how they impinge specifically on the lives of Kittitian women. To do so, I must also describe the nature of Kittitian society in general, demonstrating how, in an individuated social system with few inclusive group structures, success often depends upon how effectively one establishes and utilizes links in the social network. Relationships of women to men, other women, even to their own children, are very often consciously viewed as social resources to be tapped now or as investments that will pay off in the future. Before this discussion, however, I will provide a brief culture history of the social system itself.

ST. KITTS: HISTORY AND GEOGRAPHY

The small island of St. Kitts is a land mass of approximately 68 square miles situated in the Leeward chain of islands in the eastern Caribbean. Being of volcanic origin, it is a fertile land, even after more than 300 years of continuous cultivation. The eastern portion of the island tapers off into an arid peninsula which reaches within two miles of the smaller sister island of Nevis. The mountains of the interior of St. Kitts intercept the clouds blown continuously by the trade winds, with the result that the western end of the island is well watered and lush with tropical vegetation. Here the fertile nature of the land is apparent, today yielding great amounts of sugar cane for sale in the world market.

St. Kitts was apparently discovered first by the Arawak Indians, according to prehistoric records, and next by the Carib Indians, who called it Liamuiga, the Fertile Island. The Caribs were there when Christoper Columbus "discovered" the land during his second trip to the New World in 1493,[2] and when European settlement began in the early part of the seventeenth century. The British settlers occupied the central portion of the island, and the French the east and west ends, which they named Basseterre and Capesterre, respectively. The capital of St. Kitts dates to this period of French occupation. In an early spirit of cooperation, the French and British worked out a plan of coexistence that included the extermination of the Caribs. Despite the fact that the Indians had lived more or less peacefully with the settlers and provided them with food from time to time, they were killed or driven to other islands during the early years of colonization (Merrill 1958: 51; Parry and Sherlock 1957: 48).

During the later years of the seventeenth century, the British bought out French claims on St. Kitts, but the French and Spanish both challenged the British hold on the island repeatedly throughout the next 100 years of their occupation. By the nineteenth century, however, St. Kitts was a colony in the British Empire, and remained so until 1967 when it became an Associated State with a measure of independence.

Early colonists grew tobacco, indigo, ginger, and cotton for markets at home. However, these crops rapidly depleted the soils, and the farmers were unable to compete with the North American colonies. Thus, when sugar cane was introduced (*ca.* 1640) it quickly became the major product of the island. The establishment of sugar cane production as the economic base of the island resulted in far-reaching social change. Sugar cane requires large areas of cultivatable land, a large cheap labor force (before mechanization), and relatively expensive equipment and sophisticated technology to be profitable. The "sugar revolution" on St. Kitts and other West Indian islands had a threefold effect: first, there was a demise of independent small-scale farming and an exodus of many poor white Europeans; second, many African slaves were imported to fill labor needs; and, third, the plantation type of socioeconomic organization developed, comprised of white managers and overseers, and a large black population of dependent workers.

In St. Kitts, these effects were more extensive and enduring than on most other islands. Sugar has maintained its hold on the Kittitian economy even through years of failing prosperity. And the sugar estates have maintained their hold on the Kittitian people. On some of the larger islands of the Caribbean, slaves were encouraged to grow their own foods in order to reduce the need for expensive imported foods. On St. Kitts, however, it was deemed a better strategy for the estate owners to put all agricultural lands into cane production, and import foods for the slaves. Slaves were allowed to establish provision gardens on marginal lands, such as on the sides of ghauts, but these gardens were too small and unproductive to serve as the basis for a peasant farming economy after emancipation. In fact, emancipation of slaves in 1833 changed the life-style of most Kittitians very little. They moved out of the estate yards into independent villages, but the individuals in these villages were still dependent on the estates for their livelihood. Many are today.

During these years, many of the British colonists returned home, establishing a pattern of absentee landlordism. This later exodus of successful colonists, following upon the earlier one of poor whites, resulted in an island population that is predominantly black (98 percent "African" or "mixed") and poor. The poverty is partially a function of too many people competing for too few jobs in a single industry which has too many competitors in the world market. In an effort to enhance their position in the world sugar market, estate controllers have attempted both mechanization and consolidation, but the accompanying efficiency of production is a mixed blessing on an island with a large poor population. One historian has pointed out that at some time, presumably during the nineteenth century, the problem of a chronic labor shortage on St. Kitts became a problem of chronic under- and unemployment (Merrill 1958:98). The lack of jobs becomes even more serious as machines take over the work of men and women, but the problem in St. Kitts has been compounded by an increasingly militant and powerful labor union. When disgruntled workers stayed away from their jobs during the 1960s, the men who controlled the sugar industry were encouraged to get new machines to do their work for them. Modernization of the sugar industry has also failed to solve another perpetual labor problem, which stems from the seasonal nature of sugar work. Labor utilization—male labor—is intense from February or March until August, but for the balance of the year only occasional estate work is available.

The labor union of St. Kitts became an organized political force during the 1960s, and after the island was granted independence, the Labour Party assumed control of the government. Since that time, it has also gradually assumed control over the sugar industry, and, thus, the island's economic system. In this new position of political power, the Labour government is also attempting to stimulate tourism, which has had very little impact on the island economy up to now. Labour has not solved the ultimate problems of Kittitian economic development, but it has improved incomes for sugar workers to some degree and has helped erase the stigma of slavery from such work.

Continuing stresses from overpopulation and underemployment have been alleviated somewhat over the years through population migration. Throughout this century, Kittitians have moved off the island in response to economic opportunities—working on shipping fleets and navies, on the Panama Canal, and in the tourist hotels in the Virgin Islands. This movement of people has been important, not just because it has eased population pressures and job competition on the island, but because those Kittitians working overseas have traditionally sent a part of their incomes to their families back home. These remittances have long been an important source of income for the people who have by choice or necessity remained home. In fact, one official of the sugar industry admitted that Kittitians receive as much income from remittances as from sugar estate wages.

THE PEOPLE OF ST. KITTS

The people of St. Kitts, then, can be described as black, poor, and highly mobile. The Kittitians who remain home live in either the capital Basseterre (population, approximately 13,000) or in one of the smaller towns and villages that lie alongside the island's single major road. Out of the total population of nearly 40,000 people, more than three-quarters could be classified as "lower stratum" on the basis of occupation, level of education attained, and features of their life styles. Among these features are a low incidence of marriage, a high birth rate, and a high rate of illegitimate births. The rate of illegitimate first births, for example, exceeds 90 percent, and the overall figure for all births approaches 80 percent. (These percentages include births to mid- and upper-stratum mothers, as well; thus, the figures for the lower stratum are somewhat higher.) Many of the households, then, are headed by women, and some of these span three or even four generations. They also may include women, men, and children who are more distantly related or, occasionally, who are not kin at all. Economic necessity rather than kinship is the primary parameter of household composition. Men who are neither married nor living in a "consensual union" with a woman, may live alone or share quarters with other kinfolk; again, the major constraints are availability of space and economic necessity, rather than traditional and recognized social bonds. The nuclear family household is more common in the mid and upper strata, but in some of the villages, there are few middle-class families and the elite may not be represented at all.

Adaptive opportunism is also reflected in the economic pursuits of lower stratum folk in St. Kitts. Very few of the poorer people can afford to tap only one resource. A man, for example, may work in the cane fields several months of the year, raise a few vegetables and sell the surplus to a "turnhand" (a market woman, equivalent to the Jamican "higgler"), break rock and sell the gravel, help another man construct a house, and receive a small money gift from an overseas relative. None of these activities will bring a man much money, perhaps the equivalent of $500 to $1,000 U.S. dollars for the year. For a woman, the situation can be more serious, since there are relatively few jobs for women on the sugar estates. Lower-class women can and do garden. However, it is a long and hot walk to the gardens in the mountians, made more difficult by pregnancy (a common state) and the necessity of caring for small children. Even with the occasional help of a good friend or close relative, working the hilly land with nothing more than a heavy bladed hoe will usually yield only enough yams and sweet potatoes for family consumption. A woman with several children may have no surplus to sell to turnhands.

While these Kittitian women have to shoulder the burdens of family finances and nurturance, they also have the relative independence and self-determination that goes with being a head of household. Women in the Caribbean, and their West African ancestral counterparts, have always had significant supradomestic roles. In the plantation societies, slave women were too important economically to be merely bearers of new slaves, and their work included weeding cane fields, growing ground provisions, and marketing locally grown produce. The question of whether their gardening and marketing activities have a West African provenance or are a product of a slavery system in which men's labor was strictly controlled by and for the sugar estate is immaterial. Probably the roles are an outcome of the interaction between Old World cultural remnants, ethnohistorical trends, and continuing poverty. It is necessary only to point out that these are and have long been designated women's activities, important both for the women who participate in them and for the island economy. These roles were not restricted to the house and yard, but involved the women in the daily activities of the island world outside the household. Kittitian females move freely and independently about the towns and villages, relatively unfettered by cultural constraints which relegate women in some societies to a strictly domestic role.

The "turnhand," for example, remains the major distributor, wholesaler, and retailer, of locally grown provisions. Since the island lacks adequate transportation and storage facilities to move these fresh foods in bulk, women provide the service a few pieces at a time. Buying up extra sweet potatoes, yams, dasheens, tannias, carrots, tomatoes, cabbages, pumpkins, mangoes, and so on, they carry the items to the marketplace in Basseterre. Some turnhands are strictly "middlepeople" and sell their goods to those women who are retailers; others will rent a stall and sell. These women usually establish a network of regular customers who will buy only from them. They, in turn, will save choice or scarce items for their regulars. I was fortunate to establish a relationship such as this with a turnhand, since a friend and informant was one of the woman's customers. I discovered, in fact, that these mutual obligations extend beyond the marketplace. My friend and I bought "sweeties" for our children from a vendor woman at a cricket match in Basseterre, only to spy "our" turnhand, who was similarly selling snacks to the fans. My friend was so concerned at this slight that she purchased more candy and peanuts with her remaining money, and the turnhand reciprocated by throwing in some free sweeties for the little ones.

Gardening and marketing are among the oldest supradomestic activities of Kittitian women, but they are certainly not the only ones. In fact, women's economic roles are suprisingly varied on this small island. Most of the villagers I observed breaking rock into gravel, for example, were female. Women work in cane fields, although they do not cut or load sugar cane. They prepare food specialties, such as sugar cakes, black pudding, and souse, and sell them in the village, in Basseterre, and sometimes in the schoolyards. None of these traditional activities provide women with much of an income, but through a combination of them they can feed their families.

Women have moved relatively easily into the modernizing and middle-class Kittitian society. St. Kitts has female police officers, clerks, bank tellers, bookkeepers, factory workers, and intermediate level government officials. This involvement of women in the economic realm may, in part, be an artifact of the high rate of male migration; however, since women are now migrating too in great numbers, this is not a sufficient explanation. More important, in my observation, is that in this society the competency and significance of women are generally not challenged.

For many of the lower-stratum women, improved economic fortunes depend upon the availability of three resources over which they can, in a sense, exert no direct control: men, overseas relatives, and migration opportunities. A fortunate woman will find a man, usually the father of one or more of her children, who is willing to share some of his income with her, even if they do not share a common residence. In Kittitian society there are both social and legal pressures on men to help provide for their illegitimate children, but in fact they often do not. Although many women complain about the shortcomings of men, they very rarely use the law to enforce social expectations. Instead, they assume a fatalistic world view that it is in the nature of a woman's lot to work hard and have a difficult life. Nevertheless, Kittitian females do consciously establish relationships with a series of men or, occasionally, several men concurrently in order to maximize their chances of receiving financial support. (These strategies are discussed in some detail below.)

While Kittitians tend to see their island as a land of "limited good," the world outside is perceived in terms of economic abundance and opportunity. People who expect little or nothing from local kinfolk do not hesitate to request food, clothing, even money, from those overseas. Better yet, Kittitian men and women seek the opportunity to leave the island themselves, following their kinfolk to the Virgin Islands, to New York City, to London, and Toronto in search of work. For lower-stratum women, such a move may be of considerable importance, for domestic work—one of the few types of work for which most of them are qualified—is hard to find on small islands with few tourists. In 1972 (the last year for which there are published government figures), 18,793 men and 14,066 Kittitian women left the island for at least a short time (St. Kitts-Nevis-Anguilla 1972: Table 24). The availability of these opportunities, however, is unpredictable and fluctuates greatly in accordance with a variety of economic and political factors external to St. Kitts and beyond the control of the Kittitian people. An important feature of lower-class economic pursuits, then, is mobility and the ability to compete for scarce, fluctuating, and sometimes remote resources.

These facts of island life, following upon a history of slavery and a plantation social system, have had a profound effect upon the quality of interpersonal relationships in St. Kitts. Fragments of diverse social groups and parts of unrelated families were brought to the island as slaves, where they were seen primarily as individual units of production. The slavery system perpetuated the breakdown of kin and other social groups, as did the estate system after emancipation, as *individuals* sold their labor, and cheaply, to the sugar industry. On this small island there was no place where freed men and women might live and maintain control over resources and means of production outside the sphere of sugar industry influences. Thus, no socioeconomic groups grew in St. Kitts comparable to those in peasant societies. Competition instead of cooperation characterizes relationships, even to some degree between kinsmen. Eric Wolf (1966:82) pointed out that such an individuated and competitive social situation is common in developing states such as St. Kitts, where things come to be evaluated primarily according to economic values. In my 1972-73 study of food distribution and food habits, I found that food is considered in this light in St. Kitts. Most surplus foods are sold to turnhands or directly to customers, that is converted into cash, rather than used in establishing and maintaining local multistranded social ties. In other words, institutionalization of social relationships and groups through reciprocal exchanges (of food, service, and so on) is rare, presumably because such relationship would entail obligations difficult to meet in times of scarcity. In fact, my observations suggest that group obligations are an economic burden more often than an asset in this setting.

This lack of group structures was apparent in the village in which I conducted my anthropological field research. The community lies about four miles to the east of the capital, Basseterre, and, thus, is an easy bus ride or a long hot walk from the most "urbanized" section of the island. The village was settled by freed slaves during the mid-nineteenth century, and approximately 600 of their descendants still live there. The small frame and masonry construction houses are situated close together about the single road, but distance in social relationships is maintained through several social, physical, psychological, and even supernatural barriers which local folk have erected to ensure privacy and minimal interpersonal involvement. Most villagers, for example, have fenced in the property upon which their house is built. Fences range from fast-growing bushes to high corrugated metal structures behind which a villager may live for years with very little contact with neighbors. Reinforcing the physical separation of villagers is their shared set of attitudes concerning hospitality, visiting, and sharing. People commonly do most of their socializing on "neutral" ground of some sort, such as on the street, at church, in a bar or rum shop, or in Basseterre, where no one has an obligation to entertain and provide refreshment. Furthermore, there is little value placed on generosity in this social setting. An individual who is the recipient of a gift or loan is vulnerable to attack by village gossip, and fear of "being talked about" is a real deterrent to sharing. I have recorded nearly a dozen independent examples of people who have expressed a great deal of concern about being the object of such talk, have myself heard and been the victim of it on several occasions, and have seen many people take elaborate precautions to hide gifts to me and from me from the eyes of their neighbors. One time, for example, I was told by two women in the village not to drive a third younger woman to visit a 15-year-old friend of ours who had just given birth to her first child. The explanation given to me was that the young woman wanted to carry a few necessary items to the new mother, then return to the village and "talk about her." In another conversation, a woman with whom I have worked on a number of field research projects informed me that in the village, pregnant women could not borrow maternity clothes the way my "friends in the States" do, because "people would say 'H. is wearing P.'s dress' and talk about me." Finally, an individual who gets a reputation for generosity, may be considered weak and a mark for anyone willing to risk gossip for a free ride to town or a handout.

My research suggested that supernatural barriers may also reinforce and maintain social distance between Kittitians, especially older people. Among the few obvious cultural continuities with Africa still perpetuated in the culture of St. Kitts is a belief in magic call "obeah." An obeah man is knowledgeable about how to use such things as powders to produce magic for the control of people or events, and his skills are often in demand by those who harbor a grudge against kin, neighbor, friend, or foe. One destitute old man accused his cousin of attempting to harm him with obeah powders placed in food she brought to him to ease his hunger; another old man was thought to have been disabled by a spell put upon him by a jealous brother. In both cases the men had isolated themselves, avoiding certain kinds of social contact, from the fear of obeah, and gifts made to them were suspect because they might carry harmful powders. In a sense, the avoidance of sharing and cooperative social ventures because of fear of gossip is an extension of the more specific, more tangible obeah avoidance, and both reflect a general distrust of social involvement.

I felt the impact of this sociocultural situation throughout my research in St. Kitts. I found, for example, that the nonsharing ideology in the village extended to include people such as myself. In societies that are composed of a number of inclusive groups, such as kin groups, a field worker can usually count on being integrated into the organization by forming relationships with members of a major informant's primary groups. In an individuated social structure, however, the field worker faces what Morris Freilich called a lack of "spreadibility of rapport" (1970:218,226), requiring a relatively large number of informants, each of whom is the focus of a network of ties. Not only will a relationship with one individual informant *not* lead naturally and inevitably to ties with a circle of relatives and friends, it may actually interfere with the extension of ties, since many folk would actively discourage such attempts by making disparaging remarks about their friends and foes alike. Once I had learned the important ethnographic lesson that people, including myself, are resources in that environment, I could better understand why a friend would viciously attack her neighbors for bothering me with requests for rides to town and in the next breath suggest that we take a "little ride around the island."

Skill in the management of social resources, then, is an important aspect of a successful socioeconomic strategy in St. Kitts, as in much of the Third World. Whitten (1970:33) pointed out that by selectively opening, reinforc-

ing, and terminating dyadic ties with kin and nonkin, an individual can maximize his or her opportunities for social and spatial mobility. And in the
"marginal, fluctuating money econom/ies/" (1970:33) of the Caribbean successful strategies are often the most flexible ones, those with the greatest
number of options for social and geographic movement.

In an article by Nancie Gonzalez about the Black Caribs (1970), there is
evidence that the low incidence of marriage and matrifocal household, which
are both common features in West Indian society, are adaptive responses to
these same economic pressures. She points out that the "consanguineal household offers financial and psychological security to the female *and* to the male
and, thus, to the maintenance of a fairly stable home environment even when
jobs are hard to find and remuneration low" (1970:242). Gonzalez indicated
that there are pressures on males who have conjugal unions with women to be
"good providers"; to fail may bring rejection from a spouse but not from
consanguineal kin. The author added:

> Conversely, a woman can ill afford to cleave only unto one man,
> cutting herself off from other conjugal unions or from male kins-
> men, for in such systems the chances that any one man may fail
> are high. Should her husband disappear or fail to provide regular-
> ly, a woman needs the support of other males. By dispersing her
> loyalties and by clinging especially to the unbreakable sibling ties
> with her brothers, a woman increases her chances of maintaining
> her children and household even when any one attached male is
> incapable of helping her (1970:242).

In other words, Gonzalez has suggested that establishing a network of ties
with men, none of which are exclusive or ultimately binding (except, perhaps,
those with brothers) may be a successful strategy of women in these societies.
These anthropological perspectives are particularly useful in explaining the
lives of the women I have met on the island of St. Kitts.

THE VILLAGE SETTING

The village in which I lived with my three children, gathering cultural data and attempting to understand the problems of women, has no town hall
or other seat of government, because there is no local political organization.
There is no institution, actually, that integrates these people into an identi-
fiable group. There are no economic, political, ritual, or kin activities that
involve or even potentially involve all villagers. Church affiliation serves to
integrate communities in some of the Catholic islands of the Caribbean, but
in St. Kitts, even religion is devisive. The largest church congregation in the

village itself is Methodist, while the Anglicans, who are nearly as numerous, must walk to a nearby community to worship. There are several other smaller congregations in the village proper, Pentecostal and Gospel Hall being the most important, but members of these "sideways churches," as they are called, often are derided by their neighbors. The Methodists and Pentecostals, especially, sustain a mutual enmity. I have heard villagers laugh at those who have "become Christians" (Pentecostals), because joining this church requires one to adhere to a strict code of conduct and dress, as well as regular church attendance. Furthermore, the Methodists are either disdainful of or amused by the "dancing" of the Pentecostal participants as the true believers move in response to their preaching and music to achieve possession by the Holy Ghost. The woman who heads the Pentecostal Church, on the other hand, delivers powerful sermons, often directed at the curious nonbelievers who watch through the church doors. The only integrative feature of the churches that I have observed, is the community center that was built and is still maintained by the Methodist congregation. In it, pediatric clinics are held regularly by the Kittitian Health Department, and films are shown sporadically, most concerning religious themes or birth control. The local band uses the building for their practice, and young people play table tennis there.

More common than churches in the village, are the small shops of local entrepreneurs. These provide a variety of vital functions to villagers, who depend on them especially during bad times to sell on credit. Freshly baked bread, both lunch and breakfast for most villagers, is carried to the shops to be sold to regular customers. While most people shop in Basseterre each Saturday for fresh provisions and staples such as rice, flour, cooking oil, and tinned milk, they often find themselves lacking sufficient cash to purchase in quantity. When they run out of these staples in mid-week, they can purchase small amounts from the large tins and barrels in the shops. Most of the villagers with whom I worked and lived bought a great deal of their food from the shops on a meal-to-meal basis. In the long run, food costs are slightly higher, since quantities are small and unit prices somewhat higher in the villages, but this pattern does provide flexibility; people buy only what is immediately needed of stocks that are available with whatever money is at hand. Finally, the local shops are meeting places, where neighbors can visit, and men can play dominoes and discuss the latest cricket match over a beer.

This is the social and cultural context, briefly described, within which the women of St. Kitts live and strive. They perceive it as a hard world, and indeed it is; however, their personal strength and patterns of dealing with a harsh and unpredictable socioeconomic order have survival value. Mobility and a flexible network of kin and friends are adaptive social features in a changing society. In the next section, these features are described through lives of the women themselves.

A WOMAN'S STRATEGY: DEVELOPMENT OF A NETWORK

A woman usually faces the birth of a baby with mixed or ambiguous feelings. Most women want babies to affirm their female social identity, to care for them in their old age (more about this below), or to please a man who wishes to demonstrate his virility. Or they say they simply want a little one to love. Village women, on the other hand, are very realistic about the problems involved in raising children without money and without a husband. Pregnancy is not discussed a great deal, nor is labor and the process of giving birth. There is some embarrassment in bearing an illegitimate child, despite the frequency with which this happens, but there are also remnants of traditional beliefs which proscribe discussions of birth and babies. Jumbies, for example, which are perceived as spirits of the dead, can bother a new infant, causing it to sicken and die. Thus, little fuss is made over the new one, and its name is not to be mentioned until it is christened; older children may have asafoetida tied in their hair to keep the troublesome spirits away. (The latter practice is rare today, in part due to the counsel of government physicians.)

Men sometimes state a preference for male children, but mothers show little prejudice to either sex in the treatment of their babies. They are generally given adequate food and attention without being indulged, unless, of course, the babies come too quickly and too often. In this case, the mother may not be able to provide sufficient nourishment and care for each, and they may sicken and, too often, die. I have also known some mothers who have had to find other homes for one or more of their children, despite the anxiety this causes to mother and child alike. If a woman's own mother can assume part of the burden, the anxiety is less, because women feel that the grandmother will provide the love and care young ones are thought to require. No one else, the women told me, can really be trusted to adequately look after your children. Yet it often becomes necessary to send them to other kin, to friends, or to (sometimes) virtual strangers, who have the room and resources to provide for them.

Babies are generally fed according to a mixed feeding pattern, breast in the morning and evening, and the bottle in between. All the women with whom I spoke felt that women now do not have enough breast milk to feed their infants without supplementary bottles. In one sense, this shared concern itself causes problems since tinned milk is expensive, less nourishing for the babies, and must be mixed and stored under improper conditions. Some mothers spend up to one-third of their low incomes on milk alone. Yet the mixed feeding pattern does give the mothers something that may be more important ultimately—flexibility and mobility, should opportunity arise somewhere.

Most infants are off the breast completely by the sixth to ninth months, and as soon as the children begin to toddle about, less and less attention is paid to them by mothers or surrogates. This is a critical time for the children, both socially and physically, for their mobility brings increased vulnerability. The youngster is extricating itself, in a sense, from the mother and her enveloping network of resources, neither a dependent extension of the mother nor yet an independent and self-sufficient member of the household. He or she may not yet have a place at the table or a set of eating utensils. (Two women expressed surprise that a place was set for my one-and-a-half-year-old son.) The child is not considered "ready" or in need of adult food and may subsist primarily on gruels and porridges made with milk and meal or flour on into the second year. Since nutritional needs are changing throughout these months, it is not surprising that the diet of these youngsters is very often substandard, and is especially low in protein. Gastro-intestinal disorders plague the lower stratum toddlers of St. Kitts, as they do in many developing tropical nations, and are the most common cause of hospitalization in children of this age category.

Between the ages of three and five, boys and girls usually begin to spend greater amounts of time with peers, relatives and friends, with whom they play. Actually, much of their play involves gathering and stealing food of many different kinds. By the sea, for example, they may collect whelks, moray eel, and sea grapes; in the pastures they chase down tululu (small land crabs); and in the mountain they find mangoes, guavas, coconuts, almonds, tamarinds, gineps, and so on. Since my middle child was integrated into one of these peer groups, I had the opportunity to follow closely some of the scavengers, whose ages ranged from four to twelve. Most of the children in this particular group were siblings and cousins from a large family who had been left with an old woman who was grandmother and great-grandmother to them. Since she was ill and feeble, they actually had to watch out for one another most of the time. In fact, I observed and was told by several informants that many of these children that "run the streets"are those whose mothers have left to work overseas. While many of these youngsters fall short of the high standards for conduct held by villagers (obediency, respect for authority, helpfulness), the importance of the foodstuffs they gather in this context of marginal food resources is considerable.

During these childhood years, both boys and girls attend classes in the overcrowded one-room school house in a neighboring village. Virtually all of them stay in primary school for a few years, thus achieving at least minimal literacy, and many even complete the sixth level. However, only about 5 percent according to 1970 census figures, go on to secondary schools or other higher education (University of the West Indies 1975:156,157).

During these years of childhood, there are few major differences in the socialization of boys and girls. Both engage in active, physical, sometimes rowdy play, often involving the administration of "licks." When girls play card games, for example, they usually play "for licks," which gives the winner the right to strike the loser as hard as desired, one hit per point lost. I myself received a number of licks from the girls who came to know me well, and although they were delivered in the spirit of play and fun, I can attest to the strength and enthusiasm of the delivery!

Girls are not molded into dependent, subordinant, passive, and strictly domestic roles; such training would be obviously incompatible with the "real world" of lower-class adults in St. Kitts. Instead, girls acquire a sense of independence, a competitiveness, a resourcefulness, sometimes an aggressiveness that makes them seem harsh at times to outsiders, but that can assure them survival under the existing socioeconomic conditions. Most lower-class Kittitian women spend many years as mothers without also being wives, and many never have a man "to take care of them." In such an environment, socialization to independence is adaptive.

Despite the lack of sexual segregation of childhood activities and roles, the life-styles of boys and girls begin to diverge as they approach adolescence. Girls are more likely than their male peers to be given child care responsibilities, helping their mothers who have several more younger offspring, or caring for younger siblings left in their charge by mothers who must work. Child care is not entirely a sex-typed activity, but girls are more likely than boys to assume it. One girl of 12 was our constant companion during the summer months of 1972, when I first began my field research in St. Kitts. Because she was such a quiet, unassuming girl, I could not understand the constant criticisms I heard of her from friends and neighbors. "Don't harbor her," I was told on several occasions. I found that her mother, who was 29 years old, had seven other children which the girl was expected to look after. Her mother kept her home from school most of the time, and the other girls teased her because she could not read. Yet all the sympathy of fellow villagers went to her mother, who had such a disobedient child. A niece of my major informant was 13 years old that same summer. She was responsible for the care and feeding of five siblings, since her mother was working in St. Croix. I tried to arrange for her to go with us on outings to the beach, but her aunt always pointed out that the girl had to stay home with the little ones and cook for them. My obvious sympathy for her was not shared by my Kittitian friends, who saw the girl's plight as one of the facts of life: a woman must become accustomed to hard work and a hard life.

Another fact of Kittitian life is sexuality. Children learn of sexual behavior and reproduction early in those small houses in which the family all sleeps together. Furthermore, the body and its various functions are considered "natural," and people do not attempt excessively to hide them. Children experiment sexually at an early age, and full heterosexual relationships are not at all unusual by the age of 12. It is not surprising, then, that many girls are pregnant by the time they are 14 or 15. Health workers report that venereal disease is common among children 13 and younger; I personally know two girls who had their first babies during their thirteenth year. And of the approximately 25 village women of all ages from whom I got this type of information, all but two had become pregnant by the age of 17, most during their sixteenth year.

In this way, the adulthood of Kittitian women begins. For many of the lower-class females, this is also a difficult time—babies to care for, a household to establish if their mother will not allow them to stay, no job, and a boyfriend who bolts or has no money. I know of only one young mother who has found employment in Basseterre. A few have left the island, especially in upwardly mobile families, with the encouragement of other family members, who are embarrassed about the illegitimate birth. Most of these teenagers, however, must be constantly searching for sources of money, food, and clothing for themselves and their babies. The young mothers are now considered independent adults, no longer to be cared for by nurturing relatives, and as such they must assume adult roles and responsibilities. This independence is sometimes reinforced by the departure of the teenager from her natal home, either by her own choosing or by the choice of her relatives. One friend and informant of mine told me of her own difficult existence when she was told to leave her mother's home after she bore her second illegitimate child at the age of 17. Yet because a teenage mother *is* now adult, she must give up most of the foraging activities that provide supplementary foods for children. She is burdened with her baby, of course, but beyond that, foraging is not considered appropriate adult behavior in most cases. At this age, the search for a livelihood must take the form of an extension of one's rudimentary social network through the establishment of additional and hopefully fruitful social relationships.

Among the most significant of these relationships are those with men. During the early years of adulthood, a young woman may have a series of boyfriends—and, perhaps, a series of babies—and find not one with whom to establish a tie involving mutual economic responsibility. While these contacts with men virtually always involve sex, the women are not promiscuous, for there are recognized standards of conduct. For the duration of the relationship, for example, the couple is expected to remain faithful, although according to the local double standard this fidelity applies primarily to the female. Unless the relationship is very casual, the young man often takes a proprietary view of "his woman," and jealously guards her from attentions of other males. If a woman violates the unspoken vows of fidelity, or if her boyfriend imagines that she has, he may erupt in jealous anger and beat her. Several young women I know have either been beaten, one badly, or threatened with violence, and while they may have been given some degree of sympathy from their friends and relatives, they rarely use legal means to punish the men.

One young attorney in St. Kitts is particularly concerned with what he perceives as maltreatment of women. He told me that the men like to "chat up the girls," and, indeed, to get them pregnant as a demonstration of their mas-culine prowess. A man who does not produce offspring is sometimes said to have "sand in his seed." The young women, left with babies and no money coming in from the fathers of them, complain of their lot, but will rarely use the existing laws to force child support payments. Instead, the attorney said, they tell him that a woman's life is supposed to be hard. Further more, he had been constantly frustrated in his attempts to get women to use the law to protect themselves from boyfriends and husbands who mistreat them physically or mentally, or who use them simply as sources of income without reciprocation of duties. He said he felt that they hesitate to bring legal action because they see courts as a place for criminals; because of their resistance to swearing oaths (especially members of fundamental religions); and because of their fatalistic world view.

The existence of such a double standard in a society where women are independent and relatively free from the social constraints that inhibit women in many places, results in stormy male-female relationships. One young man told me, in fact, that "in St. Kitts, men and women don't like each other very much." While this is no doubt an exaggeration, I did observe a great deal of visible tension and outright battles between the sexes during my stay. In one case, a young married man had gone to a neighboring village to visit his girlfriend on an evening that a fete was being held at our house. We had invited the couple, so the young woman came alone. When her husband returned and found her there, he became jealous and very angry. During the argument that ensued, she screamed that she was going to kill him and went after a knife. Eventually friends restored order, but the couple's relationship was strained for some time thereafter.

Despite the potential tensions, even unmarried women generally are faith-ful to their boyfriends, and virtually always know who the fathers of their babies are. Informally, in fact, many illegitimate children use their fathers' sur-names, even though legally they should not. Even this public expression of paternity, however, does not force support. During my last field trip to St. Kitts I interviewed seven young mothers, ages 16 and 17, who had between them 13 children, most of them fathered by different men; not one of these young women was receiving financial help from any of the men.

There are, of course, a number of reasons why women still consort with men—social, recreational, and sexual reasons. Yet as I interviewed the women of St. Kitts, I could see that their reasons were often highly practical, for they would suggest in subtle ways that eventually a woman should find a man who will help her. If the man is not married and the relationship is reasonably stable and children born of it, they may even establish coresidence. Some women, however, told me the best situation is to have a man provide them with money, goods, and serivces of various kinds without moving in, since he is less likely to try to dominate and control under these circumstances. Coresidence often means the man moves into the woman's established household, and under these conditions he nearly always asserts what he perceives as his proper dominance. One informant told me she actually had some regrets about her boyfriend moving in, despite the fact that his income provided her with some economic stability. Another younger woman angrily explained that men move into your house and then run around with other women anyway. She wanted a man to help support her, not live with her.

However, the search for a stable relationship may be difficult and long. One young friend of mine (whose letter appears at the beginning of this Chapter) had had a series of boyfriends since her first baby was born when she was 15. After she found out she was pregnant for the fourth time, she told me that each child had a different father—an admission which caused her much embarrassment—and that although she "went" with men who might eventually help her out, all she got from them was a baby. I heard a number of tales such as this during my last field research on the island. While I was investigating the socioeconomic context of infant feeding, the word was spread that I was interested in talking with young mothers about the problems they have in taking care of their families; several of them came to me, volunteering to talk for no other motive than to have an opportunity to express their most important concerns.

Occasionally a young woman will marry her boyfriend after the first child is born, particularly if she comes from a middle-class or upwardly mobile family. Most young adults, however, establish and terminate a succession of relationships with sexual partners that are relatively casual, entailing neither co-residence nor a wide range of mutual responsibilities. For the young mothers, lacking a husband or steady beau, friends with regular incomes, adult children earning a living, or steady employment, these years may, indeed, be hard. In the language of network analysis, these are the years when the range of social networks is narrow; that is, the women have relatively few direct contacts and few types of contacts in their personal networks. The links that do exist in these "webs" of relationships are often not productive resources anyway, since they are usually peers who are in the same stage of life and facing essentially the same problems. To state the problem in a different fashion, at this stage of the life-cycle, most Kittitians have relatively few social resources to tap.

Another sure investment in the future expansion of social networks is expressed in the bearing of children. I am not suggesting that women make conscious decisions to have eight or ten children in order to add a number of links in their networks of social resources: most of them do not make decisions about having babies, a matter that seems to them to lie outside their control. Nevertheless, the young mothers who are struggling to feed their families now know that those youngsters will grow up to help them when they are older and, perhaps, unable to care for themselves. To that extent, children are an investment, a short-run expense that usually pays off in the long run. This view of children is a realistic one. One young women, now a mother of six children, was discussing with me the plight of an old man in the village who was ill and going blind. After 40 years of working in the sugar cane fields he had retired from the estate with a pension that provided him with the equivalent of about one U.S. dollar a week. He was the same man who rejected help from a cousin in the village who brought him food, because he feared she was trying to poison him with obeah. "If he had children," my friend told me, "he would not be hungry." Your children will feed you when you are old. Time and again I was told that the only people you can trust to help you are your mother, your grandmother, and your children. They are your social security.

My ethnographic observations confirm the value of offspring to older people. One of the women with whom I worked in the gathering of cultural data on several occasions is a 75-year-old great-grandmother. She and her husband expanded their house a few years ago, making it one of the largest dwellings in the village and comfortable for themselves and the four great-granddaughters who live with them. When we discussed her financial security, I found that her husband still works and she still gardens in the mountain; I also heard about all the friends and relatives that send her remittances. She has a large network of people—children, grandchildren, nieces, nephews, and their kin—who provide her with all kinds of goods and services, and she speaks of her success in terms of these social resources. Of course, not all the childless older villagers are living in the poverty of the old cane worker above, nor are all grandparents as successful as my informant; however, for many, having children who recognize the traditional obligations of lineal kinship is the only way to assure even a minimally comfortable old age.

The implications of this social situation and perception of the value of children for family planning programs are important. Dissemination of birth control information and paraphernalia has had little impact on the high Kittitian birth rate. Although a variety of cultural features (such as demonstrations of masculinity) interferes with the success of such programs, this need for a personal network of resources as a hedge against poverty in old age is a major contributing factor. However, a letter from a friend I received just a short while ago suggests that the problem of birth control goes beyond these simple explanations:

> Yes V. has her baby and if she dont be careful she will end up get-
> ting a next one. The baby is getting on fine for the present. A lot
> of these young girls presently now is pregnant I hope Im finish
> with that I have enough on my hand they are taking a lot out of
> me. Even those who was on the pill for a long period still find
> themselves pregnant. With the cost of living so high I just cant see
> how we will survive in this land at all. The Government here is
> seeking for independence and this place is so full of unemployed
> people? What is going to happen later.

Instead of seeing both the men and children in a woman's life as economically and, perhaps, psychologically draining, we must view them as a part of a larger strategy in which being involved in a variety of relationships with a large number of people in different geographic settings under a variety of economic conditions maximizes a woman's life chances. Either these people will send remittances to her in St. Kitts, or she may join them where they live and find work herself. Having such a social network broadens and extends the economic base of an individual female.

Other people, such as friends, employers, and so on, are incorporated into networks in the same way. I gained a great deal of information about the formation and function of social networks through personal involvement in several. During my first field trip, I met a young woman who worked for the landlord of the house I rented, who also was hired to help me with the care of my children. Our relationship was relatively impersonal for the first three months, separated as we were by social distance imposed by our racial, cultural, and class differences. Eventually, the distance diminished, and on subsequent trips to St. Kitts I hired her in the capacity of "research assistant," and we have worked together on several subsequent projects. Nevertheless, I was somewhat disturbed by the regular requests for clothing, magazines, and other items "from the States." When two other close relationships began to involve similar requests, I came to realize more clearly how important overseas ties are to Kittitians, and in what ways being kin or friend to someone on the island means being a social resource. Two of these relationships were clarified and structured recently by the extension of fictive kin ties to me. One woman, my friend and assistant, told me that I had "come as a mother" to her, and at Christmastime I received a beautiful Christmas card from her designed "for mother." I knew that she meant that I do things for her that one's mother usually does, providing economic help, support, and advice. The economic bond between us was also reinforced by affection and mutual respect. In the second case, my young friend whose plight is suggested in the opening paragraph, named me the godmother of her new baby.

Gradually, then, a young woman builds her network. If she is successful in her strategy, she may have a number of links that provide her with money and other items, either regularly or sporadically, and be fairly secure in this socioeconomic niche. Because my friend above is a hard working female, and thus a generally respected member of the village, she has been largely successful in this fashion. She has an employed boyfriend with whom she lives, another ex-boyfriend (father of her first three children) who provides money and clothes from time to time, a mother in St. Croix who occasionally sends money, a neighbor who provides food when she can, a friend in whose garden she sometimes works in exchange for produce, and myself.

The contrast between the rudimentary networks of teenage mothers, who are transitional between childhood and adulthood, and those fully developed

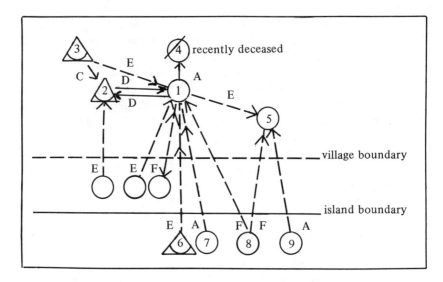

Key: ─────── Regular sharing or aid (daily or weekly)
     ─ ─ ─ Irregular sharing or aid

A. Lineal Kinsmen
B. Collateral Kinsmen
C. Employer-Employee
D. Consensual Relationship (coresidence)

E. Neighbors (most apparently nonreciprocal relationships involve gift-service exchanges.)
F. Friend, other

FIGURE 9.1
TWO OVERLAPPING SOCIOECONOMIC NETWORKS

networks of older women is generally impressive. In order to demonstrate the difference, the following figures of two overlapping networks are included. Figure 9.1, for example, presents most of the primary figures in the networks of two young women whom I know well; one was 17 when the data were collected, and the other was 29 years old. Individual number 1 is the older of the two. She, H., is the person discussed above, who is living in consensual union with her boyfriend, number 2. Both of them work whenever and wherever they can, and each contributes to the maintenance of the household, which also contains six children. Number 3 is a neighbor who is relatively well off and provides work for H. and her boyfriend, at a variety of tasks. His wife also gives them foodstuffs when she has extra items. H. gave food and money to her grandmother, in turn, until the old woman died recently. Both she and her boyfriend know people in other villages from whom they receive bits of food from time to time, in exchange for little favors, such as picking up packages for them in town, helping them dig sweet potatoes, and so on. (These in-

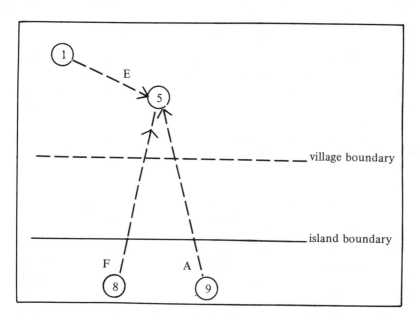

FIGURE 9.2
NETWORK OF TEENAGED FEMALE

dividuals have not been numbered.) Number 6 is H.'s ex-boyfriend, and number 7 is her mother; number 8 is the village anthropologist, myself.

H. also helps out number 5, V., when she can because V. is "something to" her boyfriend; that is, H.'s beau is a cousin of V., and H. feels some obligation to help the unfortunate girl. As figures 9.1 and 9.2 illustrate, V. has very few social resources in the form of helping relationships. Only H., her mother, and I come to her aid, and none of us is a regular patron. She and her four small children live with a cousin who is 13 and her baby in a two-room, two-bed, shack. V.'s children are all ill and grossly undernourished, their apathy and listlessness, their bloated bodies and fine, discolored hair suggesting too little protein. She herself is not well, and each pregnancy causes her increasing difficulties. The severity of her plight is exceptional, even though the general problems are common among the very young mothers. She is, in part, a victim of acts that are considered deviant by Kittitian standards: when her mother left the island to look for work, she did not adequately provide for the care of the three children she left behind, requiring V. to be essentially on her own before she was an adolescent. Furthermore, her mother rarely sends her remittances even now, as she should according to custom. The general features of her condition, however, are not unusual for a lower-class female of her age category.

SOCIAL NETWORKS OF WOMEN: A SUMMARY

The broad lines of this research on socioeconomic networks of Kittitian women indicate three major stages of network involvement during adulthood. The first begins at adolescence, when sexual behavior—and often maternity—commence. At this point, the roles of boys and girls diverge, as girls often must assume adult roles and responsibilities and their male peers "lime," which is to say, do nothing, but with a certain amount of style. Women, who perceive themselves as hardwording people, often condemn these boys as "worthless." In truth, for many of them no legitimate work is available, and they mark time until they get an opportunity to go overseas. For them there is no clear-cut rite of passage into adulthood that motherhood provides their girlfriends. Having relatively few relationships with employed males, employed friends, and potential employers, the teenage mothers have few social resources to exploit. Yet they can begin to build more ties, which can be activated in time of need, and gradually extend the range of their social networks. As adults, many of these women may be receiving help from a number of different men with whom they have had sexual relationships, friends with jobs or land to work, well-to-do neighbors, and kin in strategic places. Certainly adult women in the lower socioeconomic stratum of Kittitian society do not themselves become well off; most of them do not even become comfortable by U.S. standards. Few ever have indoor plumbing, many do not have electricity. Most continue to live in homes that are much too small for the whole family, even by their own standards. But the large majority of these adult women have enough food to feed their families adequately; many can provide sufficient clothing for themselves and their children.

As these women mature and reach the later years of adulthood—and the last stage of network involvement—network links begin to die or move on. While some older people continue to maintain small gardens by their homes or in the mountain, actual wage employment is unavailable, and income drops. Some old women try to live on the welfare payments, which are grossly inadequate. Living conditions are not so grim, however, for old women with a large number of lineal kinfolk working. Some of these women actually do quite well with all their remittances coming in regularly, especially if they have only a few relatives (such as grandchildren in the home) to support. For them there is adeqaute money and sufficient food. For old women without such kin network links, primarily those that remained childless, or for many old men, aid from social sources is minimal.

MODERNIZATION, THE MIDDLE CLASS, AND THE ROLE OF WOMEN

Much of the contemporary literature concerning women of the world deals with the effects of industrialization, urbanization, and other trends of modern society on the traditional roles that they have played in the past. A great deal of this material dwells on the destruction and major changes in the life-style of women that accompany technological and economic modification, focusing on the alterations in the basic institutions of societies, such as the family. Since women in many parts of the world were restricted to the "private" or family domain, and their major roles were those associated with being a wife and mother, changing family life virtually required changing female roles.

Some of this impact has been felt in St. Kitts. Here, however, the major changes have been political, rather than technological and economic. Over the years that St. Kitts was a British colony, and especially since 1967, when the island state of St. Kitts-Nevis-Anguilla was granted independence, there has been a trend toward self-government and democratization. Control over internal affairs now rests with the government in Basseterre, and the political bureaucracy grows each year. As career opportunities open up for black Kittitians, both men and women, the island's middle class also grows. The village in which this research was conducted contained such a growing mid-stratum, in part because of its advantageous position vis-a-vis the government and business offices of Basseterre. Only two of the women in the circle of friends and informants involved in research could be classified as middle class by virtue of their educational level, occupation, and life-style; however, ethnographic observations of village women suggested some of the ways that upward social mobility specifically affects them. First, relationships with men are different, since marriage is essential in the middle-class life-style. These women rarely have children by several different men, and they do not live in consensual union with boyfriends. They are likely to marry earlier in life than lower stratum women and to remain married to the same person, since divorce is rare. Having ties with many males, which is adaptive for poor women, is neither necessary nor proper for those in the Kittitian mid-stratum, since their men are very likely to have stable, nonseasonal, jobs or professions and adequate incomes. Furthermore, women of this class usually continue to work, as well, providing the family with two incomes. Middle-class accoutrements, such as electricity, indoor plumbing, refrigeration, television sets, are thus made possible by the efforts of two employed individuals.

Middle-class Kittitian women also lead more private lives than those in the lower stratum. Some of them interact very little with the neighbors in the village, and are rarely seen at social functions in the countryside, outside of church services. The married women of the middle class, of course, are likely to have more roles to play in the private domain, being both wives and mothers, than their lower stratum counterparts; furthermore, there is a certain amount of social distance between the classes, even in the small villages of St. Kitts. I have heard middle-class women complain that all their neighbors do is sit around and gossip, while those neighbors accuse them of snobbery. One of the middle-class women was critically called "The Queen of C. village" by some of the older children. The females in this higher social stratum tend to have more "urban" relationships, actually, than local relationships in their networks. Their employers and many of their friends live in the capital.

In a sense, there are more restrictions and constraints on the women in the higher socioeconomic levels than on those in the lower, less flexibility and less mobility. The former are tied, to an extent, to their homes by their private roles. One reflection of their different life-style lies in the narrowing of their networks, the relatively few people (men, children, employers, neighbors) with whom they have regular, sporadic, or potential relationships involving mutual help. The middle-class women depend less on a broad range of social relationships, any one of which may fail at some point, than upon a narrow network composed of generally stable links.

CONCLUSION

This ethnographic evidence indicates that the traditional patterns of life of most lower-class women on St. Kitts are changing relatively little under the impact of modernization. The history of slavery and continuing domination of sugar estates restricted the development of local groups, such as kin groups, which operated as subsistence and economic units, and in which the women might have played a specific and formal part. Instead, the individuated social structure and the patterns of social and geographic mobility developed as people, both men and women, sought ways of exploiting fluctuating and unpredictable resources beyond their direct control. The success of women, the domestic unit, and the social system itself depended upon the ability of the female to be mobile, flexible, and resourceful, rather than tied to a specific structure or role. Women were never totally relegated to strictly domestic roles; indeed, the traditional system in the lower stratum mitigated against such constraints. Because of its very nature, generalized and adaptive, rather than specifically adapted, the socioeconomic system and women's roles within it are changing relatively little. Activities and life-styles of the women in the lower stratum of society in St. Kitts need change little as long as the new technologies and economies can be reached and expoited by a link in a social network.

NOTES

1. This research was funded by NIMH grant 1 FOI MH51587-01. I conducted further work on infant feeding in 1976 with a grant from The Human Lactation Center. My thanks, too, to Ms. Sue Wolkow for the network figures, and to M. Cathey Maze for perspectives on the adaptive features of networks.

2. Christopher Columbus named the island St. Christopher, but it quickly was nicknamed St. Kitts. The official name is still St. Christopher, but the shorter "St. Kitts" is used far more commonly.

REFERENCES

Freilich, Morris
 1970 "Mohawk Heroes and Trinidadian Peasants." In *Marginal Natives,* M. Freilich, ed. New York: Harper and Row.

Gonzalez, Nancie
 1970 "Toward a Definition of Matrifocality." In *Afro-American Anthropology,* Norman Whitten and John Szwed, eds. New York: The Free Press.

Merrill, Gordon C.
 1958 *The Historical Georgraphy of St. Kitts and Nevis, The West Indies.* Instituto Pan Americano de Geografia e Historia. Mexico, No. 232.

Parry, John H., and P.M. Sherlock
 1956 *A Short History of the West Indies.* London: Macmillan.

St. Kitts-Nevis-Anguilla
 1972 *Digest of Statistics* No. 8. St. Kitts: The Statistical Department.

University of the West Indies
 1975 *1970 Population Census of the Commonwealth Caribbean,* Vol. 6, Part 3. Kingston, Jamaica: Census Research Programme.

Whitten, Norman
 1970 "Strategies of Adaptive Mobility in the Columbian-Ecuadorian Littoral." In *Afro-American Anthropology,* Norman Whitten and John Szwed, eds. New York: The Free Press.

Wolf, Eric R.
 1966 *Peasants.* Englewood Cliffs, New Jersey: Prentice-Hall, Inc.

PART III

NORTH AMERICAN SOCIETIES

10 Women in Yucatán

FELICITAS D. GOODMAN

In this chapter, the author discusses the adaptive strategies of three Maya women, whom she has known for more than a decade. Two of the women are villagers, the third is the daughter of the older one of these two. The differences in their life styles, Goodman says, arise not merely from the fact that, in age, the older woman represents an earlier generation. Rather, it appears, the older woman is, by choice, a conservative peasant, and this choice is, at least in part, motivated by family tradition. Her daughter, as the wife of a laborer, lives in a shanty town on the fringes of a port city, and views herself as an urban woman. The second villager, on the other hand, comes from a background of rural proletarians, landless laborers on the henequen ranches. Although she continues to live in the village, she has chosen a life-way that makes her into an incipient urbanite. These choices involve the women's economic roles as well as their relations with their husbands and their children. Of the three, the shanty town dweller is, apparently by her own choice, the one who is most dependent on her husband.

In this study, we will consider the question of what it is like to be a woman in Yucatan. In the most general way, the question can be answered by saying that this means for the overwhelming number of women some sort of tie to the peasant's way of life. For the peninsula of Yucatan, comprising the states of Yucatan and Campeche and the federal territory of Quintana Roo within the Republic of Mexico, is predominantly agricultural, which includes the raising and processing of sisal fiber (henequen); with an adjunct of cottage industry, light consumer-goods production, and, of increasing importance, tourism. A few introductory words are therefore in order about peasant culture, to place into context what is to follow, focusing only on one particular aspect of this complex life style.

Anthropologists, whose interest turned to this topic not much more than a generation ago, early intuited a certain instability in peasant communities. Redfield (1941: XVII) thought that such communities in the pristine state, in isolation, were places "where the native's entire view of life has this quality of organization and inner consistency." The source of social disorganization that he thought he saw in the villages he studied in Yucatan was an "imperfect juncture between elements of Spanish origin and those which are native." Others, noting similar phenomena, lay the blame at the door of urbanization and industrialization. Thus, Potter maintains, "The major sources of change in peasant societies are the cultural, technological, scientific, and ideological influences which have come in part from the Western industrialized nations, and in part from the elites of the new countries themselves" (1967:378). In fact, so strong are these influences in Potter's view that he feels prompted to predict the imminent demise of the cultural form: "In the modern world peasant societies are an anachronism and it is inevitable that they disappear."

It goes without saying that such predictions carry the mark of the euphoria created by the illusion of the unlimited availability of fossil fuels, happily dissolved by now. Also, it seems to me doubtful for internal reasons that the agricultural village ever was, even in isolation, a community exhibiting total internal consistency. The present picture of such communities exhibiting internal diversity may be older than would fit into the static picture Redfield sketches out, for in all communities of whatever life style, provisions need to be made for conflict resolution and innovation. Neither does it seem to me acceptable that the villagers are as a matter of course victims of disruptive outside, usually urban influences, and are in no position to make choices as to the acceptance or rejection of new traits. This seems to me a picture of the tail wagging the dog. At least my observations of village life, not only in Latin America, but also elsewhere, contradict such narrow ethnocentric views formulated by the observer-reporter, himself a city dweller. The truth of the matter is that it is the city dweller who is caught in a dead-end situation: there is no other, new, more satisfying way of life that he could meaningfully escape to. But for the villager, the city is part of his own adaptation. This makes sense even historically: after all, the town as a cultural form is an excrescence of the agricultural way of life, and not the other way round. What I want to demonstrate, then, is that far from being the victim, the peasant utilizes innovations proffered by the outside world, and this strategy involves conscious choices. Naturally, in the course of this process, some peasants become permanently alienated from their natal culture. What we see then is the village as a community that continually sloughs off surplus members, as a body loses surface cells. Others, however, remain peasants, again as a matter of personal preference. Women as well as men are involved in these decisions, which determine the design of the fabric of their lives. It is an intriguing task to try and unravel what factors contribute to these choices.

The following presents some material from the life histories of three women from the same village, discussing in the main their family backgrounds, the kinds of husbands they married, their subsistence activities, and their religious behavior. The data were gathered during fieldwork in Yucatan, beginning in 1969 and continuing to date.* My principal interest during this time was the ongoing history of a small Apostolic congregation, located in a populous village in the north of the peninsula. For both practical and theoretical reasons, I restricted myself mainly to a study of the life of the women—for practical reasons, because in Latin America generally, a woman alone is always suspect and possibly the target of sexual aggression. When due to my ignorance of local conditions, for instance, I rented an empty one-room house, it was not difficult to spot the ambivalence, aggression, and suspicion with which I was treated. The mood changed instantly when because of an early flood, I moved in with a family belonging to the congregation I was studying. It was not until the end of that first summer that I discovered that such houses were rented by the procurers of the village for prostitutes who came in for the weekend from other communities and from Merida, the capital of Yucatan. As to theoretical concerns, the woman's world, as we know, has generally been underreported, and Yucatan is no exception. In Thompson's (1975) book on the town of Ticul, for instance, the women are to all intents and purposes invisible. So there was a need to fill in a gap, as it were.

THE CASE OF EUSEBIA**

Eusebia was born in a small village near Chich'en Itza. Her father and grandfather, and their antecedents as far as tradition goes, were corn farmers and traders. The Maya Lowlands, where Utzpak and also the home village of Eusebia is located, have a tradition going back at least to postclassical times, of long-distance trade in luxury items. As Chapman (1957) points out, the traders engaged in it were not full-time merchants, such as the *pochteca* of the Aztecs, but rather petty nobility that carried out this trade only part-time. Eusebia remembers her father ranging on foot from one end of the Peninsula to the other, carrying relatively light-weight, valuable merchandise, and bringing home gold coin. In addition, he worked his corn fields. Of his twenty-odd children by two wives, six boys lived to adulthood, and all but one pursued this double way of life, working in the corn fields and running stores, corn mills, bakeries, or market stands in addition. A number of their children attended high school and even the university.

Eusebia's birth falls into the period shortly before the outbreak of the Mexican Revolution (1910-1920; however, in Yucatan the civil disturbances were not over until 1924). This prevented her from going to school: the teachers fled to the cities, where life was safer than in the countryside.

*Research for this chapter was supported by funds from the Denison University Research Foundation and Denison Faculty Development Grants.

**This is a fictitious name.

In her early twenties, she married Felipe, a corn farmer, coming from a background that could be characterized by what Wolf (1966:3-4) calls "householding," that is, of a social stratum consisting of "rural cultivators whose surpluses are transferred to a dominant group." Working in the *col* ("corn field") and hunting in the bush is the work Felipe was trained for, and the only kind of work he has ever done. The same is true of his two brothers. His three sisters married corn farmers, and this is what his father and his grandfather were also. He is charming, with a gentle sense of humor, and very pacific. As a young man he used to play the harmonica at the village balls, and he still knows a large stock of *jarana* melodies, which he plays expertly. When he was converted to the Apostolic faith, he learned to play the guitar. He had only two years of grade-school education, and reads and writes with difficulty.

Eusebia married the Indian way, that is, without having the marriage registered, and her children bear her name. She bore nine children, one of whom died as an infant, of what seems to have been crib death. The size of the family was not a matter of dispute between her and her husband. "I must have enjoyed getting them," she quips, "for look how many I bore." They homesteaded in a bush village, fencing several acres, a *solar* with the limestone wall characteristic of this part of Yucatan. Eventually, they built two separate one-room houses for their growing family in the traditional oval shape, and constructed of mud and wattle, as well as a kitchen building. In her solar, Eusebia eventually planted clumps of bananas, various other fruiting bushes and trees, such as avocado, *waya, zaramuy, wayaaba,* papaya, several varieties of citrus fruit, as well as tomatoes, herbs, and chiles. She raised hogs, chickens, and turkeys. As her sons became teenagers, they worked in the corn fields with their father, to raise maize and beans, both on the family's own col from the *ejido*[1] system, and as paid farm hands for one of the ranchers in the area.

In 1958, Eusebia's husband, Felipe, quarreled with the rancher for whom he worked. As a result, he could no longer find wage labor in the area,[2] and the couple decided to give up their homestead, leaving it in the hands of their recently married third daughter. Their sons sought work elsewhere, eventually drifting to the city. Eusebia, Felipe, and their two youngest children took up residence in Utzpak,* where they acquired a plot on the outskirts of the village, built a new house, and once more planted a solar.

Subsistence strategy

In Utzpak, Felipe's life continued unchanged: he grows beans and maize either on his own rented or allotted plot, or does wage labor for one of the ranchers owning large holdings around Utzpak, harvesting or weeding. Euse-

*This is a fictitious name.

bia remained as nearly self-sufficient as anyone can be in a village in contact with the modern market economy, and this is a point of pride with her. In Utzpak, which for a generation has been connected with other communities and the capital, Merida by paved highway, these skills also have become even more a source of supplemental income, than in her home village, for they are the basis for a small-scale trade with other women who have become somewhat more accustomed to rely on others for certain services and products. She has inherited her mother's sewing machine and makes not only her family's clothing, but sews men's shorts for others. She embroiders her own 'ipiles, some of them edged with *hiit puut,* a lace made with a straight needle, a technique virtually unknown in Utzpak, and sells some of these. Her hammocks are all home-made, and occasionally, she sells one to friends of her sons when she goes visiting them in Mérida. From raising poultry, there is the sale of eggs, chickens, and on occasional turkey. The annual hogs, sometimes a sow and her litter, bring in a larger sum of money used for such necessary expenses as buying palm-fronds to keep the roof of the home in good repair. For small running expenses she sells chile peppers, coriander, tomatoes, and fruit. She does not, however, have a stand in the street or a stall in the market. The women in the neighborhood know what she grows, and she is closer than the government-built market hall in the center of the village. Even small children can be sent to her solar. She is, in other words, the supplier in an informal neighborhood network. The strictly small-scale activity brings no affluence, of course, for most people in the village grow some of the same things she has. There is no variation in ecology, such as high-country versus low-lying areas close together, that might stimulate a brisker exchange of goods. But she even grows nursery stock, such as orange and avocado trees, and others, which Felipe is skilful in grafting. "It isn't much," she likes to say, "but it is something."

Recently, the daughter who was left with Eusebia's house in the home village moved to Utzpak with her husband and her eight children. The older ones of these grandchildren now market some of Eusebia's produce, especially fruit, in places where Eusebia would not go, for example, to the men watching the baseball game on the athletic field nearby, thereby expanding her clientele somewhat. However, her trading activity is only secondary to Eusebia. She is above all a householder, the needs of the family come first: she will never sell anything that could better be consumed at home. In her sixties at this writing, she sees herself as old and worn, but she is proud of what she has accomplished, rearing eight children, keeping them clean, feeding them properly even during the terrible two years when others in Yucatán were dying of starvation because of the locust plague. She is proud of all the many skills she has, of her knowledge of plants, her ways with the barnyard animals, which she keeps well by scrubbing the chicken coop and by doctoring them with aspirin when other women lose theirs to the recurring *mortandad.* She talks with pleasure of the time when she was young and strong, and all alone she would carry bundles of merchandise over the jungle paths to barter for piglets or eggs. And she is pleased that the mothers-in-law of her daughters want to learn the special recipes she has taught them, the black filling for the turkey, the soup with capers, and the many ways the earth oven, the *pib,* can be used.

She knows Mérida well, but does not yearn to live there. Occasionally, when we catch a glimpse of the interior of a house there as we walk by, and I say, "I like to see what other people's homes look like," her answer is a friendly nod, and a neutral, "Hats'uts, masimá—Pretty, isn't it?" Where she wants to be is in her solar. Every day, she sweeps its paths. Wherever she goes, she brings back slips of flowering plants, or collects seeds and bulbs, so that the area around her house is a flower garden no matter what the season. She loves and cares for her trees and bushes, instantly noting if there is something wrong, such as ants eating the roots of an orange bush, or caterpillars attacking a tomato plant. On postcards I send her from trips elsewhere, she does not note the buildings: her first comment is always about a tree or a flower. When she had to leave her original homestead, it was not her buildings she mourned, it was her trees, and when we went to visit there, she greeted each one separately recalling when she had planted it, and admiring how big it had become. When one of her turkey chicks hatched with a nervous head twitch which prevented it from eating properly, she hand-fed it until it was strong enough to make it on its own. Yet all this affection is not sentimental: animals and plants are loved as partners, for the food they yield, and there is no regret, no hesitation, when she butchers a fowl, or sells a plant.

All of these traits stamp Eusebia as a *mestiza,*[3] a Maya Indian peasant woman. A mestiza wears an 'ipil, that is the characteristic embroidered dress with a requisite shawl, the *booch* (from Spanish *rebozo*) slung over it, and who, although knowing some Spanish, speaks Maya not only at home, but also in public. If this description seems caught in superficial, easily observable elements, there is also another, less obvious one, which in the most decisive way makes her a member of the universal peasant culture. This is that her security derives from an investment in social bonds. Thus, her economic activity does not serve to accumulate capital, but to cement her relationships to others. This makes her attitude to her customers particularistic: it depends on who you are and how you behave toward her, whether she will sell to you or not. A woman who complained that Eusebia's eggs were rotten when Eusebia knew them to be fresh, in this manner violated the basis for the transaction, and no longer gets any eggs from her. A sale to another woman, therefore, is always a social occasion: most of the time is spent conversing, and at the very end there is the almost reticent request for the item, and a rapid exchange of money. Even the price demanded may vary according to who the customer is. How this manner of organizing for security plays a role also in her religious behavior will be discussed further on.

Some cash reserves are necessary in Eusebia's scheme of things not only to keep the home in good repair, and to buy seeds, lifestock, and implements, but also for medical expenses. Eusebia believes that some ailments are caused by witchcraft, such as mental aberrations of sudden onset, or paralysis. In that case, countermeasures of a witch, an *echisera,* may be effective. Mostly, however, diseases have naturalistic causes. Eusebia believes with other Apostolics that faith healing is effective; however, in the cases she has observed, such healing has been of short duration, or applied so late that the patient died anyway. In any case, she considers it only an adjunct to modern medicine. She is firmly convinced that good nutrition, such as the addition of eggs and meat to a diet of tortillas and beans fosters good health. She derides those women who sell their chickens instead of eating them, just to be able to save enough money to build a masonry house. According to her, most cases of that undifferentiated feeling of nervous exhaustion and physical weakness the women call "suffering from the nerves" is due to sacrificing proper nutrition to such ambitions. Her judgment is the same about men who bring home a deer from the hunt and then feed only the head and perhaps the liver to their families, selling the rest to the hotels in Mérida where tourists pay a good price for the meat.

In case of illness, for instance when she was having stomach pains, Eusebia first consults a *yerbera,* a woman knowledgeable in preparing herbal medicines. If the decoctions of the yerbera produce no cure, the next step is to go to a physician. Once a week, a physician paid by the government and located in the next, somewhat larger community, comes to Utzpak and sees patients. This consultation is free, but the prescriptions are not, and the price of drugs is so out of proportion with the general level of food prices and wages that buying them puts an inordinate strain on the family budget. If her savings are not enough, Eusebia will sell a pig, which in this way acts as a savings account for emergencies. For operations, the government runs various free clinics, both in a community at some distance from Utzpak, and in Mérida. There is some suspicion, however, that treatment in these clinics is not as good as that received from a private physician, and families make great financial sacrifices to consult the latter.

With both Eusebia and Felipe approaching old age, the question of how they will provide for it is also of interest in this context. I have not read any statistics on this, but it is my impression from what I have seen in Utzpak that longevity is quite common among Maya peasants. Most families speak about parents or other close kin who are estimated to have reached 80, 90, or more years of age. In 1971, a neighbor lady died some years past 100, and her daughter, herself a great-grandmother, mourned her by saying, "And to think how well she embroidered up to her last day!" Also Eusebia's father came close to that biblical age. He caught cold harvesting beans he intended to sell on the market and died of pneumonia. Yet, I have never seen or heard of any case of senility, and neither have other colleagues who worked in Yucatán, who were asked about this.

In the same way as the majority of the families in Utzpak, Eusebia and Felipe have no permanent land holdings outside their solar, and no other assets than their home and a few tools such as the treadle sewing machine which Eusebia, as I mentioned, inherited from her mother. Eusebia also considers her 'ipiles worth passing on, and talked about this with her daughters. But there is no property that would induce a son to stay home in hopes of inheriting it. Older children are expected to help until their younger siblings are reared. Eusebia's oldest grandson in Utzapk, now 17, goes to work with his father and earns the same wage, which he has to give to his mother. Should he marry, he would leave, although there are seven other siblings in the house. The oldest girl, 18, does not yet get permission to marry because she has her young brother and sister to tend. She went to Chetumal to work for a month recently, but her baby sister became ill and cried for her day and night, so she came back. As she is an Apostolic, her mother hopes that she will not elope. Eusebia's and Felipe's subsistence depends entirely on their ability to do physical labor. When they can no longer do so, their daughter may help out some, but only if most of her children are grown by that time. At present, there is hardly enough to eat in the house to satisfy everyone. Beyond an occasional present, they can expect no help from their other children either, for all, especially those working in the city, have trouble making ends meet. The entire social stratum to which they belong, the rural producers such as farm hands, artisans, corn farmers, small merchants is without social security. Only a few years ago did the Mexican govenment admit the henequen workers to the system. The only recourse Eusebia and Felipe would have in case of disability would be to go begging. This is called "andar de caridad," and there is no stigma attached to it. They would still have their home, there are no mortgage payments to be made or taxes to be paid, they would have their water as they have their own "half well" that they share with their neighbor, and the fruit of their solar. In case of illness, their granddaughters would help out, and have done so in the past. Their children would be obligated to buy their coffin. There is no price tag on a cemetery plot, which is tiny at any rate because the corpse is first placed into a temporary grave and a few years later the bones are cleaned and only those are interred permanently.

Coming to religious behavior now, Eusebia adhered in her home village to the syncretic form of Catholicism that has grown up on the peninsula from the interaction between the faith of the Spanish colonial rulers and that of the Maya agriculturalists, where the priests are liars, and most saints disappointing. The Three Kings of Tizimin, for instance, did not bring the rains Felipe needed, and although she carried out all the requisite rites, the harvest was lost. A year after she came to Utzpak, missionaries of the Apostolic church preached there, and she eventually became baptized into the sect, bringing along her two young children and Felipe. Later, she even interested her married daughter who had remained behind when the family moved, and was instrumental in her and her husband's conversion. The members of the Apostolic congregation became an important social network for her. That group shrank, however, when the congregation split into a number of descendent groups after a traumatic upheaval in 1970,[4] when some of the leading men predicted the end of the world in August of that year, and the world endured. She clung to the group that remained in the temple, saying with the others, "Not even the angels know when the end of the world will come." And she became very cool toward those who went their own way. The final blow came when the Maya ministers of the Peninsula decided to secede from the national church and form their separate organization. To her, this was a breach of faith, they betrayed not an organization but the Word of the Lord. After all, did they not change the name of the church? And in so doing, did they not drop the word *fe,* faith? She and Felipe, and her converted children were the only ones in the former congregation to take this hard line, together with Don Pedro (see below). A great deal of happy social interaction, of excitement, and contact with the larger world of the church was lost in this manner.

THE CASE OF REINA

Reina was born and raised in a village close to Utzpak, but situated by contrast in the henequen belt. Her father and grandfather were henequeneros, and one of her brothers works in the office of a *desfibradora,* a henequen processing plant. Their security depended on their relation to the *patron,* the employer. To invest in social bonds to others in more than a cursory manner could serve no useful purpose. Reina's outlook on life was strongly shaped by this home background. She sees herself as a member of the poor class, "los pobres." Receiving a postcard from a far-away place elicits the comment, "How I would love to go there too. But we, the poor ones, where can we go?" The village is understood as a unit, not an interlocking structure of social relations, and referred to as "ese cochino pueblo," this miserable village. Born in 1937, she attended several years of grade school, and reads and writes fluently. She "walks in a dress," shunning the native garb, and speaks Spanish in public and also with her small daughters, only accommodating the old people by lapsing into Maya. At 27, she married Santiago, a man three years her junior, by elopment. As she sees it, it was her last chance. To run away with a man is "the cheapest and easiest way to get married," she says. The day after she eloped, her husband sent his father to negotiate for the marriage with her father, who was quite distraught because he had wanted to see his daughter marry in the Catholic church and wear a white veil. Since she eloped, she could marry only "by register." This, her father-in-law, Don Pedro a strict Apostolic, insisted on. She was also in favor of it, because it gave her children a Spanish surname instead of her own Maya one.

The background Santiago comes from is very similar to that of Felipe's. Also his father, Don Pedro, was a corn farmer, and eventually acquired a small cattle ranch. But there are differences also. Santiago's mother was known in the entire village as a petty thief. If a chicken strayed into their yard, it ended up in her soup pot. Her oldest son became a corn farmer, but a very poor one. He is not married and is drunk much of the time. His older sister, according to the members of the Apostolic congregation, stole the money the Apostolics had saved to build a new church, went to Mérida with it, and never came back to the village. Santiago learned early that there were devious ways in which hard work could be avoided. "He looks for the soft life," they say about him in the village. He told Eusebia that he could not work in the corn fields because he was rather stout and became sore if his legs rubbed together, an excuse Eusebia thought hilarious. We had a merry time watching her in the privacy of her home, imitating his manner of walking, trying to see how he might accomplish injuring himself at work, and where.

To find the soft life, Santiago started buying and selling. He married Reina, I would say, because he recognized the advantages to him of a wife with an ability to read and write, and a mind quicker than his. And she did not disappoint him. She literally trained him, quizzing him on his transactions whenever he came home, and carefully keeping book on all income and expenditure. When a few years ago, she started getting involved in producing hammocks on a relatively large scale, she coached him on how to supervise the weavers, weighing the yarn before and after processing as a protection against cheating. Cooperation between them is made easy by the fact that they share a basic understanding: business means taking advantage of every opportunity, fair or foul. Eusebia went to Chetumal to visit relatives some years ago. Reina and Santiago asked her to purchase a long list of articles for them. In return, they would pay half her bus fare. Since she did not ask for it in advance, they never paid it. Fire wood has become scarce recently, and the householders may only cut what they need for their kitchen. Santiago started cutting for sale, and made a handsome profit until he was caught and fined. However, he has not given her a particularly easy life. Not working as a peasant, he has no solar to weed, no tools to repair, no animals to tend or fruit to harvest, so he spends much time and money in the taverns and comes home drunk. He takes marital fidelity lightly. Eusebia and I see him pass by on his bicycle, on his way to the prostitutes who work in a house down the street from Eusebia's. But Reina seems to realize that her and her daughters' economic well-being depends on his cooperation. So she works with him, does not complain too much, and to salve his pride, tells everyone that he is really very good at doing figures in his head. And she uses him.

At the beginning of his business career, Santiago traded in whatever came his way: in used bottles which he washed and then sold on the market in Mérida, in poultry that he bought on the ranches and marketed in the larger villages, and corn, which he bought wholesale and then redistributed at a profit in Utzpak in the time between harvests. When imported goods could still be bought reasonably in the free port of Chetumal, he used to make regular trips there. He resold the merchandise, such as shirts, talcum powder, umbrellas, plastic table cloths, cheese, powdered milk, and fly paper in Utzpak at a good profit. However, the government now charges import duty, and the small trade from Chetumal to the peninsula has dried up. At present, Santiago's main item is hammocks.

A few years ago, the government began taking an interest in cottage industries around the Republic, in order to stimulate local economic life. In Yucatán, the hammock seemed to offer some promise. It is the most important item of furnishing of a Maya household, and is also an attractive item for tourists. Hammocks of cotton yarn wear out in three to four years, and are continually being woven on their upright looms by all members of the family. To produce a surplus for sale, the government had an agent distribute yarn to the women of the village, and this was woven into the body of the hammock.

The women were paid a very low wage for the semifinished product, which was then completed in a government shop and taken to the tourist centers. With Santiago barely making enough to feed his family, Reina began weaving hammocks many hours a day, until she began suffering from severe shoulder and back pain. It was, in a way, her apprenticeship period. She soon understood where the profit was and began developing her own network of young girls, who now weave hammocks for her. When a hammock body is completed, they send word to her, and she is the one who puts on the strands and the fortified loops by which they hang. She pays a bit more than the government agent, so she does not lack for workers. Santiago then takes these finished hammocks to market them. In the beginning, he went to Mérida to sell them on the central market, or to the laborers coming out of the factories on payday. The new tourist playground of Can Cun on the west coast of the peninsula, developed by the government in the early seventies, is now proving much more profitable, however. Much of the peninsular trade is aimed at the foreigners with money and little knowledge of local prices who frequent its sandy beaches and fancy hotels. Can Cun is a dangerous place, the men say. They go in pairs, and do not drink there, for if a man is drunk, he may be robbed or even killed.

Reina now has three daughters, after years of seeming barrenness, during which her sister-in-law called her "mula"—mule and other insulting names, and suggested that her brother divorce her and marry someone else. A fourth daughter, named for her, died recently at the age of six months, of bronchopneumonia. She had wanted only three children, but Santiago insisted. She tried the pill for a while, but could not tolerate it. When she is angry about his demands, she tells him to go and find "a woman of the street." Basically, she is resigned to the fact that she will probably have to bear more children.

When she and Santiago were first married, her father-in-law, a widower at the time, gave them permission to live in the second house on his property. Eventually, they bought the house from him. Both are square stone houses, constructed of limestone fragments and mortar (*mamposteria*), with a corrugated tar-paper roof. This type of housing is considered to be city-style. Her solar is very small, and bare except for a few orange bushes and a tamarind tree. Her relation to her solar is quite negligent. Not only has she no produce from it, but she does not sweep it either, and she has no flowers. At one time when Santiago had quarreled with his father, the couple bought a small plot not too far from their present home, and Santiago began blasting a hole for a well. Reina was aglow with plans for an idyllic cottage with pots of flowers in front of the entrance. Soon, however, the disagreement with her father-in-law was patched up, for, as she said, Santiago did not really want to leave the house which had been their first home, and there are still no flowers by the entrance. Instead of getting satisfaction out of working in her solar, she prefers watching television. In 1969, there were about 20 sets in the village, and the owners allowed others to watch for a small fee. Since then, the number of sets has more than doubled. Anthropologists, who are used to finding in the children some of their best informants, could no longer get any help from Reina's daughters. Instead of hanging around in the streets, the shops, and the church, and then having the collected impressions fixed because the adults continually quiz them on all that they have heard and seen, Reina's children are experts on el Capitan Canguro and other children's shows. They discuss with their mother not the activities of the neighbors, but the never-never world of the Mexican soap operas with their bloated plots and one-dimensional characters, such as El Roro or Angelitos Negros. When Reina goes to visit her mother, who now lives in Mérida, keeping house for her divorced son, she is free to help sell hammocks all day because her three little girls do not move away from their uncle's television set.

Reina is not interested much in household chores either. She is a most indifferent cook, often feeding her children a breakfast of Pepsi and animal cookies instead of the beans and tortillas they are asking for, or a thin coffee with salt crackers. In the evening, they buy *vaporcitos,* a corn-meal dumpling with bits of meat steamed in banana leaves, from a neighbor who makes them for sale, or they go to the plaza and eat a watery chicken soup sold there. She does not like to make tortillas and buys them from the mill instead. Vegetables come from the local market, as does the meat and the chickens. The children snack on commercially produced junk foods. Her clothes and her little girls' clothes are made by the seamstress down the street, her husband's are bought in the store. If we accept Blanton's (1976) definition of cities as places whose inhabitants are fed by others, I would say that Reina lives as though she were a city dweller, yet she lives in a village. The only produce she has in her solar in addition to a few oranges is a small, low-grade banana crop. Even that came about recently and by accident, for the shoots were given to her as a present. The banana stalks are gradually being destroyed by her two pigs that root them out for their sweet pith. The pigs are Reina's only livestock. She used to keep turkeys, but abandoned that venture as not profitable enough. Formerly, her pigs scavenged in the streets, which fattened them faster than if they were kept confined and fed their meager home ration. One year, however, two well-grown ones contracted trichinosis from offal they had eaten in the alleys, and she received only half-price for them. Another batch wandered into a strange solar, and she had to retrieve them from the municipal office, where they had been turned in. She paid for the damage they had caused as well as a fine. Since then, she keeps them in her solar.

In describing Eusebia's life, I noted that it seemed easy to use the present tense. When I met her in 1969, her life was pretty much as it is today. There is a constancy, a permanence about her life-style, about the objects she uses and the ways she views her environment that makes the "ethnographic present" suitable. When speaking about Reina, however, I was continually aware of the fact that matters were in flux, and I had to switch into the past tense. When I first saw her, the differences between her and Eusebia were not very striking. True, she lived in a masonry house and wore dresses rather than the 'ipil. During that first year, I did not even know that she also spoke Maya. But her house had a dirt floor, and she embroidered a little 'ipil for her first daughter who was an infant then. In addition to pigs, she also had turkeys and chickens. She made her own tortillas and had the open hearth glowing in the lean-to behind her house. Her baby munched on tortillas and learned to drink bean broth from a *luuch,* a gourd bowl. Since that time, many changes have come to Reina. For instance, she used to share the well with her father-in-law, but when the latter remarried, that led to quarrels between her and her new mother-in-law. So recently, her husband paid for a new well on their own property, surrounded by a fashionable masonry wall. She uses no gourd dishes any more, and her little girls have no 'ipiles. She now cooks on a kerosene stove, quite a luxury in a village where most women have an open woodburning hearth. Above her stove there hangs a new set of aluminum pots and pans. As her husband's business ventures became more successful, she had the dirt floor of her home covered with ceramic tiles. Since the death of her father-in-law a year ago, they had the rough limestone walls plastered and painted, and electricity put into the house. The earlier small wattle lean-to that served as a kitchen, was replaced by a new room, with a roof of corrugated iron. She and Santiago spread the rumor that the antropologist sent them the money to pay for these improvements. However, village gossip has it that they stole the cash from

Santiago's father, who some years before sold his small ranch and was living on the proceeds.

Subsistence Strategy

With her solar never very productive—she buys all her food stuffs on the market, and her only profit from her solar coming from her pigs, Reina's sole contribution to the subsistence of her family derives from activity in the cottage industry. It is also so important to her psychologically that one gains the impression that it has become an end in itself. Eusebia's daughter helped her when her baby died, and was shocked to hear her say that maybe it was just as well that the little girl died, now she would not be bothered by her when she had work to do. "She did not cry very much either when the child was buried," Eusebia's daughter said. Village gossip agrees that the infant died of neglect.

To earn more money, Reina also tries new avenues, such as buying the supplies and giving women permanents. She would like to buy an electric sewing machine, to be able to do "some fancy sewing real fast. " In all these activities, Reina's attitude is strictly universalistic: anybody can weave for her, or buy her hammocks, or have her hair set who will deliver the goods and pay the price, the amount of which is determined by what the market will bear.

If illness strikes, Reina will consult first a *yerbera,* following village custom. This is what she did when during the first years of her marriage, she did not conceive. The yerbera treated her exclusively with decoctions considered "hot" in local medical lore.[5] When her first delivery was so difficult that the local midwife could not handle it, Santiago took her to a physician in Mérida. In addition, she consults the government doctor. She does not, however, recognize the role of nutrition in health care and illness prevention. If her children look wan and skinny, she feeds them extra doses of vitamins. Her own massive case of *de los nervios* she attributes to her experimentation with the pill. She said this medication made her depressed, dizzy, weak, and caused her to lose her appetite. She quit taking it, and another pregnancy promptly followed, also curing her nervous condition. It is my impression that all these symptoms, or most of them, were due to her great anxiety that Santiago would find her wanting as a proper woman, who is supposed to be pregnant as much as possible and have many children as a living proof of her husband's virility. In case of catastrophic illness, as when her mother-in-law lay dying of cancer, a pig was sold for medical expenses.

Overall, Reina at present has actually fewer assets than Eusebia, and could hardly fall back on her solar to provide sustenance for her and Santiago in their old age. She is also disadvantaged because she has no sons, for traditionally, the sons are more obligated to help their parents than the daughters. She depends less on physical labor than Eusebia, and her hope is that at least one of her daughters will be good enough in school, so that she will find employment in the city, perhaps as a school teacher. She would then be able to go to stay with her in the city, provided her son-in-law would allow it. Her father-in-law made the mistake of distributing all his remaining land and his houses among his children before he died, and thus nobody felt obligated by hopes for an inheritance to take care of him when his money ran out. She says she will not make that mistake. There was a great deal of conflict between him and his four children. The bone of contention was his second wife, who, everyone said, ate too much and was the cause for his money running out so fast.

Religious Behavior
Reina was baptized a Catholic. When she married, she showed some interest in the Apostolic faith of Don Pedro, and attended the services at the temple, which is next door to her, built on land Don Pedro donated to the congregation. Neither she, nor Santiago, however, ever spoke in tongues, and lost interest in the sect even before the millenary episode in 1970. Since then, she has had her daughters baptized in the Catholic church to please her mother— her father died a few years ago, and she now attends an occasional Presbyterian service, where some of her friends go. The Presbyterians are very worldly in the eyes of the Apostolics, and this may be the reason she favors them. After all, they permit the use of makeup, the wearing of jewelry, and the going to picture shows and amusements, and these are important to her. She does not want to become a Catholic once more because they are "too strict," demanding the attendance of masses, confession, and communion. Besides, the church is too far away.

THE CASE OF NINA

Nina is Eusebia's youngest daughter, born in 1952, in the bush village. Thus she was only six when the family moved to Utzpak, where she attended two years of grade school. She writes and reads rather well. As a teenager, she tried working as a maid in Mexico City, but became homesick and returned to Utzpak a year later. By the time she was growing up, all her brothers had moved to the city except the youngest, Chan Felipe, who became a minister of the Apostolic church and usually had village congregations. Even he no longer is a peasant. Apparently, her brothers had a stronger influence on her than her two older sisters, who married village men and remained mestizas. (There is one more daughter, Eusebia's oldest, who lives in Mérida and whom she had disowned because she is not legally married; no one in the family has any contact with her.)

When Nina was 20 years old, she married Dino, a corn farmer from Utzpak. They had met in the Apostolic church, but after they were married, he lost interest in the church. Dino comes from a family of corn farmers. His father also does other types of work, such as blasting wells and helping with the construction of houses. When Dino realized that he could not make a living working on the ranches around Utzpak, he decided to join his father and mother in Chetumal. At first, he and Nina rented a shack, but soon, Dino's father decided to return to his village in Yucatán, and sold his shack in the squatter settlement to his son. This is where Nina and Dino now live. Dino is not happy in the city. He has tried repeatedly to find ranch work again, but without success. So he learned more of construction work which at present is a good occupation to have in Chetumal, since there is a great deal of housing construction going on. He leaves for work at five in the morning, comes home about six, takes a bath, eats, and rests, even on weekends. He does not see the city. "I never go out," he says.

Nina has born four children to date. The first one was a boy, who died when they were still living in Utzpak, of an infectious disease causing large boils. Since then she has had another boy, and a girl. After the latter was born, she was emphatic about not having any more children. "They cured me at the clinic," she said triumphantly, "they put in one of those things, and there will be no more children.What money there is, will feed the two, and will not be divided among three or four." However, her IUD fell out again, and she did not have it replaced. She gave birth to another girl. Now Dino wants another boy. "He wants to prove that he is potent," says Eusebia. "Máalob, he is potent to make children, but not potent to feed them."

Subsistence Strategy

Nina is entirely dependent on Dino for income. Except for the sale of some bananas from her tiny solar, she brings in nothing. Eusebia tried to stimulate her to start growing nursery stock, but she did not take up her suggestion. She enjoys city living, and feels that the services offered by the municipal government are quite good. Thus, drinking water for household use is trucked in once or twice a week, and several blocks away, there is a pump for bathing and washing water. The elementary school is quite far away, but there is a bus going that way. In the evenings when it is cool, she takes the children to the city playgrounds on the seashore, and later, they sometimes watch the dancing by the old municipal building, where a band plays rock-and-roll music. When a hurricane swept away the squatter settlement a few years ago, there had been ample warning, everyone was evacuated, and from the windows of the large school where they were housed, she could see the roofs fly by "like giant butterflies." Afterwards, there was much assistance, food, clothing, and building material, so that Dino could rebuild their shack. For food, she shops on the city market, and there is a tortilleria nearby. She also buys charcoal, and cooks over that. Occasionally, Dino suggests that they return to Utzpak, but she will not hear of it.

Illness is a constant companion in Nina's household, hitting the children with episodes of severe fever, often accompanied by diarrhea. "It is the soil that carries all that," says Nina, and in a way, she is probably right. There are no sewers in the squatter settlement. Excrement is collected in tin cans, and then simply placed by the edge of the street to dry. When the tropical sun has done its part, the remnants are shaken out, and the tin can is used again. Dino has blasted a hole into his solar large enough that it will not be filled up soon, but this does not much improve the general situation. To cure her children, Nina relies on medication that has helped other children with similar symptoms. Most of it can be gotten over the counter, without prescription. And having learned from her mother, she tries to feed them well, with tortillas, beans, chile, eggs, some meat, and bananas from her solar. When she gives birth, she travels to Dino's home village, where her mother-in-law acts as a midwife. Taking after her mother, she has easy births.

Nina and Dino are too young to give old age much thought. They assume that things will go on as before, and that their children will take care of them, although they do not take care of their parents: that need has not arisen yet. They do not worry too much about the work running out in Chetumal either. If this should happen, Nina can take over, housework is very well paid in Chetumal, and she has done it before, in Mexico City. As a last resort, they can return to either his or her parents, although Nina is not keen on discussing that avenue.

Religious Behavior
Nina was a small child when Eusebia was converted to the Apostolic faith, and she followed her mother into baptism when she became 14 years old. She helped her brother in the congregation, when he became the minister there, playing the guitar and teaching the children to sing hymns and recite Bible verses. She went through the millenary episode and afterwards opposed the split from the central organization of the church, just as her parents did, retaining a keen interest in the further development of the church. Since she moved to Chetumal, however, there has been a gradual alienation. She no longer goes to church services, claiming that the Apostolic church is too far away. Neither does she send her little son to Sunday school, although there is one run by a splinter group she has no quarrel with, and only two blocks away. This is regretable for two reasons. This child, called Pablito, is quite poor in verbal skills, which he could improve there. Also, as so many boys in Yucatán, he has been the object of severe teasing by both grandfathers and other men of the family, a pattern not involving girls. This produces boys of great excitibility and low flashpoint. No wonder Yucatan women think of their men as uncontrollably violent. It is quite obvious that unless Pablito gets some guidance, Nina will lose control over him within a very short time.

Having no social network in the sect any more, Nina has reverted to the general Latin-American *compadrazgo* system. Now, the entire institution is abhorrent to the Apostolics, because it implies infant baptism, which they decry. The official doctrine is that infants are without sin, and need no baptism. Instead the child is presented to the congregation soon after birth, and all the members are equally responsible for its well-being, as used to be the case with the godparents, the compadre and comadre. Unnoticed by the church hierarchy, however, a Maya institution has persisted that provides the child with a godmother of sorts with practically the same obligations as before, but without involving a baptism. This is the *hetsmeek* ceremony, when a friend of the mother lets the child ride on her hip for the first time. The child is also made to touch various objects, such as money to bring it luck. It is said that if the child does not undergo the hetsmeek ceremony, its legs will not grow properly. However, the young woman who is Nina's comadre knows no Maya, and to Eusebia's horror, she has had the child's ears pierced and has given her earrings: Apostolics wear no jewelry. Nina's excuse? Her friend has no children of her own, and she wanted all this so badly.

DISCUSSION

In a comparison of various human adaptations, we find that both the communities of the hunter-gatherers and the nomadic pastoralists are in a manner of speaking open systems: conflict is resolved by the bands fissioning. The agriculturalist, at least ideally, does not allow himself this option. Too much in effort and planning is invested in a planted field. Once sowed, it must be harvested. How closed the system is ideologically becomes very clear when agriculturalist religious systems are viewed crossculturally (see Goodman n.d). Even beyond the grave, the member of an agriculturalist community is bound to serve. The most henious crime is to commit suicide, for this forever exempts him. Given general human propensities, such rigidity cannot, of course, endure. Historically, we find relatively early that ways are evolved to break out of the bondage. Buddhism, to my mind, may be viewed as such a movement. Perhaps less obviously, city living is another. It follows that I view the agriculturalist and his various escape strategies, specifically in this case, the city, not as opposing, but as complementary systems. One feeds on the other, in reciprocal interaction. This, I think, is demonstrated by the data I have presented.

Eusebia, for instance, loses her social network by the expulsion of the family from the home village. As in other human adaptations except for city dwelling, her security depends on social bonds. This is where her heaviest investment lies. Even her commercial activity is designed in such a way that it serves not to accumulate capital, but to cement these bonds. When these bonds are severed and she needs to adapt to a new community, she has to start, relatively late in life, forming a new network. Increasing her commercial activity is one way, but clearly not enough. It is entirely understandable that under these circumstances, she should be attracted to Apostolic missionizing in the village. Her intuition informs her that here, new bonds are being created. This also explains her aggressive disapproval of the schism which separated the young Yucatan congregations from the parent organization. The theological quibble is window dressing: the new independent church has no faith, because this word is left out of the name it was given; its members have no peace, since they no longer greet each other with the formula, Paz de Cristo—Christ's peace. What is truly happening is a panic reaction. The schism effectively destroyed the new network, at least in her view. She is not entirely a loser, though. Of her eight children, she has interested five and permanently converted two. In this manner, she has forged some security that in its strength goes beyond mere kin obligations, which in the present condition of rural impoverishment due to plunder by Western market manipulations is considerably weakened. The means to accomplish this were offered to her by a movement originating in the city, an urban stimulus, namely the Pentecostal movement. Joining it brought her none of the advantages touted by social scientists. It made her neither upwardly mobile, nor economically more independent. It provided her with no power, and it did not dissolve any cognitive dissonance. She used it simply as an innovation that she found capable of restoring her own traditional way of life, to enable her to live within a psychologically satisfying social configuration.

The ultimate concern of tight and solid social bonds inspiring Eusebia, is a hindrance to Reina and a bane to Santiago. In the natural course of things, they would have been the village outcasts. Reina is quarrelsome, because she lacks the early training in the many intricate ways in which social bonds are kept intact and functioning profitably. She did not learn these skills in an henequenero household. And Santiago is lazy, by agriculturalist standards, and tainted by his mother's repute as a petty thief. Local gossip, that marvelous tool for social control, for grinding down differences, would have harassed and maybe broken them. City traits provided an out in this situation, by offering them stimulation for a different, impersonal, wealth-oriented economic activity. It made it possible for them to acquire some trappings of the prestigious city life. They are not true city dwellers, of course. They do not have the skills that are needed to accumulate capital, which serves the city dweller as a basis for security in lieu of social bonds. Instead, they engage in an elaborate game of mimicry by making themselves look like town people, and of obfuscation by feeding false information to the gossip network about the source of their seeming opulence. The message they are transmitting is clear: we have made it, and you cannot touch us. One or the other of their daughters may make it to the city, as a part of the sloughing off of cells that I discussed in the introduction, and which in societies where there is a peasantry, sustains and nurtures the city.

With Nina, this process is completed. She has chosen the town, and the town is the winner. She is dragging Dino along, who, unwillingly, provides the means for her to accomplish her objective. She is not quite a city dweller yet, since she seeks to establish some permanent networks by utilizing the compadrazgo option. But she brings to the city her enthusiasm of discovery, her capacity for adaptation and improvisation. By learning the Latin-American urban social values, such as the man being the provider, the woman the sheltered, secluded homemaker and insisting on their adoption, she reaffirms and maintains what is under attack by changes wrought in the course of industrialization.

NOTES

1. *Ejido* land is federally administered public communal land; the system was introduced after the Mexican Revolution (1910-1920).

2. The situation was similar to the one Rhoda Halperin (1977) describes for Chan Kom: both the apportioning of ejido parcels and the drafting for communal labor, *fagina*, was in the hands of the same powerful family. The system lends itself to the elimination of politically uncooperative members of the village community.

3. The entire terminology has moved up a notch from earlier usage. *India* is an insult today, the old term for mixed breed, *mestiza*, substituting for it. *Ladino* for the Spanish upper class has disappeared entirely from the dialect of the region where I worked. So has the term *catrin*, often mentioned in the literature, for someone who wants to be identified with the Spanish ethnic group. In Utzpak, it is used only for men's city-type shoes.

4. This is discussed in detail in Goodman 1973 and 1974.

5. In Latin-American folk medicine a distinction is made between "hot" and "cold" substances (having nothing to do with temperature), a view supposedly going back to classical times in the Mediterranean area. Similar beliefs, however, are deeply entrenched also in India. See also Kimball, this volume.

REFERENCES

Blanton, Richard E.
  1976   "Anthropological Studies of Cities." *Annual Review of Anthropology* 5:249-64.

Chapman, Anne M.
  1957   "Port of Trade Enclaves in Aztec and Maya Civilization." In *Trade and Markets in the Early Empires*, Karl Polanyi, Conrad Arensberg, and Harry Pearson, eds. Glencoe, Ill.: Free Press.

Goodman, Felicitas D.
    1973   "Apostolics of Yucatán: A Case History of a Religious Move-
           ment." In *Religion, Altered States of Consciousness, and Social
           Change,* Erika Bourguignon, ed. Columbus: Ohio State Univer-
           sity Press, pp. 178-218.

    1974   "Disturbances in the Apostolic Church: A Trance-Based Upheav-
           al in Yucatán." In *Trance, Healing, and Hallucination: Three
           Field Studies in Religious Experience.* Felicitas D. Goodman,
           Jeanette H. Henney, and Esther Pressel, eds. New York: Wiley
           Interscience.

    n.d.   *In the Dreaming: A Theory of Religious Behavior.* (in Prepara-
           tion).

Halperin, Rhoda, and James Dow, eds.
    1977   *Peasant Livelihood: Studies in Economic Anthropology and Cul-
           tural Ecology.* New York: St. Martin's Press.

Potter, Jack M., May N. Diaz, and George M. Foster, eds.
    1967   *Peasant Society: A Reader.* Boston: Little, Brown, and Co.

Redfield, Robert.
    1941   *The Folk Culture of Yucatán.* Chicago: The University of Chi-
           cago Press.

Thompson, Richard A.
    1975   *The Winds of Tomorrow: Social Change in a Maya Town.* Chica-
           go: The University of Chicago Press.

Wolf, Eric R.
    1966   *Peasants.* Englewood Cliffs, N.J.: Prentice-Hall.

11 The Uses of Traditional Concepts in the Development of New Urban Roles: Cuban Women in the United States

MARGARET S. BOONE

In this chapter we are offered a picture of a middle-class immigrant group that has made a successful adaptation to life in a large metropolitan center in the United States. Boone notes that the women have contributed a large measure to what has been called the Cuban "success story" in this country. Settled in non-localized groups spread over the Washington, D.C., region, they have formed far-flung communication networks, that function in a manner similar to the closely knit neighborhoods in which they lived in pre-Castro Cuba. Comparing the roles of these women in Cuba and those they have developed in this country, the author suggests that their past learning has preadapted them to life in their new society. This appears to have been true of the women to a greater extent than of the men, an observation that may hold true for other immigrant groups as well, and that has, more generally, implications for theories of acculturation and social change. With regard to the Cubans specifically, Boone notes the remarkable innovative and creative capacity of which the women have made proof in the modification of their role structure.

I have learned recently (through my studies of peak experiences) to look to women and to feminine creativeness as a good field of operation for research, because it gets less involved in products, less involved in achievement, more involved with the process itself, with the going-on process rather than with the climax in obvious triumph (Maslow 1971:61)

INTRODUCTION: CREATIVITY IN ROLE CHANGE

Cuban women who have immigrated to the United States since the beginning of the revolution in 1959 come from a culture dominated by a traditional form of Latin machismo. Resettlement in the urban/administrative, Anglo city of Washington, D.C., has challenged some of their basic assumptions about relations between the sexes. It has also put at a premium their capacity for creative change. Sex roles have shifted, and their activities in the public domain have increased, without undermining the security offered by traditional interaction between the sexes.

Although the majority of Cuban immigrants are concentrated in the urban areas of Florida, New York, and New Jersey, some choose to live in northern and midwestern U.S. cities because of employment opportunities, or the proximity to kin and friends. In 1970, Washington, D.C., was the location of about 7,000 rapidly assimilating Cubans. The city attracts the immigrant who is comfortable both with the absence of a single, dense Cuban neighborhood, and with the dominance of the white-collar, bureaucratized federal government. Changes in feminine roles and their domains of activity have taken specific forms in response to Washington's dominant ethos patterns.

The majority of Cuban women in Washington are employed in service occupations that range from secretary to college professor. Since only one-eighth of all Cubans in the Washington area live in the District of Columbia, many women have adjusted to a commuter pattern of working in the city and residing in the suburbs. Their geographical spread and work patterns require them to change traditional sex-role conceptions even more than their fellow country people in Florida, who live in denser communities. Cuban women in Washington have often been forced into the public labor market by economic necessity. However, they strive to maintain a sense of cultural continuity for individual families, a sense of cohesion within networks of families, and a traditional sense of their own self-worth under financial, social, and psychological pressure that would seem crippling. However, they have succeeded in keeping their families together, and in re-creating a previous standard of living, with an ingenuity that the social scientist finds interesting, if not puzzling. As psychologist Abraham Maslow suggests, the process of creativity is found among Cuban women in a realm of daily activity that so far has received too little attention.

In Maslow's comment on creativity, he focuses on an important aspect of the anthropological study of women at all levels of culture. A great deal has been written recently on the cross-culturally prevalent difference in the domains of activity for the sexes: public or "political" for males, and private or domestic for females. Authors typically emphasize the restrictive, even stifling, quality of the private domain in which women throughout the world play out their roles as wives and mothers. This conception of the private domain is congruent with an understanding of women as the more passive participants in society. They are said to have weaker ego boundaries because of an uninterrupted identification with their mothers and daughters. The nurturance required in feeding, clothing, and tending to the bodily needs of husbands and children underscores the impression of relatively fluid feminine personalities (Rosaldo and Lamphere 1974; Chodorow 1974). In a cross-cultural survey of sex differences in socialization, Chodorow capsulizes the distinction in the title of her paper, "Being and Doing." Thus, "attainment of sex-role identity is that girls and women 'are,' while boys and men 'do': feminine identity is 'ascribed,' masculine identity 'achieved' " (Chodorow 1971: 272).

Along with many anthropologists now writing on women's roles, Maslow (1971: 90-91) feels that males differentiate themselves by a rejection of their primary identification with their mothers. Men then generalize this process in a derogation of all femininity, even the feminine qualities of their own personalities. Studies on Latin America *machismo* depict these processes in exaggerated form. Descriptions commonly include an extreme double standard, an early diffentiation between feminine passivity and masculine aggression, and an ideal cloistering of wives and daughters in the household. In modern Latin America, sex roles are changing, but very slowly. Even in post-revolutionary Cuba conceptions of the sexes are resistant to fundamental change (Rowbotham 1972).

Maslow's comment suggests a different, although complementary, view of the private domain which is helpful in understanding Cuban women in the United Sates. Both before and after immigration and resettlement, feminine roles in the domestic domain were frequently fluid and unnamed. Within that context Cuban women exhibit a type of creativity that is fostered by the milieu in which they operate. Maslow writes that the "prerequisites of creativeness—in whatever realm—somehow have something to do with this ability to become timeless, selfless, outside of space, of society, of history" (1971: 62). This description of a creative setting coincides dramatically with a picture of the private domain now emerging in the writing on women's roles. The growing literature on the role changes among female immigrants includes numerous examples of this creativity in action. However, both theoretical and ethnographic works highlight an extension of private female role development. Talents exploited in the domestic domain are used with ingenuity to achieve personal, social, and political goals in the public domain (Chiñas 1973; Riegelhaupt 1967; Collier 1974).

Cuban women in Washington manipulate their public roles with a strategy developed at home. They exhibit much of the same creativity described by other anthropologists for women in peasant and tribal groups. Their strategy includes a focus on process rather than final product, on working for the family rather than the ethnic group or society, and on exploitation of their beauty and charm as well as their intelligence and ability. Role change can be a creative and adaptive process which contributes toward personal and family security, especially in a foreign culture. Cuban women have shifted sex roles in a way that alters, without threatening, their own traditional *macho* image of the Cuban male and their own self-image as pampered, cloistered, and protected females. They have entered into the public world of work, but maintain themselves as anchors in traditional (as well as new) networks of family and friends. A veneer of ideal culture covers all their many and varied activities. This strategy could be seen as trickery of "manipulation"' in a negative sense, but this would be denying the accomplishments of Cuban immigrant women. The interpretation of these techniques as "creativity" is more useful, for their end "product" has been, with a minority of exceptions, assimilation with a minimum of social disintegration.

THE TRADITIONAL CUBAN FEMALE: CONTINUITY AND CONTRADICTION

In the United States a Cuban woman's virtue is still defined largely in sexual terms. Next to chastity and modesty, the strengths developed after immigration are secondary. As one informant said,

> The best part of a woman is her innocence. If she were exactly like a man, she would be nothing. Every time she is with a new man, something is killed inside of her... Women should never lose a delicate way of looking and feeling. If she loses feeling, she gets rough like a man, and loses *sensibilidad* (sensitivity).

There is an important social corollary to this conception of woman. Without premarital sexual restraint, a woman is unfit for a good marriage.

> I don't like freedom. One of the best things in life for a woman is marriage. You couldn't get married in Cuba if you were too free. You wouldn't be the right person to be the mother of his children.

The psychological and social importance of modesty before and during marriage is not diminished for the majority of Cuban women in Washington. However, the physical, cognitive, and emotional strengths listed by the women themselves suggest that their self-perceptions have changed. They have found new conceptual bases for the importance of marriage, work, and the family. They have developed roles in the United States which combine old and new values, concepts, and institutions. These important changes are part of an oddly self-conscious process, for Cuban women are strikingly aware of their own responses to the stress of immigration.

Before analyzing specific examples of role change, it is necessary to understand the cultural basis of sex roles, as well as the social basis from which Cuban women draw their fortitude. The traditional stereotype of the cloistered female is not consistent with the real, assertive, decisive, and highly gregarious female immigrant making her way in an urban, Anglo, northern city in the United States.

Inconsistencies between real and ideal culture have a long history in the Cuban sex-role system. However, descriptions of masculine and feminine behavior are as consistent through time as they are contradictory at any one time. For example, Cuban author García de Arboleya and U.S. feminist Julia Ward Howe focused on different aspects of the upper-class woman's life in 1860. García de Arboleya found the Cuban woman either confined to her house and carriage, or constantly chaperoned on her visits to a few selected locations such as church, shops, and the theatre. Similarly, Nelson describes her a century later as "a bird in a cage, a sheltered creature—a victim of the extreme romanticism of the age of chivalry" (1950: 175-76).

In her travel chronicles of nineteenth-century Matanzas Province, Howe pictures some of the same double standard. However, she also suggests that upper-class Cuban women were not as submissive as one might assume. She provides the following passage as evidence.

> A drive by moonlight was now proposed, to see the streets and the masks, it being still Carnival. So the *volante* [carriage] was summoned, with its smiling Roqué [the driver], and the pretty daughter of the house took seat beside us. The streets around the Plaza proved quite impassable from the crowd, whose wild movements and wilder voices went nigh to scaring the well-trained horses. The little lady was accustomed, apparently, to direct every movement of her charioteer, and her orders were uttered in a voice high and sweet as a bird-call. *"Dobla al derecho, Roqué, Roqué, dobla al derecho!"* [Turn to the right!] Why did not Roqué go mad, and exclaim,--"Yes, Señorita, and to heaven itself, if you bid me so prettily!" But Roqué only doubled as he was bid, and took us hither and thither...(Howe 1969: 155-56).

Bradley goes back even further in Cuban cultural history in his colorful book on Havana. He describes one outstanding female figure as "one of those strong-willed women who keeps appearing in Havana history in spite of the general impression that wives and daughters were subject to a sheltered life..." (1941: 77). Bradley also notes an early introduction to sexuality among the nineteenth-century upper classes. He quips that, "Albeit the image of the Virgin was the one most prominently displayed in religious processions, there must have been some misunderstanding on the part of worshippers... Half-grown children attended adult parties and were permitted such other opportunities for observation and research as are not usually achieved so early" (1941: 326). Herskovits (1937) notes similar liberties among the early wealthy planters in Haiti. Cuba and Haiti shared a frontier quality that encouraged the loosening of social structures (*cf* Price 1973; 1975). Both cultures also developed a typical two-class aristocratic social system in response to a plantation economy, as in the U.S. South and other regions of the New World.

Within an historical Caribbean context, Cuban women have always shown a degree of assertiveness and freedom from restraint, in spite of any traditional Iberian ideal. They have had an early opportunity for marriage. Although the originally Spanish feudal ideal of cloistering could be maintained by upper-class women who did not work, they were certainly not absent entirely from the public domain—from the balls, the shops, the *paseo* (public walk). Their limited confinement to the private domain failed to discourage the development of strong and commanding personalities.

Several anthropologists have tried to explain the transmutation of the Spanish ideal in colonial Cuba, and the origin of its sex-role system (Nelson 1950; Mintz 1966; Wagley 1968). Their explanations focus on the independent, decentralized agrarian economic system of early Cuba; the late arrival of the plantation system; high sex ratios, and other factors which fostered an egalitarian family form. Cuba was settled by a predominantly white Spanish population. Africans came to Cuba later than they came to Jamaica or Haiti, and never in proportionate numbers. There has been a strong tradition of freedom for a large part of the black population in Cuba.

Early in Cuban history the Catholic authorities in Spain reversed policies on interracial and common-law marriage. Some fluidity in the marriage system developed, except in the upper classes where written genealogies established strict lines of descent. The institution of marriage remained stronger than in those Caribbean societies where the plantation system required large numbers of black slaves at an early date. Cuba developed as a small-farm society in which land was available to most free men. In this atmosphere women and men abandoned the aristocratic constraints of cloistering, and, aided by the very scarcity of women, a more equal status for the Cuban female evolved. Even two centuries later in the United States, Cuban women are cherished and consulted in a manner which suggests more equality than pampering. These changes are consistent with those in other frontier societies, and some immigration situations. Economic changes can foster the rise in the social prestige and power of women.

Urban upper-class women developed their own special strengths and freedom, in spite of their close adherence to sex-role ideals. When the urban tradition later extended into rural areas via the plantation system in the nineteenth century, basic Cuban culture was established, and sex-role behavior changed little. The origin of the strength demonstrated by contemporary Cuban women in the United States can be understood in light of Cuba's unique history in the Caribbean.

> By the time the plantation system began to expand in Cuba, that colony had a society, a people, and a culture of its own. We have seen that, for over two centuries, Cuba was able to build its society slowly, without protracted disturbance from the outside... Though there were periods of isolation, and attempted invasions by other powers... Cuban society gradually took on a special quality: rural in emphasis, anti-Spanish but pro-Hispanic, folk-Catholic, creole... Cuba's near-uniqueness rested in her cultural synthesis, in the economic independence of her people, and in the protection she was provided against the spread of the plantation system (Mintz 1966: 177-78).

Mintz underscores the independent nature of early Cuban society. With the security provided by small farms, cultural evolution could proceed in relative isolation. A consistent set of strong sex roles developed, as individuality and self-assertion became typical for the female as well as the male. The ideal of sheltering a wife in the domestic domain persisted, although her economic importance in the isolated farm family lent importance and prestige to her roles. However, her contribution to the family itself derived from her chastity before marriage, her faithfulness during marriage, and her role as mother. These traits have early antecedents that extend back to the patriarchal social organization in the Mediterranean (Schneider 1971).

At the time of the Cuban revolution in 1959 Cuba was a two-class society, but the importance of the family was common to both. Its sanctity was upheld by rural families as much as by the urban upper classes and the plantation elite. Although Havana and the lowland sugar plantations had their share of poor, disintegrating families dependent on sporadic wage labor, the cultural ideal of a strong family was too entrenched to change.

The culture history of the Cuban family and its sex-role system aids in understanding the contradiction between the ideals voiced by Cuban immigrant women, and their actual behavior. The duality of submission and assertiveness, derogation with status, and sheltered pampering combined with a proclivity for the social, the exciting, the challenging, and the colorful persists today among Cuban women in the United States. Their strengths come in part from the hardships imposed by immigration. However, feminine assertion has a definite place in Cuban cultural history, and is not a new phenomenon.

Lastly, some insight into feminine behavior can be gained from Cuban national character portraits, as problematical as these can be. As in classic national character studies, these studies are implicitly more descriptive of male modal personalities than female. However, the values expressed by immigrant women in Washington suggest that women reflect national Cuban "character traits " as well, especially as their participation in the public domain increases. Among these values are: a belief in the innate worth of the individual, and a respect for unique qualities; a belief that personal dignity is maintained through close and trusting relationships, especially those in the family or based on a model of the family (*personalismo*); a strong belief in personal freedom of action, and the right to express the self in public; a belief in destiny and a tendency toward fatalism; a belief in honor and duty, but one that rarely extends beyond the family or close friends (and resembles Banfield's "amoral familism"); a belief that there is nothing one cannot do if he or she persists; a fondness of gaiety, a "hedonism," a "talent for pleasure" that find expression in care for personal appearance, dancing, music, food, and talk (Blutstein et al. 1971: 199-207; Bosch 1966).

Generalizations at this level promise to be contradictory because of their wide scope. Most incongrous in this list are a belief in destiny and luck, combined with a competitive individuality. Blutstein et al. resolve these traits in the observation that

> Success in life is measured more in terms of the fulfillment of personal destiny or spiritual potential than by the achievement of a social goal. Destiny is evaluated in terms of the competitive situation and the opportunities that present themselves at any given moment for an immediate improvement in one's personal circumstances. Thus, resignation and aggressive competitiveness are juxtaposed (1971: 202).

The contradiction is also resolved by segregating the two beliefs conceptually along sexual lines. Resignation and passivity are assigned to women, while aggression and a "zest for action" are an appropriate part of the masculine *machismo* complex (Gillin 1965: 509). As roles evolve among Cuban immigrants in the United States, these separate modes of interaction for the two sexes have blurred to an even greater extent than recorded historically. It is significant that a juxtaposition of these modes would prove highly adaptive for any group adjusting to a new society. In fact, Cuban women in Washington are characterized by an "opportunistic competitiveness" combined with resignation to life's tremendous upheavals.

THE MECHANICS OF ROLE CHANGE

Although sex is a universal criterion for role assignment, Mead (1935) and many after her show that sex roles differ among cultures according to basic conceptions of the sexes. Ideals of appropriate behavior for men and women are so basic to a world view that change in a sex-role system can cause enormous conflict and disorganization. However, sex roles do change, especially in response to economic changes.

Although Cubans come from a complex, industrializing society, they face an analogous need to shift sex roles in response to greater female participation in the public domain. However, Cuban culture in the United States has not been destroyed by these changes. This is partly because of the manner in which Cuban women have shifted sex-role content. They have been aided in this process by a cluster of inconsistent images of male and female, rather than hampered by a unidimensional concept of appropriate sex-role behavior. Some qualities derive from traditional Hispanic culture, and some developed during the history of colonial Cuba as previously described. First-generation Cuban female immigrants are assimilating successfuly because they are not restricted by an immutable and maladaptive image of what a woman is and does.

When questioned about basic male/female differences, women responded at first with surprise at such an "obvious" question. However, their eventual replies betrayed a contrasting composite of positive and negative qualities for both sexes. A traditional and a nontraditional picture of each emerged. Many of the positive qualities assigned to men and the negative qualities assigned to women are remnants of Iberian sexual ideals. Another set of more positive feminine traits and negative masculine traits complement the traditional system. They aid in understanding the mechanics of sex-role manipulation among female immigrants, and form a conceptual rationale for alterations in appropriate behavior.

Traditionally, men are expected to participate more actively in politics, and are believed to be more intelligent and knowledgeable about "the street," the world outside the home. In Cuban culture this arena includes not only business and politics, but the traditionally masculine domains of the cock-fight and the cane field. The women immigrants who list these "macho" qualities of men find some security and pride in their existence. *Machismo* has recently taken on such a negative connotation in the United States, that the more culturally "positive" aspects of this Latin American action complex are frequently forgotten. As Gillin writes, "In a sense it corresponds to an ideal type of male social personality...The cultural concept involves sexual prowess, action orientation (including verbal action), and various other components" (1965:509). It should be remembered that the traditional Cuban mother delights in signs of aggression and domination in her young sons, and looks for signs of passivity and a demure bearing in her daughters (Wagley 1968:70-71).

At the deepest level, these ideas have changed little among first-generation Cuban women. As women who foster respect within their own families, they demonstrate by their actions that it is adaptive for neither sex to give up pride in the other. However, they counterbalance their pride in the masculinity of their sons and husbands, with a recognition of their weaknesses, as

Table 11.1 Cultural Concepts of Sex Differences

	Positive Qualities	Negative Qualities
Men	physically stronger aggressive like roosters[*gallo*] less sentimental less pessimistic more responsible more sensible more wise more intelligent bossy more knowledgable about "the street"	harder for men to get sick impatient worse observers so sentimental when women wouldn't react they feel, but they don't forget more easily feel only for the moment more selfish more simple insecure immigration harder on men
Women	not as much crybabies as men can cope with more pain more energetic able to be themselves sexually now just as strong as men more patient more realistic more pragmatic more flexible more involved clever more optimistic equal (to men)	immigration physically harder on women *sexo débil* [weaker sex] sentimental pessimistic irresponsible more emotional to a degree invidious superficial

well as cultural "borrowing" of masculine strengths. As they are expressed in Table 11.1 the positive qualities of women are more than sufficient to support their greater participation in the public domain. While many work long hours in offices, commute by car and bus, and ferry their children in typical suburban fashion, they maintain that the ideal would be to stay at home and let their husbands provide and protect. They sustain a traditional although altered image of their husbands, at the same time that they increasingly recognize their own strengths and competence.

Conceptual consistency would undermine this adaptive role change. If Cuban women considered themselves the *sexo debil* [the weaker sex] they would not be so open about the weaknesses they perceive in men, nor could they rationalize their own jobs and salaries. However, if they did not overtly accept their dependence on men, they believe their family structure would be weakened.

Many of the women in Washington who live in the suburbs come from the "upper middle class" of prerevolutionary Cuba. Most of them had domestic help in their households. Some of the sexual differences they perceive are reminiscent of the *ante bellum* aristocratic ideals of the U.S. South. As both were "plantation societies," some congruency should be expected. The traditional "southern belle" certainly is not known for her total submission to masculine domination, but for her cleverness and energy. She is painted in the literature as superficial but pragmatic, irresponsible but realistic. This is very much the way Cuban women perceive themselves. The duality and contradiction has allowed them to maintain their traditional ideas of male and female while shifting sex-role behavior. The changes in Cuban sex roles have not destroyed the family or the culture.

One explanation for this cultural persistence is found in the class origin of Cuban immigrants. Why did they not develop a "culture of poverty" while Puerto Ricans frequently have (Lewis 1965)? One important factor is the relatively high level of occupational skills of Cubans, in contrast to Puerto Ricans or Mexicans. Most Cuban immigrants were not "marginal" or oppressed in prerevolutionary Cuba. They came to the United States as political exiles, and frequently succeeded in reconstituting a life-style to which they had grown accustomed in the 1950s.

It is valid to credit some of the Cuban cultural stability among immigrants to the middle-class composition of the group. However, the black or low-income Cuban women in Washington show an equal involvement in family life, an equal willingness to compete in the public domain, and equal involvement in an ethnic group. Sex-role change without the development of a culture of poverty must be explained on other than a class basis alone. Lewis offers a possible explanation in some of his more impressionistic statements. He writes that, "Puerto Rico has a much higher per capita income than Mexico, yet Mexicans have a deeper sense of identity" (1965:li). It is therefore an equally strong sense of cultural identity—in addition to class—which must explain the Cuban "success story," not only in Miami but elsewhere. As hubs of family networks, women are responsible for maintaining much of this identity. In addition, the creativity they demonstrate in role change plays a large part in the successes of the entire group.

The following discussion of Cuban women's roles is based on two branches of analysis that converge surprisingly little in the literature. Recently, a number of cultural anthropologists have focused on women's roles and feminine prestige from a cross-cultural viewpoint. They are included among those in the developing field, "the anthropology of women." There is a strong feeling among these anthropologists, most of whom are women, that some types of feminine behavior have received too little attention. Their role models stress unnamed, "nonformalized" activities (Chinas 1973:93ff). Little of their analytical scheme is based on the traditional role analysis of Banton (1965),

Goffman (1959, 1969), Gross et al (1958), and Nadel (1953). However, the students of the new "anthropology of women" are striving to solve many of the same problems of the more established role analysts. The terminologies and focus may differ, but the approaches are analogous.

For example, Chinas and Goffman offer schemes that serve some of the same purposes. Chinas writes,

> If one conceptualizes the social system as made up of roles (defined earlier as bundles of rights and obligations), one might compare a social system to an iceberg. What has been described to this point is the visible part of the iceberg, that part which includes the formalized roles. A large part of the Isthums Zapotec social system, however, is concealed in the submerged part of the iceberg. The submerged part of the social system, the nonformalized roles, is as crucial to an understanding of Isthmus Zapotec culture as is the visible part, the formalized roles (1973:93).

Goffman's concepts of "performance," "backstage region of behavior," and "impression management" are parallel to Chinas' "nonformalized role." In referring to the writings of Simone de Beauvoir, he recognizes that a great deal of feminine behavior takes place "in private," or "backstage" (1959:11-13). Both the traditional role analysts and the newer students of women's behavior try to understand the less obvious, but still predictable, patterns of cultural behavior.

The scheme developed by Chinas stems partially from a complaint concerning methodology and field work. She finds that women's activities are viewed too often as "women's nature" by members of the group, and as simply a "sex role" by some researchers. However, the difference is one of analytical and methodological emphasis, rather than theoretical basis. Chinas notes

> If the nonformalized roles are powerful, there has probably been some attempt to incorporate these into the description, often in an unsystematic way just as they occur in the field notes, leaving the reader to draw his own conclusion as to how to integrate them into the social system. Some attempts have been made to explain nonformalized roles by presenting the formalized roles as the social system and then adding data concerning nonformalized roles as "exceptions to the rules" (1973:94).

According to this formulation, both formalized and nonformalized roles are useful to Cuban women in adjusting to an Anglo society.

Although the major portion of the following discussion relies on the formalized/nonformalized dichotomy, it is also useful to look back to Linton's and Nadel's more traditional definition of the role as a set of normative expectations. The following discussion of specific roles is based on the expectations expressed by the women in this study, as a group. Whether they are stated directly or indirectly, they are broad guidelines for behavior. Many role expectations derive less from pointed explanations than from the more revealing monologues, anecdotes, and discussions. However, some expectations also emerge from the definite rights and duties that Cuban women are rarely hesitant in making clear in the informal interview situation.

From direct observation of Cuban women in interaction, it is seen that these expectations lead to, and are reflected in, patterns of behavior. Some are more widely recognized by the women than are others, and therefore the formalized/nonformalized distinction has been used. The roles remain subjective sets of expectations of the women themselves, and reflect their husbands' and children's desires only as indirect perceptions.

The dichotomy between expectation and "real behavior" becomes problematic in a group of informants with a high level of self-awareness. Only rarely did behavior and reports of behavior conflict with each other, or with expressions of ideal behavior. More common was a self-conscious ac-accounting of the conflict between "how things should be" and "how they really are." Because of their self-awareness, the women in this study rarely pictured ideal roles without comments about the discrepancies between real and ideal. Their expectations took on a realistic and pragmatic quality. In such a case, the "emic" and "etic" blend. Because of their self-analytical nature, the Cuban women in this study create a continuity between normative expectations and reported behavior.

In the following sections roles are distinguished as to their formalized or nonformalized quality, and as to their domain of activity. Chiñas distinguishes roles according to their place in the public domain. However, in a pluralistic society a new domain emerges that is both public and private: the domain of the ethnic group. In the heterogeneous locale of the modern metropolis, this domain becomes especially important for family and individual security. Support is provided among Washington Cubans along widely ramifying network lines, and less so within discrete, localized ethnic groups. In fact, Cubans in Washington do not self-consciously belong to one national identity group. Although efforts to create a sense of unified Cuban ethnicity have been made, associations have met with apathy especially on the part of the more wealthy suburbanites. Success in the United States for this group remains an individual family matter, although they continue to socialize mainly with other Cubans. If they could be assigned to a group, it would be "Latins with money, status, and/or high social aspirations who live in the suburbs." On the other hand, poor and black Cubans belong to a group of "poorer, black and mulatto Latins who live for the most part in the Adams Mill-Morgan area of the District of Columbia." Still, this would not include all Cuban immigrants in the area, as many find support in smaller networks in the nearby suburbs of Arlington, and Alexandria, Virginia.

The ethnic group as a domain of activity can be divided potentially into classes, racial segments, and occupational groups (which are especially important in the nation's capital where the work ethic dominates most lives). For present purposes, roles will be distinguished as to their place in the private, ethnic public, or national public domain. The ethnic public domain is defined most inclusively in this study as "Latins in the Washington SMSA".*

The roles of wife, mother, and worker are formalized roles, while the role of the *chismosa,* the *belleza,* and the *tia* (loosely translated as the "gossip," the "beauty," and the "aunt") are nonformalized. Table 11.2 indicates the predominant domain of each role, and arrows show any overlap between domains. Each role is important for the adjustment of Cuban women to a new society. Some are old roles that have changed because of new circumstances, and some are largely new. In all cases they strengthen the security of the women, their families, and to some extent their ethnic networks.

Table 11.2 Female Roles and Their Domains.

	Private		Ethnic Public		National Public
Formalized	wife	→		←	worker
	mother	→			
Nonformalized	*tía*	←	*belleza*	→	
			chismosa	→	

THE WIFE: A PRIVATE AND FORMALIZED ROLE

Most first-generation Cuban women are married and immigrated to the United States with their spouses or at about the same time. Marriage is considered the most normal and satisfying mode of existence for the Cuban women, and is valued as an institution above and apart from the roles of husband and wife. To be a wife has a broad meaning for the Cuban woman, as she came from a society in which the extended family was an important unit of social organization. Prerevolutionary Cuban society placed relatively light emphasis on associations outside the family. In a sense, the family was more important than the nation itself, in that political leaders fashioned their roles on the contract and trust relationships typical of the family (Blutstein et al. 1971: 206). Pseudokinship relations—of the *patrón* (a mutually responsive arrangement between a wealthy, powerful man and a man of lesser status and his family, where protection is given in return for allegiance); and the *compadre* and *comadre* (where the godfather and godmother extend familial protection to nonkin in exchange for social prestige and influence)—were very important in prerevolutionary society. Remnants of them persist in networks established by Cuban immigrants in the United Sates, although they are much more important in southern Florida than in Washington, D.C.

*Standard Metropolitan Statistical Area

The role of wife implies not only a marriage relationship but a tie between families, as in all cultures where the extended family is important. The Cuban woman traditionally shows as much interest in her husband's relatives as her own, and the Cuban women in Washington exhibit this kind of concern. The behavior is an extension of the traditional idea that the wife is more than simply a wife. She is an anchor in family networks. In Washington she is a communication node in an extremely effective "grapevine" within and between families of a certain class level, and a source of aid in times of need to a wide range of Cuban friends and kin. Her role as wife is not simply as a single stranded link to one man, but the focal point in a system of social relationships.

However, the wife-husband bond is the most important strand in the network rather than the parent-offspring bond, as in many societies where the extended family persists. Cuban women in Washington consider their husbands as good and lifelong friends in a manner which would appear atypical for a Latin group, where sexual segregation is rather stringent. Furthermore, many Cuban women feel closer to their husbands since the time of immigration. Elizabeth Bott (1971:290) offers a generalization which explains this, the "conjugal bond/network density hypothesis." She generalizes that where dense, supportive networks of kin and friends exist outside the conjugal relationship, the latter will be relatively weak, or "segregated." Where these networks are looser (as for the Cuban immigrant woman), the conjugal role evolves into variable forms and frequently becomes closer, or "joint."

In a test of Bott's network density/conjugal bond hypothesis, Cuban women were asked if relations (1) between them and their husbands, and (2) between them and their other relatives, had become more, less, or were just as important as in Cuba. In general they replied that they were closer to their husbands and more distant from other relatives. Geographical distance was the most frequent reason for a decrease in importance of other relatives. Bott finds this factor significant elsewhere in loosening dense familial networks (1971:106-8; 126-28). In spite of the constant use of the telephone to maintain close family connections within and between cities, the fact remains that many Cuban families have "scaled down" to approach a suburban nuclear family. A grandparent or collateral relative is often included in the household; consolidation of generations in one household occurs at times; and no woman ever lives alone. However, the basic family linkage is the husband-wife, and they form the nucleus of the typical immigrant household.

Cuban women explained that the relationships with their husbands changed after immigration, and are different from the way they would now be in Cuba. The women say that husbands and wives need each other more, and that they have learned to share and cooperate in ways they could not have learned, and were not necessary to learn, in prerevolutionary Cuba. They attribute these changes to the hardships of resettlement and the increased mutual need between husbands and wives. There have been some broken marriages due to the shifting role obligations between husbands and wives, but these appear to be minimal in Washington, and certainly less prevalent than in Miami, according to Washington Cuban women. Bott's hypothesis and the body of theory that developed from following studies show that these changes are adaptive. If the extended Cuban family is now less important in spite of attempts to reconstitute it, then the husband and wife must find in each other the kinds of aid and reassurance that same-sex relatives once offered. Networks of female kin and friends, although still important, have become less dense among Cubans in Washington, and the conjugal relationship has become more important in terms of providing a confidant, a source of emotional and financial support, and one with whom to share household and extrahousehold tasks. Cuban women find preexisting role models in the suburban lifestyle in the United States, but they have chosen selectively those aspects of family and community life that are consistent with their own traditional values.

For example, they have not completely abandoned the value placed on the extended family. When questioned as to their families' reasons for settling in Washington rather than elsewhere, they mentioned primarily the availability of employment. At the same time, they state that one reason for their contentment with Washington is the presence of kin and friends. These two factors—employment and personal support networks—did not mitigate against one another in the process of resettlement. Frequently the search for a job and the location of relatives overlapped either directly or indirectly. If relatives and friends from prerevolutionary Cuba did not directly function in finding employment, then they provided the moral and/or the financial support needed for resettlement. Very few Cubans in Washington received government assistance. Very few were relocated under the government-sponsored program to disperse refugees throughout the country and relieve the problems developing in south Florida in the 1960s. This attests not only to their relatively high social, educational, and motivational levels, but to the strength of mutual aid networks based on the extended family and friendship.

Even among the first refugees to arrive, choice played a part in the decision to live in Washington. This choice revolved around the location of relatives when the necessity of finding employment was satisfied. Families tend to choose the same city and neighborhood when possible. Initially the husband, and sometimes the wife also, used a connection formed before the revolution with a friend in the United States, a government agency, or a Cuban relative, to find a job. Then as the phase of language learning, capital accumulation (although some were able to bring funds with them), and emotional adjustment passed, efforts to consolidate the family persisted. The distribution and location of friends and kin within the Washington area suggests that their presence is not simply a matter of chance, but choice, and that choice played an increasingly large part as families became more settled. Cuban women say that one basic difference between Cubans and people in the United States is that a Cuban would always choose to be near his family rather than take employment elsewhere. They view the U.S. mother's encouragement of independence in her children, and the "make-it-or-break-it" nature of the isolated nuclear family as heartless and unnatural. By exercising the considerable amount of influence they have in the family because of their traditional focal position, Cuban women have helped to reconstitute the extended family to the greatest degree possible. The money made by some and the communication lines exploited by all have facilitated this process. Second-generation women find the extended family less important.

One unexpected dimension to the role of wife emerged. It underlines the strength of women in the husband-wife relationship, and the leadership of women in the extended family. In many cases, Cuban women in Washington made the final and overt decision for their families to immigrate. In all cases, women had input into the decision-making process. It was not unusual to hear that the wife encouraged the husband to leave Cuba in spite of the husband's resistance. In the same way, older first-generation women encouraged their brothers, sisters, and cousins to leave and come to the United States.

One basic assumption of Latin culture espoused by Cuban women is that the weaknesses, or "softer virtues," of femininity—such as being more emotional, more sensitive, and "weaker" than men—develop in the context of marriage. The continued value placed on marriage now has an added dimension in the context of immigration. Marriage is valued for the support and companionship it provides as well as a milieu in which sensitivity [*sensibilidad*] and "innocence" can flourish. The overt conceptual rationale for marriage has shifted from an emphasis on female weakness and male strength, to a combination of strengths and weaknesses for both sexes. Experience has shown Cuban women that they are not physically, intellectually, or emotionally weak. The concept of the vulnerable and chaste woman was an Iberian ideal image, and an effective basis for marriage. Traditionally a woman passed from the protective hands of her father to those of her husband. This ideal is still superficially maintained among immigrants, but the entrance of women into the public domain has shifted the conceptual basis for marriage. Table 11.3 summarizes this shift.

The traditional and nontraditional models coexist. The second does not negate the first, just as contrasting conceptions of each sex exist together, and do not negate one another. The continuing importance of marriage has been extremely adaptive for Cuban immigrants. It has allowed women to keep and cherish traditional feminine qualities, while allowing them to develop the more covert qualities of patience, realism, pragmatism, flexibility, cleverness, and involvement. Without contrasting sets of ideas about women, this shift could not have occurred so easily. If the creative process were sought in everyday accomplishments, then surely the role of wife among Cuban immigrants could be seen as quite an imaginative product.

Creativity can also be seen in more detailed daily behavior of wives and husbands. Since most of the women in Washington came from households

Table 11.3. Marriage Models

	Traditional Iberian Model	Non-Traditional Immigration Model
Cultural, Conceptual Basis	Women are physically weak and vulnerable to predation	Women are physically strong and capable of acting in the public domain without danger.
Social Institution	*Marriage needed* to protect the moral purity of females	*Marriage needed* to provide companionship and support in a new society, where women frequently work, or, are involved in public activities by choice
Personal Qualities	*Positive qualities* of women (emphasis on traditional innocence and *sensibilidad*)	*Positive qualities* of women (emphasis on flexibility, pragmatism, cleverness, and involvement)

with at least a minimum of domestic help, their present complaints center on the duties of cleaning, cooking, and performing chores that are completely new for them. They especially dislike cooking, although many are fond of sewing, or even make money sewing. Most Cuban women in the Washington area finished high school, and sewing was a skill that prerevolutionary schools emphasized for girls—but cooking was not.

In the redistribution of tasks between husband and wife, which was necessary because of the lack of domestic help, wives have become the cooks where there is not a grandmother or maiden aunt to assume some of the burden. In one household the wife had to enter a hospital, so she put little signs on the drawers to help her husband find things in the kitchen. There were even signs on the food containers in the refrigerator. This follows a traditional male/female distinction, in that one of the privileges of the Cuban husband was coming home to well-prepared meals. Cuban wives sometimes find their husbands very demanding about specific dishes or deserts that they enjoy. They feel somewhat burdened by this pressure since they are not accustomed to cooking, and some work long hours. Where no relative resides with the nuclear family, daughters perform some of the cooking, although there remains a general prohibition about sons' performing kitchen tasks. They help at times with other household chores. The notion that females belong to the private domain is still strong, and the most private and domestic part of that domain is the kitchen.

The private domain has increased in scope for some families to include all arenas of activity to which the husband does not have access because he works away from home. Because of longer commuting distances, the work/home differential has increased. Men seldom come home in this northern Anglo city for the traditional midday meal and siesta. Time has been reorganized around the eight-hour workday for both men and women. The commuter syndrome has been adopted. Socializing among couples occurs mainly on the weekends because of time, distance, and fatigue. In one home the wife extended the household to include washing the cars and having them fixed. Men shunned manual labor in prerevolutionary Cuba if they were of a certain social standing. The gardener or the chauffeur was expected to wash the car. In the United States, the wife, because of her greater conceptual, if not actual, participation in the private domain, has at times taken on some of the tasks of gardener and chauffeur. However, in some families both husband and wife garden. Beyond cooking and child-tending the organization of these tasks is highly variable. Families were refinishing rooms in two households, and in both the husband assumed the task of putting up paneling or wallpaper. A number of wives commented upon how helpful their husbands were with household chores, and how they had learned to share these duties. Many, sometimes with surprise, noted how handy their husbands were when they were sick or visiting relatives. Praise and complaints alternate, but in general their comments betray a discomfort with the isolation of the nuclear family household, and pride that they and their husbands have adjusted. The loudest complaints come from those women who work full-time and then come home to take care of a house. They find the time and energy conflict overwhelming, as do many wives in the United States.

Cuban women are extremely talkative and gregarious. They complain about hardships, but in a context of general conversation and with a tinge of the martyr syndrome so common among Latin American females. However, the complaints rarely extend so far as to disavow the role of wife or the importance of marriage. They consider it the most favorable form of existence they could assume, no matter how numerous and strenuous the wife's tasks. They are culturally "comfortable" with being wives. The role of wife has a dignity steeped in tradition and central to Cuban culture. In attempting a national character portrait, prerevolutionary politician Juan Bosch made the following impressionistic comment about the honor accorded to women.

> The Cuban wants money in order to render homage to his wife. This is the historical theory I have come up with in order to explain to myself the traditional lack of honesty which exists in the country in the administration of public money... And I have come up with my theory, half because of its humor and half because every day the opulent beauty of the Cuban woman amazes me. Hence when a stranger asked me why it happens that in pub-

lic offices so much money is stolen from the people, I answered, pointing to the first girl who passed by: for that reason—because women so beautiful require, even though they don't ask for it, an environment of comfort and splendor. Her presence alone inclines man to offer her the finest and most beautiful (1966: 202).

The Cuban wife offers her husband a status that he cannot obtain in any other way, even with a mistress (who offers a different kind of status). The Cuban wife is ideally a combination of chastity and beauty, the Virgin Mary and Caribbean bombshell.

THE MOTHER: A PRIVATE AND FORMALIZED ROLE

Cuban women have great difficulty with the role of mother in the United States. Most of the problems faced by Washington mothers involve differences in the domain of appropriate behavior for children and adults, boys and girls. They find it difficult to allow their children, especially their daughters, to enter the public domain in ways that they, or U.S. youngsters, do so. Although a number of women voice the opinion that boys should be treated the same as girls, the women's anecdotes and informal comments betray an underlying double standard. They believe that girls should stay close to the home until a later age than boys; in fact they believe that girls should never really leave the protective atmosphere of home and family until they marry. Even when they do marry, Cuban mothers expect to keep in close contact with their daughters, and expect other family members to look after their daughters if they move away from the city where their parents reside. The "grapevine" functions to communicate information about relatives in other cities and even countries, so in a sense the daughter never does leave home. If a girl should shirk her obligations to stay in close contact with her parents, the news is quickly broadcast. As one woman said, she *thinks* that girls and boys should be treated the same, but she just does not *feel* this way. The women in Washington explain this in general terms of "social history" or "just the way we were brought up." They are defensive about the double standard, afraid of a single standard, and remain strongly resistant to change. While their values remain the same, their actions are forced to change, resulting in a great deal of conflict.

When questioned about chaperoning, the conservative nature of their values is obvious. Most women in Washington were chaperoned themselves when they began "dating" in Cuba. Usually a brother, an aunt, or a grandmother would accompany a group of young people to public nightclubs, private clubs, or parties. Pairing off was considered a definite sign of engagement, which was typically several years in length. One woman remembers walking home with her fiancé when they were both in college, and her grandmother's admonishment not to be seen alone with him in public during broad daylight.

People would talk. In fact, her grandmother had been sent with her to the town where she attended school, specifically to keep an eye on her.

When the Cuban women in Washington were asked if they believed their daughters should be chaperoned, they generally said "No, but..." They believe there are too many temptations for dating girls in the United States, and several mentioned that their own daughters were frightened and confused by the manner in which boys in the United States made advances. A complementary viewpoint is held by young Cuban men who date U.S. girls. One woman said that her younger brother felt these girls were "just for fun," but that dating Cuban girls was a more serious matter. The mutual comfort about these conforming ideas is evident in the fact that most young second-generation Cuban women do, in fact, marry Cuban men, or others from Latin America where sex-role standards are similar. The age differential, once 5-7 years between males and females, is now narrowing.

Cuban mothers feel that some form of supervision should be continued until the girl is 18-20. Until this age, they feel that social activities should occur in groups, with parents, relatives, or friends, and preferably in the home. Because of school activities and the greater assimilation of their children into U.S. society, this ideal is frequently not realized. Some mothers suggest "double dating" as a compromise, so that a girl will not be alone, but others feel strongly that even this is inadequate.

Another form of indirect chaperoning is prevalent for the second generation. Because the girl is expected to date only young men whose families the parents know, a girl is "chaperoned" even when she is alone with a boy. As one woman expressed it, the parents will know who is responsible "if anything happens." So in a sense, the chaperone is present in absentia. The first postrevolutionary immigrants in Miami tried to keep the custom of chaperoning alive, but the girls whose families followed this tradition were, in one woman's terms, "boycotted." The general feeling was that the chaperone was interested in going out, herself, as many families had little money for entertainment when they first arrived. A young man frequently could not afford this extra guest. So, the chaperone was dropped. The one-piece bathing suit had a similar fate in Miami. Girls whose families forbade their wearing bikinis were similarly "boycotted."

The cloistering of women and girls is not dead in the United States, but it does take different forms. The perpetuation of courtship customs is the result of two strong and traditional belief systems. First, the idea persists that single encounters between boys and girls "who are not mature" invites irresponsible behavior on the part of the girls. Sexual advances on the part of young men are not considered irresponsible as much as they are "naturally mischievous." However, this does not diminish the concern of the parents. Since chastity before marriage for girls is still a mark of family responsibility, if not status, it is highly prized by both males and females. From all accounts, it is not simply

an ideal but a reality. Sexual instruction is minimal, although second-generation mothers feel some need to be more informative. Sexuality is a matter
that mothers traditionally refrain from discussing with their daughters. The
eventual husband of the girl, because he is usually older and supposedly more
experienced, is expected to provide all the instruction needed. This is mainly
true of heterosexual relations, as most mothers are more sympathetic and informative about menstruation and body development. Discussion of sexual
matters is thought to invite experimentation, as is single dating. A belief in
male predation persists, which causes mothers of both sexes concern. Cuban
women were accustomed to much more stringent supervision by relatives,
maids, and school officials in Cuba. The neighborhood, itself, functioned as a
chaperone and as a general guardian. In the United States, Cuban mothers
worry about their children walking distances to bus stops, or being alone anywhere outside the household.

The second strong belief system which functions to perpetuate conservative notions about dating is the deep pride and joy which all Cubans take in
children. Just as the modesty of wives is a symbol of family status, children
are a symbol of the wife's and husband's continued integration into a wide
family network. The adequate provision for children is a symbol of social responsibility and conformity. The Spanish Civil Code and later Cuban law specified that it was the duty of parents to clothe, feed, and educate their children.
Neither men nor women take the responsibilities of parenthood lightly. The
strength and security of the family is too important to leave their children's
upbringing to outside associations, or chance. Cuban women are uneasy with
their children's participation in activities outside the home, although at the
same time they desire their assimilation into U.S. society.

Cuban women's comments about the responsibilities of motherhood reveal some conflict. On one hand they describe a Cuban system in which the
child's welfare was in the hands of many people: mothers, grandmothers, collateral relatives, older siblings, neighbors, and domestic help. They long for a
situation which relieves some of the burden of mothering in the more isolated,
suburban household. But they are not sure whom to trust. They try to maintain the old system of caring for friends' children while the mother is ill or
busy, but as so many mothers in the United States know, this is often incon-
venient or impossible. They live in neighborhoods where many people are
strangers, and friends are not within walking distance. Those women who do
have the time and energy to maintain a general concern about others' families
are accorded a great deal of respect, and a general attitude of concern is expected of all. Women who isolate themselves are not considered altogether
human. One Cuban woman told a story of aiding a child in a playground
when he fell. She said that no one else would help. Now his mother is her
thankful friend. Cuban mothers do not comprehend the lack of involvement
on the part of many U.S. mothers. They are accustomed to neighborhoods
where all know and care for each other's children.

In a sense, the Cuban mother has taken over the duties that were once not only hers, but those of the rest of the family and neighborhood. They report that the good Cuban mother does "everything" for the child to make him feel more secure, "even handing him a glass of water." It is probable that not only the mother accorded the child this type of attention. Others were available to assume some of the burden. Therefore, Cuban women are under the strain of maintaing an ideal of constant supervision and protection, while not having the traditionally large household to help. For the working mother the conflict can be extreme, and in these cases there is often a relative residing in the house who cares for the children. Husbands still maintain their position as *dueño de la casa,* master of the household, and do not share a great deal in the daily and intimate tasks involved with child-tending. From some reports this is changing, but slowly. "Women and children" are still set apart as a category of people whose appropriate domain is private, and whose status within that domain is subordinate to the father's. The Cuban mother considers it one of her duties to foster respect for the father. However, she is also quick to speak out for her children's own individual interests. The mother cultivates the mutual respect of all household members. Cuban women trace this emphasis back to the extended family in Cuba, where mutual respect was essential if a large number of people were to live together peacefully.

In spite of an emphasis on the individual although dependent worth of the child, and a conscious and concerted effort to maximize his security, Cuban children appear to have a minimum of adjustment problems. According to the Cuban ideal, no expense is spared for their happiness. Unlike the second generation among so many immigrants to the United States, Cuban children are reported to be handling the conflict between traditional Hispanic and modern Anglo cultures well. No doubt a great deal of their adjustment can be attributed to the values that derive from the relatively high social class of so many Washington Cubans, and the family-oriented method for regaining lost status and wealth.

When asked if their children have any difficulties in assimilating, Cuban mothers usually report, with a certain amount of envy, "No, they were born here." With some despair they report that their children reply to them in English when Spanish is spoken in the household. Second-generation Cuban children rarely have even a trace of an accent when speaking English, dress in blue jeans and other "unisex" clothes, and play and tease in public. They share their parents' gregarious nature and fondness for gaiety and music. Although they seem to enjoy some of the freedoms of other youngsters in the United States, and worry their mothers when they venture out alone or in groups, they appear to remain conservative in two general areas: relations between the sexes, and the importance of the family. When asked what they would most like their children to retain from their Cuban background, mothers indicated the importance of the family and the Spanish language. Some women hoped their children would retain a "sense of morals," but for most women "morals" and the family are one and the same. Sex-role behavior is subsumed under a more inclusive set of values about the family.

It would appear to some that the emphasis on the family creates extremely dependent women and children, but Cuban women do not feel this is true. They refer to the dependence of the U.S. child on his mother as "pathetic," while criticizing the independence that these mothers cultivate in their children. At the same time, they believe that the women in the United States are more subject to sexism than Cuban women. "She is tied to the home because she has no help," is not an uncommon observation of the U.S. woman's condition, and to some extent of the immigrant Cuban's. However, the principal difference between Cuban and U.S. women as they perceive it, is the latter's "independence." This is frequently explained in terms of socialization. Cuban women are brought up to be dependent, while women in the United States are taught to be independent. These conflicting ideas suggest that first-generation Cuban women are experiencing some frustration with their roles as mother and homemaker. Their responsibilities have multiplied as they strive to maintain their traditional values in the United States.

The role of mother does not require as much of a shift in feminine self-conceptions as it requires a shift in conceptions about children. Because they go to school or shopping by themselves in the United States, children must be seen as somewhat more independent and responsible than tradition dictates. This change reflects back onto the mother. Is she being irresponsible in allowing her children more freedom than she had? The question would not have arisen in prerevolutionary Cuba in the same, everyday, gnawing form of self-criticism that Cuban mothers face in the United States. In fact, a number of women report that immigration has increased their level of self-awareness, and has made them question their actions in ways that they would not have in Cuba. Their own children's questions create this necessity. Cuban mothers complain that their children do not obey them in the United States without an explanation. This process itself requires that women become wiser, responsible, and "knowledgeable about the street." They are painfully aware of the problems of drugs, crime, and early sexual experimentation—or as they express it, "morals." Becoming a mother to "American" children—that is, their own—makes it necessary to borrow some of the qualities that are traditionally reserved for men.

When questioned about their first reactions in the United States, they recount tales of physical and emotional stress as newly arrived refugees. However, they maintain that they had a job to do, and they did it. As wives and mothers they held their families together. They did so by changing old roles to fit new circumstances. As they look back now with some astonishment and a certain fatalism, they frequently say that "I just didn't think about it." When they do think about immigration now, it is without doubt the role of workers which was initially the most traumatic and eventually one of the most satisfying.

THE WORKER: A NATIONAL PUBLIC AND FORMALIZED ROLE

Most first-generation Cuban women in Washington were not brought up to work. Some lower-income individuals grew up with an awareness that they would be employed, but this is a minority. There are professional physicians, architects, and college teachers, who received most of their training in Cuba, but they are a minority as well. On the other hand, very few first-generation Cuban women were or are totally devoid of skills needed for employment. Most of them finished high school before they immigrated, and learned office skills, facility with another language, or sewing. Talking is a skill that a number of women have used: one as a real estate agent, another as a saleswoman for goods sold at her family's store, and another as an employee of the telephone company. Their general facility with language, spoken or written, was obtained before the revolution and—literally—capitalized upon in the United States. A traditional emphasis on appearance, cleanliness, and beauty has no doubt aided them in their search for employment, and counterbalanced some of their difficulties with English. Lastly, they are aggressive and gregarious in the public domain. They are willing and able to stand up for themselves in work situations. At the same time, they balance this stance with a traditional demure bearing. The combination of these factors has meant that work is available for the Cuban woman in Washington if she wants it and her husband agrees.

Cuban women maintain that both they and their husbands would prefer a situation in which the wife did not work. (The professionals are an exception.) They also report that their children want them to stay home. However, many women explain that their husbands encouraged them to get work and keep themselves busy and happy. The contradiction implies that there was some confusion about the wife's working. Where there was an initial cultural resistance to the idea of a working wife, the decision was rationalized in terms of the family. Few women express a long and deep desire for a career, but those who do work enjoy it. In reply to a standard question which asked the most important things that had happened in the past day, week, and year, those who worked always mentioned something about their jobs. Their responses show them to be competitive, ambitious, and deeply involved. They frequently mention work situations before they mention family incidents.

The 1970 census indicated that slightly more than half of the Cuban women in the United States were in the labor force. Although statistics have not yet been published, it appears that a higher percentage of Cuban women in Washington work. Women who do not work are generally of two kinds: those with young children whose husbands can provide adequately, and those who left Cuba with enough resources to continue a desired life-style without an intermediate period of lowered income and saving. Women in those upper-middle-class families who were not able to bring money with them, and who have slowly climbed their way back up to a previous standard of living, continue to work now that they have resumed a higher standard of living. They are faced with a situation that many people in the United States face: they are dependent on the wife's full-time income in order to maintain an acceptable life-style. Washington is an expensive city in which to live. Housing costs are higher than in any other U.S. city, including New York. In the face of this pressure, Cuban women report that their husbands recognize and accept their working even if they do not prefer it. Women's incomes become the property of the family. Decisions about spending their salaries become family decisions that are made by husband and wife. Cuban women do not have, nor do they want, sole control of their income. The concept of "my own income" becomes meaningless in the context of the family.

Traditional Cuban culture has a strong work ethic, although it differs in some ways from the Puritan work ethic in the United States. The continued Spanish influx into Cuba is partly responsible for a heavy emphasis on work. Spaniards had a reputation for industriousness, and a reliance on hard work to succeed. Cubans see this in part as "materialism," which they despise (Blutstein et al 1971: 203). However, many Cuban women in Washington go to great lengths to stress their Spanish ancestry. The covert implication is that Spanish heritage is a mark of status. When asked why Cubans have succeeded in obtaining work, women frequently refer to the Spanish heritage which is indirectly a characteristic of Cuban culture, and directly a characteristic of many families in Washington, especially the higher-status Cubans.

An interesting contradiction lies in the fact that, according to the Iberian ideal, the person with a very high social status is beyond work. When one woman asked her parents what her grandfather did, they replied, "he had money, he didn't have to work." Therefore, a dual notion of work has been inherited from Spanish culture, and from the Cuban experience with the plantation system. Hard work is highly valued, but self-support without work is a definite mark of distinction. Cubans in Washington rarely come from families in which the "ideal of nonwork" was achieved. The women from the high-status families point out that those Cubans in Washington, and in the United States in general, are not those from the uppermost reaches of Cuban society. Many come from the upper middle class (or the "lower upper" in one woman's scheme), but few come from the smaller *clase rica,* the upper-upper class. The women in Washington come from families in which working for one's living was a way of life, no matter how much they valued leisure and comfort.

Blutstein et al resolve the contradiction between a dislike for materialism and a fondness for high standards of living, in terms of personal competitiveness discussed earlier.

> For those who could afford it, and even for many who could not, a conspicuously extravagant standard of living was essential to the public appearance of success before the Revolution. Expensive cars, hotel entertainments, country estates, clubs, weddings, and

funerals, clothes, and education were as much marks of distinction in the republican era as noble connections and coats of arms were in colonial times. High standards of living were characteristically a personal competitive accomplishment...(1971: 204).

In a sense, the combination of a strong emphasis on work, a dislike for materialism ("working just for things, not the family"), and a penchant for the good life, is extremely adaptive for the Cuban immigrant. Goals are clear-cut: to hold the family together, and to achieve a high standard of living. The method for achieving these goals is equally clear-cut: hard work. Combined with a blustering self-confidence noted among both men and women, Cubans have often succeeded where other immigrants have not.

When the concept of work is extended to women, it takes on a broader meaning. It is true that women have to some extent borrowed from men the values of working for the family and competing in the public domain. However, the totality of women's work becomes an expression of a general cultural proclivity for action and involvement. Those women who do not work are extremely busy with family, friends, and sometimes clubs. It is rare for a Cuban woman to do little but keep house, unless she has a number of children and no domestic help. One Cuban woman recalls that as a little girl she told her grandmother that she had nothing to do. The grandmother punned in reply, *No sea burra*. This can be translated literally as "Don't be a donkey, a burro." However, if one slips over the words, it can also be heard and understood as "Don't be bored, or boring," *No se aburra*. In any case, her grandmother found her complaint tiresome, and implied that to be bored and unoccupied was to be like a donkey. It becomes difficult to keep in mind the cloistered, pampered Latin female when Cuban women recount their past and present experiences. It is much easier to picture Julia Ward Howe's tempestuous woman in Matanzas Province.

THE CHISMOSA OR THE "GRAPE": AN ETHNIC PUBLIC, NONFORMALIZED ROLE

Unlike the peasant group studied by Chiñas, where nonformalized roles predominate among women, the most important roles of Cuban women are formalized. This is probably true of individuals in all complex, urban societies where roles are standardized through law and communications. This is not to deny the importance of nonformalized roles, especially among members of an immigrant group. In the case of Cubans, the continued importance of certain nonformalized roles creates a sense of familiarity within the ethnic group and the family, and therefore increases the security of their members. It is through nonformalized roles that Cuban women have maintained a strong sense of their cultural identity. Detailed, intimate, and everyday behavior that goes unnamed is most resistant to change. Where these roles do not mitigate against the fulfillment of formalized roles, they can be extremely adaptive for the group adjusting to a new culture. An interesting nonformalized structure exists among Cuban immigrants in Washington, the United States in general, and throughout the world. This is the "grapevine," a communications system maintained largely by women. It functions to transmit information about Cuban family members and to create a sense of belonging. It also serves to prevent actions deemed inappropriate to the ethnic group and to the class level of the members of the grapevine. Not all Cuban women acknowledge the grapevine's power to check the behavior of family members. "A Cuban does what he wants to" is in keeping with the traditional emphasis on the dignity of the individual, and, especially for refugees from a Communist revolution, an emphasis on freedom of action. Yet some women admit to the power of the grapevine to check, guide, and prevent certain behavior. They describe its power as "stifling" at times, although they also recognize its usefulness in providing security. Ideally, when a Cuban moves to a new city, the grapevine immediately transfers this information through friends and kin, and the newcomer is at once enmeshed in a network of Cubans. This function is most important among the higher-status Cubans in Washington, and extends only down to a certain class level. The dividing line is the status of the family rather than occupation or wealth. The grapevine is partially cross-cut by social "groups" of couples, and group inclusion is usually mutually exclusive. "Group" inclusion is not characteristic of all members of the grapevine, as some Cubans choose to socialize more than others. Traditionally, maids and subordinates at work functioned as vertical communication links between those who are better off, and those who are not. This persists to a minimal extent among immigrants in Washington.

The speed with which information travels the grapevine is at times startling to the Cuban women themselves. One woman told of receiving some information about a friend from a relative in Florida, and then transmitting it to her grandmother. However, her grandmother had been visiting in Paris and had already received the information from a friend there. The telephone is essential in maintaining the grapevine, and letters only slightly less important. Telephone bills to relatives and friends in other cities can be high. Nevertheless, the communication is seen as a method for preserving the family, and is rationalized in terms of it. Through the grapevine the woman's traditional role of anchor in an extended family is to some degree preserved.

Cuban women in Washington recognize the "gossip" in a narrow sense. She is an exaggerated type, a woman who transfers more negative information than positive, and who obviously does so for her own purposes. Beyond this, general gossip is not the object of scorn. In fact, the woman who keeps to herself and who does not engage in chit-chat is considered somewhat abnormal, if not actually ill. Women feel little sense of shame in "just letting something slip." Exchange of information about friends and kin is a normal and necessary role for women. It is part of daily social interaction and helps to cement relations between family members and friends. Within the smaller networks of Cubans in Washington, gossip also serves to check extramarital behavior. There is little way to keep secret a liaison with another Cuban.

The role of communicator is ideally suited to women because of their central position in the family and some of the basic cultural conceptions about women. Women still perceive themselves as somewhat more superficial and irresponsible than men, and present themselves this way in mixed company. Gossip is a direct outgrowth of this self-perception as well as their importance in the extended family. The Cuban proclivity for talk is also an extension of the general-action orientation previously discussed. Cuban women laughingly report that all Cubans place a high value on talk, loud and continuous talk. In traditional Cuban culture the verbal artist and the orator are as much heroes as the military man, the athlete, and the cane cutter (Blutstein et al. 1971: 201). Although women's traditional communicator role lay more in the private domain, they have extended this to the ethnic public domain in the United States. Since the neighborhood can no longer be a real social unit in cities where there is a low density of Cubans, the grapevine must substitute. The telephone conversation replaces the casual walk and talk.

THE BELLEZA OR "BEAUTY": AN ETHNIC PUBLIC, NONFORMALIZED ROLE

The very high value placed on personal grooming and attractiveness among Cubans cannot be denied. Women spend as much time as their present circumstances will allow on arranging their hair, polishing their nails, and fixing their make-up. The skin is of special concern, and among white Cubans a soft, white, *nacra* skin combined with dark eyes is the ideal. Except in very relaxed moments at home, care is taken to dress attractively, whether it be in slacks among the more Americanized or in heels and stockings among those who maintain Cuba's beauty ideals of the 1950s. Although the type of beauty standard varies between black and whites, the wealthy and the poorer, there is a consistent emphasis on cleanliness, dress, and color. As a result, first-generation Cuban women do not "look their age" according to U.S. standards. One woman notes that the second generation may look older, "because life in this country kills you."

In discussing the role of wife, Cuban women suggest that it is a duty to their husband and to themselves to maintain their looks. They also feel it is important to set an example for their children, who more often than not are seen in jeans and other informal clothes. Teenage daughters generally follow the dress codes of their peers in the United States, although they go back to their mothers' standards in high school. Mothers describe the delight and surprise in their daughters when they switch dress codes and are approached differently by their friends. However, the transition is not always easy, and mother-daughter fights are not uncommon. The status of the traditional Cuban family is vested in the chastity of wives and daughters. When modesty becomes an issue related to dress, then traditional standards reassert themselves. Yet they do so in modified form, as Cuban mothers do not absolutely forbid the faddish and the stylish, nor do they shun it themselves.

The role of the *belleza* should not imply a plastic, unnatural image, as its social implications are many and varied. A good personal appearance is important not only for women, but for men as well. However, the role of the *belleza* may have a special implication for Cuban women vis à vis men. Through this role the Cuban woman serves not only as a model for her children and as a symbol of the family's status in general, but as a status symbol for her husband also.

In prerevolutionary Cuba it was common for a husband to take a mistress, although this was by no means true for every man who could afford it. The mistress was frequently slimmer and more fashionably dressed than the wife. In the United States a mistress is a status symbol which Cuban men cannot use in a traditional manner. Having a Cuban mistress could alienate other Cuban families, or count for nothing in the eyes of others in the United States. It is probable that in her role as *belleza* the Cuban wife is taking over some functions of the Cuban mistress. Social interaction, for example on a dance floor, strongly suggests that this is the case. Flirtation and exhibition are part of normal interaction, but they are of an extremely mild and shallow nature. There is no doubt in anyone's mind as to the lack of seriousness among those who are married.

A shift in beauty standards supports the existence of this wife-mistress function. Women note that Cubans are more weight conscious than they were in Cuba, where sweet desserts and starchy meals of black beans and rice were the rule. Heavyset people of both sexes were more common. Very few Cubans in Washington are truly fat, and women report that this is a change. In Cuba there was a widespread acceptance of overweight, as the term of endearment, *gordita,* implies. It translates "little plump one," and continues to be used even when the person is quite thin. Although the ideal Cuban woman in the United States bears no resemblance to the Madison Avenue model, she is not fat. According to one man, she has an "opera singer look," with pronounced bust and hips, and hair piled high on the head. Women in Washington are diet conscious, a fact which may correlate with the changing wife-mistress aspect of being a *belleza.* Women are changing a social role as well as a beauty concept and their diet, all the while maintaining a traditional value on general personal appearance. The role of *belleza* combines old functions and new in the ethnic public domain, and enhances women's chances for success in the national public domain.

THE TIA: A PRIVATE, NONFORMALIZED ROLE

The role of the *tía,* which means literally "aunt," has evolved in the United States because of the dual pressures of working and motherhood. When the wife works and children remain at home, it is not uncommon to find a grand-mother, aunt, or cousin residing with the family as a combination housekeeper-nurse. This provides advantages for the husband, wife, children, and the female relative. All continue to receive well-prepared meals and to enjoy a well-kept house despite the long absences of the wife at work. The female relative enjoys a home life and care when she is sick that she could not find elsewhere.

The attitude toward these female relatives is mixed. They usually speak little English and only occasionally leave the household. They are therefore considered "old fashioned" by the younger members of the household, and are sometimes teased or chided. However, they receive a large measure of re-spect at the same time. They serve as language models for children who speak less and less Spanish, and are sometimes the only ones to whom children must communicate in Spanish in order to be understood. They know traditional re-medies for illness, and recount stories of prerevolutionary Cuba. Their very presence reminds children of the extended family which was once so strong, and of the importance of caring for all relatives. In a small number of cases, the *tía* may actually live with relatives other than those for whom she cares. Several elderly and unmarried or widowed relatives may live together and make it their duty to call upon those relatives or friends for whom they are "responsible." These actions provide a form of security and closely knit net-work which both first- and second-generation Cubans enjoy.

The role of *tía* is not altogether new, as female relatives rarely lived alone in prerevolutionary Cuba. It was not considered proper. The morality, how-ever, is more a matter of family responsibility than cloistering an unmarried woman. A family is not respected if it does not care for its elders, nor do the family members feel comfortable with themselves. Children are taught the re-spect of relatives at an early age, especially older relatives. The resident *tía* functions to pass on this particular family value.

IN CONCLUSION

The roles of Cuban immigrant women have changed according to the new challenges they face in the United States. There is an obvious continuity be-tween their present patterns of behavior and those that were important to women in prerevolutionary Cuba. Likewise, there are important consistencies between the new role obligations and more traditional conceptions of the sexes. To support these new role elements, Cuban women have not become "American" but have used a repertoire of familiar yet more covert notions about the nature of femininity. In addition, they have "borrowed" some of the characteristics of men, especially when they assume the role or worker in the public domain.

An important male/female distinction in Table 11.1 underscores not only the more minute deviations in individual roles, but the entire process of role change. Cuban women point to a present-time orientation for males, as opposed to the longer range and wider view which they believe women have. Many women claim that men feel or think only for the moment—that they want things rapidly and all at once. One woman uses a standard reply to her husband when these more immediate desires are thwarted. *Tú te ahogas en un vaso de agua:* "You are drowning in a glass of water." In saying this she is not only encouraging him, but implying that his view of the situation is too narrow. This conceptual difference is most evident in the reports that Cuban women frequently made the decision to immigrate even when their husbands were hesitant. When questioned about this process, women suggested that their husbands were so involved with their positions in Cuba, they often could not conceive of immigrating to a different country. The implication was that their lesser participation in the public domain in Cuba helped them in coming to their conclusions.

This is a strong possibility. With less investment in public roles, they could conceive of moving the entire household because their own most important roles would remain the same. They did not envision the changes the immigration would necessitate in their roles as wife and mother, nor did they fully appreciate the economic situation that would call for their future employment. Their view of the situation was simultaneously wider than their husbands' and more narrow. Their self-conception as protected women allowed them to risk a change, yet they did not fully appreciate the consequences.

Maslow suggests that creativity is fostered by a sense of timelessness, of "being outside of history." In a sense the cloistering of women in the private domain may make this possible. Given a set of conceptions about women that both conform to the ideal of cloistering yet enable them to rationalize activity and competition in the public domain, Cuban women were in an ideal position to create patterns of behavior that aided them in the United States. Their pragmatism and forcefulness is evidently not new. The Cuban woman was not a complete "victim of the age of romanticism." Cuban cultural history suggests that women were able to develop a parallel set of self-concepts that balanced their image as "birds in a cage." Their traditional cleverness, pragmatism, and involvement served as excellent preadaptations to the situation faced as immigrants to the United States, as did the traditional emphasis on family, language ability, and personal appearance.

The real creativity in daily manipulations of the Cuban woman's role comes in her ability to prolong the importance of certain values in new contexts without an overreliance on them; of playing traditional roles with certain behavior modifications; and of covering her new and nontraditional behavior with a cloak of idealism. The satisfaction of Cuban women with their accomplishments is evident, although the strain on them is also obvious. In one light, the best proof of their success may be found in the relatively easy adjustments made by their children. In Washington these children display few of the obvious traits of Cuban culture. However, at a deeper level, they demonstrate the benefits of family solidarity and a strong set of ideals about relations between the sexes. They are the best evidence that Cubans are assimilating into U.S. society with a minimum of social disintegration.

REFERENCES

Banton, Michael
  1965 *Roles: An Introduction to the Study of Social Relations.* London: Tavistock Publications.
Blutstein, Howard I. et al.
  1971 *Area Handbook for Cuba.* Washington, D.C.: Foreign Area Studies of the American University.
Bosch, Juan
  1966 "The National Psychology." In *Background to Revolution: the Development of Modern Cuba,* Robert Freeman Smith, ed., pp. 201-207. New York: Knopf.
Bott, Elizabeth
  1971 *Family and Social Network.* New York: The Free Press.
Bradley, Hugh
  1941 *Havana.* New York: Doubleday.
Chiñas, Beverly L.
  1973 *The Isthmus Zapotecs.* New York: Holt, Rinehart and Winston.
Chodorow, Nancy
  1971 "Being and Doing." In *Woman in Sexist Society,* Vivian Gornic and Barbara K. Moran, eds., pp. 259-91. New York: New American Library.
  1974 "Family Structure and Feminine Personality." In *Woman, Culture, and Society,* Michelle Rosaldo and Louise Lamphere, eds., pp. 43-66. Stanford: Stanford University Press.
Collier, Jane Fishburne
  1974 "Women in Politics." In *Woman, Culture, and Society.* Michelle Rosaldo and Louise Lamphere, eds., pp. 89-96. Stanford: Stanford University Press.
García de Arboleya, José
  1860 *Manual de la Isla de Cuba.* Havana: Pérez y Cía.

Gillin, John
    1965   "Ethos Components in Modern Latin American Culture." In *Con-temporary Cultures and Societies of Latin America*. Dwight B. Heath and Richard N. Adams, eds. New York: Random House.

Goffman, Erving
    1959   *The Presentation of Self in Everyday Life*. New York: Doubleday Anchor Books.

Gross, Neal, Ward Masons, and Alexander McEarchen
    1958   *Explorations in Role Analysis*. New York: Wiley.

Herskovits, Melville
    1937   *Life in a Haitian Valley*. New York: Knopf.

Howe, Julia Ward
    1969   *A Trip to Cuba*. New York: Frederick A. Praeger. (orig. 1860)

Lewis, Oscar
    1965   *La Vida*. New York: Random House.

Maslow, Abraham H.
    1971   *The Farther Reaches of Human Nature*. New York: The Viking Press.

Mead, Margaret
    1935   *Sex and Temperament in Three Primitive Societies*. New York: William Morrow and Company.

Mintz, Sidney
    1966   "Industrialization of Sugar Production and Its Relationship to Social and Economic Change." In *Background to Revolution*, Robert Freeman Smith, ed. pp. 176-86. New York: Knopf.

Nadel, S. F.
    1953   *The Foundations of Social Anthropology*. Glencoe, Ill.: The Free Press.

Nelson, Lowry
    1950   *Rural Cuba*. Minneapolis: University of Minnesota Press.

Price, John A.
    1973   *Urbanizaion in a Border Culture*. Notre Dame: University of Notre Dame Press.
    1975   "Reno, Nevada: The City as a Unit of Study." In *City Ways*. John Friedl and Noel J. Chrisman, eds. pp. 71-85. New York: Thomas Y. Crowell Company.

Riegelhaupt, Joyce F.
    1967   "Saloio Women: An Analysis of Informal and Formal Political and Economic Roles of Portuguese Peasant Women." *Anthropological Quarterly* 40:109-26.

Rosaldo, Michelle Zimbalist and Louise Lamphere
    1974   Introduction. In *Woman, Culture, and Society*, Rosaldo and Lamphere, eds., pp. 1-15. Stanford: Stanfod University Press.

Rowbotham, Sheila
    1972   *Women, Resistance and Revolution.* New York: Random House.
Schneider, Jane
    1971   "Of Vigilance and Virgins: Honor, Shame, and Access to Resources in Mediterranean Society." *Ethnology* 10:1-24.
Wagley, Charles
    1968   *The Latin American Tradition.* New York: Columbia University Press.

12 The Life of Sarah Penfield, Rural Ohio Grandmother: Tradition Maintained, Tradition Threatened

ROSEMARY JOYCE

The author of this chapter offers us a picture of Appalachian Ohio and the changes the region has undergone through most of the present century through the life history of a single individual. Much of this is given in the subject's own words, making the account direct and vivid. Joyce suggests that by studying an actual individual in a society, we can begin to understand not only the depth of the influence of tradition, but also the implications that result for personal conflict in women during this period of rapid societal change in the United States. In the case of Mrs. Penfield, we see that tradition tends to be a conservative as well as a pervasive influence. It continues to leave its mark on women, even though they move increasingly in nontraditional directions. The reader may ask, to what extent the life story of this rural Ohio grandmother reflects the experience of middle-aged and older women in the United States generally, perhaps even in sectors of the society that are neither rural nor relatively remote and conservative.

The life history has long been recognized as an important research tool in anthropology. This chapter utilizes the life history approach to depict the life of Sarah Flynn Penfield,[1] a 74-year-old woman from a traditional, rural community in southeastern Ohio. Generational continuity in her life patterns is the focus here, with emphasis on her conception of social change in woman's role, and of the effects of social change on her life and her family's lives. Through this example I intend to illustrate the need for similar study of other women's lives. Such information will become increasingly important as women's roles continue to undergo rapid change, with underlying potential for conflict. For one of the results of social change has been conflict for Sarah (and possibly for other women as well): conflict stemming from the confusing reality of both the cognitive dimensions of her awareness—woman is equal—and the affective dimensions of that awareness—woman is inferior. Can the resulting ambivalences thus offer a paradigm for conflict in other women? Or is she idiosyncratic in her own community as well as in the larger society? Regrettably there is a dearth of literature dealing with the role of women—in southeastern Ohio, in the larger region of Appalachia, and even in the still larger area of the nation.[2] The study of women's lives has received neither attention nor impetus until recently. Answers to such questions will be only conjectural then until further research is documented on woman's role in the various layers of society.

Its borders only political, Ohio is composed of three distinct geographic zones: the Lake Plains of the northern end, remnants of a diminishing Lake Erie; the Central Plains of the center and southwest, rolling and then flattening into the western prairies; and the Allegheny Plateau of the eastern half. This plateau is divided into two distinct areas: the northern and western glaciated sectors, and the eastern and southern unglaciated sectors.[3] This southeastern unglaciated portion is marked by steep valleys and narrow ridges cut up by streams. It is more valuable for its coal deposits than for its agricultural products.[4] Mid- and southeastern Ohio is recognized politically as part of Appalachia by its inclusion in the 13-member Appalachian Regional Council; this is a federal/state venture founded in 1965 to combat the severe problems of the region, such as lack of transportation networks, lack of adequate medical facilities, a large percentage of poverty-level families. Sociologically it is generally treated as Appalachian; popularly it is often referred to as the "foothills of the Appalachians." However, many native-born residents do not agree with this designation, and consider themselves only "Ohioans." Little literature treats southeastern Ohio as an entity. Thus, only further research could point to differences between these Ohio residents and the southern Appalachians dealt with primarily in existing cultural studies.

Though occupying 33 percent of the state's total land area, Ohio's "Appalachia" received only 15 percent of the 1971 farm production income.[5] Nonetheless, industrious families, especially in the valleys and less convoluted central counties, have wrested a living from this less hospitable soil. It was in this center of Appalachian Ohio, in Bay Township, that both the Flynn and the Penfield families settled in the mid-nineteenth century. Today Sarah lives on the farm to which her husband's ancestors emigrated. She has resided all her 74 years in two houses—her father's and her husband's—just three miles apart.

The area was typified by subsistence farming originally, but now farmers there concentrate on raising livestock and livestock products.[6] Farmhouses of the region are approximately one-half a mile apart, and each one is dwarfed by its cluster of outbuildings—usually a large barn for storing hay and wintering stock, plus at least a smokehouse, chickenhouse, tool shed, and spring house. Farms average around 175 acres, a somewhat misleading figure, since often large portions are steep, rocky, or wooded, and thus untillable.[7]

Demographic and economic features have changed through the century. Agriculture and forestry employment dropped off nearly 100 percent in Appalachian Ohio between 1960-70.[8] Farm population fell nearly 50 percent even in the central counties.[9] Though farmers have always sought supplementary employment, in 1969 not only did the number of farms drop substantially, but 60 percent of the farm operators worked 100 or more days off the farm.[10] Wives and daughters, too, joined the working force, with well over twice as many women from the area employed in 1970[11] as in 1940.[12] Commuting to town jobs has become a fixed pattern, dramatically changing the complexion of the once-agrarian locale. The landscape itself has changed: trailer home sites proliferate, as farmers sell off untillable land, and former city dwellers respond to exurbia's call. In 1970 the rural nonfarm population was over 1000 percent greater than the farm population.[13] The one-room country school, where both Sarah and her parents were educated, gradually has given way to graded schools in nearby small towns for Sarah's children, and to consolidated school systems in the larger towns for her grandchildren.

These changes in the region during the evolution of the twentieth century find a parallel in Sarah Penfield's changing life patterns: she grew up on a subsistence farm, raised her family on a farm demanding increased outside resources, and now observes her children and grandchildren living as exurban commuters or urban dwellers. They face rapid social change temporally and spatially, in the traditional framework transmitted by Sarah; she learned these folkways in turn from her parents, they from their parents.

For amplification of the following account of Sarah's life, her narrative is inserted wherever possible, since it paints a vivid scene of the social settings. One must bear in mind that these are remembrances, and not necessarily validated or recorded occurrences.[14]

SARAH'S GRANDPARENTS: THE FIRST GENERATION
OF FLYNNS IN OHIO—1853-1895

Sarah's grandfather, John Flynn, was an original settler in Bay Township, emigrating to Ohio from Ireland in 1853. Apparently an enterprising, hard-working young man, he bought or managed a large hotel, and purchased considerable acreage nearby. Marrying a young German woman, he sired eight children. Father, mother, and children had definite roles in the subsistence paradigm. Little else is known of this period in the family, except that grandfather was a "terribly hard" worker who consequently died very young—"he just killed himself!"

His sons continued to live on the family farmstead with their mother. Soon Sarah's father, Joseph William, met and married a newcomer to the valley, lively young Sally Mae Powers. She joined the family, widowed mother and three sons, in their log house.

SARAH'S PARENTS: THE SECOND GENERATION, HER NUCLEAR FAMILY OF ORIENTATION—1895-1927

After the marriage of Joseph Flynn and Sally Powers, the subsistence farm operation was soon enlarged. Following their widowed mother's death, one brother married and moved to a nearby farm, and Joseph bought more land. His family grew as well: 11 children were ultimately born to Sally and Joseph. A large white frame house replaced the original log structure, but retained the bucolic setting: a small rise of land overlooking Bay Creek as it cut through flat rich fields and drained the high wooded ridges guarding each side, north and south. Typically, the house was built close to the road for easier access.

Life was primitive, often rugged, sometimes rewarding. There were few amenities: roads were scarce and often barely passable in bad weather; crops brought no money, since transportation to market was impractical or nonexistent; stores were distant; cash was scarce; summers were hot, winters cold; electricity did not come to the valley until 1943;[15] free gas came with wells drilled on the property around 1918, but Joseph—fearful of its explosive potential—refused to install a furnace, and continued to heat with wood, which was "free," too, but with a cost high in human effort; all the cooking, all the water heating, were done on a temperamental wood stove; all water—for drinking, bathing, cooking, cleaning, laundering, watering stock—had to be drawn from a spring each day; oxen, horses, and mules were the only source of power, besides human muscle.

Farming was a subsistence operation: "everything that we used practically was raised back in those times." This included sorghum for syrup, buckwheat for flour, cane for sugar, apples for cider and apple butter, corn for cornmeal. They raised and butchered their own meat: at least two beefs, two mutton, and twelve hogs. Eggs came from their chickens, and milk, cream, and butter from their cows.

To supplement a scarce supply of cash, Joseph, like most farmers of the region, sought outside employment the few times possible: "Father worked whenever he had a chance." The gas company drilled wells throughout the area in the teens. Not only did Joseph receive royalties for the wells drilled on his property, but he also worked in the gas fields, drove his horses and sled to meet workers at the railroad stop, and boarded drillers. A county road tax was levied, but could be—and always was—paid out in work rather than in precious dollars.

The women were also dedicated workers. Her mother, Sally, raised a huge garden, and canned thousands of jars of fruits and vegetables to feed her growing brood. As Sarah recalls these childhood scenes, her sister's comments also augment details of this period:

> S: We had our own potatoes, we had all the vegetables we ever had. We didn't buy vegetables. Anything we had. Mother even raised celery. You can even can cabbage and keep it beautiful, you know. Cabbage, everything we picked, we canned.
> Sister: We had a cellar. We didn't have actually what they do today. They kept things good, and it was always full of things. Then Dad buried turnips and things like that.
> S: Well, if you bury them they keep wonderful. They just keep like they're growing.

They made their hominy; they made their soap:

> See, our parents did all those things. It was the only way you could get them.

Clothes, however, were a difficult item:

> The garments were all handmade. You didn't go to the store and buy, even the coats and things usually were made.

> My mother could just really sew, and she made the clothes.

> I can't remember when they spun their own cloth, but I do know they made their own carpets 'n things. My mother did that even. Carpet rags. No, they have a loom [they are not braided]. It is really pretty....I can remember 'bout her covering a whole room at a time with them. Done by hand. Lots of work.

> I can remember mother making us the cutest little dresses. She sewed so much; she sewed real well....I can remember when mother gave three cents a yard for calico; we called it calico then, today I don't know what they call it. It's be red with little white dots and blue with little white dots, but we were so proud of those little, she really was a good sewer, we were so proud of those little dresses.

> Mother could just, she could crochet anything.

Farm and family required constand work, by parents and by the children, too, as they came along.

S: [My father] would do any kind of work; he was a terribly, terribly hardworking person.

S: Everything was done the hard way then. We had no conveniences. We had lots of cows. We had to help dig out the barn.... There were actually fourteen in the family. Three big meals a day, a lot of washing and ironing.

Sisters in chorus: A lot of everything!!!

Sister: Years ago if a child went out and made a little money on the side, the parents usually took it.

S: Yeah, you know we picked blackberries to get our clothes.

Sister: We certainly did!

S: For 25 cents a gallon! or 20. Carry 'em for miles. You can't find the blackberries today, can you? So don't think you can go out and make a fortune. You can not find blackberries today.

Sister: First teeth—the first work I ever had done to my teeth I picked blackberries.

S: We sure picked gallons of 'em.

Sister: People used to come from the city, and picked 'em up for wine.

(Access then to money as children?)

S and Sister together: It was very, very little!

With only one boy older, the first three girls helped outside as well as in:

Sister: We had this one brother, then there were three girls in a line, then the next boys were too young. During the First World War, our brother was taken into the service, and the girls had to work right out on the farm like boys.

Turnabout was not fair play, however:

S: Oh, I believe girls have a harder time of it, don't you, because we had to work outside....Yes, and the washing and everything had to be done by hand and everything...and we milked lots of cows.

Sister: We worked outside as well as inside.

S: We always had to get outside and bring the horses and things in from the pasture in the morning.

The disparity was obvious: both Sarah and her sister hooted at the merest suggestion the boys might have also helped inside. "*NEVER!*" was the simultaneous reply. Yet their mother helped in the fields.

Sister: Well, you see, there were three girls that were much older than the boys. The boys were not actually old enough for quite a number of years there. The boys were not old enough to do much work, so the girls filled in, because a farmer couldn't afford to hire

hands. So whoever was in the family did the work. Like my mother, went out in the fields *all* the time. Oh yes, she did!

When queried as to whether then the father worked inside too, Sarah's reply
was:

Yes, I'm sure he would, uh-huh.

There was little doubt in the minds of either Sarah or her sister that girls
worked harder than boys, and that significantly, this carried on into later life,
with women working harder than men, in most families:

Oh sure they did! They went out and worked in the field with
their husband and they'd have the home all to do, too, to take care
of.

In spite of her grueling daily schedule, Sally Mae always made time to attend to more than her family's physical needs:

My mother was especially education-minded....Oh yes, she was interested in education.

She loved to read. Mebbe she would read all night and work all the
next day. She loved to read 'n things. She kept up on things. Yes.
She was very much interested in getting us in school. Of course
we had nothing but the little one-room school.

Yeah, I saw her with my oldest brother. He didn't want to study
and he'd cry and he'd cry and he'd fight and she'd make him study
anyhow....He hated school, but she sure did make him study.

Surprisingly, none of the six boys were educated, and all the five girls were!
Two became teachers, and one a store saleswoman, and two nurses.

Well, she was for the boys too....Yeah, but the boys wouldn't take
it....No, not to amount to anything.

Though the family was unusual both in having their daughters educated
and in using their labor in the fields, the mother was traditionally conservative
in wanting to keep her children close by, especially the girls:

S: You know a mother can keep the girls closer, and I think they
watch over them closer. I think that mother watched over us closer than she did the boys, don't you, because she didn't have the
control over the boys she did over the girls.
Sister: The boys were allowed a lot more freedom.

S: They had the silly idea that the boy could do the same thing,
be guilty of the same thing as the girl, but it didn't hurt him like
it did the girl. And people would forgit that! But they wouldn't
forgit it if the girl did it.

Social life consisted, then, of simple pleasures, close to home: walking, climb-
ing hills, berrying, nutting, swinging on grapevines, riding horses, swimming in
the creek, sliding down haystacks in the summer, snow-covered hills in the
winter. Simple, but apparently effective:

I think your happiest period is when you are going to school....It's
a carefree time.
There was more of a sociable life then.

At the old hotel (which had been their grandfather's) "old-fashioned musicians" still played for "old-fashioned dances," but

S: Mother wouldn't took us very much. But they had all that sort
of thing, dancing, 'n ice cream, you know. But then we always got
out and played a lot—games outside, like, well, different, like "Old
Dan Tucker," you don't have to dance it you can play it, and
"Down the Old Ohio" was one.

As they grew older there was more exposure to the surrounding community,
with parties—often taffy pulls—held at different neighbors' homes.
The three institutions which served then as socializing agents were the
home, the school, and the church. The school often served as a focal point:

The little country schools, township schools, were the center of
the social life for the country people. You can just put it that way
because that's the way it was.

They [older men] would go maybe in the winter when they didn't
have anything else to do, you know. It was a kinda of entertainment—they played ball, it was their social lives. They'd have box
socials, and they'd have spelling bees at night in the school houses.
And really the school house was about the only place they had social gatherings. And they had old-fashioned spelling bees. You
know, they would choose sides and then they would have what
they call—which was a lot of fun, they don't do that any more—
they would choose sides and then they would take a subject—De-
bate! They had so many debates. And the older men, the lawyers,
the educated people would come in and they would have those debates. Really to tell the truth, I think they knew more about enjoying themselves than we do today....

Next to the school, the church:

> Church, really church was the center next to the school. They
> went to church for entertainment. Then they had what you called
> Protractive Meetings, and had church singing....United Brethren
> and Methodist. Nearly everybody went to church.

Even omnipresent work was turned to a form of socializing when possible—
barn-raisings, beanhullings, cornhuskings, butchering, harvesting. Families and
neighbors—often one and the same—developed a relationship of mutual dependency through sharing: heavy tasks were thus possible, lonely isolation was
thus eased. Threshing, for instance was a grand occasion: hot, dusty, difficult
work for all, but laced with an air of festivity, a feeling of community:

> **Sister**: Mother would always save her last ham, smoked ham, for
> the threshers, remember? The table they set out in the lawn on a,
> it was made on a, saw horses they called it, not boards. And the
> farmers came from all around to help at each farmhouse.
> **Sister**:And some of the women—they cooked all day. Then they
> stayed two or three days. And the men would sleep in the hay
> mow and work the next day.
> **S**: So you changed—worked back and forth—you didn't give them
> money, you went to your neighbor and worked, then he'd come
> to your place.

The women, too, cooperated. Sally's mother, "Grandmother Powers," just
down the road, was a great help to her daughter. Evidently a strong person,
Grandmother also played a significant role in the larger community:

> She had a horse and she rode this one—I wish we'd a kept that—
> but she had this sidesaddle, something you never see today, and
> she rode all over the country all hours of the night and delivered
> babies...I 'spect she was as good as a doctor at that time, you
> know, I mean the old doctor...Yes, she went all over the coun-
> try, everyplace. She rode this horse, and went everyplace and
> delivered babies. They couldn't've even got a doctor then, we
> were so isolated...It was all gratis; it was never any impression of
> it being paid for...Well, see doctors here would refuse—they
> wouldn't go to your house...They were very friendly people
> [the women]; helped each other at harvesting time and every-
> thing, free gratis they went back and forth ...[Training was] just
> by experience, teaching each other, sure, by being with the doc-
> tor in some cases. They never lost a case that I—natural child-
> birth, it's just what you would call natural childbirth.

This at a time when even the one-mile trip to school was difficult:

It was an awful trip. That would be an awful walk, because it was up the hill and down...There was a little brook that went through this place and you'd cross this little brook on stones, stepped from stone to stone to get to the school.

Helping was reciprocal, of course. Sarah's older sister went to stay with her grandmother when she became ill:

Sister: They took my oldest sister—older than I—and she cried and wouldn't stay and she got homesick, so they took me over and I stayed with my grandmother [at age eight].

Sally's first six children were delivered by her midwife mother, before the mother's death. The last five were born with the aid of a local midwife, except one:

Sister: It runs in my mind that one of those children were born when there was no midwife there and Dad cut the cord, yes, uh hum. Which one of us was it?
S: I don't know. I don't remember, but I remember he did.

Life continued, its poverty and toil remembered the most clearly by some of the Flynn children, its halcyon days of family togetherness and "sociable" times by others. The children began to leave home: the oldest to work for the gas company upon his return from the army after World War I, the second to teach school in a nearby town, the third to marry. Sarah, the fourth, attended high school by living first with her maternal aunt in Bayville, seven miles from home, and then with the school teacher sister in Northfield, three miles away.

I stayed with my aunt down in Baytown...two years, then I came back to Hillview in my third year and they divided—they petitioned the school off and had a teacher down from York and there was about ten of us that started in, I think there was five that finished the year, and he was able to give me my third year and then I went to Northfield. My sister was teaching and I went to Northfield and stayed with her and went back—there was a group of children back and forth to Bay creek—and graduated that year.

She then attended a "rural country college" in Athens, two summers and one winter, receiving a diploma to teach in the primary grades. She returned home to live, and taught in a nearby country school, Pine Bluff, one room for all eight grades.

Oh yes, we didn't even have a music teacher!

During her teaching career she met a young man who had also lived all his life in that same township, except for several short periods of employment in Columbus. She remembers little of their courtship, but believes she met him as a friend of her brothers'. Plays and programs at the school, Friday night spelling bees, were courting fare, with occasionally a movie:

> **S:** Yes, we'd go to the movies. And mother and father they didn't have a car 'n they'd go with us. We'd all go as a family, yes. Neither one of us cared for that sort of thing—pictures. We went visiting you know, family sometimes. It's been so long ago-...But there wasn't too much, if we didn't go to church or something at the school. That was all the social thing of the community. If you went to a little picture show you had to go as far as Bluffton.
> **Sister:** To start with, mother didn't want us to go.

Medicine shows plied the circuit, for a welcome change, as did "Chatauquas":

> **S:** We'd drive the horse and buggy down to Southfield, watch the medicine shows. Well, they sold medicine, I don't know what kind, snake—was it made from snakes? What was that medicine that they'd sell?
> **Sister:** Sort of like a carnival in a small way.
> **S:** Yeah, they'd have, probably somebody'd play a guitar or something, a little music, tell some jokes with it.
> **Sister:** Usually a man, usually a girl, the girl would get up and sort of dance.
> **S:** 'N the man'd tell stories—
> **Sister:** The man'd tell this particular medicine would cure anything—snake bite or anything else. I think it used to sell for a dollar a bottle.
> **S:** It was a cure-all, I know that.
> **S:** Chatauquas used to come around. Yeah, they'd put up a tent. I believe it was kind of a religious...Chatauquas were about the same thing [as revival mettings] except on a bigger scale, and mostly music, hymns, musical hymns, maybe a speaker or two. They used to have Chatauquas all over the country.

The young man who courted her finally convinced her to marry him, to move with him "over the hill," three miles away.

The second generation of Flynns, Joseph and Sally, ran a subsistence farming operation on land which had been his father's. The primitive conditions meant onerous labor in the house and in the fields for the parents and their 11 children, including the girls. Though little outside employment was available, any such opportunity was utilized to add cash to the family economy. Education was prized, and all the girls were educated beyond the available one-room schoolhouse and all had some kind of career before or after marriage; none of the boys availed themselves of educational opportunity. The girls were, traditionally, kept close to home, and social life was simple. School and church provided almost all available social activity besides work-sharing parties. Sarah's life was characterized by stability and continuity: she was born and raised in the same house; attended three years of high school away from home during the school week, but lived with close relatives; returned home after two summers and one winter 50 miles away for teacher training; lived at home for three years while teaching; married and moved to a farm just three miles away.

SARAH'S MARRIAGE, BIRTH OF CHILDREN, NUCLEAR FAMILY OF PROCREATION—1927-1947

After her marriage in 1927, Sarah moved just three miles from her birthplace to her husband Robert's farm. His family also demonstrated continuity in their residence in Bay Township: Penfields—believed to be English—had owned the farm since mid-century, their deeds tracing ownership "clear back to the government." Robert's grandfather was the original settler and raised 11 children in a log cabin. Robert's father built the present Penfield home, a large white frame house, for his parents. Robert was born in the house.

After his marriage to Sarah Flynn, their children were all born in the same house, with the exception of their first; she was delivered by the family doctor from Johnstown at Sarah's parents' home, "because the roads were so bad." Soon Robert moved his wife and new baby to Columbus to escape the problems of cold winters and impassable roads. However, work as a conductor was monotonous and confining, and within six months Robert and Sarah returned to the family homestead.

Life changed little thereafter: stability and continuity were maintained; the patterns of living grounded in childhood were perpetuated. Just as her mother had borne a large family (11), so did Sarah. Six children—three boys and three girls—followed the first girl in the next 18 years. (None of Sarah's ten siblings had large families, however, averaging only 1.4 children.) These six were born at home, under a doctor's care, because in the hospital "you're exposed to others' germs." Her mother was with her for each of the births, certainly offering excellent experience, as *her* own mother, Sarah's grandmother, had been a midwife, too.

> Mother followed in her footsteps. Mother went quite a few places, but then they got so they could have doctors, you know, then. But we still—you see, we were knee-deep in mud in the winter, James was born when this highway was started across here

[her third child]. Across the old Hogan Road was the road, and then this was cut through up here, and we give the right of way in order to get a better road, and that's when James was a baby that was built. We were pretty much isolated...After Dennis [her mother's last child] was born [c 1920] I don't remember her going any place...Finally you could get doctors. It was gratis. Friendly. They helped each other, just like harvesting.

Subsistence farming was pursued in this generation as well:

It was probably a follow-up of my parents' life, because we lived on a farm...you really provided nearly all of your living....We've always been people that's raised lots of our living—self-sufficient.

However, the complexion of agriculture and of subsisting was changing both regionally and nationally, and many farmers worked at other jobs as well. Robert was forced to seek all available outside employment through the ensuing years, hauling with his team of mules and team of horses, threshing, sawyering, repressuring gas wells.

Sarah was involved as well in contributing to the family's subsistence and maintenance. She taught three different years at nearby country schools. She raised chickens and sold the eggs. She kept cows, milking them herself, and sold the milk. Though she handled those monies herself, it went for necessities:

I never gave it much thought, we just, you know, when we—'cause if the children needed clothes, they needed clothes. If they needed food, they needed food. That come first. That's what you worked for. That's what we live for, isn't it? That's what money's for.

Really, to tell the truth, if either one of us had money, if we needed it, well, we just never gave it a thought, really, to tell the truth. We just go one to the other....I usually got my milk checks 'n we used 'em for whatever we had, you know, and our egg money 'n things, and that more or less all went in one—whatever we needed for...[Milk checks yours?] Yes, well, I would help pay some, I would pay so many of the bills out of them, you know, the children's clothes. Sure, the clothes and things like that....No, it wasn't my money. If there was any left over then it went for whatever we needed....Yes, I don't think we ever had much money—or trouble over that, over finances. I mean we used what we had, and if we didn't have it we didn't use it, that's what I mean.

As the children grew they were expected to contribute to family maintenance. As the boys grew older they helped in the fields, plowing, planting, harvesting; they fed the stock, gathered the eggs. The girls worked in the house. Sarah stood firm that her girls would not work in the fields or in any job requiring heavy lifting. She was determined to spare them the physical problems she observed as stemming from this. Occasionally they rode the work horses during harvesting to fill the hay mow, or held the cows' tails while their mother milked, "to keep them from switching her in the face." The whole family "broke spruce," in the early winter, that is, cut hemlock branches from their woods into bundles to sell to florists for Christmas decorating.

Much of the work revolved around feeding the ever-growing family. They butchered their own meat, at least two steers, two lambs, and up to ten hogs, as had Sarah's parents—"we still followed that out"—with Sarah's canning the meat, sugar-curing and smoking the pork hams, shoulders, bacon. She planted and tended an extensive garden, using a single-blade, hand-push plow to plant and cultivate, and time-honored "signs" to guide (gardening was considered a "woman's job"). She canned the always bounteous harvest; every autumn the "fruit cellar" shelves boasted row upon row of gleaming jars of fruits (apples, applesauce, peaches, pears, cherries, rhubarb, blackberries, grape juice), vegetables (beets, broccoli, cabbage, corn, peppers, carrots, tomatoes, tomato juice, green beans, wax beans, lima beans, soup beans, spinach, brussel sprouts), pickles and relishes (corn relish, tomato relish, catsup, dill pickles, bread and butter pickles, watermelon pickles, mixed pickle, garlic pickle, sweet pickle, chili sauce), jams and jellies (strawberry jam, elderberry jelly, blackberry jam, raspberry jam, apple jelly, peach preserves). Potatoes, onions, apples, winter squash, pumpkins were also stored in the cool cellar, as were crocks of sauerkraut and sausage. Wheat was taken to the mill to be ground into flour:

> I'd never leave Saturday go by without baking at least two cakes.
> I never baked one cake at a time. I always kept baked things for
> my children. They never were without jelly on their table.

Sarah sewed nearly all her children's clothes, even to their night clothes:

> They put up chicken feed in the real pretty print sacks, and I never let one of those go to waste, so I made pajamas and things out
> of those...pillow cases, yes, I've made beautiful pillow cases, I've
> got them with lace like this, I'd crocheted lace, and I've got a dra-
> werful of them with lace on yet...pillow cases, curtains, clothes
> [the kids] wore to school, all from feed sacks.

Little cash, then, was mandatory. Sugar and shoes were purchase items, as were some school clothes, though Sarah utilized feed sacks for many of those also. The closest town, one-and-a-half miles away, boasted a general store which met many needs: hardware, nails, needles, thread, corsets, shoes, bolts of material, canned goods, bologna, wheels of cheese, and--her husband's great treat--"kags of salt fish," which Sarah boned and soaked overnight.

The children were taught these same survival skills, as Sarah had been taught by her parents, with one cardinal virtue overlaying all: work.

> And he [her father] *should* teach us to work! Keep us out of mischief!

> They'll be lots happier that way [sharing work]. That's what keeps a family close together, is to work together.

And today every one of her children is an indefatigable worker, none more than Sarah herself, whose day still begins at dawn, and ends with little break in the strenuous routine.

Socializing was incidental to surviving; there was seldom occasion for simply visiting. Yet neighbors were friends-in-need, and even work times were potential fun times as well. Butchering still provided such dual opportunity, as did threshing, though barnraisings were mostly past history; baling machines packed hay into small bundles, precluding need for the old-style large barn. Though life in the rural area was still generally characterized by omnipresent work, there still were some institutions which answered a need, not only for socializing, but concomitantly for building foundations of community and reciprocity. Many of these were associated with school or church; PTA, basketball games and tournaments, Farmers' Institutes, 4H Club, Oddfellows Lodge, Grange, all were popular.

The word "segregation" was not in common usage, but the practice was subtly present. Sex roles were unconsciously circumscribed. At threshing and butchering the men formed a tight circle of workers outside, while the women stayed close to their traditional domain: the kitchen and dining room. They prepared and served huge meals to the male "workers," threshers or butchers, then ate afterwards. Men were usually the officers of the clubs and chairmen of the various committees. Here, too, women played a traditional role:

> Well, another thing that we had quite a bit...was the Parent-Teachers' Organizations and things like that and we'd always have suppers and serve; the families would go together, especially the parents.

> In the churches they's have what they call Ladies Aid; the ladies have their meetings, and they do things at Christmas time, make baskets for the poor children, and make quilts and things and send them across [overseas]. There's a lot of different things they have for entertainment.

Funerals also brought families--and neighbors--together again, with women playing a predominant role:

I can remember back years ago when a couple a the neighbors went and laid, they called it laying them out, and they bathed them and got them ready for the grave, instead of the undertaker taking them in and doing it see...At funerals two or three of the ladies would always come in and help a big dinner after the funeral...and set up all night. They used to have wakes, you know, when people died.

Most often relatives formed the nucleus of social gatherings:

We always were having company...Oh, we had lots of company ...Lot of it, lot of it would be relatives, yes.

Another course of constant help and companionship was Sarah's mother, who lived in her own home at Hillview until after all Sarah's children were born. Supportive of all her own ten children (one had died in childhood) and 21 grandchildren, presumably she felt special empathy for Sarah's position in having the largest family. While one son also lived close to her, the others remained within a 50-mile radius except for one daughter, who left the state after marriage. All described their mother as a woman who remained exceptionally alert and active throughout her life.

Thus, we have seen in this period how Sarah maintained the patterns of living established in childhood. Generational continuity was evidenced by both Sarah's and Robert's grandfathers' emigration to Bay Township in the mid-nineteenth century. Continuing the subsistence farming operation carried on by the previous generations Sarah and Robert also raised a large family. Everyone contributed to the family economy. Sarah considered her parents, particularly her mother, a model for living, and for supplying physical, spiritual, and emotional needs to her own seven children. The extended family was the base of social and work groups. In addition, the neighborhood was still close-knit, with work chores traded, and school and church activities the center of community social life.

SARAH'S LIFE CHANGES: CHILDREN
LEAVE, WIDOWHOOD—1947-1977

Little could be recovered concerning this period in Sarah's life, perhaps because nothing noteworthy could be recalled, possibly because it was a painful time of traumatic loss.

Gradually inexorable change took place. World War II factories introduced a whole new spectrum of employment opportunities in Columbus some 50-miles distant. Commuting began as a way of life for many local residents. The natural beauty and open country of the region attracted the beginnings of recreation/leisure-time devotees, and "summer people" brought rural residents into further contact with different customs and viewpoints and life-styles. The Penfield children grew, and one by one left home to marry and start homes of their own.

Death brought the most drastic change. In the early 1960s Sarah's sister-in-law (and close friend) was killed in an automobile accident. Five months later Sarah's oldest son died from a rare disease acquired serving in the Korean conflict, and in four more months her husband died of cancer.

Finally the youngest--and last child at home--married, though she and her husband worked in Blufton and continued to live at home for two years. When their first child was born, they moved to Blufton. After a lifetime of being surrounded by family, Sarah was alone.

She continued her strenuous daily routing, however. No matter the table was set for one, instead of nine. The huge garden was still planted and tended; the fruit cellar was still loaded with the bounty of nature--and her partner, Sarah. Children and grandchildren would need to eat. Amenities softened the stark house: one son installed a bathroom; another laid kitchen carpet; a son-in-law added a kitchen countertop; a freezer supplemented fruit cellar shelves.

Two jobs interrupted the normal routine briefly. She taught in the Catholic school in Blufton for one year, and through a daughter's political connections was made temporary postmistress of nearby Harrington.

She apparently preferred private life, however, and pursued no other potential employment situations. Loneliness was an overriding problem. She lived alone for over ten years, though there were usually one or more members of the family visiting for lunch, a Sunday afternoon, a day of canning or freezing or sewing, or several days of "staying at Grandma's." To solve the problem, in a characteristically open-hearted manner, two years ago she invited her Florida resident sister--whom she had not seen for thirty years--to share her home. The company and the care has improved the sister's poor health far beyond expectation.

SARAH TODAY: FIFTEEN YEARS A WIDOW--1977

Today at 74, fifteen years after her husband's death, life continues to retain the patterns, the habits, and the values originating and cemented in a happily remembered childhood. She still embodies the concept of perpetual motion, and is an unflagging worker, both inside the house, and outside in yard and garden. Even when she sits, her hands remain busy, picking nuts, sorting vegetables, mending, quilting. Her speech mirrors this incessant activity--machine-gun staccato. She still practices most of the traditional methods of folk life which have acquired recent fame through the *Foxfire* books: preserving (meats, fruits, vegetables, pickles, relishes, jams, jellies, sauerkraut); cooking with recipes handed down for generations; making soap; planting a garden by the signs; using home remedies for illness; crocheting and quilting. She has an abiding interest in the farm, its operation carried on skillfully for her by son, James. After he plows, she plants an immense garden, still weeding it with the ancient hand tiller, still canning and freezing prodigious amounts of the *always* bounteous harvest. One son gives her meat for her freezer. She gathers berries and nuts; she does not, however, keep chickens for eggs now. She painted the *out*side of the two-story house again two years ago--relenting enough to allow her son to paint the third-story eaves.

Life did and does revolve around home and family.

Your children are you. They're your life. And your future.

Her conversation is usually person-oriented, and reverts to emphasis on family —name, kind, number, and character of the children, place of residence—no matter the original topic. All her children are married; two live in the immediate neighborhood, one daughter, and one son who farms her tillable acreage; three live ten to 14 miles away (one of these is her eldest son's widow, remarried but in relatively close touch); one lives 20 miles away, and one 50 miles. One son works for the gas company and farms; the other holds numerous jobs much as his father did, in addition to a significantly larger farming operation. Her four sons-in-law have city jobs, but all live in a rural setting, where they either farm or have extensive gardens. In this way each has remained "in touch with the land," insofar as practical. Each maintains a garden, varying in size from large to huge. Each daughter and daughter-in-law cans and freezes extraordinary amounts of the produce to assure her family a well-laid table throughout the coming year. Each bakes as a matter of course. Sarah assists them whenever possible:

> I was there [daughter's] at daylight picking peas, and they didn't know it...Pretty soon here come little Penny out to the patch, and she stayed with me. And Paula--her bedroom is on the side next to the garden, and she says when she gets up she always looks out there 'cause the cattle pastures out there too. And she saw I and little Penny. And she said to George, "What do you believe, my mother's out here stealing my peas!"....So I had them all picked before they got up. And she had little errands she had to run, so I hulled them. I'm going to paper, Susan, I'm going to help her paper her house. They'll have a nice home when they get through with it. James has been working on it a lot this summer. Really three or four rooms. The kitchen I papered a long time ago, all I have to do is just kind of go over it. The paper's really nice, only a few places and she's got enough to fix that. I did Shelly's room. It's nice. I helped Susan pick out the order for her paper.

Each of her daughters sews as well:

> Ann did lots herself. Claire can sew, too. Helen is a beautiful
> sewer. She makes Bud's suits. You should see them! She tail-
> ors 'em. She makes all their clothes, coats.

And, like their mother again, each takes pride in a well-kept home:

> Helen is a beautiful housekeeper. So's Claire. So's Paula. So's Ann.
> Did you ever go to Paula's?....I was gonna say, her house is al-
> ways just spic 'n span, with all those little kiddies. She makes
> them get around and help, too, she's teaching them to work.
> You'd be surprised what little Sarah can do. Really it's wonder-
> ful, she's teaching them to work. They have their own beds to
> make, 'n she goes in and inspects them. Even that baby! Even
> Penny makes her own bed. She does.

In addition, all but one has worked, or is working, at either a part-time or a
full-time job at different periods in her married life. This is a difficult proposi-
tion for Sarah. She firmly believes in woman's place as being *in the home*;
nonetheless she also attempts to understand the financial necessity behind
their work. No other reason, such as a need for expansion of horizons, or desire for a career, or relief from monotony, would be tolerated so long as children remain at home, as they still do in each one's case. She has 21 grand-
children--as did her mother--of whom she is inordinately proud.

The cooking, preserving, baking are primarily, of course, for the children
and grandchildren. Her relationship to them all is very positive; most visit her
often, all are concerned for her welfare. As her sister said, "She is lucky; she
has a very unusual family." She is independent, nonetheless, and instead of
asking for assistance, she is always helping them, from picking peas and wall-
papering to canning tomatoes and mending blue jeans. She tries especially to
lighten the burden of her youngest daughter, eager to take one or more of the
six children. Perhaps she identifies more with this daughter than with the
others, who average only 2.4 children. (No doubt she had received similar
special help from *her* mother, since Sarah was also the only daughter who had
raised a relatively large family.) She babysits for the younger grandchildren,
and is a "buddy" to the older ones. Just as one daughter remembered, "Mom
always had a little egg money if we needed something special," so now does
Grandma manage to help each of the grandchildren with "something special,"
buying a bathing suit for a tot or quilting a comforter for a teen. She always
smiles broadly and becomes even more animated than usual when discussing
any of the grandchildren.

Travel still holds no fascination for her. "I don't like it" is her simple
and definitive statement. Trips to the doctor for her and her sister, and an oc-

casional shopping trip constitute far more time-consuming trouble than she would prefer. Visiting the children offers the only real pleasure away from home:

> Oh, the old folks in Blufton, they have so much, Blufton has so much for their senior citizens, you know. I don't know maybe we'd enjoy some of them if we were in there....Well, I pieced one quilt and quilted it this winter and then I pieced another one and uh, things like that and I'm not much for--unless I can just mix up the cards and--I won't play cards. To me it's a waste, see. I want something I can have.

Though she decries television for its effect on family life and neighbor relationships, she has a new set, and she and her sister watch it fairly regularly. "Grand Ole Opry" is a favorite, and she becomes personally involved with its participants.

Predictably, as with all older persons, health is a predominant concern. Stories of friends' illnesses dot the conversation, and the rising cost of sickness is a constant threat. Life in an old-age home is a grim specter, especially since her sister has had first-hand experience. Resentment is deep against those who seemingly get rich from others' misfortune, particularly the doctors, the lawyers, the undertakers.

Resentments run high, too, when Sarah discusses change in their lives, change she neither asked for, wants, nor enjoys, yet change she feels powerless to control. The ubiquitous "they" receive much of the blame. As she and her daughter discussed aspects of socializing, past and present, her daughter stated:

> See, time has taken care of all this. There's no more thrashin', people aren't together any more for this kind of stuff. Funerals, everyone goes to the funeral home. You just take it down, really, 'till there's no reason for people to get together any more....They took the school away, that did away with the--Sarah interrupts: Yeah it took, that took away your community, when they take your children away; it takes your interests 'n everything'. And the people fought about it terrible....They took our children away, and to tell you the truth, we had *awfully* smart children up here. They could go to college or *anything,* they really were prepared up here....And they took away the school and when you take the school away you've taken *everything* away.

Modern equipment has in fact made each farmer more self-sufficient. Sarah's two sons and one of her sons-in-law farm; they trade labor and equipment regularly. Yet the machines handle crops so quickly, with so few laborers, that traditional big dinners are no longer an accompanying institution to harvesting. Lack of neighborliness is blamed on television as well, and on city-job commuting. Since everyone has a car or cars, no one stays home, precluding neighborhood visiting.

Neighbors are nonetheless still friends. Funerals bring neighbors together; even though funeral parlors have displaced customary wakes, women neighbors always bring food to the bereaved family. Sarah is unable to detail how she knows most all that happens in the community--which she does. But family is always first, in all matters, and nearly all her socializing revolves around one or another member of her family.

One of the most compelling areas in which she sees change is in that of women's roles, their status, and opportunities. When Sarah was young, there was almost no opportunity for women to work outside the home unless they taught school. A few did housework; two dollars a week was considered a big salary! But not many families could afford such "expensive" help. During the depression any women who were working were fired if their husbands were employed. Gradually jobs in other fields opened up, though they were not always high-status types; for example, they were hired as lookouts in the fire towers of state parks, at low pay. Today women have moved into the public sector, as bookkeepers and tellers in the banks, as township clerks and trustees, even as preachers. Nearby Bluffton, with a population of over 6,000, boasts a woman vice-president in one of the banks! Sarah is quite aware of the differences in women's lives today. Nearly every home has a bathroom (a quite recent addition for her), washers and dryers, "all the conveniences."

Today Sarah lives in the house to which she came as a bride over 50 years ago. She maintains the energetic pace and the patterns characteristic of her whole life. Family remains the central core of her existence, and most of her activities are centered around the needs and desires of her seven children and 21 grandchildren. She has witnessed great change in social climate and conditions in her 74 years. She cites consolidation of the schools, increased mobility, and television as the most cogent factors in the breakdown of family and community cohesiveness. One of the greatest areas of change she sees is in that of opportunities for women in their changing status in all roles, public and private.

CHANGE CREATES CONFLICT

The changes Sarah has observed over the century's progress have been enormous in scope, far reaching in effect. But they are not necessarily all for the better. She regrets the poor quality of service in stores, and the fact that men no longer rise when a woman enters the room, or give her a seat on the "street cars." While only the rich had private transportation when Sarah was young, now everyone expects it. Women *have* to work to pay for the two or three cars per family, the fancy houses. And:

that's where the trouble starts.....They plunge themselves so highly in debt, and then, just start in fussing.

Oh, I think there's a round about change today, really I do.
Sometimes I think the mothers just *push* their daughters out.
You know they seem to want them to get married s' young. I
think that's the one reason for the divorces today....too early
marriages. They're not prepared.

For whatever reasons, she reveres the past.

It wasn't like it is today.
They're doing everything the easy way now.
There was more of a sociable life then....your happiest period.

Yet she recognizes some good in the present:

...a wonderful period in some ways. Because there's work and
there's money for people to make. Where we've lived through the
Depression when you didn't know whether you could buy the
second loaf of bread or not. So in a way it's a wonderful time
and in a way it's a terrible time.

This ambivalence is particularly marked in her attitudes toward the
changes in woman's role. Change for her, as for nearly everyone, is unsettling.
Some changes are expected, such as the changes of life, *les passages*. Though
these have usurped her youthful vitality, her nuclear family, and, in fact,
much of the reason for existing, they are still "in the picture of life." They
can be--and are--met with courage, with stoic pride:

It could be made a beautiful place [neighboring rundown farm].
....put a fence around it and just buy your hay and keep a good
herd of cattle. Oh sometimes I wish I was young again!

My father used to say "when you get ready to live, you die."
And you know sometimes that is true.

Everytime he [a neighbor] would see my son, he'd say, "If I
could have my youth back, I'd give all my money away!" He sure
wanted his youth back....No, I don't. No, it isn't in the picture of
life....No, it's all in the picture of life, and God has it all fixed up
for you.

But some changes are *not* in the picture of life. The changes which Sarah
observes in woman's role--the private increasingly displaced by the public--are
not. They call forth widely ambivalent attitudes. Her positive image of woman is evident on one hand:

I don't care what you say, nine times--at least five times out of ten--the woman has more brains than the man.

There isn't anything younger than a man! [agreeing with daughter] Why are men running the world when women are much more capable, thoughtful, and stable?

We find that some of our great minds come from females. And why would the males be so smart if they didn't have a smart mother? *Sure* they're as important!

I do think that some people say women are inferior. I mean it is very, very wrong.

She has strong feelings about the injustices women have borne, possibly remembering the inequities in her own childhood, when the girls worked in the fields, but the boys *never* worked in the house.

No, I really don't think it was right [lower pay, few job opportunities], especially if some women had to support themselves.... You know they can go out and do the same as a man why not get paid the same as a man?

And I think if a woman stands up and works in a factory beside her husband, when her paycheck comes, it should be just as much as his, if she does the same thing equal. All right, then when she comes to wash her dishes, then he's got just as good a right to get a dishrag and wipe 'em as she has to....Yes, I think that they should share and share alike.

Oh, as long as they keep the price down and the girl doesn't get as much money for the same work, naturally they'll get the jobs, won't they....If you can hire a girl, she will work more steady than a man will, and if you can hire a girl cheaper, you're going to hire her, aren't ya?

We found the doctors have their nurses and the dentists...it really isn't fair because women do a lot of work men get the big money for.

(This very positive image could, according to Chodorow, be attributable to her mother's having been a strong character, and the ultimate role model for Sarah:[16]

Mother was the ruling member of our family--there's no doubt about that--not that she was the domineering type.

I don't think father ever made any decisions without going to her and asking her about it....I'm that way too. I always went to my Mother, I always asked her advice, even after I was married.)

On the other hand, her underlying conception of woman as "the second sex" also emerges:

> Men have more strength....And then I think that they can made decisions and be stronger, don't you? When it comes to a tight, serious question, I think that--yes, like President of the United States I think will always be a man...women are, I think they're weaker. They are more sympathetic and I think that a man is stronger in that way in making decisions.

> Eve destroyed man in the Garden of Eden and women have always destroyed men.

> You know the Bible says that a woman should not get up in the church and speak....It says to ask her husband. The things that she does not know, to go to her husband for advice.

> [Concerning local woman made trustee] She didn't know, I don't imagine, anything more about digging a ditch than anything in the world....And I think people went and voted for her for the fun of it. They thought, "That's funny." And mebbe she's a good trustee, [doubtful tone] I don't know.

Change unleashes inner storms for Sarah. Her whole pattern of living has been founded on her belief in home and family as the nucleus of the universe, with the mother at the center. Woman's place is in the home and nowhere else, her job is to raise children.

> I really think it's a mother's place—a woman's place is in the home and early life of her children.

> Just to go out and neglect her children, I wouldn't think of that... In their early life they need you so much. After that why shouldn't she have a few years of her own?

> So the home's falling apart, and they ask why, well that's it [women are working]....And when she comes home she's so tired, that probably she don't see much of the children, don't know much about what they're doing, too tired to ask 'em what they've done today or where you've been.

> Yes, I think to be a good wife and to be a loving wife that you have to have a good meal on the table, your house clean, your children clean and nice and respectable to their father and that then is the big thing in a home.

> What is the world coming to, what is our world coming to when there those young girls are out with men. They're going to get what's coming to them....It's terrible!

> They say that now they're wanting to be in the fire department, go out on the fire wagons, which a woman doesn't belong at night out on the fire wagon, and climbing on the ladder. They're asking to be embarrassed and the men'll embarrass them....They're just not nice women to begin with or they wouldn't put themselves there....I think there are some jobs women are not intended for.

Yet the knowledge that her daughters have worked—or are working—is reflected by qualifying statements on public roles for women:

> Well, the thing today is that two working can't dress and clothe their children.

> I don't think it is wrong for a woman to go as far as she can today. Because I think even in politics she's gonna be more honest. A woman in the White House would *never* have done what those people have done.

> But let 'em go as far as they can. I think they have rights. Like even a woman if she is smart enough to be president, why not let her try? She *couldn't* do any more than they've been doing. No indeed. And do you know, I think we'll have one.

> But it takes really two checks today to live, doesn't it? So we have problems, don't we? Who's gonna solve them?

Ambivalence is demonstrated, too, in the dichotomy between optimistic bearing and pessimistic outlook. Her demeanor, her actions are brisk, positive, optimistic, jovial. But doom-singing proclivities are woven into her speech. (Always devout and interested in church, the Bible, and religion, Sarah became active in a specialized sect about six years ago, and some of her fatalism and pessimism may simply reflect the normative for that group.)

> I think it's a terrible time to bring—I think it's so hard on the babies and parents both—a terrible time to bring the little things into the world. There's just nothing but suffering ahead for us....What kind of future have they got?

> It's in the last days. You see, the Bible says that the families will really turn against each other. Which is happening. All those things are coming to pass....isn't it horrible?

Thus ambivalence, the outward expression of inward conflict, is evidenced by Sarah's real versus ideal ambiguities. Her revered and idealized past is one in which woman's role—however limited—was still comfortably circumscribed. Ideally she decries unequal treatment of women; realistically she cannot approve the mores accompanying present movements toward equality. Ambivalence surfaces, too, in a strange admixture of her doom and gloom proclamations with her buoyant life-style. Ambivalence/conflict becomes then a feature of her personal ethnography. It is difficult to assess on which levels these ambivalences and conflicts are manifested: conscious or unconscious. The ambivalences, and their accompanying contradictions, appear to be on an unconscious level for Sarah, revealed only by assessing many conversations with her over a period of several years. However, conflict, on a personal and on an interpersonal plane, appears to be both conscious and unconscious as well, affecting her thoughts, feelings, and behavior without always entering her awareness.

Change is threatening the foundations of the world as she views it. Inner conflict becomes a hallmark of living, as real and ideal concepts wage their private war. The basic need to parrot the societal line—woman is the second and inferior sex—battles furiously with concomitant awareness of the reality of woman's equal potential. Sarah has steadfastly and courageously fulfilled the personal and societal expectations defined by her spatial and temporal reality. However, the addition of emotional stresses to onerous physical demands has exacted a heavy toll—inner conflict.

For Sarah Penfield some of the rapid changes of this century have been expected and "in the picture of life." Others have been worse than disturbing. While she has a strong, positive image of woman, her abilities and her rights, Sarah is concerned that the new freedoms are undermining woman's ordained place—in the home. Divergent conceptions of the female sex—from equal to inferior—erode her conceptions of herself and her children, of a healthy, positive future for her grandchildren. Inner conflict is a sharpened reality.

CONCLUSION

The life of Sarah Penfield, 74-year-old wife, mother, and grandmother in rural southeastern Ohio, has been chronicled here, a history characterized by generational and residential continuity. Sarah was raised on a nearly self-sufficient farm with ten siblings. As a child she worked in the fields with her brothers, as did her mother with her father. She received two years of teacher training after high school, and taught in elementary schools both before and several times during her marriage. After marrying another native of the township, she moved only three miles from home, where she participated in a subsistence farm operation similar to her parents', and raised seven children.

Her mother was a strong role model; Sarah's own involvement in the subsistence patterns of both her nuclear family of orientation and of her family of procreation, contributed to a strong image of women in general, herself in particular. Nonetheless, she projects definite ambivalent attitudes toward the role of woman in a rural community, and in the larger society of state and nation.

This has been intensified even further by social changes which have shifted women's roles further and further from Sarah's ideal of the private role to the real role of public involvement. Presumably, conflict could be even more dysfunctional for those whose childhood situations gave less opportunity for strong role identity than Sarah's. One can only speculate on the extent to which this same conflict has troubled women in other rural areas, in urban centers, in other age brackets.

Mechanisms for dealing with this conflict arising from countercurrents of social change have slowly become available to women since the late 1960s, primarily through consciousness-raising groups. But these were not an alternative for Sarah, for rural women in general, nor for most women beyond 30. They have faced conflict alone, with no cohorts to ameliorate their private monologues of distress. Definite portents of such conflict are the recent popularity of the "Total Woman" concept, the animosity of female audience members directed at women speakers fighting for equality, and the heavy mobilization of women's groups to fight against passage of the Equal Rights Amendment.

Are Sarah's conflicts, her attitudes, and feelings shared with other women—in her own age group, in middle-age brackets, in younger levels, in urban neighborhoods, in ethnic enclaves? Can Sarah's ambivalences—woman is equal versus woman is inferior—offer a paradigm for conflict in women in general? Or is Sarah simply idiosyncratic, representative of no one, older, rural, or female?

Ideally, comparison could be drawn here between studies of women in other societies and Sarah, between their roles, their attitudes toward those roles, and Sarah's role and attitudes. Yet this is nearly impossible. As indicated earlier, there is little literature which treats southeastern Ohio as it is or is not typical of the larger area of Appalachia. Further, there is no literature on women in southeastern Ohio; there is little on women in Appalachia. In fact there is a notable deficiency on the study of women's lives in general.

An unpublished thesis, written because "only Appalachian men's traditions have been studied" provided viable comparisons.[17] It depicted the lives of seven Kentucky women; the youngest—a mere 65—was the "most adaptable," and all practiced traditional folk ways and crafts. The house was the center of activity, and there was basic agreement on woman's role: milking, tending small animals; gardening, any task revolving around food preservation and cooking; quilting, weaving, sewing, caring for the family's clothes. In addition almost all did fieldwork ("I can do anything a man can do") and it took precedence over housework, at least the cleaning portion. Even recreation was work-oriented: wheat threshings, pea-shellings, cotton-pickings. All wanted to keep active; life is work. They, too, seemed to have a positive image of themselves, despite the overt patrifocality of the Appalachians.

Personal fieldwork with women in southern Ohio and Appalachia underscored similar life patterns: happy childhood memories, close-knit families, a particularly close relationship between mother and daughters, recreation a socialized work form (molasses parties, barn raisings, quilting parties), omnipresent hard labor, women and girls performing mens' and boys' tasks—and strong self-images.

In *The Isthmus Zapotecs: Women's Roles in Cultural Context* Beverly Chiñas provides a relevant cross-cultural comparison.[18] Parenthood is one of the culture's central values; the mother is mainly responsible for socializing the child; boys of all ages are allowed a great deal more freedom than girls, and fewer demands are placed upon them; the household is the basic social unit, though only babies and toddlers receive open displays of affection; Sunday afternoons are the traditional time for married daughters to visit their mothers; the Zapotec ideal is that social relations between siblings will always be close and cordial, and kinship will include mutual trust and cooperation—an ideal seldom realized. Matters of inheritance give rise to conflict, but those adult siblings who are friendly have the closest relationship beyond the household unit. There is little intimacy with neighbors unless they are also kin, but they can be counted upon for help during special occasions—ritual, economic, threat.

There is, then, a paucity of extant literature concerning the culture of southeastern Ohio, the role of women in Ohio, or in the larger area of Appalachia, or even in the still larger area of the nation. This scarcity is unfortunate, because it precludes our depicting change in that role as it might be developing from past to present to projected future. Again, it also precludes making comparisons here with Sarah's role and the changes therein. Thus, valid comparative statements are impossible to formulate at this time.

I suggest there is definite need for further study of women's lives to identify: social patterns of women's roles; attitudes of men and of women toward those roles; the presence or absence of ambivalence/conflict toward change in woman's role in rural groups, in urban groups, and in differing age categories.

For sex roles are changing. This is recognized even by Sarah, an older, rural, heretofore isolated, traditional woman. It is experienced by her daughters and granddaughters. Women's longevity has increased dramatically.[19] Women are marrying later, divorcing more often, remarrying less frequently, and bearing fewer children.[20] Women are entering the labor force in increasingly greater numbers and proportions,[21] even during childbearing and childraising years.[22] Sarah's daughters are examples. One salient fact emerges from these statistics: a very different nuclear family makeup than has been considered standard is now emerging. And the projections for the next two decades promise even more drastic change. There will be new family structures, new housing patterns, a fragmentation of traditional roles.[23]

Nonetheless, data from a survey of college women reveal that ideologies—systems of belief transmitted implicitly—are based on a woman's concept of what kinds of behavior are appropriate to her role as a female.[24] We have observed this both in Sarah and in her daughters: though either circumstances or choice dictated their entering the labor market, they continued, however, to manifest strong traditional patterns, attitudes, and values concerning woman's role.

If ideology does indeed shape women's lives, and if many women today have been exposed to similar traditional upbringing, then talk of equality between the sexes through enlarged public roles is certainly premature. It will not matter what strides are made by individual women in the arts, in commerce, in athletics, in government, in any one of a myriad of potential careers. A true status of equality for women will depend first upon their own perceptions of themselves as equal to men as inheritors of the fruits of the earth and of their own labors.

From available statistics and projections it seems certain that both girls and women will attempt to or be forced to break out of the traditional wife/ mother role. This real change in mores, without concomitant changes in ideal attitudes toward *appropriate* behavior for women, can be viewed only as having a dangerously dysfunctional potential. There is profound need for broader understanding of conflict in women, and a recognition of the power of its real versus ideal ambivalence, circular in treadmill motion, with all the frustrating connotations of the dog-chasing-tail syndrome.

NOTES

1. All proper names are fictitious, in order to ensure the anonymity of both the consultant and her family.

2. Even more pertinent, according to Michelle Rosaldo and Louise Lamphere, eds., in *Woman, Culture, and Society*, there is almost no theoretical appartus for understanding or describing culture from a woman's point of view (Stanford: Stanford University Press, 1975), p. vi.

3. Eugene H. Roseboom and Frances P. Weisenburger, *A History of Ohio* (Columbus: The Ohio Historical Society, 1969), p. 4.

4. Ibid., p. 3.

5. Community Development Division, *Ohio Appalachian Development Plan* (Columbus: Department of Economic and Community Development, 1974), no paging.

6. United States Bureau of the Census, *County and City Data Book, 1972* (Washington, D. C.: Government Printing Office, 1973), p. 377.

7. Ibid.

8. Community Development Division, no paging.

9. United States Bureau of the Census, *County and City Data Book, 1972*, p. 376.

10. United States Bureau of the Census, *County and City Data Book, 1972*, p. 377.

11. United States Bureau of the Census, *Census of the Population, 1970: General Social and Economic Characteristics*, Vol. PC(1)-C37, Final Report, (Washington, D. C.: Government Printing Office, 1972).

12. Ohio Bureau of Unemployment Compensation, *Labor Force and Employed Workers in Ohio, by County and Industrial Group, 1940*, adapted from Census of Population, United States Bureau of the Census (Washington, D. C.: Government Printing Office, 1942).

13. United States Bureau of the Census, *County and City Data Book, 1972*, p. 376.

14. The term "memorate" to denote personal narrative has been coined by the Swedish folklorist, C. W. von Sydow. For a discussion of "true experience" stories, see Linda Degh's "Folk Narrative," in *Folklore and Folklife*, ed., Richard M. Dorson (Chicago: University of Chicago Press, 1972), esp. pp. 77-80. See also Lauri Honko, "Memorates and the Study of Folk Belief," in *Journal of Folklore Institute* I (1964):5-19.

15. Date verfied by research of Reno Robinette, South Central Power Company, Lancaster, Ohio, on November 29, 1977.

16. See Nancy Chodorow, "Family Structure and Feminine Personality." in *Woman, Culture, and Society* (Rosaldo and Lamphere) for further discussion: for example, "the care and socialization of girls by women ensures the production of feminine personalties. . .with a comparatively secure sense of gender identity," p. 58.

17. Linda White, "Study of Woman's Role on the Traditional Farm," unpublished Master's Thesis, Western Kentucky University, 1975.

18. New York: Holt, Rinehart and Winston, 1973.

19. "Over the 73-year period 1900 to 1973, the average length of life of females increased from 48.3 years in 1900 to 75.3 years in 1973, that is by 27.0 years. For men, life expectancy at birth increased only 21.3 years over the same period, advancing from 46.3 years to 67.6 years"; charts and tables further illuminate these statics in *Current Population Reports: Series P-23; no. 58*, United States Bureau of the Census (Washington, D. C.: Government Printing Office, 1976).

20. Ibid., pp. 15-20.

21. "Their [women's] phenomenal growth in the work force is illustrated in the tables and text of this year's databook," United States Department of Labor, Bureau of Labor Statistics, *Bulletin 1977*, (Washington, D.C.: Government Printing Office, 1977), p. iii.

22. In *Current Population Reports, Series P-23, A Statistical Portrait of Women in the United States,* this fact is underscored: "a phenomenal increase has been occurring among women 25 to 34 years of age. Their labor force participation rate advanced by 12 percentage points to 57 percent between 1970 and 1976, and reached 59 percent early in 1977. This is a remarkable increase because of the majority of women in this age group (64 percent) are married, live with their husbands, and have children at home, factors which traditionally have tended to keep women out of the labor force," p. 1.

23. Jean Lipman-Blumen, "The Implications for Family Structure of Changing Sex Roles," *Social Casework* (February 1976): 67-69.

24. Jean Lipman-Blumen, "How Ideology Shapes Women's Lives," *Scientific-American* (January 1972): 34-42.

REFERENCES

Chiñas, B. L.
  1973 *The Isthmus Zapotec.* New York: Holt, Rinehart and Winston.

Chodorow, Nancy
  1975 "Family Structure and Feminine Personality," In *Woman, Culture, and Society,* eds., M. Rosaldo and L. Lamphere. pp. 43-66. Stanford: Stanford University Press.

Crane, Julia
  1974 *Field Projects in Anthropology.* Morristown, N. J.: General Learning Press.

Davis, Kingsley
  1949 *Human Society.* New York: Macmillan.

Degh, Linda
  1972 "Folk Narrative." In *Folklore and Folklife,* ed., Richard M. Dorson. pp. 53-83. Chicago: University of Chicago Press.

Dorson, Richard
  1972 *Folklore and Folklife.* Chicago: University of Chicago Press.

Edgerton, Robert B., and L. L. Langness
  1974 *Methods and Styles in the Study of Culture.* San Francisco: Chandler and Sharp.

Ergood, Bruce, and Bruce E. Kuhre, eds.
  1976 *Appalachia: Social Context Past and Present.* Dubuque: Kendall/Hunt.

Friedl, Ernestine
  1975 *Women and Men.* New York: Holt, Rinehart and Winston.

Goldstein, Kenneth
  1964 *A Guide for Field Workers in Folklore.* Hatboro, Pa.: Folklore Associates, Inc.

Honko, Laurie
1964 "Memorates and the Study of Folk Belief." *Journal of the Folklore Institute* I: 5-19.

Kahn, Kathy
1973 *Hillbilly Women.* New York: Doubleday.

Klingaman, David C., and Richard K. Vedder, eds.
1975 *Essays in Nineteenth Century Economic History.* Athens: Ohio University Press.

Kluckhohn, Clyde
1945 "The Personal Document in Anthropological Science." In *The Use of Personal Documents in History, Anthropology, and Sociology,* eds. L. Gottschalk, C. Kluckhohn, and R. Angell. New York: Social Science Research Council Bulletin 53.

Langness, L. L.
1965 *The Life History in Anthropological Science.* New York: Holt, Rinehart and Winston.

Lipman-Blumen, Jean
1972 "How Ideology Shapes Women's Lives." *Scientific American* January: 67-79.

Lipman-Blumen, Jean
1976 "The Implications for Family Structure of Changing Sex Roles." *Social Casework* February: 34-42.

McMillen, Wheeler
1974 *Ohio Farm.* Columbus: Ohio State University Press.

Ohio Bureau of Unemployment Compensation
1942 *Labor Force and Employed Workers in Ohio, by County and Industrial Group, 1940,* adapted from Census of Population, United States Bureau of the Census. Washington, D.C.: Government Printing Office.

Ohio Community Development Division, Department of Economic and Community Development
1974 *Ohio Appalachian Development Plan.* Columbus: Department of Economic and Community Development.

Pelto, Pertti J.
1970 *Anthropological Research: the Structure of Inquiry.* New York: Harper and Row.

Rogers, Everett
1969 *Modernization Among Peasants.* New York: Holt, Rinehart and Winston.

Rosaldo, Michelle, and L. Lamphere, eds.
1975 *Woman, Culture, and Society.* Stanford: Stanford University Press.

Roseboom, Eugene H., and Frances P. Weisenburger
1969 *A History of Ohio.* Columbus: The Ohio Historical Society.

Santmyer, Helen H.
  1962   *Ohio Town.* Columbus: Ohio State University Press.

Spindler, George, ed.
  1970   *Being an Anthropologist: Fieldwork in Eleven Cultures.* New York: Holt, Rinehart, and Winston.

United States Department of Commerce, Bureau of the Census
  1972   *Census of the Population, 1970: General Social and Economic Characteristics,* Vol. PC (1)-C37, Final Report. Washington, D.C.: Government Printing Office.

United States Department of Commerce, Bureau of the Census
  1973   *County and City Data Book, 1972.* Washington, D.C.: Government Printing Office.

United States Department of Commerce, Bureau of the Census
  1976   *Current Population Reports: Series P-23; no. 58.* Washington, D.C.: Government Printing Office.

United States Department of Labor, Bureau of Labor Statistics
  1977   *Bulletin 1977: U.S. Working Women: a Databook.* Washington, D.C.: Government Printing Office.

White, Linda
  1975   "Study of Woman's Role on the Traditional Farm." Unpublished Master's Thesis. Western Kentucky University, 1975.

Wigginton, Eliot
  1972   *Foxfire* I. Garden City, N.Y.: Doubleday.

Williams, Thomas Rhys
  1967   *Field Methods in the Study of Culture.* New York: Holt, Rinehart and Winston.

13 The Economic Role of Women in Alaskan Eskimo Society

LYNN PRICE AGER

A description of women's contributions to the economy of Eskimo society, this chapter is a counterbalance to the heavy emphasis on male hunting activities which dominates most ethnographies of Eskimo culture. The author argues that the popular stereotype of a predominantly male-oriented society in which hunters provide nearly all raw materials, manufacture highly specialized equipment, and trade their wives to cement social relationships is not without some factual basis, but it tends to obscure the important complementary role of Eskimo women. She notes that a woman's importance to the comfort and survival of the hunters is acknowledged by the men's insistence on having a woman traveling companions for long trips. In addition to the domestic activities women perform, they are responsible for making the tailored garments which make it possible for men to survive in a harsh winter climate. Women are the converters of many raw materials into products which men use in their hunting activities. Thus, the cooperative and complementary nature of men's and women's activities in Eskimo society is more easily understood by this focus on women's contributions.

The traditional Eskimo economy was based on a hunting and gathering subsistence technology in which the unit of production was also the unit of consumption: the nuclear or small extended family. The only full-time specialization of labor was that based on sexual division. Eskimos thus had one of the simplest economic systems known. This chapter will deal with the women's role in that system: her contribution to the acquisition of raw materials; the conversion of resources into consumer goods; the distribution of those goods and her services; ownership of property; and her part in the wage economy of contemporary acculturated society. Finally, there will be a brief discussion of the status of Eskimo women.

In all known hunting and gathering societies, men are primarily hunters and women are primarily gatherers. Recent research into one hunter-gatherer group, the Kalahari Bushmen, demonstrated that women's gathering contributes more to the total diet than does men's hunting (Lee 1968). We are now taking a second look at women's subsistence activities in all societies and discovering that, in many cases, women provide a great deal more than was formerly recognized. But what about Eskimo societies in which hunting, rather than gathering is, in fact, the major source of food and raw materials? What role do women hold there?

Eskimos inhabit a wide range of environments, from the high Arctic of Siberia, North America, and Greenland to the forested Pacific coast of Alaska. The ecological diversity—from Arctic tundra to Pacific coast forest to inland riverine environments—is tremendous and has given rise to cultural diversity largely ignored by all but serious students of Eskimo cultures.

All Eskimos speak a dialect of one of the two Eskimo languages: Yupik and Inupik. Yupik speakers include the Siberian Eskimos, St. Lawrence Islanders, and Alaskan Eskimos south of Unalakleet on Norton Sound. Inupik speakers include Alaskan Eskimos north of Unalakleet, and all Canadian and Greenlandic Eskimos.

Linguistic differences between Yupik and Inupik Eskimos are merely part of the cultural diversity. Population size and density, settlement patterns, focus of subsistence activities, social organization, and other cultural traits also differentiate Eskimo groups. This chapter will deal exclusively with the Yupik speaking Eskimos of southwestern Alaska.

Southwestern Alaska may be the oldest area of Eskimo habitation in the new world. The sheer complexity of Yupik culture, technologically, linguistically (there are three dialects of Yupik in southwestern Alaska alone), and ceremonially, indicates a longer period of development than that of the simpler northern Eskimo cultures. The population of southwestern Alaskan Eskimos is currently greater than anywhere else, and prehistoric settlements indicate that aboriginal populations were probably also larger here than elsewhere. Thus, it is fair to say that southwestern Alaskan Eskimos, or Yupik Eskimos, represent a major Eskimo cultural pattern. Yet little has been written about them compared to the volumes published on Arctic populations.

The southwestern Alaskan coastline and river valleys are richer in both abundance and diversity of resources, such as vegetation, driftwood and fauna, than the Arctic tundras. Yupik Eskimos have easier access to these resources too as the climate in this area is generally milder than it is farther north. In that sense, perhaps they have less romantic appeal than do the Arctic Eskimos, who are pictured stereotypically as struggling incessantly to fend off imminent starvation and danger from cold and wild animals. This may explain, in part, both the layman's and the anthropologist's fascination with Arctic Eskimos. In Alaska, it may also be due in part to the longer period of contact between Anglo-Americans and Inupik Eskimos. Whales, furs, gold, and more recently, oil have lured white entrepreneurs and adventurers to the north, with mission-

aries, teachers, and then anthropologists in their wake. The scarcity of commercially exploitable resources along much of the southwestern coast of Alaska and the barrier to ships caused by shallow water along much of that coast
have resulted in less invasion of that area by outsiders in the past.

The Eskimos have probably been the most studied group of aboriginal
peoples anywhere in the world. Yet it is remarkable that, in 1973 when I first
began my fieldwork in Tununak, Alaska, I was the first anthropologist to
have conducted more than a brief visit to Nelson Island. The closest settlement
for which there exists a published ethnography is Nunivak Island, 20 miles a-
cross the Etolin Strait, where Margaret Lantis (1946) began her observations in
1939. There is no close community on the mainland for which we have comparable data. I mention all this by way of explanation; for a discussion of traditional Yupik culture, I relied heavily on Lantis' findings for Nunivak; I used
my own data for the discussion of contemporary society. The study is, therefore, somewhat limited. Although there are some similarities among all Eskimos, there are also differences from village to village and even more from area
to area. The data presented here are applicable only for the southwestern Nu-
nivak-Nelson Island coast, and the reader must be cautioned not to generalize
too much for Eskimos beyond that area.

In this chapter, I want to present a counterbalance to the stereotype perpetuated in much of the literature, namely, that the Eskimo woman is a subservient individual with little economic value because of the fact the Eskimo
men provide all raw materials and food. While this stereotype *may* approach
reality among certain Eskimo groups, most likely those in the central Canadian Arctic, it does not hold true for the majority of Eskimo women, that is,
those of the most populous group, the Yupik speakers. And even among northern Canadian Eskimo groups, the cooperation between men and women has
been emphasized (Briggs 1974).

TRADITIONAL SOCIETY

The southwestern coastal Eskimos have traditionally been sea mammal hunters and fishermen. The land and sea provide a comparatively rich harvest
with only the mid-to-late winter as a season of scarcity. Seals are available
throughout most of the year except when the winter pack ice offshore is
thick and unbroken (there seems to be no tradition of seal breathing hole
hunting here). There are also occasional beluga whales, walrus, and sea lion in
spring, summer, and early fall. Fish are available year round, including large
runs of salmon and herring netted every spring off the coast as well as individual fish caught with hook and line. In the spring and summer, vast flocks of
ducks and geese nest in the marshy tundra around Nelson Island and adjacent
delta flats. The only large land mammals there today are musk-oxen, intro-

duced by the Department of Fish and Game a few years ago, but these are off-limits to hunters. A reindeer industry was attempted in the 1920s and 1930s, but it failed and the animals have disappeared. Some men travel to other parts of southwestern Alaska to hunt moose, but between sea mammals, fish, and wildfowl, a man need not travel far from home to obtain all the meat his family needs.

Eskimos divided their labors almost entirely on the basis of age and sex. No real economic specialization developed; each man hunted, fished, and conducted limited trading with groups inland, while each woman performed domestic tasks and processed raw materials. This simple, complementary division worked well in a society where a married couple possessed all the knowledge and skills necessary for self-sufficiency and where the family was the unit of consumption.

In Alaska, even in the comparatively milder southwestern area, the climate is stormy for much of the year. A man's comfort and sometimes even his survival depended on protective clothing. Eskimo women have a well-deserved reputation as seamstresses and designers of carefully tailored garments specific to the season and activity. Winter clothing and boots were of warm fur while spring clothing was often made of waterproof sealskin. Raincoats of sealskin intestine protected the hunter in his open kayak at sea. Eskimos recognized that adequate clothing was essential, and women who were especially skilled earned prestige as skin sewers and were highly desired as wives. By providing proper clothing, bags and containers for equipment, and waterproof boat covers of skin, women contributed indirectly to their husbands' success as providers. Once game and fish were caught and retrieved, women handled the processing and distribution of the catch. The knowledge and effort involved in cleaning, butchering and distributing meat, preserving food, cooking, and manufacturing the necessary items from these raw materials is considerable. Sea mammals are skinned; the layer of fat or blubber is cut away, entrails are removed; the carcass is butchered; meat is distributed, preserved or cooked; intestines are cleaned, blown up to dry, then split to use in sewing raincoats; fat is stored until it melts into a golden oil, used extensively in the diet; the skin is scraped, dried and stretched, then scraped again, softened or tanned, cut and sewn into garments, boots, bags, or cut into ropes. Sinew is dried, then pounded, shredded and twisted into thread. These steps also consume more time than the actual hunting does. Whereas men expend energy in brief bursts out hunting, then loaf for days at a time, women are constantly busy with their tasks. During the spring fish runs off the coast of Nelson Island, for example, men might spend two or three long, hard days fishing, but it then took women from 10 to 14 days, 12 hours a day, to clean the fish, lay the eggs out to dry, braid the fish into grass ropes, and hang them up to dry. Women were responsible for the majority of the processing of animal products men contributed through hunting. The scarcity of wood (only driftwood is available along the treeless coasts) and suitable stone, and the absence of metallurgy meant that Eskimo technology depended on raw materials from animals more than on any other kind. Skin, sinew, bone, antler, walrus ivory, and intestine were converted to boat covers, drum covers, tools and weapons, equipment, and all clothing and footwear (with the exception of grass "socks" to line skin boots).

In addition to the separate but complementary division of tasks, men and women also occasionally cooperated on the same projects. For example, they built houses together, and occasionally a husband and wife team handled a seine together in fishing.

> The high economic value of both sexes and the fact that neither was just a drudge for the other were unconsciously demonstrated in various ways. Both used exactly the same types and quality of baskets and carried them in the same way. Although the shapes of dishes and buckets varied for the two sexes, all were decorated in the same manner. Their clothing was equally fine and equally decorative (with the possible exception of men's fancy caps for festivals), and both sexes wore nose ornaments, ear ornaments, and labrets.
> ... Although men's and women's labor and crafts were different, neither sex was thereby made independent of the other. It was just the reverse. The mere fact that each sex performed specialized tasks meant that each was dependent on the other, producing an economic unit, the family, characterized by full cooperation within itself. It is true that man's position was higher than women's. Baskets were not wealth, sealskins were. This sums up the difference (Lantis 1946: 246).

So far we have merely outlined the use of animal products as food, clothing, and other items. A detailed account of all the processes involved is beyond the scope of this paper. But it is clear that, as Lantis puts it, "woman's most vital work was the conversion of raw materials into consumer goods" (Lantis 1946: 245).

The distribution of meat and most manufactured goods was also the responsibility of the woman. She had control over food stores and their allocation. She decided who received gifts of food and who received gifts of her handiwork. She had her own partners, as did the men, with whom she shared food she collected and with whom she exchanged gifts (Lantis 1946: 161). The tools made for her and her own handiwork were her personal property, to dispose of as she wished or to leave as an inheritance for her daughters (Lantis 1946: 252).

Women manufactured items from raw materials they themselves obtained as well as from materials provided by their husbands. Women in southwestern

Alaska, unlike Eskimos in most other areas, manufactured crude pottery from local clay. These dishes were used as seal oil lamps; the only source of heat and light, and as cooking and eating utensils. They also gathered and dried long grasses to use as boot insulation and to weave into coiled baskets, loose net-like bags, socks, and mats. Another independent contribution of women was in gathering and in supplementary fishing. Women fished with hook and line from ocean beaches and river banks and through holes in the winter river ice. They gathered shell fish, sea weed *(Fucus)* and sea anemones from tidal pools along the shore, freshwater plants from shallow ponds, and young greens and berries from the tundra. Wildfowl eggs were collected in the spring, and herring eggs clinging to seaweeds *(Fucus)* in the shallow saltwater close to shore were gathered in summer. Such gathering activities provided variety and important additional nutrients in the diet. The literature suggests that plants were of relatively minor importance in the diet of northern Eskimo groups. In the southwest, however, plants were more abundant and were used to a great-er degree. (Approximately 40 species of a total of 170 identified on Nelson Island were used as foods, medicines, or as raw materials in 1973-74, accord-ing to an ethnobotanical study by Ager and Ager). Since extensive knowledge of plant uses is today held only by older women, it may be that this know-ledge is passing from the culture and was even greater in precontact times. Greens, eggs, and berries were also preserved to eat in winter. Lantis estimates that fish, shellfish, greens, eggs, and berries constituted nearly one-half the diet on Nunivak (p. 245). Admittedly, this is higher than any other area re-ported, but I think it reflects the detailed attention to women's contributions by a female anthropologist. Perhaps even Eskimo women in the harsher Arc-tic environments contribute more to subsistence than male anthropologists have been able to record, although available plant and shallow water resources are more limited in the northern areas.

Both males and females could become shamans whose focus was on the cause and cure of *disease,* but *symptoms* were generally treated with cures made from plants. Women were the most knowledgeable herbalists since they were collectors of plants and did most of the preparation of plant remedies. In some cases, curers were given a gift or small fee for their assistance.

In a manner consistent with their values on individualism, Eskimos marked children's transitions, not in group rites performed at some arbitrary stage of development, but by recognizing ceremonially such tangible signs of maturity as a girl's first menstruation or a boy's first killing of a major game animal. These were known as "firsts" ceremonies (Oswalt 1967: 200). "Firsts" could be observed when a boy shot his first seal or caught his first fish, or when a girl gathered eggs or berries for the first time. Ceremonies of recognition did not necessarily take place on every one of these occasions, and generally the boys' achievements were celebrated more frequently than the girls', but the mother played an important role in ceremonial observances of these achievements. A boy's first bird, for example, would be skinned by his mother and saved for later hanging in a place of honor at the annual Bladder Feast to propitiate the souls of animals killed in the previous year. She observed the same taboos as her son when he killed his first seal. She helped him distribute his catch and prepared a feast for the men as part of any "first" ceremony. Her contribution was, in this way, an integral part of the public recognition of children's achievements. In addition to "first" ceremonies for children, there were "first fruits" rites for the first seal taken by a hunter at the beginning of each annual cycle. The hunter and his wife frequently observed the same taboos, and the wife was in charge of handling the game in a prescribed ritual manner (Oswalt 1967: 225-26). In many ceremonies, gifts were exchanged and food was distributed. These events were, thus, occasions for movement or redistribution of resources. Those with more to give gained prestige by providing a greater share of the feasts and gifts or by sponsoring such feasts individually. Ceremonial exchange, feasts, and partnership exchanges were the primary mechanisms for mobility of resources and goods beyond the family circle, that is, to nonrelatives or distant relatives.

The role of women in the social structure as well as in the economic system was traditionally separate from, but complementary to, that of men. Eskimos had no highly developed political institutions and no formal public offices. There were few specialized roles of any kind; the role of shaman was usually only a part-time occupation. Men and boys over the age of about five lived, worked, and slept in a communal men's house called a *qazgiq* (or *kasigi*), and food was brought to them there by their wives or mothers. The *qazgiq* also served as a village ceremonial center. Individual dwellings were matricentered, with female inhabitants controlling the domestic activities; men were really only visitors in their wives' or mothers' houses, although technically they were owners. The public and private domains were thus clearly segregated, with men governing the public sector and women in charge of the domestic sphere. Women were not public figures. Individually and privately, they could, and sometimes did, wield considerable influence through relationships with their husbands, grown children, and friends, but they were circumspect and inconspicuous in public, at least until they were quite old. Lantis says,

> ...a woman might be influential in the community through her gossip, her industry and maintenance of high standards of workmanship or of generosity, or her domination over some important man; but this was unofficial, indirect, and variable. Hence, only the men's roles are formally stated (p. 246.)

It is important to note, however, that circumspection and a low public profile were generally valued among all Eskimos, regardless of sex or age; both men and women strove to live within the extreme emotional restraints imposed by Eskimo concepts of ideal behavior. The behavior of women was not, therefore, necessarily an indication that they were subservient (Lantis 1946: 256).

A case has been made for the subservient position of women in northern Alaskan Eskimo society (Friedl 1975), a case based on the dependence of women on men as producers; and although my discussion pertains to southwestern Eskimos, it might be useful for purposes of comparison to quote from a primary source on northern Alaskan Eskimos.

> The economic aspect of the husband-wife tie was considered by the Eskimos to be of equal importance to that of childbearing in both traditional and recent times. During the interviews in which informants were asked to evaluate specific examples of this relationship, economic considerations were always at the top of the list (the bearing and care of children being taken for granted.)....
> She was...in charge of game, practically from the moment a kill was made until the meat was eaten, her duties including retrieving, skinning, butchering, storing, cooking, and serving. In addition, wives brought in a fair amount of small game themselves. They hooked for fish, and snared ptarmigan and rabbits in all districts; along the Kobuk River, they were in complete charge of the crucial summer fishery. Women were responsible for the acquisition and storage of all vegetable products—berries, greens, leaves, roots—which constituted a more important resource than most authors recognize. Women were in charge of operating the oil lamps which constituted the only source of light, and the primary source of heat in traditional times. It was the [wife] who got the wood for the one cooked meal of the day. She fed and generally cared for the dogs, and she probably drove them more often than her husband did, both when retrieving game and when traveling. (Burch 1975: 88-89).

Because of the greater prestige value attached to male activities, especially hunting, we cannot say that women held equal status in traditional society. The public domain, especially politics and warfare, was dominated by males, with one or two of the oldest females serving as influential advisors on some occasions. But the women's economic contribution may be nearly as important as the males', and within the private domain, their power was considerable.

CONTEMPORARY SOCIETY

Itinerant Roman Catholic priests have visited Nelson Island since the last decade of the nineteenth century, and a Bureau of Indian Affairs school opened there in the first third of this century. The people have converted to Christianity and adopted many technological changes (for example, rifles, snow machines, outboard motors). The outward appearance of life in the villages is one of great transition, since the visible aspects of life, that is, material culture, have changed most dramatically. But their social life remained less influenced by contact until the recent past. In spite of a hundred years of U.S. territorial status and statehood, many adults speak only Yupik. There are still local curers who practice bloodletting and prescribe teas brewed from local plants. Older men still know how to construct kayaks; and the ancient dances are still performed, although in a social context rather than in a religious one. Traditional semisubterranean houses were still homes for a few families until a decade ago.

Men still depend on hunting and fishing to support their families. Stores in the village now stock nearly everything a family really needs, but the people seem to prefer their traditional diet and buy store goods primarily as supplements or special treats. Tea and pilot crackers are an exception; these are now considered essential.

Because the annual subsistence cycle is still intact, women continue to perform a viable economic role in subsistence activities. They still carry out gathering activities and process all fish, sea mammals, and wild birds. Because of the availability of manufactured clothing, tools, and other household items from mail-order catalogues and local stores, however, women can spend more time at activities that will earn cash income. Rather than using all skins for their family's clothing, Eskimo women can sell some of them for cash. Seal oil is now also sold for cash by coastal Eskimos to those who live inland (formerly it was traded for pelts of inland fur animals). Crafts now occupy a greater proportion of some women's time than heretofore. Baskets sell from $20 to $200 to tourist shops in Alaskan cities. Women also buy white reindeer hair from herders on Nunivak Island and make dance "fans," carried by women while dancing traditional Eskimo dances. These can be sold either to other Eskimos or to tourist shops in the cities for $15-$30 a pair. Ivory carving is not prevalent here; only one man has any recognized talent and earns income from his carving, but there is at least one woman who carves small ivory earrings for occasional sale and others who make necklaces from glass beads. Women's basketry is presently the only local industry of any consequence in Tununak, but there is no women's organization or cooperative; all business arrangements are made by individual women with tourist shop owners elsewhere.

Women, in addition to their independent economic enterprise in basketry, also assist their husbands in joint economic ventures, such as operating small stores or movie houses. Culture change and the introduction of a cash economy have brought jobs to the villages. Women find full- or part-time employment as school cooks, teacher aides, babysitters for teachers' children, postal clerks, social work aides, medical aides, assistant medical aides, and so on. The cash from these jobs is a significant, and in some cases the major income for families.

In addition to their direct economic contribution as gatherers and converters of raw materials, as wage earners, and artisans, women participate in other ways in the economy of the villages. The Alaska Native Claims Settlement Act of 1971 provided for 40 million acres of land and $962.5 million plus revenues from royalties on leases to be distributed to the Alaskan natives through their 12 regional corporations. Generally speaking, men hold positions of control in these corporations, but many of the decisions regarding land selection and future local economic development are made by the village level organizations or village corporations. At the village level, women are now becoming active participants in the public sphere. Women hold positions of secretary, treasurer, or even vice-president of native councils and corporations. I do not know how much actual decision-making power women in these offices hold, but it is significant that they are elected to office by the village at large.

In Tununak, the village where my fieldwork was conducted, women's activities are the primary mechanisms for mobility of wealth. Two afternoons a week, the village council sponsors bingo games to raise funds for community activities. Bingo is the major acceptable outlet for gambling, especially among women who form the majority of players. Some women lose up to $20 in an afternoon of playing, while others can win that much. Wins and losses probably all even out in the long run, but a woman who has just won at bingo is more likely to splurge by buying extra goods at the stores or by taking her entire family out to the movie that night than she would if the same amount of money were a regular, expected income.

Another important leveling mechanism is what is called the "seal party." Seal parties are the modern counterparts of "first" ceremonies for children and "first fruit" rites for adult hunters. Two kinds of seal parties are given: one for men and one for women. Either or both can be given to observe the same occasions: a child's first contribution or a man's first seal of the year, or for a favorite child's birthday. Both are hosted by a woman for her child or her husband. For the women's party, the hostess buys as many small items from the stores or mail-order catalogue as she can afford: yard goods; thread and other small packages of sewing notions; plastic baskets or bowls; barrettes; hair clips; toilet paper; cans of soda pop; packages of gum or candy; bars of soap, and so on. The more money a woman has, the more she can purchase (that is, the more money she pumps into the local native-owned businesses). She prepares *agutuk*, or Eskimo "ice cream," which is distributed to guests (all the other women of the village are invited) as they arrive outside her door. After everyone is assembled and food has been distributed, gifts are distributed to the guests outside, usually by throwing them up in the air and letting the women scramble to grab as much as they can. It is all in fun and is accompanied by great laughter. The party is then over, and everyone goes home with what she has caught. Women who have more money to spend not only distribute more gifts at each party, but also give seal parties more frequently. A poor woman might be able to celebrate her son's first seal hunt, but women with more cash income find many excuses to celebrate and may give two or three seal parties a year (for example, one affluent woman gave a big party to honor her only son's first running in the 4th of July race). Women gain prestige from frequent seal parties, but these are nevertheless not ostentatious. In spite of some differences in amount of cash income, there is no great discrepancy in the standard of living in small Eskimo villages. Seal parties are simple economic leveling mechanisms carried out in the guise of a social event. And like so many other similar mechanisms, the giver earns prestige.

The men's seal party is also the responsibility of the hostess, though her husband is the ostensible host. She prepares a feast to serve all the men in the *qazgiq*. The more variety and quantity of food, the more admiration for the host and his wife. Sometimes, gifts, such as packages of cigarettes, are distributed to the guests if the host can afford to do so. Again, everyone shares in the feast, regardless of whether or not he can respond in kind. Moreover, while poorer families may have to choose whether to sponsor a woman's party or a man's feast on a special occasion, a wealthier hostess will give both to observe the same occasion. Wealth not only moves from the "richer" to the "poorer", but since many manufactured goods are bought locally (store goods have more prestige value than even the loveliest locally hand-made crafts), the local merchants profit as well.

The influence of missionaries resulted in abandonment of the *qazgiq* as a men's communal dwelling, and now husbands live with their wives. In the majority of homes I visited, I got the impression that there was an equality in the marital relationship. A few husbands were known to dominate their wives, but there were also wives who dominated their husbands. We could speculate that the loss of the men's house has resulted in men's attempting to exert more influence over their private households, but I have no data to support or refute this. Men do continue to gather together in the native store daily, and they also join the National Guard which provides them a place to gather once a month for a weekend together. And many spend considerable time in the local pool hall.

Both males and females now attend school and have equal opportunity for higher education. Young women seem to be successfully resisting parental pressure to marry young, and many are pursuing jobs or higher education. Men still hold most of the positions of leadership available in contemporary village politics, but women are participating to a greater extent directly in the public domain by becoming members of school and church advisory boards and officers on the village council, and indirectly in the traditional way: as advisors to their husbands, brothers, and sons.

During the early 1970's, an 800 mile oil pipeline was built from the north slope of Alaska to the pacific coast of the state. Benefits to the Alaska Natives were expected in the form of jobs, but few natives were actually employed on a permanent basis, and I could discern no impact of that project on the residents of Tununak, who were not located anywhere near the route along which the pipeline was built.

Young married women are still expected to be industrious; being seen frequently in public is interpreted as a lack of responsibility at home. But the liberated young are beginning to ignore some of the old restrictions and spend more time visiting each other.

The oldest woman in the village today has a great deal of prestige. She decides when the annual "Special Dance" is held (a modified and local version of the traditional Messenger Feast), and what kinds of goods will be exchanges: store bought or traditional. Other older women are influential as advisors and are viewed as moral leaders. Even well-established, middle-aged men are said to consult their aged mothers on important decisions.

In the traditional system, the primary family was both the unit of production and the unit of consumption. Women were providers of supplementary raw materials (clay, grasses, small driftwood collections) and foods (shellfish, seaweed, green plants, berries, eggs). But their major function was the conversion of resources into usable items of food, clothing, household equipment, boat covers, and other equipment. The distribution of wealth took the form of exchange, through partnerships and the medium of ceremonial gift giving and feasting. There was also movement of resources within the kin group, as women distributed food, and to a lesser extent, their handiwork, to family members.

In the contemporary society, the traditional subsistence economy continues to function, but a market economy has been superimposed. Women still have the primary responsibility for gathering and for processing and distributing game provided by the hunters. In addition, cash income is earned by some women through jobs and the sale of crafts. Women also participate to a large extent in the cash flow of village life. They order most of their families' clothing and domestic equipment (for example, pots and pans, furniture, and so on) from mail-order houses and thus decide how a significant part of the family income is spent. They do much of the shopping at local stores, participate in bingo games, and often dole out money for the children to spend at stores and movies. The seal parties they host are the most significant economic leveling mechanisms within the confines of a village.

In the aboriginal culture, women's skills were considered so vital that no man would undertake a long journey without a woman to accompany him. It has been suggested that where men and women contribute equally to subsistence, where there is a demand for goods produced by females, and where women are respected, their status tends to more closely approach equality to men (Sanday 1974). It would appear that traditionally, women approached true equality to men only in their later years, whereas today young women actively seek it earlier. Still, the measure of equality in individual relationships depends on the personalities of the people involved and can range from nearly complete subjugation of a young wife to the domination of an older woman over her husband. As a group, Eskimo women are not subservient. They have always contributed vital skills and knowledge to the economy of Eskimo society, skills that while not as prestigeful as hunting, were nevertheless of equal economic value and essential to survival.

REFERENCES

Ager, T.A., and L.P. Ager
    n.d.   An Ethnobotany of the Eskimos of Nelson Island, Alaska. Manuscript under publication review.

Briggs, J.L.
    1974   "Eskimo Women: Makers of Men." In *Many Sisters*. Carolyn J. Matthiasson, ed. pp. 261-304. The Free Press.

Burch, E.S., Jr.
    1975   *Eskimo Kinsmen, Changing Family Relationships in Northwest Alaska*. American Ethnological Society Monograph, No. 59. St. Paul: West Publishing Co.

Friedl, E.
    1975   *Women and Men: An Anthropologist's View*. New York: Holt, Rinehart and Winston.

Lantis, M.
    1946   *The Social Culture of the Nunivak Eskimo*. Transactions of the American Philosophical Society, Vol. 35, No. 3, pp. 156-323.
    1959   *Folk Medicine and Hygiene of the Lower Kuskokwim and Nunivak-Nelson Island Areas*. Anthropological Papers of the University of Alaska, Vol. 8, No. 1.

Lee, R.B.
    1968   "What Hunters Do for a Living, or, How to Make out on Scarce Resources." In *Man the Hunter*, R.B. Lee and I. Devore, eds. pp. 30-49. Chicago: Aldine.

Oswalt, W.H.
    1967   *Alaskan Eskimos*. San Francisco: Chandler.

Sanday, P.
    1974   "Female Status in the Public Domain." In *Woman, Culture and Society*. M.Z. Rosaldo and L. Lamphere, eds. pp. 189-206. Stanford: Stanford University Press.

PART IV

CONCLUSIONS

14 Comparisons and Implications: What Have We Learned?

ERIKA BOURGUIGNON

Our discussions of the situation of women in a dozen different settings have told us a good deal about the diversity as well as about some common trends found among these settings. We must now attempt to sort out what we have learned, assess our findings, and attempt to account for them. We may now see what we have discovered, and what is new in our materials.

THE IMPACT OF REGIONAL TRADITIONS

Our twelve socio-cultural settings span the globe. They range from South East Asia to West Africa and on to the Western Hemisphere. There they move, with a series of stops, from Southern Brazil to Western Alaska. Yet, in fact, they may be grouped within six major cultural traditions each of which has great historic depth; they include beliefs and concepts concerning the nature of men and women, and of sexuality. They embody value systems and beliefs that are both causes and rationalizations of behavior and its control. It is therefore important for us to understand how the traditions affect those aspects of culture and society that we are particularly concerned with.

Which Traditions?
The six traditions represented in our twelve cases are that of South East Asia, as found in Brunei, two quite distinct Native American traditions–those of the Maya and the Eskimo, respectively–the Mediterranean tradition, the tradition of West Africa, and the Anglo-Protestant tradition.

The Mediterranean Tradition.
This tradition appears in two variant forms, the Islamic and the Ibero Catholic. Islam, in its expansion from its historic source in Arabia, carried important aspects of the culture of the Mediterranean basin to South East Asia and West Africa. The Spaniards and the Portuguese brought their versions of the Mediterranean tradition, itself influenced by centuries of Arab rule of the Iberian peninsula, to their colonies in the New World. In our cases, the Is-

lamic tradition appears in its classic form in Saudi Arabia, and, in somewhat modified form, among the Malays of Brunei. It is also seen among our two West African groups, the Dioula of the Ivory Coast and the Hausa of Niger, both of whom now live in multi-ethnic nations that were once French colonies. The Ibero-Catholic tradition is represented by our Latin American examples: the Brazilian cities of São Paulo and Rio Grande do Sul, the Yucatán Peninsula of Southern Mexico, and the Washingtonian Cubans.

Honor and Shame

The Mediterranean tradition, both in its Islamic and its Ibero-Catholic form, embodies concepts of key importance with regard to the status and roles of women. In her discussion of Saudi Arabia, Deaver speaks of the values expressed in the concepts of *honor* and *shame*. The basic pattern she describes, although in somewhat modified form, holds for both Islamic and Ibero-Catholic cultures. In all of these societies, males are responsible for the behavior and the reputation of their sisters, wives, and daughters, and in the absence of other appropriate male relatives, of their mother as well. A woman's offense against the rules of sexual purity brings shame on her kin group. To save the honor of the family, the men must punish any violations. In an extreme case, a father may kill his daughter. Therefore, to avoid the dangers of shame, female seclusion and veiling exist as barriers to temptation and the infraction of the rules of modesty. Temptation always exists because sexuality is perceived as a force that is not subject to internal controls, and women are believed to be more highly "sexed" than men. They are, therefore, dangerous to men, who must not be exposed to temptation. John Gulick (1976) has argued that, contrary to the idea that this puts the women into a key position, in fact it places the "burden" of family honor on them. The existence of such a burden is seen in the control that men exercise over women, whose violations of the rules they seek to prevent, and, if they occur, to punish.

A number of authors have shown the interrelated themes of honor and shame to be part of a general Mediterranean pattern of values (Peristiany 1966, Schneider 1971) and some explicit comparisons have also been made between the world of Islam and that of Latin America (Youssef 1974). Quigley (1973) speaks of a "Pakistani-Peruvian axis," meaning that there is a single cultural complex, of great historic depth, that extends from Islamic Asia to South America. In the context of the present volume, it may be said to extend from northern Borneo (Brunei) to southernmost Brazil.

In West Africa and in the Americas, the Mediterranean tradition encountered another cultural tradition, namely that of West Africa. This tradition is illustrated by the Hausa and the Dioula, and it also appears in Brazil and in Cuba, countries to which West Africans were brought as slaves. There, the African traditions have influenced, to a greater or lesser extent, not only the direct descendants of the Africans, but also population groups of non-African ancestry. St. Vincent and St. Kitts, both outside the sphere of the Mediterranean cultural tradition, also are peopled by blacks, and there, too, the West African tradition is evident in significant respects.

West Africa and the Economic Independence of Women

A central theme of the West African and Afro-American tradition is the economic independence of women. In Africa, this appears in the context of exogamous lineages, held together by the solidarity of a group of brothers. Here there are strong ties between mothers and their children, but weak affectional ties between husbands and wives. The primary concern is with carrying out one's responsibilities, and, as Robert LeVine (1976) has noted, material transactions are stressed in interpersonal relationships. All of this is in great contrast to the Islamic Mediterranean pattern, where kin groups are ideally endogamous and the preferred form of marriage is between a man and his father's brother's daughter. Families, as we have seen, are held together by the honor of their men and the modesty of their women. When these two contrasting patterns come together, one key question is this: how can women be economically active and maintain independence without challenging the honor of their men? The accommodations that have been worked out merit our attention.

In the New World, slavery to a large extent destroyed the African family unit, and for lower-class families, a widespread pattern of matrifocal consanguineal households resulted. Where the Spanish legacy came into contact with the Maya tradition, as among the peasants of Yucatán, there is little evidence of the honor/masculinity complex (*machismo*) that so strongly characterizes northern Mexico (Paz 1961).

The Anglo–Protestant Traditions

The third cultural tradition, that appears several times and in a number of combinations, may be termed Anglo-Protestant. It is represented in our cases in clearest form in Appalachia. It is also found in the Anglo-Caribbean, where it appears in combination with elements of the West African tradition. Moreover, it is the dominant tradition in the United States, to which Cubans and Eskimos alike must adapt. The Anglo-Protestant tradition is in many ways different from both the Mediterranean and the West African tradition. It shares certain features with each, yet places stresses on different qualities and goals. In contrast to the emphasis of both of the other traditions on lineages and large kin groups, the Anglo-Protestant tradition emphasizes the independent, self-reliant individual, and beyond the individual, the nuclear family. Sexuality is seen as essentially evil, and individuals must be brought up to develop internal controls. In the words of a Mexican observer, "the North American hides or denies certain parts of his body and, more often, of his psyche: they are immoral, ergo, they do not exist. By denying them he inhibits his spontaneity" (Paz 1961:37). Women are less sexed than men, so that it is easier for them to be in control of themselves and they must see to it that men are held in line. There are no veils, no walled compounds, no chaperones.

A clear picture of this Anglo-Protestant tradition can be seen in the life of Joyce's Sarah Penfield: the self-reliant, hardworking, Ohio farm family of the first decades of this century, the rules by which children were brought up, the sexual double standard. Because controls are supposed to be internalized, there is a good deal of external freedom for young people here. The Cubans in Washington find this one cultural difference with which they must learn to cope. Many elements of this tradition are couched in religious terms and are expressed in Protestant fundamentalism. In this form they can be seen in the Pentecostal and Apostolic churches of the Caribbean and Latin America. In our cases, they are discussed with reference to St. Vincent and Yucatán.

Cultural Transformations

A word, finally, must be said about one additional factor that affects the kaleidoscopic variations of culture, namely "Westernization" or "modernization," terms that are often used synonymously. To a considerable extent, this involves an export version of Euro-American culture. Its most visible aspects are various forms of technological and economic change. As such, it constitutes one element in each of our cases, yet, with regard to the status of women, as we have seen, its impact is not always the same.

The 12 studies presented in this volume all deal with complex, stratified societies. Only the Eskimo were until relatively recent times a "tribal" group, with little internal differentiation. Several of the societies are also multiethnic in character. Although a number of the chapters deal with two or three groups and contrast their ways, the concern is never with the society as a whole but only with the localized segments, that could be studied by fieldwork. Yet the situation of women in a particular local group cannot be understood without reference to the larger society, or indeed, to the major cultural traditions, the values and systems of meanings they embody.

THREE CENTRAL CONCERNS

In our introduction we set out three central concerns for our discussion of women's lives: the economic roles of women, the utility and applicability of the concept of domains (public versus private or domestic) for our understanding of women's status, and the effects of culture change. As we discuss these topics we shall need to keep in mind the cultural traditions to which each of our 12 cases belongs, and to consider the effect the core values of these traditions have had on women's lives, on the roles they play, and the status they occupy.

The Emic and Etic

In the anthropological literature discussions concerning women's work, the subject of the domains, and the role of culture change are based on conceptualizations that are intended to allow cross-cultural comparisons. Yet a reading of the chapters in the present volume makes it quite clear that there is a serious danger in such universalistic or *etic* preoccupations, for they may distort and overwhelm the specific cultural or *emic* reality as it is experienced by the people themselves. We have therefore not only provided the ethnographic contexts in which work takes place and in which the domains are structured, but have also paid attention to the ways in which women perceive themselves. This has led us to raise the question of women's self-respect and self-esteem.

Balancing the cross-cultural, *etic* perspective by an *emic* one is especially important because the suspicion arises that much that passes for "scientific," supra-cultural or *etic* anthropology may be no more than a reflection of our own local cultural concerns. Before considering our data, it may therefore be worthwhile to illustrate the point at issue. The U.S. sociologist, Jean Lipman-Blumen has sought to explain the segregation of social institutions by sex in Western societies. She argues that women are excluded from what she terms the "male homosocial world" because they do not have the kinds of power and resources that make men "useful and interesting" to both other men and to women. Here she lists such attributes as territoriality, exclusivity, dominance, and resource accumulation. As a result, Lipman-Blumen says, "by ignoring the existence of women outside the domestic, sexual, and service realms the male homosocial world relegates women to the sidelines of life" (Lipman-Blumen 1976:31). According to this author, the resources of Western women are limited to sexuality, beauty, charm, service, and parenthood; therefore they must emphasize their capacity for sexuality, motherhood, and service to be allowed to share the men's world at all.

Although many of the societies under discussion in this volume exhibit a sharper sexual segregation than that which exists at present in the United States, it does not necessarily follow that women in these societies perceive their limitation to "sexuality, motherhood and service"—if they are indeed so limited—in quite the same way. It may therefore be helpful to place Lipman-Blumen's assessment of women's roles into the context of U.S. culture and society. Here the observations of an anthropologist from a non-Western tradition such as F.L.K. Hsu (1970), who has considered American society from his own Chinese perspective, may be of particular value. He notes that the core value of self-reliance and independence tends to separate family members from each other and makes for intergenerational conflict. The emphasis on the husband-wife tie rather than on the family line makes families temporary units. In the autobiographical account of Sarah Penfield, presented by Rosemary Joyce, we note how, over a period of the last couple of generations, interdependence and cooperative ventures among farm neighbors and relatives has declined as a result of economic specialization and technological advances. The fact that her children and grandchildren keep in touch with her suggests her sister's comment: Sarah has an unusual family! These reflections are important with regard to Lipman-Blumen's assessment of women's position in U.S. society. She is talking about a system in which *individuals* hold power and have assets, not kin groups, and in which the capablility to produce children may offer private satisfactions, but not authority, power, or be considered a resource.

Taking our cue from Lipman-Blumen's discussion of U.S. society, we may ask: why do men need women? What resources and powers do they control, to which men seek access? If sex segregation exists, does it "relegate women to the sidelines of life?"

How Stratification Effects Women's Social Position

Women's roles and status in stratified societies are affected to a significant extent by class position. In such societies, women hold social positions as wives and daughters of men of particular classes. Class position affects not only the economic role of women but also their other activities, as well as the scope and range of their movements among the several domains. It influences the women's perception of their position, and the effect of social change on all of this. Class position is expressed in the availability of resources and in the size and structure of households. Status is validated by the way in which the household is run and how it interacts with other segments of the community, both economically and socially. If women are responsible for the operation of various houshold functions, this means that important aspects of status validation are assigned to them.

As we turn to a consideration of our 12 case studies, we should note that generally the women, whom anthropologists have studied in class societies, belong to the lower stratum; they are peasants and, sometimes, members of urban slum groups. Some in our sample are middle and upper class: the urban upper-class Saudi women, the middle-class Cuban women, the Brazilian middle-class group in Rio Grande do Sul and the upwardly mobile lower class in São Paulo, and upwardly mobile groups among the Hausa and the Dioula.

WOMEN'S WORK: A COMMENT

A discussion of women's work cannot be easily separated from the subject of domains. Also, since the societies we deal with are all undergoing rather rapid changes, this topic, too, becomes central to our understanding, for change affects both work and the separation, or interaction, of the domains. Most of our societies include both traditional and modern, or modernizing, sectors. However, these may, in most instances, be best regarded as the ends of a continuum, rather than separate social and cultural compartments.

A reading of these chapters suggests that women's tasks are highly diverse, yet share a core of common feaures. These center about the household and its management, including the production and rearing of children, and cooking. Childcare, though work, is not, strictly speaking "economic" since it produces neither subsistence goods nor income. Indeed, to the contrary, in their early years, at least, children increase a household's subsistence needs. After the early years, however, children become part of the work force. Women can frequently get help with childcare, from various female relatives, and particularly from their older daughters. Schooling, as one aspect of modernization, by taking children away from work, increases the workload of adults. This is particularly true for girls' schooling, since they usually are drawn into childcare and household chores earlier than boys. Kimball reports that in Brunei, where some young women join the work force in the modern sector, they receive assistance with childcare from female relatives, but the household chores remain to be done by them when they return from their jobs.

WOMEN IN MEDITERRANEAN SOCIETIES

At the same time, as Ellovich points out specifically for the Dioula, where children are sent to shcool, women's role in their education, particularly that of the girls, is diminished. Among the tasks women carry out within the household, one has received little attention, and that is the effective management of the members of the household as a working unit. It is interesting that the important managerial skills women need to fulfill their household tasks have often been overlooked. For example, Deaver tells us that among wealthy urban Saudis, male servants do much domestic work. Within the households of their employers such men become, in effect, socially neuter: they do "women's work," they take orders from women, they enter the quarters of the women, who remain unveiled and ignore their presence. The inclusion of servants in the household, and often of dependent relatives, modifies the workload of the women. On the one hand, it reduces the amount of physical labor done by them; on the other hand, the supervision of servants and of a large, diversified household becomes one of the responsibilities of the woman who is the female head of the domestic organization.

Hausa and Dioula Women

For the Muslim Hausa women, who participate in the subsistence economy, the structure of the household in which they live is a significant factor in their ability to carry on income-producing crafts. Seclusion and polygyny are both considered to be desirable because they reduce their household workload. In such a complex family a senior wife has authority over junior wives, dependent children, and daughters-in-law. She has a demanding role that yields respect for the competence with which she carries on the management of a large organization and its resources. The abolition of polygyny, which some advocate as part of modernization, would abolish this authority position. It would also severely reduce the freedom and mobility of women, for it would reduce the demand for wives. It is this demand that gives Hausa women a considerable advantage over men in the "marriage game."

The high rate of divorce and remarriage among the Hausa underlines the need that men have for wives. They depend on wives for various things they cannot do without but cannot provide for themselves: cooked food, household management, full adult status, achievement of the status of head of household. Although Islamic law makes divorce easier for men than for women, women, in effect, remain married by choice.

Cooking is central to women's household roles, and the kitchen or the hearth their central "inside" location. Cooking is linked to nurturance and the care of children, but in relation to husbands, it is often symbolically tied to sexuality. Not only can a Hausa man, for example, not cook for himself, but when there are several wives, they rotate their roles in relation to the husband. The woman whose turn it is to sleep with the husband is also the one whose turn it is to cook. Similarly, cooking and sex are linked among the Dioula.

Brunei Women

Cooking and serving food is also central to various ritual functions. In Brunei, the husband's dominance is expressed symbolically by the fact that he is offered all dishes first. Yet behind this formal gesture of deference, there lurks a threat; men may demand deference and they may beat their wives, but women may poison their husbands.

In Brunei, as in Saudi Arabia, women have major responsibility for hospitality. Their importance in this regard is most clearly seen in the presentation and organization of weddings, the primary ritual expression of kinship and family status. For well-to-do families a wedding involves a series of activities extending over a period of time, and includes repairs to the house, preparation of the wedding chamber as well as entertainment and food for large numbers of guests whose presence may last more than a week. Such an event entails major expenditures of resources and of effort, requiring planning and organization of work activities, provisions, and supplies. These are also important occasions of exchange of help with other families. Women are clearly in charge of these events and their skills in management are fully appreciated. Kimball says they "boss" the occasions. Yet the formal act of cooking on the appointed day is left to the men. It is tempting to interpret this as a symbolic expression of the myth of male dominance.

Saudi Women

In these complex societies, women are seen as playing a significant role in the validation of their husband's and kingroup's status. For example, the Saudi man's status is validated by a number of factors: the hospitality he is able to offer, the continuation of the family line, and the strictness with which the honor/shame code is observed. With regard to all of these, women hold key positions. The prestige that accrues to a man as a result of generous hospitality, is in large measure due to his wife's skill and organizational ability and, indeed, to her cooperation. Saudi women, as Deaver tells us, recognize that they are the only source of children. As Gonzalez (1974:44) has pointed out, in criticism of Sanday's thesis, in some societies, "lives themselves may be resources."

Because the societies are ranked, women's status in them is directly related to the status of their menfolk. Status validation is, in part, a woman's function. Yet women also have reputations of their own. In Brunei, they may be famous for their cooking or baking, or as healers or midwives. Among the Hausa, they may be particularly skillful in their crafts.

In the traditional sector of these four Islamic societies there is an ideological basis for the explicit and clear-cut separation of the domestic/private and the public domain. This is associated with a firm separation and clear complementarity of sex roles. In actual fact, only in the case of the secluded Saudi women does this mean that women are limited to the domestic domain. Even the secluded Hausa women, who constitute only a minority of wives, participate in the public domain by means of their economic activities for the marketplace. Other Muslim Hausa women participate more directly in the public sphere, either through their economic activities, their utilization of divorce courts, and some as courtesans. The lives of the women among the Brunei Malays and the Dioula are less circumscribed.

Two further points need to be considered here, the subject of women's self-esteem and that of culture change. For each of these societies we are told that women are aware of their powers and have high self-esteem. In each case, women are necessary for men to reach significant status positions, and women know this. Where this is the case, women are not marginal to the life of their society. Self-esteem results from an achievement of the goals developed in the individual during socialization, that is, from living up to one's ego ideals, and their confirmation through the esteem of significant others. It is important to distinguish this from etically defined criteria of social status.

These cases, most particularly the extreme situation of the urban Saudi women, are important as tests of our ethnocentrism. It is possible to be secluded, to have self-esteem and, indeed, to pity the Western women who cannot rely on men to support them, who may deprive themselves of motherhood, who do not play a pivotal role in a complex of honor and shame, and who do not perceive themselves to be sensual creatures.

Our Islamic cases also show that culture change, as influx of money, may serve to reinforce existing values rather than to change them. On the other hand, where Western schooling for girls leads to salaried jobs, women's situations increasingly approximate those of Western women, and this, as Mintz (1971) has shown, may in fact involve a reduction in their "individual prerogatives." This may be linked, however, to an increased role in the public domain.

Ibero-America

The cases of the Brazilian and Cuban women reflect traces of the Mediterranean tradition, as shown in the virility/virginity complex, that marks these societies. Culture change is seen here in two forms: rapid economic development in Brazil, and for the Cubans, adaptation to the United States. Our two Brazilian studies focus on variants of the rapidly growing Umbanda religion. As Pressel (1973) has pointed out elsewhere, Umbanda not only facilitates sociocultural change, it also constitutes a symbolic expression of that change.

Possession trance cults are a very widespread phenomenon in many parts of the world, particularly in sub-Saharan Africa, Afro-America and South East Asia. In Brazil they represent a very interesting integration of elements drawn from African and non-African sources, and show the power and prestige of the African traditions among people of European ancestry. In most of the societies where they exist, women play a predominant role in cults of this type, often as leaders, always as mediums. Why this should be is a question that has been only preliminarily answered (Bourguignon 1975; 1979). In most general terms we can say that the presence of possession trance gives expression to key conflict areas in a society. Pressel and Lerch, considering two aspects of Umbanda, find complementary answers. For Pressel, the cults are a neutral domain, neither domestic nor, indeed, public. The magic and countermagic she discusses illustrate well Nadel's point (1952) that the person who deviates from the cultural norms—in the Brazilian case, the unattached single women— becomes the scapegoat of witchcraft accusations. Umbanda provides women with an area of initiative, personal power, and authority. Lerch shows that it may also provide them with a following and with information that may lead to a redistribution of goods and services. When women become cult entre- preneurs, the cult, in some sense, becomes an extension of the home, where sex roles are, to a degree, reversed. Lerch sees the domain of the cult as non- domestic, therefore public, and the goods and services as part of the economic, hence public, sphere. Yet the economy is not that of the marketplace, and the relations upon which the networks are built are private, personal, and in- dividual. Indeed, the public aspects of the cults, the local and national federa- tions and their legal and political aspects, are in the hands of men. Yet at the base of the organization are the women, who find in the cults a means of alle- viating their situations. This may involve a balancing of the stresses of domes- tic situations or those caused by the economic development of the country. Psychologically, mediumship allows women the possibility of acting out powerful roles, often those of important and aggressive male spirits, thus giving them some vicarious satisfactions. Most importantly, the cults offer lower- middle-class women the means of affecting their own destinies.

THE ANGLO–CARIBBEAN

It is interesting to compare Umbanda and its functions for women in the developing society of Brazil with the Spiritual Baptist church of St. Vincent, as described by Henney. Here we are outside the orbit of the Mediterranean tradition. The Anglo-Protestant and West African traditions form the context of this study. The former is most clearly seen in the formal ideology of the church, which concerns itself with sin and salvation rather than directly with healing and the resolution of practical problems of daily life, as is the case in Umbanda. Whether there are traces of the West African tradition to be found in the possession trance pattern may be debated; however, the economic position of women in the public domain certainly links the Vincentian pattern to that of West Africa. With regard to values, instead of the Mediterranean virility/virginity complex, we find a conflict, for men, between the goals of *respectability* and *reputation,* as proposed by Peter Wilson (1973; 1975) for other parts of the Anglo-Caribbean. As elsewhere in the region, lower-class women on St. Vincent have access to a degree of economic independence. In the context of the church, women offer men deference of a type that exists more in the ideal than in the real conditions of the society. Henney sees this as a ritual expression of the myth of male dominance. It is the women, she tells us, who, both as mothers and as adults interacting with adult males, shape and perpetuate "the ideal image of the male as virile, aggressive, active, and dominant." The women, who gain self-esteem and satisfaction in other aspects of their lives, are less dependent than the men on the roles the church provides for those who wish to opt for respectability.[1] Outside the church sex roles are more flexibly defined and there is less complementarity between them than we observed in the Mediterranean societies discussed so far. Women can be self-reliant adults, without attachment to fathers or husbands. Henney's discussion of the different satisfactions men and women gain from the church is of particular importance since in this instance, in terms of compensation for a low social position, men here have more to gain than women. This is contrary to the thesis derived by I.M. Lewis (1971) from his Somali data, one which he generalized to women's role in possession trance cults in other parts of the world. Is the church part of the public domain? It is certainly separate from the major economic and political institutions of the society. Relations are quasi-familiar, with the use of fictive kinship terms, such as "mother," "sister," and "brother," but not "father." The church sets itself up, in some sense, in contrast to the world of sinners, and thus seeks to create a domain of its own, a counterdomain reversing some of the patterns of the actual public domain.

Henney's comparison between ritual trance and the psycho-physiological states of sexual intercourse is of considerable interest. Possession trance states are often referred to in the literature as "orgiastic," but serious analyses of the kind presented here are woefully lacking. The similarity between the phases of possession trance and female orgasm suggest one answer, if the findings can be duplicated elsewhere, as to why more women than men have generally been reported to be possession trancers (or "mediums") in rather widely differing societies. Also, where both men and women participate, we hear references to female but not male orgasms as occuring under ritual conditions. Men who participate in possession trance are often referred to as effeminate, and in the literature on Brazil, in particular, we frequently find references to male cult homosexuality (Landes 1947; Leacock and Leacock 1972).

St. Kitts

Gussler, in her discussion of St. Kitts, focuses on some different aspects of women's positions in this nearby island of the Anglo-Caribbean. In contrast to St. Vincent, St. Kitts has a plantation economy, which influences all aspects of the social as well as the economic life of its people. However, it shares with St. Vincent a respectability/reputation ideology that dictates much male behavior. Women here, too, engage in a great many different kinds of work and in neither of these societies are they in any sense limited to the domestic domain. Yet being married, supported, and not having to work outside, part of the respectability ideal for women, is aspired to. Both of these societies show us a contradiction between the self-reliant but often difficult lives of women and the ideal state of social aspirations and elevation involving a decline in personal freedom which closer approximation of the ideal norm of the traditional Western middle-class woman implies. While women perceive themselves as, by nature, having a hard life, they also live in a society in which their self-reliance and competence go unchallenged. It is interesting that in this society of self-reliant, highly independent people, there are no structured kin groups to fall back on and hospitality and generosity are not virtues that are valued. The contrast between the Anglo-Caribbean and the Mediterranean pattern could not be greater.

By Contrast: Some Modern Mayas

Where the rural women of St. Kitts live in what Eric Wolf (1966) calls "open" peasant communities, the traditional Maya live in "closed" communities. In Utzpak, situated on a motor road to Merida, both styles of life are possible side by side. Like Ellovich, Goodman compares three individual women and looks at their lives as based on a series of choices, each having her own adaptive strategy. The peasant woman's life is stable, the pattern essentially set. This author's bias, in contrast to much of what we read in the U.S. ethnographic literature, is clearly on the side of the peasants. The two other women, urbanizing and urban, are seen with a much more critical eye. The peasant woman contributes substantially to the subsistence of her family, and does so with a great range of skills. Her home and garden are the center of her world, although she engages in trade and, in earlier years, traded at a distance. She has been a powerful influence in the life of her husband and of her children and grandchildren. Indeed, the husband who works as a ranch hand appears marginal to the life of his family. The second woman, Reina, shows the transformation of a peasant woman into an entrepreneur, as well as a worker in whatever moneymaking activities arise in this rapidly urbanizing area. She has strong economic ties to the public domain, and she and her family lack the virtual self-sufficiency of the peasant. The third woman, the daughter of the first, actually lives in a city and is totally dependent, economically, on her husband. These women show great contrasts in their adaptations, their attitudes toward themselves and others, their willingness to bear and rear children, their perceptions of themselves as persons. Goodman suggests that the older peasant woman, Eusebia, has the greatest self-esteem and the greatest authority in her family and, indeed, in her community. In each of these cases, Goodman perceives the women as the principal actors, the men depending on them to a large extent in their choices of their own strategies. This is seen in Eusebia's religious conversion and her influence on her husband and several of her children to join the church, in Reina's economic skills without which her husband could not operate, and in Nina's wish to move to the city and be an urban housewife, if only in a shanty town. The women's access to resources vary, the urban woman being tied most closely to the domestic domain, yet, apparently, because she wishes to limit herself in this way. Moreover, the women's range of work and of influence vary greatly in scope; however, male and female spheres and occupations always differ.

THE ANGLO-PROTESTANT TRADITION

The process of urbanization and culture change we note in Mexico is one that we have found in all of our cases so far, and it reappears in the instance of Joyce's Mrs. Penfield, the rural Ohio farm woman. She and the Maya peasant woman Eusebia also share the distinction of being grandmothers, who look back on long and productive lives and on the changes they have experienced. They force us to deal with another aspect of women's lives, which we have not yet addressed directly: the significance of different stages in the life cycle. If it is not possible to generalize about women in a stratified society without looking at class differences, neither can we understand women's status without considering the pattern of the life cycle. When are the peaks in a woman's career, when the low points? For Eusebia, the high point appears to have come somewhat later in life than for Mrs. Penfield, whose role in the public domain is severely reduced. For both, old age brings a narrower range of interactions.

An Appalachian Woman

The story of a long life allows us to view change through the eyes of our informant. For Mrs. Penfield, as well as for Eusebia, there have been great transformations, with the influence of urban ways on rural life among the most important. Urbanization in rural Ohio has meant, among other things, the centralization of schools and the loss of control over education by the local community. Such centralization stands in direct contradiction to the traditional values of self-reliance and independence, and leads to a sense of powerlessness. Peasants in Mexico or in the Anglo-Caribbean have long been aware of their lack of power, so that innovation has not brought them this type of conflict. Education is often seen as a means of culture change and of personal advancement. In rural Ohio, as elsewhere, it can lead to salaried jobs for women. Although women here have worked in the fields when there were insufficient male hands, this real pattern is somewhat at variance with the ideal separation of roles. When men and boys were available for work, girls could, and did, stay in school longer than their brothers. Marriage here has been later than in, say, Brunei, where education is also free, yet girls tend to drop out to marry and have children. For Mrs. Penfield, as for women in all of our rural samples, life has been a sequence of a great deal of hard physical work. Like the Mexican Eusebia, she has a broad range of domestic skills and takes pride and satisfaction in her work and in its appreciation by others.

One of the most interesting aspects of this report is its identification of this woman's internal conflicts. There is a life-long view of women as inferior to men, yet this does not imply personal feelings of inadequacy or a lack of self-esteem. There is a revision of the view that sees women as weaker than men, perhaps under the impact of the women's movement, yet this conflicts with a sense of what is right and proper for a woman to aspire to. Some of the traditional views are buttressed by religion, an institution that in recent years has taken on major significance in this woman's life. We do not have much information on this point, but one may wonder whether the church represents, at least in some sense, a supplement to Mrs. Penfield's activities and relationships in the domestic/private domain. The relationship between social ties and religious memberships, it will be remembered, is explicitly noted by Goodman for her Mexican peasant woman.

Cubans in Washington

The substitution, or shifting, of personal involvements from relationships in one domain to another is an adaptional mechanism we note also among the Cubans in Washington. Indeed, the substitutions of networks and grapevines for tightly knit neighborhoods is stressed by Boone in her discussion of the creativity evidenced by Cuban women as they adapt to a radically different sociocultural environment. Boone also draws our attention to the possible preadaptation of roles, that allow for an optimal shift of actors from one cultural setting to another. What is meant here is a "positive preadaptation." Mrs. Penfield's case may make one wonder about the possiblitly of "negative preadaptations." The conflict between self-reliance and centralization may be an example of such a phenomenon.

In her discussion of Cubans in Washington, Boone distinguishes between two types of public domains: the ethnic and the national. In some sense, the ethnic group provides a region of safety and implicit shared understandings beyond the family and the private domain. This is evidenced by Boone's identification of nonformalized roles for women in this ethnic public domain, roles that would be incomprehensible in the national public domain. We have here an interesting question about the existence of such ethnic public domains in plural societies generally: for example, a Malay as well as, say, a Chinese ethnic domain in Brunei. When Appalachians move from their region to northern cities, they may find there their own "ethnic public domain" as well as the national public domain.

Boone's distinction between formalized and nonformalized roles, which builds on the work of Chiñas (1973), suggests a possible distinction between the domestic and the private, that we have not worked out previously: if the domestic domain is limited to the household, the private domain may include a network of relationships that extends beyond the physical confines of the domestic sphere. Many of the nonformalized roles that exist in the setting of the public domain involving patterns of personal interactions, may then be private also.

A large percentage of the Cuban women contribute to their families' subsistence by working at salaried jobs. Some of these are defined as "women's work" in the U.S. context, others, such as real estate agent, are not sex-specific. Whether a woman holds a job depends largely on family need; the ideal is for women not to have to do so. Among those who are earners, satisfaction comes from job success, however, as well as from the fulfillment of traditional goals within the domestic domain and the private sphere: homemaking, child rearing, hospitality, management of relationships and maintenance of the network. Certain qualities are rated high by both women and men: beauty, grooming, verbal skills. Together with domestic skills, they allow women to validate their sense of themselves as sensual creatures and also their husbands' status. The role and position of mother is highlighted by its contrast with that of the "tía," the dependent female relative. (There is no parallel role for dependent male relatives). The emerging concepts of male and female identities show us the world of Mediterranean values confronting adaption to a cultural reality dominated by the Anglo-Protestant tradition.

Status validation is a subject to which we have returned a number of times. For the Cubans, it involves status in the ethnic public domain primarily, and only to a limited extent in the national public domain. There the women's role is much more marginal and can affect the husband's position only to a limited extent. The specific form status validation takes depends to some extent also on class position and the availability of resources. For example, in the Anglo-Caribbean and in Mexico, where we have dealt with the lower strata of society, a woman's childbearing gives public evidence of a man's virility. The status, here, is that of the male, not that of a particular rank or class.

Alaskan Eskimo Women: Then and Now

Here the example of the Southwest Alaskan Eskimo—both traditional and contemporary—may offer us a significant test case. In spite of the fact that this was, and remains, a small-scale society with limited resources, no stratification and little rank differentiation, women play an important role in the validation of their menfolks' status. Here the prestige of hunters and the first achievements of young children are valued and publicly recognized through the women's generosity in gift giving and the excellence of their hospitality. The Eskimo case suggests that what is at issue here is the area of cooperation and interdependence among the sexes. For the Eskimo, the division of labor between women and men is highly complementary, neither sex being able to survive without the contribution of the other. By contrast, in the Anglo-Caribbean among seekers for reputation in the lower social stratum, sex and procreation appear to be almost the only area of complementarity among adults. Here each sex can do most of the work of the other, and there is great dependence on money for the acquisition of goods. The couple is in no sense a self-sufficient unit.

Ager documents the great economic interdependence of men and women among the Southwest Alaskan Eskimo, in the contemporary society as well as in the past. This situation continues to exist in spite of the inroads made by the money economy, in the form of salaried employment, and wage labor, the store, the mail-order catalogue, funds from Native Claims, and so on. Women played a major role in the distribution and redistribution of wealth in the traditional economy, and they still do so. Moreover, they contributed substantially to the local economy and they do so now, though in somewhat modified form. Although the men's hunting and fishing produced the major sources of food and material culture, these were not usable until the women had transformed them through their skillful and time-consuming processing. Through gathering, they also contributed directly to the supply of food and resources. The fact that the women took over the animals directly after they were killed and distributed shares even before major processing, suggests that their role in the subsistence economy was traditionally recognized. Their skills brought them prestige; it made them desirable as wives. In response to a question raised earlier, we must say that, because of their crucial contribution to physical survival, it is clear that the Eskimo women's place in society was never marginal, in spite of the fact that they played no role in the limited political organzation or warfare.

In spite of the great economic interdependence, there was, traditionally, much social segregation between the sexes. Men and boys lived in a communal house, while women, girls and young children lived in individual houses. This suggests that in Eskimo village life there were, in fact, two kinds of domestic domains, since there were two sorts of residential units. The house, owned by the men, but occupied by the women and children, was, in fact, a workshop, where raw materials were processed into food and artifacts for family use and redistribution. The communal house was a place where males ate and slept, passed their spare time and kept some of their gear. It can be called "public" only because many of the men were only distant kin, if at all related.

Under the influence of the missionaries, the communal residence has been abandoned and the men now live with their wives and children, or, when younger, with their natal families. The distinction between the domestic/ residential doman and the public/social domain now is drawn in the familiar Western fashion. During the last generation, the economy also has been transformed, and although hunting, fishing, gathering, and processing are still basic subsistence activities, money plays an increasing role. Some of the women's handiwork is now being produced for the tourist trade; only the women had the traditional craft skills available to tap this source of income. The fact that women hold elective office gives evidence that they are recognized as competent individuals in the public as well as the private sector.

The Eskimo are the only hunter-gatherer society in our sample. They present a striking contrast to our other examples and their modern situation raises a number of questions. When tribal agriculturalists are integrated into nation states they are often transformed into peasants, if not into marginal urbanites. They contribute to local and often also to world markets. The Eskimo continue to produce most of their own food but have little to offer the national market, from which, however, they increasingly draw equipment that becomes more and more necessary to them. Women, as workers, earners and consumers, make an important share of the decisions that will affect their future.

SUMMARY AND CONCLUSIONS

Our discussion of women's lives suggests a number of tentative conclusions and hypotheses. Readers may find in these rich data leads to other propositions.

Work and Domains

In all of our local settings in the 11 societies described women's work includes child care and homemaking. Yet this simple and platitudinous statement tells us nothing of the great variation in the scope and difficulty of the tasks involved, or how much help women receive from other female relatives, and servants. We have stressed the important managerial aspects of women's domestic responsibilities.

In all our rural groups women contribute directly to subsistence. However, only among the Brunei Malay do they play an important role in farming. Elsewhere they raise gardens and small animals (including pigs) and they also engage in gathering and some fishing. The scope of the subsistence contribution of Eskimo women in Southwestern Alaska, both in the past and under present-day conditions, may require the revising of a widely accepted picture of Eskimo life. In all of our rural and most urban groups women also work at some income-producing activities. The preparation and sale of items of food and handicrafts is frequently a source of money. For the great majority of the women in our diverse groups there is much hard physical labor and a constant round of activities. The greatest variation occurs with regard to the control of the products of women's work. Does money, specifically, become part of a shared household fund, does it go directly to the husband, or is the woman free to utilize her income as she chooses?

Seeking to deal with our materials within the conceptual framework of contrasting domains has required a critical examination of these concepts. Only in the Mediterranean cultures, particularly the Islamic ones, could the bipolar scheme of domains be applied readily, for the division of the world into male/female, public/private, and a series of other related pairs of opposites represents the ideological underpinning of these cultures. Elsewhere we struggled with situations where the concepts of opposing domains proved applicable only with difficulty, if at all. We found the synonymy of supradomestic/public/male, contrasted with domestic/private/female, to be questionable. Domestic and private spheres may overlap only partially, and males as well as females may have important roles in both of them. The scope of the domestic domain varies as does the number of individuals and their relationships to each other that a household, or other residential unit, may include. Similarly, the number and variety of tasks performed within its limits also varies. The domains may, in some sense, interpenetrate each other; for example, among the Hausa, work for the marketplace is carried on within the domestic context. The same is true of the hammock weaver in Mexico or of the Brunei seamstress or healer. Also, the physical limits of the domestic domain may be defined differently. Among the Brunei Malays, it might include the agricultural land basic to family subsistence, as well as multifamily residential units.

In addition to these variations in definition and scope, we found other complexities. For example, there may be neutral domains that serve to mediate the polarities between the domestic and the supradomestic, as Pressel suggests for Brazilian spiritist religions. Also, there may be several types of public domains; Boone suggests this for multiethnic societies. Perhaps we can visualize a family within an ethnic group as being surrounded by a series of public domains forming concentric circles about it, each representing a greater degree of social distance as we move from the domestic/private core to the periphery.

We need, furthermore, to consider the articulation of the domains, whether these be defined as domestic/supradomestic, private/public, or female/male. It appears that where the domains in each pair are clearly separated and defined, there are also highly complementary role patterns, and families and kinship units whose survival requires the contributions of both women and men. Where money and wage labor predominate, complementarity and interdependence of the sexes in the economic sphere decreases for money can purchase goods and services from anonymous unsexed sources. Individuals in such contexts become interchangeable. This has been the case, to a considerable extent, in Appalachia, where Mrs. Penfield's traditional women's skills are remnants of an earlier, much more highly interdependent, complementary and sex-segregated society. It is also largely true in the Anglo-Caribbean.

It is a commonplace of sociology that in Western, urban, industrialized societies a great number of what were once functions of the family have been taken over by various institutions in the public domain—the sphere of home and family—voided of much of its substance, women may well perceive themselves, and be perceived by men, as placed on the margins of such societies. Some traditional and modernizing societies may offer us a different picture. Here we need only to think of Eskimo men, socializing in a communal hut or talking at the local store and playing in the pool hall, whiling away the hours between the occasional high expenditure of effort on hunting trips. At the same time, women, in their home/workshops are engaged in a continuous flow of work, transforming carcasses into food and the necessary articles of daily life. Locating the center and the margins of a society under such circumstances appears to depend on the position of the observer.

A CHALLENGE TO STEREOTYPES

Culture change reported in our studies consistently includes urbanization and education. Education for women constitutes potential preparation for salaried jobs. Such work opportunities in the public sector for women who previously did not have them does not necessarily give them greater freedom or increase their power, authority, or status. In fact, it may weaken their overall position; the effect will depend on the preexisting pattern of roles. In situations of culture change, a range of individual adaptive strategies may come into play.

Our findings challenge a number of stereotypes. The following are particularly striking:

1. Culture change may reinforce rather than modify traditional values and increase the opportunities for their realization. Women may perceive seclusion and polygyny as desirable. Both may offer advantages in the contexts of prestige and self-esteem, but also of a practical economic nature. Seclusion, moreover, is not incompatible with economic participation in the public domain. The stricter the division of the domains by sex, the greater the control women have over their own domain may be. Divorce may offer greater opportunities to women than to men. Westernization and education may not enhance

women's status, neither may jobs in the public domain, nor may they reduce women's overall workload. Adoption of patterns of family organization that resemble those of the West may not be due to imitations of a Western model but to pressures of urban living and to some of the same causes that gave rise to the contemporary Western patterns in the first place.

2. In many societies, women are necessary to men both to achieve important statuses and to validate their statuses. It may be argued that it is the absence of such functions for women in modern urban, industrial, Western societies that has brought about the marginality of women's roles in the domestic private domain.

3. Traditional roles may be preadaptive for successful survival in new situations. Managerial skills and personality qualities fostered in one setting may be unanticipated assets in new social and cultural situations.

4. Attention should be given to ceremonial occasions that constitute ritualized statements of kinship relations and sex roles. Where ritual deference is offered by one sex to the other we should be alert to the possibility that this may represent an expression of a myth, the affirmation, in a formal context, of a denial of some aspects of the reality of day-to-day life. (Note that Euro-American patterns of etiquette between the sexes have long been a target of feminists.)

5. The appeal of novel religious groups may lie in the opportunity they offer for the creation of private networks of power, influence and authority in a nondomestic setting. They may therefore be of particular value to women who need to balance the power and authority of men either in the domestic domain or in other nondomestic spheres. In such contexts women may obtain power and authority by overt behavior that appears to indicate their abdication. In spiritist religions[2] women may relinquish their personal identities to powerful male spirit personae, through whom they act (while the spirits appear to act through them). Yet possession trance religions may offer men compensation for social inferiority—even vis à vis women. Such cults are not always expressions of female inferiority.

6. Boone, in her examination of the adjustment Cuban women have made to life in Washington, stresses their creativity in the modification of their roles and the contribution they have made in this way to the Cuban success story. Creativity is also seen in a great range of other examples we have considered, whether evidenced in religious innovation and the utilization of spirit roles or the modernization of Eskimo life. Creativity is at the heart of human adaptation to novel problems; women anthropologists are in a favored situation in seeking to discover the problems women in other societies face, the choices they make, and the capabilities they bring to the resolution of their problems.

NOTES

1. Gussler (n.d.) points to the quest for respectability that is expressed in the adherence to churches of a similar type on St. Kitts.

2. This applies to trance healers among the Brunei Malay as well as to Umbandistas in Brazil.

REFERENCES

Bourguignon, Erika
   1975   "Importante papel de las mujeres en los cultos afro-americanos."
          Montalbán 4:423-38.

   1979   *Psychological Anthropology, Introduction to Human Nature and
          Cultural Differences.* Chapter 7: "Altered States of Conscious-
          ness." New York: Holt, Rinehart and Winston.

Chiñas, Beverly
   1973   *The Isthmus Zapotecs, Women's Roles in Cultural Context.* New
          York: Holt, Rinehart and Winston.

Gonzalez, Nancie
   1974   "Sex Roles and Cultural Domains." Review of Women, Culture
          and Society, M.Z. Rosaldo and L. Lamphere, eds., *Science* 186:
          43-45.

Gulick, John
   1976   "The Ethos of Insecurity in Middle Eastern Culture." In G.A.
          DeVos, ed. *Responses to Change.* New York: Van Nostrand.

Gussler, J.D.
   n.d.   " 'Sideways Churches' and Respectability in St. Kitts." (Unpub-
          lished paper.)

Hsu, F.L.K.
   1970   *Americans and Chinese: Two Ways of Life.* Rev. ed. New York:
          Abelard-Schuman.

Landes, Ruth
   1947   *City of Women.* New York: Macmillan.

Leacock, R., and S. Leacock
   1972   *Spirits of the Deep.* Garden City, N.Y.: Doubleday.

LeVine, Robert
   1976   "Patterns of Personality in Africa." In G. DeVos, ed. *Responses
          to Change.* New York: Van Nostrand.

Lewis, I.M.
   1971   *Ecstatic Religion.* Baltimore: Penguin.

Lipman-Blumen, Jean
 1976 "Toward a Homosocial Theory of Sex Roles: An Explanation of the Sex Segregation of Social Institutions." *Signs* 3:15-31.

Mintz, S.W.
 1971 "Men, Women, and Trade." *Comparative Studies in Society and History* 13:247-69.

Nadel, S.F.
 1952 "Witchcraft in Four African Societies," *American Anthropologist* 54:18-29.

Paz, Octavio
 1961 *The Labyrinth of Solitude.* New York: Grove Press.

Peristiany, J.G.
 1966 "Introduction." *Honor and Shame: The Values of Mediterranean Society.* J.G. Peristiany, ed. Chicago: University of Chicago Press.

Pressel, Esther
 1973 "Umbanda in São Paulo: Religious Innovation in a Developing Society," In E. Bourguignon, ed.: *Religion, Altered States of Consciousness and Social Change.* Columbus: The Ohio State University Press.

Quigley, Carroll
 1973 "Mexican National Character and Mediterranean Personality Structure." *American Anthropologist* 75:319-22.

Schneider, Jane
 1971 "Of Vigilance and Virgins: Honor, Shame, and Access to Resources in Mediterranean Societies." *Ethnology* 10:1-24.

Wilson, Peter
 1973 *Crab Antics: The Social Anthropology of English-speaking Negro Societies in the Caribbean.* New Haven: Yale University Press.

 1975 *Oscar: An Inquiry into the Nature of Sanity.* New York: Vintage Books.

Wolf, Eric
 1966 *Peasants.* Englewood Cliffs, N.J.: Prentice-Hall.

Youssef, N. Haggag
 1972 "Differential Labor Force Participation of Women in Latin American and Middle Eastern Countries: The Influence of Family Characteristics." *Social Forces* 51:135-53.

INDEX

INDEX

NOTES ON CONTRIBUTORS

LYNN PRICE AGER holds an M.A. from the University of Alaska and a Ph.D. from The Ohio State University. Having lived and traveled extensively on several continents, she acquired an early exposure to cross-cultural experience. She has taught anthropology at several universities, most recently at George Mason University. She spent two years in Washington, D.C. as legislative assistant to the congressman from Alaska, working on Alaska Native issues. Maintaining her interest in applied anthropology, she is employed by the Legislative Council of the State of Alaska Legislature, working on the planning of an internship program to train college students for legislative staff work.

MARGARET S. BOONE holds a Ph.D. in anthropology from The Ohio State University. As the holder of a National Science Foundation Public Service Science Residency, she is connected with Georgetown University's Center for Population Research. Her investigation into Washington's high rate of infant mortality is centered at the District of Columbia General Hospital. She has taught at several universities, most recently at Georgetown University, where her main field of instruction was urban anthropology. As a result of her work in 1978 as staff assistant to the Select Committee on Population, U.S. House of Representatives, her research interests have shifted to fertility related behavior.

ERIKA BOURGUIGNON is Professor and former Chairman of the Department of Anthropology at The Ohio State University. She received a Ph.D. in anthropology from Northwestern University. She is editor and co-author of *Religion, Altered States of Consciousness, and Social Change* and co-author, with Lenora Greenbaum, of *Diversity and Homogeneity in World Societies.* Her other books include *Possession* and *Psychological Anthropology: Introduction to Human Nature and Cultural Differences.* Her long-term research into the social and cultural correlates of altered states of consciousness has led her to a special interest in the important role women hold in possession trance cults in all parts of the world.

SHERRI DEAVER holds a Ph.D. in social anthropology from Washington State University. Her research interests include the Middle East, and more generally, world view with particular emphasis on the cultural definition and uses of space. She is the author of "Concealment versus Display," published in *Dance Research Journal* (1978). Among her current research activities is a study of van art in the United States. Sherri Deaver is at present Assistant Professor of Anthropology at The Ohio State University, Mansfield Campus.

RISA ELLOVICH is an Assistant Professor in the Department of Sociology and Anthropology at North Carolina State University at Raleigh. She received her Ph.D. in anthropology from Indiana University. Her dissertation concerned Dioula women, among whom she lived for eighteen months in 1972-74. During her stay in the Ivory Coast, her fieldwork centered on Dioula women and their adaptation to urban living.

FELICITAS D. GOODMAN holds an M.A. in Linguistics and a Ph.D. in Anthropology from The Ohio State University. She recently retired from Denison University, where she taught linguistics and anthropology. She is the founder of the Cuyamungue Institute in New Mexico, and devoted to teaching and research in anthopology, with special emphasis on religious behavior. She is the author of over thirty articles and of several books, including *Speaking in Tongues: A Cross-cultural Study of Glossolalia;* with J.H. Henney and E. Pressel of *Trance, Healing and Hallucination: Three Field Studies in Religious Experience;* and the forthcoming *In the Dreaming: A Theory of Religious Behavior.*

JUDITH D. GUSSLER received a Ph.D. in anthropology from The Ohio State University. She has taught at Franklin University where she was chairman of the division of social sciences and where she is currently an adjunct member of the faculty and co-instructor of a course on women in the work force. A research specialist at Ross Laboratories in Columbus, she is continuing her long-standing study of the social and cultural context of food habits and infant feeding patterns on the island of St. Kitts, as part of her larger investigation of changing infant feeding patterns throughout the developing world.

JEANNETTE H. HENNEY teaches anthropology at Capital University, where she is an Associate Professor in the Department of Sociology. She received a Ph.D. in anthropology from The Ohio State University. Her publications include *Trance, Healing, and Hallucination: Three Field Studies in Religious Experience,* which she co-authored with F.D. Goodman and E. Pressel.

ROSEMARY JOYCE is a doctoral student in an interdisciplinary program in American folklore at The Ohio State University. She maintains a primary interest in woman's role, particularly as it is reflected in the traditional role of motherhood. This stems in part from her own experiences in making the transition from wife, and mother of five children, to wife and "mature student."

LINDA A. KIMBALL holds a Ph.D. from The Ohio State University. She was a Senior Fulbright Exchange Lecturer for two years (1972-74) in Malaysia, where she taught anthropology in the Malay language at the Universiti Kebangsaan in Kuala Lumpur and, for one year, also at the Universiti Sains in Penang. Her publications include the forthcoming volume *Borneo Medicine: The Healing Art of Brunei Malay Indigenous Medicine.* She is Assistant Professor of Anthropology at Western Washington University.

PATRICIA BARKER LERCH is Dean of the Weekend College and Assistant Professor of Anthropology at Hiram College. She holds a Ph.D. in anthropology from The Ohio State University. Her interests include the extension of opportunities for higher education to adults. Her current research includes an analysis of census data to discover the impact of modernization and industrialization on Brazilian women in the 1970s.

ESTHER PRESSEL is Associate Professor of Anthropology at Colorado State University and a post-doctoral fellow at the University of California, Los Angeles, under a grant from the National Endowment for the Humanities. She holds a Ph.D. in Anthropology from The Ohio State

University, and she returned to that institution under a post-doctoral fellowship from the National Institute of Mental Health in 1975-76. Her present research interests center on the psycho-biological aspects of altered states of consciousness. Her publications include *Trance, Healing, and Hallucination: Three Field Studies in Religious Experience*, of which she is co-author with J.H. Henney and F.D. Goodman.

MARGARET O. SAUNDERS earned the Ph.D. in Social Anthropology from Indiana University. As a Visiting Professor in the Department of Agricultural Economics at Purdue University she currently carries on research dealing with economic development in Francophone West Africa. She combined interests in social organization, demography, and urban anthropology in her research on marital stability among the Hausa. Her fieldwork on this subject was conducted in the Hausa town of Mirria in the Niger Republic in 1973-74 and in 1975.